Monuments Decolonized

ALGERIA'S FRENCH COLONIAL HERITAGE

Susan Slyomovics

STANFORD UNIVERSITY PRESS
STANFORD, CALIFORNIA

Stanford University Press
Stanford, California

Publication of this book is supported in part by a grant from the Graham Foundation for Advanced Studies in the Fine Arts.

Printed in the United States of America on acid-free, archival-quality paper

Library of Congress Cataloging-in-Publication Data
Names: Slyomovics, Susan, author.
Title: Monuments decolonized : Algeria's French colonial heritage / Susan Slyomovics.
Other titles: Worlding the Middle East.
Description: Stanford, California : Stanford University Press, 2024. | Series: Worlding the Middle East | Includes bibliographical references and index.
Identifiers: LCCN 2023057995 (print) | LCCN 2023057996 (ebook) | ISBN 9781503632899 (cloth) | ISBN 9781503639485 (paperback) | ISBN 9781503639492 (epub)
Subjects: LCSH: War memorials—Algeria. | Monuments—Algeria. | Art and history—Algeria. | Decolonization—Algeria. | War memorials—France—Colonies. | Monuments—France—Colonies.
Classification: LCC NA9330.A4 S59 2024 (print) | LCC NA9330.A4 (ebook) | DDC 355.1/80965—dc23/eng/20240402
LC record available at https://lccn.loc.gov/2023057995
LC ebook record available at https://lccn.loc.gov/2023057996

Cover design: George Kirkpatrick
Cover painting: *Aux libérateurs l'humanité reconnaissante* [To the liberators, humanity is grateful]. Ahmed Benyahia (1973, revisited in 2013), 172 cm × 192 cm, oil on canvas. Artist's collection, reproduced by permission of Ahmed Benyahia.

MONUMENTS DECOLONIZED

WORLDING THE MIDDLE EAST

To Nadjib Berber (1952–2023), artist, husband, father

CONTENTS

ACRONYMS

ADDVRC Association de défense du Vieux Rocher Constantine / Jamʿiyya al-difāʿ ʿan al-ṣakhr al-ʿatīq (Association to Preserve the "Old Rock" of Constantine)

ALECSO Arab League Educational, Cultural, and Scientific Organization

AML Archives municipales de Lyon (Municipal Archives of Lyon)

ANFANOMA Association nationale des français d'Afrique de Nord, d'outre-mer et de leurs amis (National Association of French from North Africa, Overseas, and Their Friends)

ANIFOM Agence nationale d'indemnisation des français d'outre-mer (National Agency for the Indemnification of Overseas French)

ANOM Archives nationales d'outre-mer (National Overseas Archives)

APC assemblés populaires communales (elected municipal city councils)

CDHA Centre de documentation historique sur l'Algerie (Center for Historical Documentation on Algeria)

CSCO Collectif sauveguarde des cimetières d'Oranie (Collective to Protect the Cemeteries of Oran)

CIVIC Comité d'initiative et de vigilance citoyennes d'Oran (Oran Citizen Initiative and Vigilance Committee)

DAF déserteurs de l'armée française (deserters from the French army)

FIS Front islamique du salut (Islamic Salvation Front)

FLN Front de libération nationale (National Liberation Front)

FNR Front national des rapatriés (National Front of the Repatriated)

FSNA français de souche nord-africaine (French of North African origins)

GPRA Gouvernement provisoire de la République algérienne (Provisional Government of the Algerian Republic)

GPV grand projet de ville (major city project)

JORA *Journal Officiel de la République Algérienne* (*Official Gazette of the Algerian Republic*)

JORF *Journal Officiel de la République Française* (*Official Gazette of the French Republic*) Although the usual abbreviation is *JO* for *Journal Officiel*, *JORF* is used to distinguish from Algeria's *Journal Officiel* or *JORA*.

MIR Mission interministérielle aux rapatriés (Interministerial Mission for the Repatriates)

ONAC-VG Office national des anciens combattants et victimes de guerre (National Office for Veterans and Victims of War)

ONM Organisation nationale des moudjahidine (National War Veterans Organization)

OAS Organisation de l'armée secrete (Secret Army Organization)

OS Organisation spéciale (Special Organization)

PLO Palestine Liberation Organization

SHD Service historique de la défense

ILLUSTRATIONS

NOTE ON TRANSLATION AND TRANSLITERATION

Unless otherwise indicated, all translations from Arabic and French are my own. When available, I have used existing translations into English. Algerian names for people and places follow forms based on French colonial orthography and transliterations because these transcriptions are still in use by Algerians in the press, on their identity cards, on road signs.

The transliteration system for Algerian Arabic dialect adopts Algerian vernacular spellings in Latin script, including ch for the letter ش, and ʿ for the letter ع, as most appropriate for rendering the vernacular language in the same way its speakers do. The *International Journal of Middle East Studies* (*IJMES*) transliteration is used for Modern Standard Arabic.

MONUMENTS DECOLONIZED

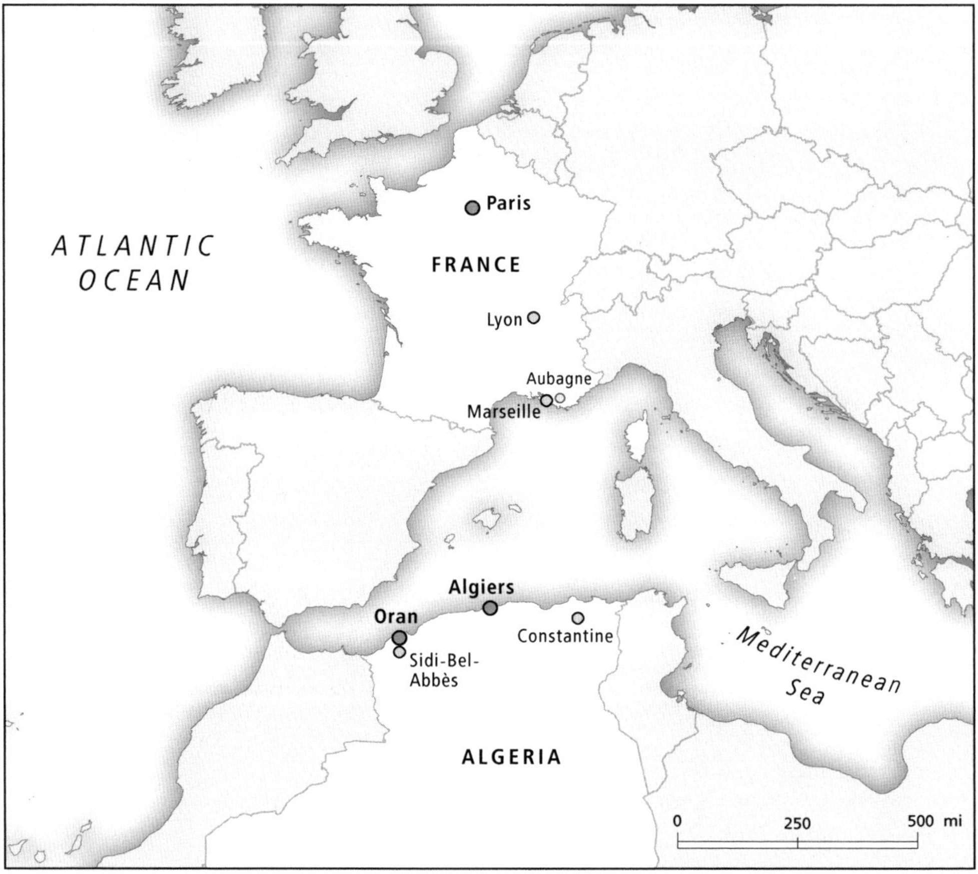

FIGURE 1. Map of sites of monument movements, from Algeria to France. Map by Erin Greb Cartography.

INTRODUCTION

MONUMENTS AFTER ALL

THE IDEA OF WRITING ABOUT monuments from colonial-era Algeria first came to me in Lyon, France on November 11, 2013, during Armistice Day commemorations, as former settlers of French Algeria were singing "The Song of the Africans," their unofficial anthem,[1] and I was contemplating the statue of an Algerian soldier whose bust was fused to his Senegalese and French counterparts (figure 2). I am rehearsing Edward Gibbon, who, in his autobiography, describes the epiphany that inspired the *Decline and Fall of the Roman Empire*, "at Rome on the fifteenth of October 1764 . . . amidst the ruins of the Capitol, while the barefooted friars were singing Vespers in the temple of Jupiter."[2] In Gibbon's Rome, preserved Roman ruins attest to the destruction of an empire, to a Christianity triumphant over paganism, and to materials cannibalized for new structures. My own epiphany evidenced the same fascination with the melancholic ruins of an empire's transported and renewed materiality. Where Gibbon was contemplating the vestiges of Roman ruins, I was looking at the World War I war memorial to soldiers from Oran, Algeria, who had fought for France. This colonial vestige from Algeria had been moved to the northwest quadrant of Lyon, France, the arrondissement of La Duchère, a neighborhood created after World War II. During my year of research in Lyon (2013–2014), I learned that the three soldiers atop the memorial had been removed from their base in 1968 and brought to Lyon to be placed in a new district for European settlers who had left Algeria in 1962 at its independence from France. Every year, Lyon's Oran monument attracts former settlers from Algeria who, like their monument, come from a dismantled French colonial empire.

I wanted to analyze French colonialism and its aftermaths in France and Algeria through war memorials, the "monuments after all" that survive in both countries.[3] They are the many visible aspects of French colonialism, and since 1962, when Algeria won its independence from France, are among colonial artifacts in France as well. Standing before Lyon's war memorial from Oran, I wondered how, why, and when a war memorial bearing the name of Algeria's second largest city came to a new public square in Lyon. Since when did France's Armistice Day commemorations for the dead soldiers of World War I and World War II include ceremonies for Alge-

FIGURE 2. Front of the colonial war memorial of Oran, Algeria in Lyon, France. Photo by author, November 11, 2013.

rian Muslim auxiliary troops who fought against Algerian independence?[4] Which actors are safeguarding the patrimony of French Algeria amid the noisy claims of ownership over the patrimony of the source community to whom this colonial statue of Algeria in France putatively belongs?

My reactions to this peculiarly placed Algerian monument in Lyon reflect my deep attachment to the city of Oran, Algeria. These responses to Lyon's statue are a formative condensation of happy memories from when I lived intermittently in Oran between 1990 and 1992 and discovered my strong affinity for the place, my research subject, and met the man whom I married. During those two years, I often walked by the *Stèle du Maghreb* (figure 3), which sat prominently on the palm-lined corniche overlooking the Mediterranean bearing an explanatory dedication by the Algerian poet Moufdi Zakaria. I had assumed it was Oran's war memorial that commemorated the Algerians who had died fighting for independence from France during the Algerian War of Independence (1954–1962). On its plinth and column had stood three sculpted soldiers that were now in Lyon.

In two different countries at different times, I confronted at least two

FIGURE 3. ***Stèle du Maghreb*****, the war memorial to the martyrs of the Algerian Revolution, Front de Mer, Oran, Algeria. Photo by author, spring 2014.**

monuments, or two different parts of a single monument: in Oran, the footprint and pediment that had formed the base of the 1927 monument were still traceable at the original emplacement; in Lyon, three sculpted World War I soldiers symbolized those who had fought and died for France. What I glimpsed then in Lyon and had previously seen in Oran shaped my understanding of the monuments that filled the Algerian landscape. These memorials, columns, cenotaphs, pillars, crosses, and statues were not merely aesthetic creations; they were a structural component of colonial French power and violence. Bold, confident, intrusive monuments stood on land that had been allocated by a succession of French military governors to the largest European settler colonial population among France's overseas colonies. They adhered to French canons of beauty and civic order and signified the territorial dispossession of the colonial native subject. Algeria's history as a French colony from 1830 to 1962 is written in and by an abundance of statues and war memorials built for and by Algeria's European settler colonial population. Their story—how, where, why, and how many were built under colonial rule and what happened to them at Algerian independence—is told in this research across detailed case studies. Monuments are important for visual and written records of the history of France in Algeria; indeed, a study of the region could "start with art."[5]

COMMEMORATIVE WAR MEMORIALS: REMAIN OR REMOVE?

A monument was erected to France's 1830 invasion of Ottoman-ruled Algiers that began 132 years of French colonial rule over Algerian territory. On the Mediterranean coast just west of Algiers, a massive amphibious French military force of 37,000 soldiers and 27,000 sailors landed at Sidi Fredj, vastly outnumbering the 3,000–5,000 Algerian troops. They were the first wave of France's murderous military campaigns, which continued until the defeat of the great nineteenth-century Algerian resistance leader, the Emir Abdelkader (ʿAbd al-Qādir ibn Muḥy al-dīn, 1808–1883) in 1847. At his surrender, the French army in Algeria numbered over 100,000 men. A hundred years after the French landing, a fifty-foot monument was erected to commemorate the centennial festivities of French Algeria in 1930 on that spot at Sidi Fredj—the Arabic name which became colonial Sidi Ferruch.

Sculpted by Algiers-born artist Émile Gaudissard (1872–1956), the monument depicts a standard-bearing allegorical female France embracing a smaller female Algeria counterpart. The inscription summarizes France's imperial "mission to civilize" (*mission civilisatrice*):

> Here on the 4th of June 1830/ By the order of King Charles X /under the command of General de Bourmont / the French Army / came to unfurl its flags / liberating the seas / giving Algeria to France / 100 years later / the French Republic / having brought justice to this country / a thankful Algeria / pays homage to the mother land / the homage of its everlasting attachment.[6]

The Sidi Fredj / Sidi Ferruch sculpture bookmarks the existence of French Algeria—the victorious invasion of 1830 celebrated at its centenary of 1930, and the 1962 Algerian independence celebrations when joyous Algerians chiseled away the monument's inscription (figure 4). Just before Algeria's official independence day of July 5, 1962, the French military swiftly dismantled Gaudissard's monument. Sections of it now sit in an outdoor museum complex in France's southwestern Mediterranean port of Pont-Vendres, facing Algiers.[7]

France's conquest of Algeria was commemorated by monuments that were erected everywhere and on a grand scale. War memorials outnumbered the monuments to great men. Approximately 36,000 war memorials were erected in France, which included Algeria (integrated as France's southern departments or provinces) and in its other overseas colonies.[8] "Statuomania" refers to these vast numbers of statues including those brought to the Algerian colony.[9] The practice of systematically recording and identifying by name the dead in military cemeteries began in France after World War I even as local war memorials provided sites for mourning and remembrance by families bereft of loved ones who were buried on distant battlefields.[10] French war memorials were first erected in large numbers after the Franco-Prussian war and continued for the two world wars; war memorials began appearing in large numbers in Algeria after World War I. Conquered Algerians could see an unprecedented number of statues and monuments—three-dimensional representations that shaped them into a "picture-minded people."[11] Historian Arthur Asseraf claims that the groundwork for visual literacy was laid even among illiterate Algerians by the vast output of illustrated newspapers and magazines in circulation in the colony between 1881 and 1940 at the height of French colonial power.[12]

A war memorial was part of the template for a French town center. These

FIGURE 4. **"Celebration of the independence below the monument commemorating the French landing in Sidi Ferruch in 1830, July 2nd 1962." Marc Riboud (1923–2016), photographer. Reproduced by permission © Marc Riboud / Fonds Marc Riboud au MNAAG / Magnum Photos. On his photography at Algerian independence, see Marc Riboud, "Interview by Sylvie Hugues,": http://marcriboud.com/en/texte/algiers-july-1962-marc-riboud/.**

omnipresent monuments were integral parts of most settler town layouts in French Algeria in the interwar years, if not earlier—the towns are unimaginable without them. Monuments were typically sited adjacent to the colonial military-prison complexes that protected settler spaces. Immediately after World War II, another generation of war memorials was erected in France and its colonies; these were new memorials, or occasionally simple additions to the World War I monuments inscribed with the names of newly fallen soldiers. Where erecting these monuments in France was a ceremonial sign of postwar bereavement, erecting them in Algeria was a material expression of colonialism as a state of war to eliminate the native population and their claims to land. These monuments, war memorials, and statues erected by French imperial power in settler colonial contexts—a legacy of French statuary—were later reshaped by Algerian decisions about their fate and existence. Modified in contemporary postindependent spaces of Algerian towns and villages, the street grid often converges on a central square bordered by a former church, a post office, a municipal building, a school, and a war memorial. After Algerian independence, during the decade of the 1960s, many colonial-era memorials were rededicated to the Algerian War of Independence.[13]

The history and context of many French colonial monuments must also account for the removal of some or some parts of war memorials from Algeria to France, processes tied to the different communities in the colony. The dramatic exodus of most European settlers began in the early 1960s after a war of independence that lasted seven years (1954–1962) followed by massive departures from Algeria. This exodus reversed the nineteenth-century arrivals of Europeans, and also, in part, the implantation of commemorative French monuments. The defeated French army returning to metropolitan France, the Catholic Church whose properties and personnel were reduced, and individual settlers all played a role in uprooting these particular signs of French domination. Military and colonial archives attest to the many ways that colonial monuments were moved out of Algeria, destroyed, or replaced. They never explain why. It is settler colonial studies that provide theoretical approaches that confront French ideas, in contrast to Algerian ideas, to understand these as acts of patrimony, what it means when people move with their objects across the Mediterranean. The displacement and removal of communities and things are part of the colonial legacy that endures long after Algerian independence and affects French and Algerians in fundamental, visible, and quotidian ways. In France and Algeria, commemorative war memorials trigger a nostalgia for and a memory of French Algeria that binds Algeria and France materially and emotionally.

"REPATRIATES," REPATRIATED OBJECTS, AND THE "PIED-NOIR"

To regulate the end of the Algerian War of Independence and the loss of France's last North African colony, the Évian Accords of March 18, 1962, stipulated that by July 5, 1962, the French army would leave most of independent Algeria, with the exception of its military sites in the Sahara.[14] But to insure an orderly removal of archives and monuments, approximately 80,000 French troops remained for twelve months at Oran's nearby naval base, Mers-el-Kebir. France negotiated an additional fifteen-year lease for the naval base to make it easier to transport people and objects out of Algeria, which ended earlier by 1968.

In the first years after Algerian independence, two-thirds of the settler population of some 1,300,000 people—the majority of whom were French citizens—departed. More than half left between January 1, 1962, and December 1963.[15] They and their artifacts were "repatriated" to France. Where the departing settlers were legally deemed repatriates, their artifacts were not. Depending on highly divergent definitions of the term "repatriation," the removal of artifacts was considered legal or spoliation. "Repatriate" was initially defined by the French law of December 26, 1961, as applying to a specific trans-Mediterranean mobility of French persons from former French colonies: "Those French, having had to leave or feeling obliged to leave because of political events, a territory in which they were established and that had previously been under the sovereignty, protectorate or trusteeship of France."[16]

The new set of laws to support the "repatriates from Algeria" (*rapatriés d'Algérie*) conferred legal and political legitimacy and provided state financial indemnification, housing allocations, and more in France. Those who fled Algeria precipitously might have been deemed exiles, asylum-seekers, refugees, migrants, emigrants, expatriates, or *immigrés* (immigrants) in a diaspora, but the only designation for those migrating post-1962 with their belongings across the Mediterranean—to France in the main, but also to Spain, Malta, and Corsica—ever to have stuck was repatriate.

Colonial settlers were not the only group of "repatriates." Counterintuitively the majority of native Algerian Jews, who had been granted French nationality by the 1870 Crémieux Decree, were also considered repatriates. This rare extension of French citizenship to an entire Indigenous religious community in a settler colonial setting enabled Algerian Jews to integrate French institutions such that by the time of the Algerian War of Independence and definitively by the time of their exodus in 1962, the autochthonous Jewish community (*israélite indigène*) was assimilated into the category of *pied noir*, the popular term for the settler colonialists of European descent.[17]

While most historians believe that the term *pied noir* emerged post–World War II, its origins are numerous and colorful.[18] It has been translated literally as "black foot," associating the European settlers with the Native American tribe of the same name or with the black military boots of the conquering French army. Others considered that settlers blackened their feet with their grape-trampling winemaking.[19] My preference is for Pierre Bourdieu's definition of *pied noir* as a deformation of *pionnier* (pioneer) and a pure creation of French Algeria, in keeping with the approach taken in settler colonial studies: "There is a good deal of unfairness in the attitude of these Frenchman who make the pieds-noirs their scapegoats and blame all the tragic happenings in Algeria on their racism . . . it is colonial Algeria that has produced the pied-noir and not the reverse."[20]

In this study, I replace the French lowercase italicized *pied noir* into the English uppercase hyphenated Pied-Noir to designate them as a group and a community marked by their historical, geographic, and communal upheaval. I use "Pied-Noir" as the indexical term to reference the vast literature on social agents, affective continuities, and material objects written about and by all the European settlers post-1962 who left for France, and that also encompasses the native Algerian Jewish community.

These repatriates—European settlers and Indigenous Algerian Jews—received social benefits, relocation subsidies, and social services; unlike a third group of Algerian Muslims who had fought for the French during the Algerian War of Independence but could not be considered repatriates and indeed received few benefits.[21] Sometimes subjected to retaliation by Algerians during and at the end of the war, they were labeled refugees in France. While they did eventually become French citizens, they were designated citizens called "French of North African origins" (*français de souche nord-africaine*, FSNA) and endured social marginalization in France.[22] The colonial Muslim *indigène* retained the name of Harki brought from Algeria to the metropole but was affected by evolving legal designations and practices. These boundaries of French Algeria's populations on which constantly changing legal practices rely and get defined have recast the colonial Muslim *indigène* in the colony as the Harki in the metropole. As historian Lorenzo Veracini emphasizes, settler colonialism projects a future of a society to come.[23] Even "repatriated" to France, the settlers' ideas about settlement and Indigenous peoples matter: just as they could not imagine their place in a future Algeria without a vocabulary that was specific to French Algeria, so too, categories for the Harki were fixed when in France.

The former French colonial populations of the provinces of Algeria reconfigured their stories of group belonging and formation by 1962. Their repatriation implied an ingathering of settlers as opposed to a diaspora. Settlers who had gathered in French Algeria subsequently gathered in France where they retained their identity as settlers, having brought with them their statues. They had arrived in the hundreds of thousands as settlers and colonists on North African shores as of the early nineteenth century as migrants; their decolonization became what anthropologist Andrea Smith calls the story of an invisible return—of people coming "home," propelled by postindependence political tumult not only in Algeria but also in the formerly French North African colonies of Morocco and Tunisia.[24] These European settler repatriates of Algeria comprehended their chronologically divided and distinct existences on two shores of the Mediterranean Sea through doubling, repetition, and reinvention. From 1961 to 1963, the end of French Algeria and the first years of Algerian independence, the European settler community that departed Algeria en masse referred to the experience as a "loss" (*perte*), "exodus" (*éxode*), "wounds" (*blessures*), and "wrenching heartbreak" (*les déchirements*). Similarly, after the sea crossing, the Pieds-Noirs use an imagined binarism characteristic of settler colonial contexts according to Patrick Wolfe.[25] In various interviews, they told me that they find themselves exiled in the metropole although they are *français d'outre-mer* (overseas French); they are "here" or *ici* in France versus *là-bas*, "over there" in Algeria. They live among *français de souche* (original French stock) rather than among themselves as Pieds-Noirs who may be *français de racine* (of French roots) or *français de coeur* (emotionally French). Time is laid out in futureless contrasts between *actuellement* and *anciennement* (currently and formerly; life in France and life in French Algeria), their official status as "repatriated" versus *éxil* and *exode* (popular expressions of "exile" and "exodus"), where they live in *pays d'adoption* versus *pays natal* (an adopted country versus land of birth). While this may not be surprising to anyone who has shifted countries, the fiction of legal repatriation is that they moved back home.

Repatriation as a process and explanation undertaken and given by French colonialism lives uneasily with theories of decolonization demanded by an independent Algeria. Where material and geographical studies examine ongoing settler colonies in the United States, Canada, and elsewhere, the native Algerian and the European settler interacted and navigated colonial power in physical spaces that were sundered in 1962: French occupation and the settler colony in Algeria were no more. Settler colonialism is a structure, insists historian Patrick Wolfe, and the mass exodus from

Algeria to France that created repatriates but preserved the settlers intact, even as they vacated, will be investigated in this study as innovative structures. And a statue is literally a structure meant to be looked at.

Rescue strategies for French Algeria's objects were integral to the chaotic events during that first year of independence marked by violence and fear on all sides.[26] The exit of French imperial power from the decolonized spaces of Algeria throughout the decade of the 1960s included messy moves and removals of people, monuments, sculptures, and objects. For now, the term "removal" shies from calling out the legality of the move, by and for whom. Whereas the removal of French war monuments from Algeria to France was called repatriation, no legislation covered it or addressed the monuments. The 1962 Évian Accords that negotiated Algerian independence did not mention these monuments. The term *rapatrié,* much too vague after its original collective designation of human beings, was borrowed and applied to objects and statues and even actions. But its application to cultural objects was contested as perceptions and definitions of this "repatriation" ranged from destruction or spoliation to preservation to reuse. Moreover, most removals were undertaken without consulting the provisional Algerian government. They became integral to the wrenching experiences of decolonization and exile from the lost settler colony. This special category of monuments taken/repatriated from French Algeria to France includes colonial statues, church bells, and war memorials uprooted from their original sites. Their removal during the waning years of France's control of its overseas provinces of Algeria reflected among other things the belief that the French monuments faced imminent destruction from a newly sovereign Algerian state during this major geopolitical rupture. In response, many institutions and networks in France and the colony were activated to remove them. The French army and navy coordinated their passage across the Mediterranean Sea. Repatriates took them as they departed. Public art moved out of Algeria was designated *rapatrié* to hide the economic processes and complex transnational circuits through which large artworks were dismantled, packed, and transported from Algeria to their presumed place of origin in France. There, they were installed in new sites of colonial memory in France making parts of France into a memorial for its own settler colonial monuments and settlers. A major geopolitical rupture, a French belief that the monuments faced destruction from an independent Algeria, and the capacity and will to transport them elsewhere by the "repatriated" drove this.

HOW TO REMOVE ALGERIA'S COLONIAL MONUMENTS

Contemporary heritage standards require that objects be identified by their provenance, which entails a history of their creation and custodianship. Subsequent chapters of this study will revise French metropolitan descriptions of Algerian destruction of statues on the basis of information from the military archives housed at the Château de Vincennes near Paris, a major point of collection and dispersal for removed Algerian monuments. There among the file boxes, I found documents with clearly articulated objectives for the "repatriation of *souvenirs militaires*," where *souvenir* denotes "monument."[27] Documents laid out the plans to have the French army remove preemptively monuments in January 1962, six months before independence. Box 1R 368 of the French military archives delineates a roadmap for monument removal, although oral consultations among military and ministry staff typically preceded written directives in all likelihood. Protocols were thus charted months before the March 1962 ratification of the Évian Accords separating France from Algeria and before the July 1962 countrywide referendum that confirmed independence.

Correspondence between the headquarters of the Ministry of Armies and the Superior Command of French Forces in Algeria (CSFAFA) to local commanders throughout Algeria involved requests for lists and descriptions of monuments on the blank forms (*fiches descriptives*) that were provided. These included indispensable war memorials and sculptures slated for shipment to France. The combined military forces of the French army, navy, and engineering corps were instructed to cull objects and statuary deemed important for safeguard, preservation, and transportation to France. A diagram limns the military decision-making hierarchy (figure 5). Red, blue, and black lines and circles delineate the central roles of the Ministry of the Interior and the Ministry of the Armies. Information about proposed monument removals was collected from municipalities, collectivities, and individuals in coordination with the French Embassy and transmitted to central command headquarters. Three army divisions were put in charge of removals and transport at monument sites corresponding to Algeria's three French *départements*: the 20th division for central Algiers Province, the 4th division for western Oran Province, and the 2nd division for eastern Constantine Province, all reporting back to the central command.

So, in the months before official independence, the military established bureaucratic avenues and infrastructural networks to remove monuments.

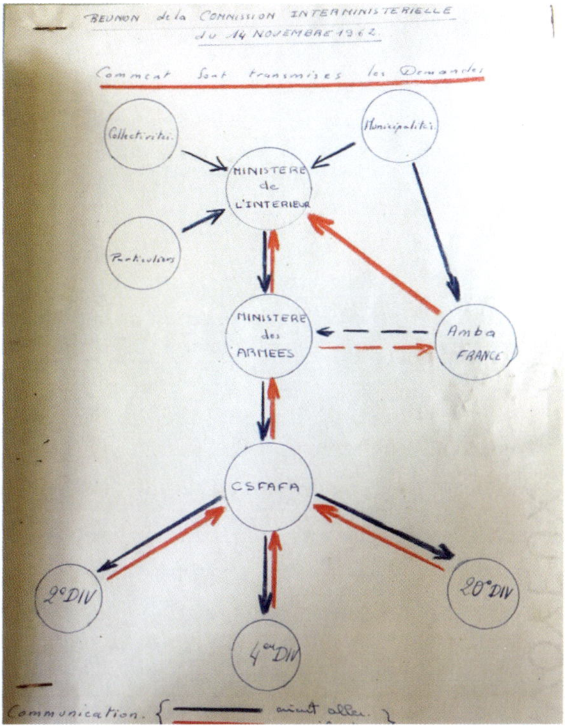

FIGURE 5. Military diagram for repatriation requests and removals, Château de Vincennes SDH 1R 368. Author's cellphone photo.

In addition, museum contents were also slated for "recuperation." The Laclotte Mission of July-August 1961—named for art historian and museum director Michel Laclotte (1929–2021)—surveyed Algeria's museum riches and advocated for art objects.[28] Concurrently, the settler population was aided by the colonial civil bureaucracy in retreat even without the support of the French army or top-down military instructions to undertake private initiatives. For objects, "repatriation" was seen to entrench rights to artifacts from the colony by settlers, who became France's metropolitan repatriates.

In France and Algeria, the demise of colonial North Africa promoted new heritage-formations and performative ceremonies. Augmented, repurposed, saved, de-territorialized, or destroyed monuments become emblematic of settler colonial, postcolonial, and decolonization worlds. When we look upon such monuments that seem to speak to material processes of hybridity, resistance, mimesis, or assemblages, we also look at the shared desires of former settlers and the formerly colonized to safeguard and preserve. In many ways, which this book explores, Algerian statuary and monuments participated in the colonial encounters that had reconfigured the North African littoral into French overseas provinces (*départements*) for 132 years.[29] Altered and removed, the monuments, statues, and war memorials took on unintended meanings, were seen in new ways, and became new objects. Many colonial-era plinths, pedestals, and figurative sculpted representations confront viewers in both countries to this day. They arrive before our eyes as the contemporary *terminus ad quem*, "the limit up until which," that signals the decolonization process, wholly or in part, whether by removal or patrimonial preservation.

PATRIMONY, *PATRIMOINE*, *TURĀTH*

Monuments, it seemed to me, were essential to French urban life.[30] I was living in Lyon in 2013–2014, at a time when the city was considering its long-standing local involvement in preserving and restoring ruins. Issues of patrimony had long been gaining currency. Three international charters—the 1931 Athens Charter, the 1964 Venice Charter, and the 2000 Krakow Charter—have declared that "the question of the conservation of the artistic and archaeological property of mankind is one that interests the community of the States, which are wardens of civilization."[31] Such guidelines for preserving monuments in or outside national boundaries reflect assumptions about the general value of artifacts of civilization. The complexity of the issues has led to many additional agreements, charters, and conventions: the Moveable Cultural Property Convention (1954), the Convention on the Means of Prohibiting and Preventing the Illicit Import, Export and Transfer of Ownership of Cultural Property (1970), also articulated in the World Cultural and Natural Heritage Conventions (1972). In the aftermath of World War II, UNESCO established the transregional Tunis-based ALECSO (Arab League Educational, Cultural and Scientific Organization) for the Middle East and North Africa in 1970. A set of rules evolved to insure, protect, and when possible, enforce "the layered metacultural operations that constitute heritage in the first place—the host of regulatory steps, actors and institutions that transform a cultural monument, a landscape or an intangible cultural practice into certified heritage."[32]

From such official (and culturally contingent) contexts, nation-states interacting with international bodies define *patrimoine* whose semantics range from "cultural property" to "history" to "inheritance," less commonly "patrimony," and often as "heritage" or "cultural heritage." These words effectively designate what many inhabitants of Lyon regard as their patrimony with its double links to France and to Roman Lugdunum. French Algeria's artifacts thus belong to European settlers who trace a long line to Rome. The preservation of objects and shared values and collective memories constitute patrimony or heritage, according to cultural theorist Robert Shannan Peckham, in his terms:

> On the one hand, [heritage] is associated with tourism and with sites of historical interest that have been preserved for the nation. Heritage designates those institutions involved in the celebration, management, and maintenance of material objects, landscapes, monuments and buildings that reflect the nation's past. On the other hand, [heritage] is used to describe a set of shared values and collective memories; it betokens inherited customs and a sense of accumulated communal experiences that are constructed as a "birthright" and are expressed in distinct languages and through other cultural performances.[33]

But Algeria and France have opposing (and overlapping) notions of patrimony. For architectural historian Nasser Rabbat, *patrimoine* in Arabic has a "lost-in-translation effect," in which the word *turāth* connotes "inherit." [34] Thus, it may include French colonial artifacts. On the eve of Algeria's hard-fought independence from France, the National Council of the Algerian Revolution (Conseil national de la révolution algérienne, CNRA) adopted the "Tripoli Program" to embed Algerian heritage in a culture of resistance such that the quest for freedom and independence intersected with heritage insofar as the civilization was said to support national resistance. The Arabic language needed to be returned, having been endangered when French was the designated official language of colonial Algeria.

> [Algeria's] economic prosperity, the exceptional vigor of its people, its traditions of struggle, the fact that it belongs to a culture and civilization common to the Maghreb and to the Arab world, have all long supported national resistance. . . . . The necessary creation of a political and social mindset informed by scientific principles and fortified against erroneous ways of thinking makes us appreciate the importance of a new conception of culture. Algerian culture will be national, revolutionary, and scientific. As a national culture, it will in the first place be about returning its dignity and effectiveness as a language of civilization to the Arabic language, the very expression of our country's cultural values. To do so, it will endeavor

> to reestablish, revalorize, and promulgate the national heritage and its twin classical and modern humanism in order to reintroduce them into the intellectual life and education of the population's sensibility.[35]

Patrimoine is thus a form of cultural resistance against the colonial European elimination of local languages and the reinvigoration of Indigenous approaches to ethnographic research that had come under attack during the French colonial era.[36]

To discuss *patrimoine* in Algeria, architect Yassine Ouagueni uses the image of phased house building. Just after independence, legal ordinance number 67-281 of December 20, 1967, called for protecting historical sites and monuments. Ouagueni dates the more substantial concern for Algeria's cultural heritage to Law no. 98-04 of June 15, 1998, which complemented or extended legislation.[37] Law no. 99-07 of April 5, 1999, added a historical and cultural heritage regime or set of rules when it amended the privileges and rights of fighters and martyrs of the Algerian revolution. Articles 52–54 identified commemorative stelae and specific sites as national revolutionary symbols that included torture centers, forced regroupment camps, prisons, battles, archives, and films. It mandated the preservation of this material historical patrimony, or heritage: "it is prohibited to transfer, in whatever form, parts of historical and cultural heritage."[38] The initiatives also include Executive Decree no. 03-322 of October 5, 2003, on protected cultural elements; the Decision of May 29, 2005, establishing interventions for protected cultural elements; the Decision of May 31, 2005, providing a list of interventions on protected cultural elements; and the Decision of November 5, 2007, to pay the costs of interventions of protected cultural elements. For Ouagueni, these initiatives raised questions about the concern for patrimony and its protection:

> In other words, it is appropriate to ask when and why this idea [of patrimony] arose in the daily life of Algerians: Was it driven by colonization? Did something entirely new emerge at specific moments of the post-colonial period? Should we see it as culminating an endogenous process or as the effect of contact with France? . . . In sum, during the colonial period (1830–1962), the colonized society saw patrimony in economic terms: a building's value was based on its materials (marble or volcanic tuff columns, marble or terra cotta tile floors, walls lime-washed or adorned with painted faïence tiles) and extended spaces, especially patios. From 1863 to 1896, colonial society considered that the only economic value of local heritage was in attracting tourists, even before the associations created by the first coloniz-

> ers identified the Roman presence in North Africa with French colonialism and made it into another foundation of colonial memory.[39]

Ouagueni's examination of France's colonial-built heritage in Algeria is important for Oran and Sidi-Bel-Abbès, the focus of two chapters. With its majority European settler population, Oran's center was long considered to have the longest continuous inhabitation of French and Spanish in Algeria.[40] But because Oran had no ancient center or "primitive" Arab element, it was unfavorably compared during the colonial era with more picturesque walled cities such as Fez, Tlemcen, Rabat, Algiers, and Marrakesh known for labyrinthine streets and homes with interior patios invisible to outsiders.[41] Although Algeria maintained French colonial heritage laws after independence, especially those that focused on precolonial architecture, until the 1999 revisions, these laws did not prevent changes, often seen as forms of decolonization, to war memorials and monuments in many Algerian cities and towns in the 1960s and '70s. No one claimed them as Algerian heritage.

DECOLONIZATION AND MONUMENTS

Why study monuments, war memorials, and statues? In 1878, art critic Henri Auguste Jouin (1841–1913) celebrated the French "genius of sculpture" vindicating the transhistorical appropriations between France and Algeria:

> Statuary, we have said is powerful. We would like to now demonstrate that sculpture is a French art. Two characteristics distinguish our race. We French people are, above all logical and social beings. . . . France has produced sculptors. They have populated the country with their masterpieces. . . . Space is an obstacle that must be overcome. Has French sculpture become a master of space? Has it conquered? Have neighboring and distant nations recognized the supremacy of our nation in the art of statuary? Which is the modern metropolis of statuary? Where are the colonies?[42]

Specific to French Algeria, aesthetic forms of eighteenth- and nineteenth-century French sculpture were catalysts for epic national representations that indexed and mediated powerful colonial-era structures of commemoration. Monuments were figurations of power and beauty governed by sculptural conventions "inseparable from the logic of the monument"; these conventions, writes art historian Rosalind Krauss, are historically contingent rather than universal:

> By virtue of this logic a sculpture is a commemorative representation. It sits in a particular place and speaks in a symbolical tongue about the meaning or use of that place. . . . Because they thus function in relation to the logic of representation and marking, sculptures are normally figurative and vertical, their pedestals an important part of the structure since they mediate between actual site and representational sign. There is nothing very mysterious about this logic; understood and inhabited, it was the source of a tremendous production of sculpture during centuries of Western art.[43]

Mainly, monuments in colonial settings are actors in colonization and decolonization. They commemorate resistance fighters in Algeria and elicit nostalgia and amnesia in France because decolonization, I will show, brings about both substitutions and additions. When France's colonial empire in Algeria ended, the afterlives of monuments—as with my encounter with the Oran war memorial split and removed to Lyon—inscribe geographical and affective provenances in at least three realms: between Algeria and France, within France toward the large numbers of returning European settlers from Algeria, and within Algeria in relation to postindependence histories written after 1962. I rely most on the temporal term "postindependence" to characterize Algeria after 1962 and the complicated interlocking histories and geographies of monuments between France and Algeria, despite slippages toward the "postcolonial" as anthropologist Ann Stoler has observed:

> Despite the warnings of those who rightly insist that [postcolonial theory] is not a time period but a critical stance . . . the term "postcolonial" often references a critical perspective on a past colonial situation (too easily made distinct from our own) or on those who bear the costs of living in a space that was once colonial and is no more.[44]

The object biography of each war memorial dedicated to those who died fighting for France uncovers political and social forms of grief that generated monument-making after World War I in both Algeria and France.[45] Public art, monuments, and sculptures expand geography and history to trans-Mediterranean spaces that link Europe and Africa. France stretched from Dunkirk in the north to Tamanrasset in the southern Algerian Sahara, or so politicians and soldiers of the empire proclaimed. They compared the Mediterranean Sea between France and Algeria to the Seine River running through Paris. This enforced geopolitical union ignored the racialized fissures within French Algeria, which was, as Frantz Fanon observed,

> [A] world cut in two. The dividing line, the frontiers are shown by the barracks and police stations. In the colonies, it is the policeman and the soldier who are the official, instituted go-betweens, the spokesmen of the settler and his rule of oppression. . . . In colonial countries, . . . the policemen and the soldier, by their immediate presence and their frequent and direct action maintain contact with the native and advise him by means of rifle butts and napalm not to budge . . . the agents of government speak the language of pure force.[46]

The native Algerian population understood the significance when colonists implanted stone statues. Architectural historian Françoise Choay relates the word "monument" to the Latin root *monere,* meaning "to recall" and "to warn."[47] Iraqi-American artist Michael Rakowitz notes that "demonstrate," "remonstrate," and "monster" come from the same Latin root:

> I started to think about monuments as monsters. Throughout history, humans have believed that monsters were sent from above to warn us about something. So, you could think of the removal of a monument as a completion of the sculpture: a way of defeating the monster by creating the opportunity for us to understand it as a warning. At least, as a warning to certain people.[48]

Monere may also refer to a surveyor's stake on the land that legally delimits property. Boundaries, warnings, monsters, and threats are implicit in Frantz Fanon's apt depiction of the causal connection between form and function, signifier and signified: "[A] world of statues, the statue of the general who carried out the conquest, the statue of the engineer who built the bridge; a world which is sure of itself, which crushes with its stones the backs flayed by whips."[49] Fanon acknowledged visceral Algerian experiences of a statue's physical presence where war memorials were another embodiment of colonial world-making. Fanon practiced psychiatry in Blida-Joinville from 1953 to 1959, where a twenty-three-foot bronze *Winged Victory* war memorial had been inaugurated in 1925. This female figure, sculpted by Émile Oscar Guillaume (1867–1954), was poised on a bronze globe placed on an elevated plinth and was visible from everywhere in the colonial town center. The statue disappeared after independence.[50] If land dispossessions, unequal repressive legal practices, military garrisons, and colonial administrations directly controlled the noncitizen Indigenous population, monuments reflected indirect control.[51] Fanon perceived colonial statuary as aggressive and obtrusive with theatrically anthropomorphic objects that commanded the surrounding space and largely forced the spectator to behold. Statuary embodied land and landscape-centered projects of native dispossession through the logic of elimination that Patrick Wolfe theorized, of dispossession encoded and marked by the monument.[52]

Fanon's assessment of materiality as a basis for concretely actualizing unequal power relations between colonizer and colonized links unexamined colonial practices on the ground to an early use of the word "decolonization." In his 1836 essay, "On the Decolonization of Algiers," Henri Fonfrède (1788–1841) attached the Latin prefix *de-* to the word "colonization" a mere six years after France's 1830 invasion of Algiers. Fonfrède's aim was to convey his urgent opposition in the "de-" to mean "come away from." In fact, he advocated that France cut its losses by reversing its conquest from the North African overseas colonial project. Elaborating on his title, *De la décolonisation d'Alger,* in an apostrophized epigraph, he writes: "Algiers, give us back our millions!" (Alger! . . . rends-nous nos millions!). Fonfrède was a political journalist in Bordeaux who covered France's maritime commerce with the colonies in the West Indies and the Ottoman Regency of Algiers. For classically educated, nineteenth-century readers, he was clearly alluding to the shocked outcry of Emperor Augustus to General Varus, the military leader responsible for losing three Roman legions to an alliance of Germanic tribes at the battle of Teutoberg Forest in 9 CE. As with the Varian tragedies and similar failed attempts to establish Roman settlements or *coloniae* in northern Europe, the conquest of Algiers would also result in massive losses according to Fonfrède. France's soldiers, honor, and economy confronted "nomadic hordes of Arab centaurs, more horse than men who fly along the sand faster than any French tax-collector."[53] He believed it was better to tend to his list of national treasures that included the nation's precious monuments. Fonfrède's coinage of the term "decolonization" targeted his French metropolitan audience as France was on the threshold of renewed imperial military entanglements across the Mediterranean Sea. He also foresaw something like the "blue water rule," adopted by the United Nations on December 16, 1952, which defined "decolonization" in Resolution 637 VII: "to be eligible for decolonization, the presence of 'blue water' between the colony and the colonizing country or a discreet set of boundaries would be needed."

The aftermath of the decolonization of French Algeria, the birth of the new Algerian sovereign state, and a French nation-state less its overseas territory are also long processes.[54] Arabic-language phrases for "decolonization," translated for me, were *mukhallafāt al-istiʿamār* (aftermaths of colonialism), *istirjāʿ al-istiqlāl* (reacquiring or recuperating independence) and *taṣfiyāt al-istiʿmār* (liquidating colonialism). Philosopher Ariella Azoulay adds: "Unlearning imperialism involves different types of '*de-*,' such as decompressing and decoding; '*re-*,' such as reversing and rewinding; and '*un-*,' such as unlearning and undoing."[55] The making, unmaking, and remaking of colonial monuments is part of a process of decolonizing the material lived world of French Algeria's monuments that was gradual, paradoxical, messy, and seemingly never-ending. Frantz Fanon is relevant here once again:

> Decolonization, which sets out to change the order of the world, is, obviously, a program of complete disorder. But it cannot come as a result of magical practices, nor of a natural shock, nor of a friendly understanding. Decolonization, as we know, is a historical process: in other words, it cannot be understood, it cannot become intelligible nor clear to itself except in the exact measure that we can discern the movements that give it historical form and content.[56]

Defining decolonization as a historical rupture and the birth of a sovereign Algeria in 1962 inadequately reflects the passions and violence surrounding the Algerian War of Independence. The word cannot measure French and Algerian bodies traumatized, tortured, and killed.[57] A million-and-a-half French conscripts served in the Algerian War of Independence war between 1954 and 1962, of whom an estimated 25,000 were killed. Algerians calculate a million-and-a-half of their own people dead during the war in the face of French counterclaims of 400,000 or even fewer. These figures do not take into account the two-and-a-half million Algerians, approximately half the rural population, who were forcibly moved from their lands into "regroupment camps," which were never more than open-air mass internment areas. More displacements affected over a million European settlers and allied Muslim and Jewish populations after Algerian independence, most departing to France and categorized as decolonization's migrants.

The studies that follow describe the complex process of moving/vandalizing, and preserving/redesigning/reinscribing monuments and objects. In France and Algeria, what are people doing with the vestigial monuments and objects of decolonization that remain from fallen empires? Commemorations involving French sculptures in Algeria irrevocably changed in postindependent Algeria once familiar entanglements among settler municipalities, the Catholic Church, and the army were dissolved. How do the structural, architectural, and political changes in an independent Algerian society intersect with new monuments or repurposed colonial models erected in nodal urban sites? After 1962, when decolonizing Algeria's artistic worlds was front and center, how did new and existing museums, galleries, art schools, and collectives connect with the biographies of Algerian artists claiming visual artistic spaces?[58]

RESEARCH AND CHAPTER OUTLINES

Monuments are meant to be immoveable although most are not. Drawing on the anthropology and folklore of art, on critical heritage studies, and on settler colonial studies, this work examines France's monuments in and from Algeria on the move. Since 1991, I have visited and lived in Algeria with my husband Nadjib Berber, an Algerian cartoonist, to whom this work is dedicated. He introduced me to overlapping familial, artistic, and academic circles. In addition, I observed, measured, photographed, delved into personal and official documents, and interviewed people in France and Algeria in French, Algerian Arabic, and English, who are involved in acts of creation, preservation, and the movement of monuments. I zigzagged between war memorials removed to France and French colonial monuments still in Algeria. I discovered that the former French empire finds new aesthetic configurations to reevaluate older statues both in France and independent Algeria. In Algeria, beyond marking the initial 1830 French conquest and subsequent settler colonial projects, new generative postcolonial monuments can be tracked because war memorials and statues have lived on after independence in 1962 even if some, but by no means most, were removed from Algeria to France. They are physical and social forms tying sculptural and artistic production to art and anthropology. Even more, so many French colonial-era monuments remained in place on Algerian soil before, during, and after the country's hard-fought independence that they have brought about affective relations with the former colonizer. As well, the new Algerian monuments—representational, figurative, and abstract statues—found everywhere in public places, can be studied ethnographically through local styles adopted postindependence. Algeria is a Muslim-majority postcolonial country, but it does not necessarily conform to the "essentialist paradigm" attributed to "Islamic cultures" that assumes "a quasi-pathological aversion to figuration."[59]

Chapter 1, "Encountering Monuments: Postcards and 'Nostalgeria'" focuses on my fieldwork, interviews, and rephotography of colonial postcards to compare monument removal from Algeria with what remains in Algeria. I analyze the visual appropriation, repurposing, and memory work that characterizes the circulation of the French colonial postcard archive of Algeria.

Chapters 2, 3, and 4 take up issues of iconoclasm, here broadly defined as Algerian transformations and French removals of monuments that some sought to preserve and renew by erecting them in new sites or replacing them with new statues in their previous settings. I met a variety of individuals and institutions involved in this process—repatriated settlers, the French military, the Catholic Church, Algerian bureaucrats, and artists. I was helped by members of three active local Algerian preservation associations in Oran, Sidi-Bel-Abbès, and Constantine, whose generous understanding of their French colonial heritage deepened mine. I describe who destroys and why, who preserves, and who transforms and why.

Chapter 2, "Moving War Monuments: From Oran Province to France," comes full circle to my introductory paragraphs. It describes the rare case of a *legally* removed war memorial from Oran to Lyon. My initial ignorance that Oran's war memorial in its new Lyon home was a "removal" attests to my inescapable enmeshment in the material world of French Algeria, where the memorial once stood. As it turns out, the Oran war memorial installed in Lyon in 1968 anticipated by a decade the first monument dedicated to the French fallen of Algeria and their native allies—usually considered to be the Troyes monument in France erected in 1977.[60]

Once relocated to France, Algeria's removed colonial statues condense emotions, rituals, and new performances of settler exile identity. While scholars have analyzed Pied-Noir commemorations and monuments by considering the nostalgia, trauma, or melancholy and mourning they provoke, I examine how the vibrant afterlife of French Algeria appears in practices surrounding the memorials, as manifestations of heritage emerging from the vast material destructions of two world wars and the Algerian War of Independence. Indeed, as philosopher Étienne Balibar posits, "Algeria is irreducibly present in France just as France is in Algeria."[61] Historian Hosni Kitouni likens this enduring relationship to that of a shattered family disputing items from a formerly shared household: "[W]e are still in a horrible neurotic discussion with the French, as if we were caught in the drama of an endless divorce where neither party wants to leave without taking everything in the house with them."[62]

The counterpoint is a discussion of the French colonial statues that remained in Oran, Algeria's most European precolonial urban center, and which were destroyed, repurposed, or safeguarded. This chapter explores folklore and anthropology's contributions to heritage studies and how Franco-Algerian *patrimoine* is locally lived, defined, revisited, received, realized, reinvented.

Chapter 3, "Dismantling a World: Sidi-Bel-Abbès and the French Foreign Legion," looks at how monuments construct the image of French Algeria and continue to resonate to this day. Algeria possesses an abundance of French monuments and Roman ruins, the latter assimilated in powerful foundational ways to France's colonial identity in North Africa and exemplified in this chapter by the French Foreign Legion.[63] Sidi-Bel-Abbès was the cradle of the French Foreign Legion whose headquarters remained there until 1962, at which point vestiges of the command post were moved to southern France, to Aubagne, replete with statues, films, a museum, and an archive. Indeed, the storied French Foreign Legion was created in and for Algeria after the 1830 French military occupation, and many monuments were erected in support of French and Christian revisionist histories. Drawing on the concept of "dissonant heritage," I describe the fates of Sidi-Bel-Abbès's two war memorials as an example of how independent Algeria responded to the residual statues, stelae, monuments, and other representations of the colonizing military past.[64]

Chapter 4, "Creating Provenance: Ahmed Benyahia and Public Sculptures in the Constantine Region," follows the 1972 statue commemorating Algerian war hero Zighoud Youcef (1921–1956), which was cast using the melted bronze of the interwar 1922 war memorial to settler and native soldiers from French Algeria killed fighting for France on the battlefields of World War I. The creation, emplacement, disappearance, and reappearance of the Zighoud statue sculpted by artist Ahmed Benyahia for Constantine are the story of postindependent Algeria's efforts to decolonize public space. This chapter considers the ways in which decolonization can lead to the capacity to value, the will to appropriate, and the activity to preserve the departed oppressor's objects and architecture. I draw on possibilities of reciprocal repatriations and mutually beneficial interdependence as expressed by Régis Debray at the Goncourt Prize award ceremony for Algerian author Kamel Daoud. For his *Meursault, contre-enquête,* Daoud rewrote and gave a name, a family, and a history to the anonymous "Arab" of Albert Camus's *The Stranger.*[65] Debray, a member of the Goncourt jury, remarked on reciprocity of the events: "You repatriated *The Stranger* to your culture. You have made Albert Camus into a French author who talks about you, to you. So we, the Goncourt jury, we are repatriating your [novel] *Meursault, contre-enquête* [*The Meursault Counterinvestigation*] into the treasury of French literature, the treasury of all literature."[66]

The conclusion offers a close reading of the cover artwork of this book by Ahmed Benyahia. His aesthetic and material practices are grounded in postindependence transformations and appropriations of Western figurative art that reflect an artistic commitment to represent French-Algerian histories of violence and their sculptural afterlives. Monuments erected before, during, and after France's rule over its Algerian provinces call for anthropological approaches to settler colonial studies, art and material matters, and heritage formation broadly, yet critically conceived. The proliferation and aesthetics of monument-building throughout Algeria that had been assumed to be imported from France also draws on Roman antiquity, the Ottoman era, and local socioreligious beliefs and practices for remembering and honoring the dead, the famous, and the divine. Decolonizing French Algeria's monumental heritage is a chronology of France and Algeria acting on their respective environments through iconoclasm, preservation, and renewal. Monuments and statues in motion between Algeria and France suggest possibilities for reconfiguring entanglements and power imbalances between the two countries. These may be deemed modes of colonial domination intrinsically exhibiting postindependent relations of power, but they also convey the human experience of things in place that marks the sociospatial nature of decolonization. The narrative of decolonizing Algeria's heritage of French public art—the contentious heritage battles, paradoxical reversals, controversial actors (humans or inanimate artworks), unfinished aesthetic renewals, uncanny familiarities—makes it urgent to imagine and represent transformative action.

CHAPTER ONE

ENCOUNTERING MONUMENTS

Postcards and "Nostalgeria"

IN 1990, I BECAME A deltiologist, someone who studies and makes a hobby of collecting postcards.[1] I joined in the brisk trade of colonial images at the many postcard stalls lining the street in front of the Algiers Cinémathèque. I wanted to use postcards of French Algeria as historical documents and looked for those showing the monuments that I was seeing in France or Algeria. To reproduce the images for my study, I also sought out the commercial firms that had produced, marketed, and seldom control copyright for these postcards, which rarely name the photographers. Colonial tourist postcards, I quickly realized, often showed images of monuments typically from the front whereas I looked also at the back, a visual blind spot. They were imprinted with generic captions and generalized identifiers, making the façades synecdoches for colonialism.[2] In Lyon, Nîmes, Aix-en-Provence, Cannes, and online, I found a considerable and informed trade in colonial postcards fueled by the European settler community.

Postcards, photography, and Algeria overlap. Photography was an established medium by the time of the invasion of Algeria. The camera had been invented in the late 1820s, claimed by the Frenchmen Joseph Nicéphore Niépce and Louis Daguerre. In 1837, seven years after the French occupied Algiers, the Commission des monuments historiques was established to inventory and classify historical and architectural monuments in France using photography and, later, using postcards.[3] The technology was not so easily accessible in Algeria and reinforced disparities between conquering and subjugated populations. Photography, a visually extractive technology, can capture only parts of the whole within a frame. Ariella Azoulay describes the photographic practice in this way: "It [the picture] commands what sort of things have to be distanced, bracketed, removed, forgotten, suppressed, ignored, overcome, and made irrelevant for the shutter of the camera to function, as well as for the photograph to be taken and its meaning to be accepted."[4]

For European settlers of Algeria and for recipients in the French metropole, these postcards offered a form of civic instruction on colonialism.[5] People rarely figured in them, thereby ensuring that the colonial monument postcard remained faithful to a genre that presents Indigenous-free landscapes and objects. The native inhabitants of French Algeria figured in a separate category of postcards presenting "scenes and types" that created categories and stereotypes of natives. And while postcards did not depict scenes of violence, they implicitly showed the empire's grip on the visual archive and on the monuments and inhabitants of the colony. These photographs became the principal introduction in France to the people in Algeria.

Malek Alloula's path-breaking *The Colonial Harem* charts how French Algeria's postcards allowed for the easy reproduction of image-making:

> Photography steps in to take up the slack and reactivates the phantasm at its lowest level. The postcard does it one better; it becomes the poor man's phantasm: for a few pennies, display racks full of dreams. The postcard is everywhere, covering all the colonial space, immediately available to the tourist, the soldier, the colonist. It is at once their poetry and their glory captured for the ages; it is also their pseudoknowledge of the colony. It produces stereotypes in the manner of great seabirds producing guano, the fertilizer of the colonialist vision.[6]

Algeria's efficient colonial postal service created soon after the 1830 conquest helped disseminate the reproduced images shaping French visions of Algeria in France and the colony.[7] After 1962, as military monuments were being destroyed, repurposed, relocated, or reduced to vestiges, these postcards became souvenirs for the French settler community of a remembered French Algeria. They also served in many films, graphic novels, television programs, and websites illustrating and reconstructing the villages and towns of French Algeria. Even as the photographs of the monuments and stereotypes persevere, they also lend themselves to new narratives. "The photograph is out there, an object in the world, and anyone, always (at least in principle), can pull at one of its threads and trace it in such a way as to reopen the image and renegotiate what it shows, possibly even completely overturning what was seen in it before."[8]

For Algerians and former European settlers, these old postcards confirm or jog memories of historical experiences.[9] As they circulate on settler websites, postcards document what never needed to be said before. Now commentaries are lengthy.[10] Often posted as first-person narratives on public web pages, they typically juxtapose an image of a war memorial serving as a background for family photographs of a school or sports team. The focus is on collective memory. European settlers, Algerian natives, and anthropologists all see the postcards differently, however, and measure the changes in image and meaning.[11] After independence, many Algerians discovered these postcards along with memorial books and websites saturated with settler nostalgia. Various European settler communities download, print, and upload these virtual repositories of pre-independence images of their hometowns. Colonial photographs decorate many Algerian cafés not because Algerians are nostalgic for their colonial past, but rather because not much good contemporary Algerian photojournalism tells the story of independent Algeria, according to photographer Abdo Shanan.[12] French colonial postcards are rich resources for Algerians, for historians, and for anthropologists seeking a visual archive by and about French Algeria. As an entry point into this account of colonial military monuments moved from Algeria to France, I begin with the visual archive of Alain Amato.

ALAIN AMATO: MONUMENTS EXILED TO FRANCE

In 1975, during a family vacation near Nantes, Amato chanced upon a seventeen-foot bronze statue and plinth of General Louis Juchault de Lamoricière (1806–1865). The general stood with an upraised hand brandishing a sword and wearing the uniform and *chéchia* cap of the Zouaves, the light infantry regiment of North Africa that he reorganized after serving as a Zouave officer. Missing from the Nantes site were the original sculptures of a female *France* protecting a female *Algeria* who proffers fruit while a Zouave soldier trumpets the call to battle.[13] The statue stopped Amato in his tracks.[14] Born in Constantine, he had felt acutely alienated from his childhood memories of Algeria and out of place and time in his French environment. Coming upon the statue was painful and productive; it sparked a project of sentimental salvage through documentation about Algeria's European settlers and their monuments.[15]

Amato undertook a partial census of colonial Algeria's displaced monuments. He began his research over a decade after the mass exodus of French settlers. In 1979, he published *Monuments en exil* listing some two hundred artifacts, concentrating on war memorials, statues, and church bells, organized alphabetically by their site of relocation in France. Where European settlers who returned to France after 1962 spoke of their "exodus" from Algeria, Amato focused on "monuments in exile":

> Over the years, those memories now evoke with great acuity the symbol of the lost homeland. I use the qualifier of "exiled" for them because I think that monuments and statues are always created as a function of the place and space they will occupy and that after Algerian independence, they were reinstalled far from these places and the spaces for which they were originally destined.[16]

The Lamoricière statue that spurred Amato was inaugurated in Constantine on April 25, 1909, in the presence of its sculptor Jean-Baptiste Belloc (1863–1919) and of Lamoricière's daughter (figure 6).

It was removed by the French Army Engineering Corps (Génie militaire) days after Algerian independence on July 8–9, 1962. Amato detailed the stages of moving French colonial monuments from Algeria to France often by order of the French Ministry of Defense. It fell to the corps of engineers typically to dismantle the statues and war memorials for eventual transfer and storage in the port of Marseilles in early 1962, before Algeria's official independence. Gradually, the monuments were dispersed to regional depots often linked in some fashion to the statue's subject:

> Then came independence, and in a single night between July 8th and 9th 1962, the statue was unbolted and shipped to Marseilles by the French Army corps of engineers. It stayed on the docks of Marseille until June 1963 and was later transferred to Nantes; the Minister of the Armies having assigned it to de Lamoricière's hometown. At its arrival, it was stored in sections in the Moutonnerie warehouse. About a year later Mr. Pennetier, Mayor of Saint-Philbert de Grand Lieu and general counsel of the Loire-Atlantique, learned of its existence and had the idea of claiming it for his town. In fact, the family takes its name from a small place called "La Moricière" two kilometers from Saint-Philbert. Five years would pass during which Pennetier lobbied energetically. His tenacity was rewarded on June 29, 1969, he inau-

FIGURE 6. Constantine's monument to General Lamoricière, sculpted by Jean-Baptiste Belloc (1863–1919). Postcard, Collection Idéale P.S. Author's collection.

gurated the statue facing an audience of two thousand people. The body of General Lamoricière lies in the chapel of the Saint Philibert cemetery.[17]

After independence, the sites where the statues had stood, and indeed the towns and public squares, were renamed. After Lamoricière's statue was ripped from its Constantine emplacement in 1962, the eponymous square was renamed Martyrs Square (Place des Martyrs).[18] Commander Larbi Berredjem, who took charge of Zone 2 (Wilaya II) that included Constantine, threatened to destroy all French colonial statues and artifacts unless they were immediately eliminated. As expressions of postindependent emotions of bereavement for the Algerian war dead, he positioned two symbolic tombstones on the emptied site of Lamoricière's statue in the summer of 1962 seeking to reaffirm Algerian ownership of the space after the French military "repatriation" of the statue.[19] Berredjem's symbolic tombstones were considered inappropriate for the heart of the Constantine, and the site eventually became a traffic circle embellished with flowers, grass, and a fountain until 2014. For the 2015 festivities celebrating Constantine as the capital of Arab culture, an abstract sculpture representing a dove was erected and attributed to a Chinese construction company. A large, polished brass globe bearing sharp porcupine-like quills sat atop the statue, which locals called the "duck." It was later renamed the Corona for its resemblance to the COVID-19 virus (figure 7).

FIGURE 7. "Corona" monument in Place des Martyrs (formerly Place de Lamoricière), Constantine. Photo by author, July 3, 2022.

PAIRED POSTCARDS, MONUMENT ERASURES

Two decades after Amato launched his pioneering project memorializing French Algeria's former monuments in France, I traced some of his steps in Algeria. I looked at portable church bells, small religious statues, plaques, busts, large war memorials, and even exhumed remains of bodies that were in the process of being removed from Algeria to their presumed place of origin in France. I rephotographed postcards—my visual portal to monuments, statues, and war memorials—and juxtaposed them with my own photos to create a "before-and-after" method of visual comparisons.[20] I read colonial photographs as moments in the biography of an artifact that capture the recognizable erasure of formal features.[21] Postcards of monuments show me now the details of missing pieces—a broken sword, a missing cornucopia, a disappeared limb. Describing monuments that remain identifiable despite their obvious modification or relocation, Richard Wrigley uses the term *sous rature* or "under erasure."[22] Recognizable erasures mean that a colonial monument remains a colonial monument, while still evoking in the viewer who recognizes them a sense of loss and melancholy. The dismantling of French colonial monuments followed by Algerian iconoclasm and the conservation practices of the French colonial heritage, in addition to French-Algerian disputes about ownership and preservation, has led to many recognizable erasures. My fieldwork offers a visual ethnography about remnants of Algeria's colonial heritage.

My first pair of images show a plinth that once supported a war memorial in the Algerian landscape (figure 8). A train traverses a pediment—formerly the foundation of Oran's war memorial commemorating the railway workers who died on the battlefield for France. A bas-relief depicting a train in movement, in front of the empty plinth at the main entrance to Oran's "neo-Moorish" (*neo-Mauresque*) train station designed by architect Albert Ballu (1849–1939) is all that remains.[23]

Figure 9 shows the original monument. Two stalwart soldiers, nudes, and a large round plaque are placed to suggest a train engine. The postcard gives a partial view of the upper grouping, but no information about the damage or removal. This is a recognizable erasure sited in front of a well-preserved French colonial architectural complex in Algeria.

The war memorial is attributed to Jules Dugaret, a French settler from Oran, trained at the École des Beaux Arts in Paris. At its installation, the

FIGURE 8. Empty plinth of the colonial war memorial to the railroad workers, Oran train station. Sculptor Jules Dugaret, ca. 1930s. Photo by author, May 2014.

FIGURE 9. Original Oran train station colonial war memorial to the railway workers (*monuments aux morts des cheminots*) of Oran Province who fought and died for France. The Serra postcard collection is housed in Musée Nicéphore Niépce, France. Reproduced by permission: © Fonds Combier, Musée Nicéphore Niépce, Ville de Chalon-sur-Saône.

contemporary colonial press lauded Dugaret's intricate mortuary statues in cemeteries throughout western Algeria.[24]

Another Oran war memorial of World War I sailors who died at sea sits in Oran's public Promenade de Létang (figure 10). The verdant promenade is like a balcony offering panoramic views of the port; the city's iconic Mount Murdjadjo is visible in the distance. Figure 11 is paired with figure 10 documenting the monument's decline and the legible inscription identifying a colonial war memorial.[25]

Anonymous photos of the intact column circulated online until 2000 at least. The shaft was wrecked sometime between 2000 and 2018, therefore, and pieces of column were strewn about suggesting the fragility of French military structures when no one cares, or that broken columns are left in place to beautify the park, attesting to Algerian familiarity with the preserved sites of Roman Algeria in various states of decay. The fragments of the French colonial war memorial in Oran's Cheikh Ben Badis Park may have been left as a warning, making the destruction the message.[26]

Twenty-five miles northeast of Oran on the seaside boulevard facing the port of Arzew, another "erased" navy memorial commemorates sailors who died for France. The memorial was transformed postindependence. Little is known about the sculptor beyond a reference in the weekly colonial satirical journal *Oran-Spectacles*, where Isaac Sarraude, the Algerian Jewish marble-maker (*marbrier*) who completed the work in 1958, was characterized as affable and talented (*sympathique et talentueux*).[27] Sarraude's workshop in Oran's Mdina Jdida still stands (see chapter 3). After independence, the sculpture was painted azure, navy, blue-green, and powder blue (compare figures 12 and 13). The blue for the nautical apparitions of a mermaid and an anchor transform a somber war memorial into a vision of oceanic depths. Playful aspects are emphasized in this colonial military war memorial locally referenced as *la sirène* (the mermaid).

FIGURE 10. Plinth of the colonial war memorial to French naval troops on the former Promenade de Létang (today's Promenade Cheikh Ben Badis) with Mount Murdjadjo in the background, Oran. Photo by author, June 10, 2018.

FIGURE 11. Colonial war memorial to sailors, repaired and re-erected in 1939 on the Promenade de Létang, Oran. Postcard, no publisher. Author's collection.

FIGURE 12. The Arzew colonial war memorial to sailors (*Le monument aux marins*), inaugurated November 11, 1958. Postcard, Ed. Alexander Sirecky, Oran, no. 12. Author's collection.

FIGURE 13. Postindependence painted Arzew war memorial. Photo by author, May 2, 2019.

Simple columns, obelisks, and cenotaphs (empty tombs) were also erased. Many exceptionally reusable, unadorned, freestanding columns commemorating the Algerian dead of the two world wars became artistic commemorations of the Algerian War of Independence. Many of the columns standing in western Oran's provincial towns of Gdyel (formerly known as Saint-Cloud, which also lost her female *Winged Victory*) and Arzew's main square were changed by the addition of new signs or plaques and, often, a plaster relief sculpture of the Emir Abdelkader, Algeria's preeminent nineteenth-century hero.

Bas-reliefs of the Emir Abdelkader added to columns are popular, exemplified in Oran where the French removed the ground-level statue on a colonial-era obelisk in Place d'Armes (a name that stuck despite its official renaming as First of November Square). The 1898 monument by Jules Dalou (1838–1902), sculpted of Algerian marble and imported stone (figure 14) is crowned by a bronze female nude *Winged Victory*, a familiar allegorical

FIGURE 14. Monument to the Battle of Sidi-Brahim, main square of Oran, erected 1898, sculpted by Jules Dalou. Postcard, LL (Léon et Lévy) no. 119. Author's collection.

figure on World War I monuments.[28] Her stance and the dynamic movement of her robe allude to the *Winged Victory* of Samothrace (second century BCE), which inspired so many French writers and sculptors who saw it in the Louvre as of 1884.[29] Dalou placed the female sculpture of France at the base of the Oran war memorial celebrating the French soldiers who had perished at the 1845 Battle of Sidi-Brahim won by the Emir Abdelkader.

Writer Maurice Dreyfous provided a rare, detailed description of the colonial sculpture:

> At the top stands a statue of *Victory* and on the small base, a woman, seen from behind, symbolizing *France* fully clothed, one knee buried, finishes writing at the bottom of the obelisk the last names of the soldiers renowned for the Sidi Brahim affair, a list covers the entire front of the monument. Her left hand holds a flag, whose upright shaft and restrained folds follow the oblique line of the obelisk. Next to her rest on the pedestal sit the high shako cap and the large rifle of the older troops of Algeria. Above, *Victory*, stretches her arms, her palm and laurel wreath hover in space. The head, in a supple gesture, slightly bent towards the left shoulder, seems to sing. The body is full draped, below the loins, sitting on the hips and revealing the lower abdomen and the left groin, recalling, by the ensemble of its arrangement in this square, the drapery of the Venus of Milo that hugs her legs and moves left in a floating fold. The erect and very supple naked torso emerging from the folds of the fabric thus attracts all the light. Behind it, two small eagle wings stretched and flapping, moderate and harmonize the Ion imbuing the feet posed at the top of the obelisk with a sense of flight; their lines balance that of the drapery that flutter as the wind blows. The statues are bronze, the obelisk is made from Algerian marble. A vast cartouche, crowned with a running and hanging garland, decorates the façade. This is where the dedication is etched.[30]

Dreyfous pointed out that no other work by Dalou took so much time to complete. After casting the statue, the despairing sculptor destroyed all the plaster models making it necessary to travel to Oran to see Dalou's *Victory*. The statue of France at ground level was among many statues and war memorials slated for removal by the French military at Algerian independence; this one was selected because it was easy to move. On April 1, 1963, it was transported to France to be installed in Périssac.[31] In figure 15, the *Winged Victory* still dances high up on the column in Oran, inaccessible to Algerians or French in the early postindependence years when these monuments were moved.

After independence, Algerians replaced the French inscription and

FIGURE 15. Monument to the Battle of Sidi-Brahim, erected in 1898 and modified in 1969 in the former Place d'Armes, now Place du 1er Novembre, Oran. Sculptor Jules Dalou. Photo by author, November 4, 2019.

affixed bust-like reliefs of the Emir's face on all four sides of the obelisk. Mohamed Cherfaoui, an art student in Oran's École des Beaux Arts in the 1960s, explains that he and fellow students were asked to fabricate the four reliefs of the Emir.[32] They called on Oran's famous marble-maker Mohamed Bouledras (known as Hamani), who was responsible for changing another of Oran's other war memorials (see chapter 2). The French inscription, "Comrades, defend yourselves to the death," was replaced with the Quranic Sūrah Āl ʿImrān 3:169 that appears on many postindependence Algerian war monuments: "And never think of those who have been killed in the cause of Allah as dead. Rather, they are alive with their Lord, receiving provision." Today in Oran, the monument is reread as a doubling of two Algerian victories—1845 and 1962—when the long colonial night ended. Colonialization remains visible in the recognizable presence of a French colonial war memorial column topped by the bronze allegorical statue. The Algerian reliefs and the missing statue of France measure two erasures. Tunisian writer Albert Memmi offers this understanding of the process:

> We then witness a reversal of terms. Assimilation being abandoned, the colonized's liberation must be carried out through a recovery of self and of au-

> tonomous dignity. Attempts at imitating the colonizer required self-denial; the colonizer's rejection is the indispensable prelude to self-discovery. That accusing and annihilating image must be shaken off; oppression must be attacked boldly since it is impossible to go around it. After having been rejected for so long by the colonizer, the day has come when it is the colonized who must refuse the colonizer.[33]

The most spectacular recognizably erased monument to the war dead stands in downtown Algiers. Erected in 1928, it was sculpted by Paul Landowski (1875–1961) and Charles Bigonet (1877–1931) from creamy limestone (*pierre de Lens*). Landowski named it *Le Pavois* (*The Shield*). The elaborate composition includes a corpse lying on a bier-like shield upheld by an Algerian spahi and a French cavalryman on horseback enveloping a female Winged Victory, a lesson in fraternal cohabitation. Below the two soldiers, ambulating men and women represent the bereaved wartime settler and native communities. Landowski described the female mourners as embodiments of intercommunal solidarity:

> [I] completely switched around the rear group of the Algiers monument. Two Arabs will be the background. A sort of warrior from the south. The main group will consist of a French woman and an Arab woman in each other's arms. Effect is starting to be excellent. The dead man is cast.[34]

Bigonet's bas-reliefs portrayed stretcher-bearers, soldiers, and more members of the mutually supportive lives of Arabs and Europeans in the colony (figure 16).

Landowski's monument remained unscathed from 1962 until 1978 when the Third African Games were held in Algiers, and for which a collective of Algerian artists and art students led by M'hamed Issiakhem (1928–1985) was commissioned to destroy and replace it with a memorial to the Algerian Revolution. Their radical solution was to surround Landowski's work with a new concrete Algerian sculpture. The statue was wound with wire mesh (known as "grillage Zimmerman" in Algeria), which formed a new skeletal framework onto which white cement was slapped. Landowski's colonial troops bearing the shield that protected the colony was erased by Issiakhem's sculpture of a protective shield. Two clenched, raised fists breaking their chains jut out from the base and an Algerian combatant, assumed to be the artist's self-portrait, is at the back (figures 17 and 18). Architectural historian Zeynep Çelik reflects on Issiakhem's shrouding and manipulation:

FIGURE 16. Sculptors Paul Landowski and Charles Bigonet, *monument aux morts* entitled *Le Pavois*, Algiers, 1928. Reproduced by permission of Marc Landowski and Elizabeth Caillet.

> [Issiakhem's] powerful intervention, referred to simply as "*bétonnement*," is open to multiple interpretations. Is it a celebration of Algerian independence? Or is it a constant reminder of its colonial history? Does the roughness allude to the violence of the colonial rule and the decolonisation war? Is colonialism buried alive here? Is this hence a unique "sarcophagus in concrete"? Certainly, the idiosyncratic structure still standing in one of the most prominent locations of Algiers does not leave the casual passerby unmoved but prompts multiple reactions and has a shocking impact.[35]

The Landowski-Issiakhem sculpture has been variously interpreted as a hidden artistic dialogue, a literal palimpsest, a protective enclosure, interlocked memories, a sarcophagus, and an echo chamber. Writer Tahar Djaout saw it as a shell waiting to be opened to recuperate the colonial monument.[36] In 2012, when cracks appeared in the concrete exostructure to reveal the hidden interior of the French marble memorial, artist Amina Menia referred to stacked memories, a metaphor for French-Algerian relations before the state repaired and re-covered it:

> This monument covering a second monument brings to light the stacking of memories. It seems to me that it might be the absolute metaphor of the

FIGURE 17. Sculpted by M'hamed Issiakhem, Algiers, 1978, front and side view. Block sticking out covers Landowski's bronze horse head. Photo by author, November 13, 2019.

FIGURE 18. Sculpted by M'hamed Issiakhem, Algiers, 1978, rear view facing downtown and port. Photo by author, November 13, 2019.

> relationship between Algeria and France. In this silent dialogue, we face avoidance, diversion, the unsaid and unfinished. By extension, this overlay represents the two nations, the two histories that intersect without caressing, that collide without touching.[37]

COLONIAL PRESERVATION IN ALGERIA

Established as a French military colony during the conquest of western Algeria as early as 1837, Misserghin lies ten miles southwest of Oran. Its intact World War I monument stands inside the gated city hall enclosure (figure 19). After independence, a statue of the Virgin Mary taken from the town's former Catholic Church (since transformed into a mosque) joined it (figure 20). The colonial past was preserved by removal and maintenance, gestures that safeguard *le rouge et le noir*, the army and the church, the twin pillars of colonialism, standing together in the outdoor garden.

As I photographed the main square, an early example of French colonial town planning, a municipal worker pointed to one side of the colonial war memorial's pedestal where, during the Dark Decade, the incised names of dead Algerian Muslim soldiers had been inexpertly cemented over to efface their names whereas the French names of soldiers were left intact, just as ancient Romans struck names inscribed on monuments—*damnatio memoriae*—as a "condemnation of memory." The Misserghin colonial war memorial thus no longer commemorated the heroic sacrifices of Algerian conscripts in the two world wars, which still touch Algerian families to this day. Its defacement reflected an amalgamation of Algerian Muslim service to France in two world wars to the role of the Harkis, the Muslim auxiliary soldiers who fought for France during the War of Independence. Conflating the current Algerian regime and the former French colonial state into a single enemy to be overthrown, iconoclastic acts such as this one were common during the Dark Decade of the 1990s, dramatically lashing out at municipal property: soldiers who served warranted being effaced.

Obvious symbolic desecrations target colonial necronominalism, a term defined by historian Thomas Laqueur as "a moral imperative to hold on to them [war memorials] in public settings . . . to inscribe them in stone or steel . . . to treat them as if they were actual remains."[38] Partial destruction translates into partially legible Algerian Muslim names; this "public secret" is that all who enter the building "know what not to know."[39] The town of Misserghin had opted to preserve the monument and statue through ac-

FIGURE 19. Colonial war memorial in front of the Misserghin town hall. Photo by author, May 2017.

FIGURE 20. The 1897 statue of the Virgin Mary was removed from the former church of Misserghin to the enclosure of the town hall. Photo by author, May 2017.

cretion, entropy, and clutter. Nor did the municipality erase the traces of the attempted erasure, perhaps to make it as a warning and an expression of state power to despoilers. The partial destruction of this particular interwar monument was relatively easy to chart because, like so many French memorials, this one relegated the names of "native" Algerian Muslim soldiers to one quadrant devoid of the names of any European settlers. The presence in Misserghin of intact French colonial statues belonging to the military and the church is not unique. In town squares throughout Algeria's western Oran province, abundant examples reflect very different responses to memorials from the colonial past and the celebration of struggles for independence.

Preserving French colonial statues and architecture is one aspect of twenty-first century Algerian urban life and patrimonial consciousness that came to my attention in May 2017 when I visited El-Maleh (former colonial Rio Salado, thirty-five miles southwest of Oran) and sat in a café enjoying a delicious grilled kebab dinner. I had with me a sepia-colored postcard of a statue of France's victorious, helmeted Marianne flanked by an armed infantryman, inaugurated on December 9, 1923 (figure 21). The sculptor was Camille Alaphilippe, who was born in Tours in 1874 and settled in Algeria after military service in World War I where he remained until his death in 1934.[40]

In the place of the former war memorial by Alaphilippe stands an Algerian monument dedicated to the martyrs of the Algerian Revolution massacred in the region by French soldiers in 1957.[41] A pair of oversized hands clasp an open book, *al-kitāb*, a popular iconographic representation that anthropologist Mohamed Hirreche Baghdad relates this to the message of Islam (*al-risāla*) (figure 22).[42]

The café proprietor pointed to the colonial photos and photocards that he had downloaded from the internet and put on his walls. Using the images, he discussed the current layout of the square directly facing us. The church that was built by the Algiers-born architect René Vasselon (1902–1967), who designed schools and hospital buildings throughout Algeria, often with his associate Georges Garnier (1881–1956), did not appear in the postcard. The town's church bell is dedicated to Saint Monique, or Saint Monica, mother of Augustine of Hippo, both often claimed by Catholics as early Christians in Algeria. It was removed to the church of Saint-Pierre-de-Chanel in Rilleux-la-Pape near Lyon, under the auspices of Cardinal Léon-Étienne Duval (1903–1996), Archbishop of Algiers from 1954–1988 as

FIGURE 21. Sculptor Camille Alaphilippe (1874–1934). Undated colonial postcard, "Rio Salado—the war memorial and town hall." Creative Commons license CC BY-NC-SA 2.0 FR: https://www.geneanet.org/cartes-postales/view/5904095#0.

FIGURE 22. El Maleh (ex-Rio Salado) Algerian war memorial and town hall. Photo by author, May 24, 2017.

part of the "rescue" (*sauvetage*) of hundreds of church objects in the years immediately after independence.[43]

In town squares throughout Algeria's western Oran Province, we find examples that speak to very different relationships to the colonial past and independence struggles. Algerian war memorials are often located on the site of former French monuments, for example. An Algerian monument dedicated to the martyrs of the Algerian Revolution massacred in the region by French soldiers in 1957 replaced the missing statue of Marianne in El Maleh's main square.[44] Streets have been renamed; for example, El-Maleh's main street was renamed Jean Coutant to memorialize the death of a European settler tortured for his allegiance to Algeria's national liberation. El-Maleh's monument to the martyrs of the Algerian Revolution is an example of Algerian monuments supplanting French monuments whereas Misserghin preserved its colonial statues by moving the Virgin Mary statue and by erecting, in the main square directly opposite its municipal enclosure, a newer monument to martyrs of the Algerian War of Independence (figure 23). The names of Algerian Muslims link the proximate war memori-

FIGURE 23. Misserghin's cenotaph to the Algerian War of Independence on the main square stands close to monuments in figures 19 and 20. Photo by author, May 2017.

als, juxtaposed to emphasize the twentieth-century's three murderous wars in which Algerian combatants died—World War I, World War II, and the Algerian War of Independence.

After photographing El Maleh's postindependence Algerian monument, I entered the 1904 town hall (shown in the postcard) that still operates. The predominantly Spanish-speaking settlers of Rio Salado had embedded an engraved stone plaque, which remains untouched in the entrance way. I was warmly greeted by the mayor, who grasped my hands and repeated in French, "Welcome back home, we saved your war monument to the dead!" I am the same age as a returning Pied-Noir and may even resemble a child of Rio Salado who departed in 1962. From the mayor, I learned about a second preserved colonial war memorial in the walled Christian cemetery of El Maleh.

Christian cemeteries were often used to relocate war memorials in the first years after the war, at least temporarily. In the village of Trois Marabouts (now Sidi Ben Adda), 60 miles southwest of Oran, frightened settlers collectively removed their war memorial of a French *poilu* infantryman on the eve of Algerian independence by destroying the plinth and installing the sculpture in the European cemetery where it remained until 1989. Ultimately, the statue was reinstalled in the necropolis of the Petit-Lac military cemetery near Oran, home to sculptures and tombs of 10,000 French, British, and American soldiers who died during World War II (figure 24).[45] In 1962, the cemetery and its care were transferred to France.

In the town of Batna, a magnificent *Winged Victory* war memorial by Algerian Jewish sculptor Joseph Ebstein was moved after independence from the central boulevard to the Christian cemetery (figure 25).

Initially, it was replaced by a bland pyramid-shaped structure, but in 1997, during the Dark Decade, a bust of revolutionary hero Mostefa Ben-Boulaïd was installed on the site. In 2014, on the sixtieth anniversary of the November 1, 1954 revolution, during a large, festive ceremony paid for by the municipality, Hossine Mazouz, Governor of Batna Province, inaugurated the bust having worked with members of the Ben-Boulaïd family. It stands on an outsized square pedestal. Each side displays different photographs of the six historical figures of the Algerian Revolution and a newspaper image of Ben-Boulaïd's arrest in Tunisia in 1955 (figure 26).[46]

In Batna and El Maleh, I learned about French colonial war memorials preserved in the walled Christian cemeteries. I also experienced the welcome afforded a departed European settler who makes the return visit. The

FIGURE 24. *Poilu* at parade rest, formerly the colonial war memorial of the village of Trois-Marabouts, installed in Oran's Petit-Lac Cemetery minus the plinth. Photo by the author, May 7, 2017.

FIGURE 25. Joseph Ebstein, sculptor, *Winged Victory* war memorial moved from Batna's town center to the Christian cemetery. Photo by A. F. Chenni, June 10, 2021. Reproduced by permission.

FIGURE 26. Monument to Mostefa Ben-Boulaïd installed in 1999 to replace Joseph Ebstein's *Winged Victory* statue in downtown Batna. Photo by author, June 11, 2022.

El Maleh mayor especially acknowledged and authenticated the performative parameters of exiled settler nostalgia for Algeria in the sentimental tour I received of the cemetery and war memorial as if I were a returning Pied-Noir visitor. More visits in Algeria led me to these two object biographies that describe how Algerians and French view their contested, shared tangible heritages: one of the Sétif statue, which is preserved in Algeria, and the second, of a Bugeaud statue, removed to France and replaced by another statue in Algeria.

SÉTIF AND ALGIERS: DECOLONIZING MONUMENTS

I first visited the Sétif monument in 1990 during my two years in Oran with my partner. My stay was cut short in 1992 at the beginning of Algeria's internal civil strife, often referred to as the Black or Dark Decade (*décennie noire* in French, *al-ʿushriyya al-sawdāʾ* in Arabic). In the country's first contested national elections between December 1991 and January 1992, the Islamist political party, the Islamic Salvation Front (Front islamique du salut, FIS) was facing the National Liberation Front (Front de libération nationale, FLN), the single political party in power since independence in 1962. The outcome of the first round of elections—where the FIS was well ahead—set off a political upheaval. On January 11, 1992, I watched Algerian television amid a roomful of disbelieving Oran friends listening to President Chadli Bendjedid read his resignation. His forced retirement led to the suspension of a second-round run-off between the two leading parties followed by a military takeover seeking to forestall the impending Islamist victory.[47] A decade of conflict ensued. An estimated 60,000 to 200,000 Algerians were killed or went missing.

This Dark Decade will run like a ruinous thread throughout this work because colonial and postindependence monuments and statues were targeted and protected during these years. The situation of French colonial statues during this decade tells a different postindependence story since 1962 about France's statues after their original colonial implantation. My example is an intentional iconoclastic gesture from December 18, 2017, at the central statue and fountain of Sétif, a town 167 miles southeast of the capital Algiers. The statue in Sétif is by Francis de Saint-Vidal (1840–1900). He sculpted the fountain complex of statues entitled *The Five Parts of the World* that were to embellish the surroundings of the Eiffel Tower, erected for the Paris Universal Exposition of 1889. The five nudes represented five continents, each physiognomy signified different intellectual and emotional levels: Europe is a studious female nude surrounded by philosophy books; America is personified as industrialized thought and money; and Asia, including the Algerian colony as an extension of Asia and the Arab Middle East, stands for rampant sensuality: "Asia, in the figure of an undulating odalisque softly reclining in a sensual attitude, on its left the narghileh, is it not thought self-absorbed in the search for the refinements of pleasure and veiled by the languor of pleasures as well as the sybaritism of the countries of polygamy and harems embalmed by the intoxicating perfumes of the East?"[48]

Below Asia, Africa incarnated the state of nature and was followed by Oceania, a brutal savage. Personifying continents was a popular nineteenth-century artistic practice using hierarchically arranged nude female allegories to encompass the world. The center of the fountain housed mythological figures—Night, Day, Mercury, Clio, Sleep. The sixth figure, Love, was closely paired with Asia. Naiads were associated with water in Greek mythology and were treasured by nineteenth-century French sculptural traditions that drew on classical motifs of Nereids. These were found throughout Roman North Africa where mosaic nymphs decorated the nymphaeum, fountains, palaces, and baths. French sculptors alluded easily to the Roman ruins of nymph depictions in Algeria and elsewhere thanks to their classical training that connected the ancient Roman motifs and artifacts with the French empire.[49]

Formally, the crowded fountain of female figures closely approximates Saint-Vidal's Sétif nude through its repetitions of twisted female torsos and coyly raised legs. A naiad came to Sétif at the request of the city's mayor, a gift from the director of the Paris École des Beaux-Arts (School of Fine Arts). This provincial delegate had come to the metropolitan capital in search of an appropriate symbol for his expanding colonial town center. Given the prevailing practices at the time of producing duplicate models, there may have been a spare nude in Saint-Vidal's Paris atelier to be palmed off on the overseas colony. The economically driven Paris world fair celebrating the latest scientific and technological breakthroughs became associated with the aspirations of Sétif's colonial municipality through this sculpted nude female. The nude figure that shipped from Paris subsequently marked Sétif's rising importance as an interior provincial center having grown since its creation in 1847. Originally an interior garrison city between Algiers and Constantine, the town became accessible thanks to the new 1882 railroad connection to Algeria's coastal cities. The donated fountain sculpture was installed in Sétif in 1899, like its counterpart in Paris (figure 27).

FIGURE 27. Model of Francis Saint-Vidal's fountain in Paris, 1889. Lithograph. Author's collection.

Much loved by most inhabitants from both the settler and native communities, the naiad statue in Sétif endured through postindependence as a vision of a female water sprite reclining on a rock above trickling water, fountain, and basin. In fact, whereas Sétif's municipal monument had been translated and appropriated into Arabic as Aïn Al-Fouara, referring to the precolonial "gushing spring" and the fenced in, colonial-era sculptural unit, the breasts and face of the town's nude statue (*timthāl ʿarī*) were damaged during the Dark Decade, by a man armed with hammer and chisel, described by Algerian media as a deranged Islamist-Salafist. Nicknamed *Bou Martou* ("hammer-man" from the Arabic *abū* and the French *marteau*), he was stopped by locals who surrounded their fountain and pelted him with rocks until he was arrested by the police.[50] As I watched the video of the attack, I recalled my 1991 trip to Sétif and the pride of the Algerian colleagues who had brought me to see the city's famous central statue. This latest attack was the third attempt in twenty years to destroy Sétif's nude—the first took place at the height of the Dark Decade in 1997 with a homemade bomb, and a second in 2006 with a hammer. There were different attitudes toward this mutilation. Some Algerians argued for nationalist claims to preserve a beloved downtown place-marker for accessible spring water, while others, the insurgent Islamist-Salafists, were iconoclasts, who saw the naiad as a shocking intrusion in the city too close to Sétif's central mosque. The protection and swift repairs of the statue burnished the state's legitimacy as the institutional safeguard of heritage in general. Colonial female nudes that remain in Algeria's urban spaces can become the locus of struggles over representations of gender and Algeria's revolutionary past (figure 28).

FIGURE 28. Aïn El-Fouara after the third repair, Sétif, Algeria. Photo by Amine Kasmi, December 8, 2019, reproduced by permission.

Like fountains elsewhere, drinking of these waters ensures a return visit. I returned to Sétif in 2022, thirty years after drinking the statue's waters and saw that the naiad had been preserved again. The statue's formal properties and uses—a place to celebrate weddings, take selfies or, it is said, ask for fertility—are different from its colonial provenance. In 2018, the glossy red tram cars of the newly launched light rail system, coursing along the spine of Sétif's central east-west axis, made a significant detour (figure 29). The tracks were deliberately rerouted around Aïn El-Fouara to form a fenced traffic island in the city's main thoroughfare to preserve the statue. According to the authorities, the constant flow of trams protects the tourist site unique to Sétif so that it can be seen: "The *Wali* [provincial governor] had also emphasized the need to avoid the fountain of Aïn El-Fouara 'which is part of the built heritage of the city.'"[51]

The central avenue of the colonial city center with its fountain, public square, parks, theater, and school remain important urban reference points for the residents of Sétif.[52] Statues left in Algeria—including the sculpted

FIGURE 29. Mosque, tramway, and Aïn El-Fouara statue, Sétif. Photo by author, June 24, 2022.

breasts of an idealized nude—are to be defended according to some but not all Algerians.[53] But when the statues left by the French are defaced with hammers, the perpetrators are declaring their position in the civil strife of the Dark Decades when Algerians fought one another, with state history, and with colonial and postindependent monuments in public squares, traffic roundabouts, and cemeteries. So, for example, on December 2, 2022, a man described as drunk (or, by his family, psychologically damaged) attacked the statue's breast and was stopped by bystanders. His act was considered vandalism (*takhrīb*) against the state, according to the case filed by the city's Directorate of Culture. A monument is clearly "a statement of power and presence in public" that continued to have meanings and agency beyond its original contexts and into Algeria's Dark Decade.[54] Preserving colonial-era statues after independence was not embraced by all Algerians. The afterlife of Aïn Al-Fouara—imported from France and preserved in Algeria—is not unique.[55]

In my second example, I tell the story of a colonial-era statue imported from France, removed in 1962 to France to be preserved, and replaced in Algeria with another statue. In 1991, when I first photographed the bronze equestrian statue of the Emir Abdelkader brandishing his sword over the eponymous square in Algiers, I knew only that the sculptor, Marian Konieczny (1930–2017), was famous for creating this monumental statue and notorious for a grandiose statue of Lenin in his native Poland (figure 30). The statue of Algeria's great resistance leader had been erected in 1987, merely four years before I first viewed it, to replace a smaller 1968 statue of the Emir from an Italian workshop that had been considered insufficiently grand. The Italian sculpture was regifted to the town of Mascara, near the Emir's birthplace.[56] Yet Konieczny's version seemed to me to belong to the central French colonial-era plaza adjacent to other revolutionary tourist spots commemorating a vanquished colonialism. New statues and new meanings for the intact French architecture conveyed the reversals of history. The nearby "Milk Bar" in the 1990s was an iconic site where bombs placed in the European quarter in 1956 symbolized the ongoing Algerian Revolution exploding in the heart of the European city.

In 1962 at Algerian independence, the French military removed the statue of General Thomas-Robert Bugeaud (1784–1849) from central Algiers and sent it into "exile" to the French countryside.[57] Sculpted by Auguste Dumont (1801–1884) and inaugurated in 1852, Bugeaud was the anointed conqueror of Algeria, honored for having captured, imprisoned, and exiled

FIGURE 30. **Place Emir Abdelkader, Algiers (formerly Place Bugeaud, rue d'Isly): Leslie Thornton, Madeleine Nieto, Tom Zummer, and my husband, Nadjib Berber, on the right. Photo by author, December 28, 1991.**

his fierce enemy, the Emir Abdelkader. Bugeaud's imperial projects to settle the land, establish agricultural communities, and bring in statues figure in every chapter of my study. Astride his horse, his equestrian statue dominated the new European public square of Algiers. In the photo postcard of the sculpture, we also see the colonial stamp with the image of the same statue (figure 31).[58]

Bugeaud was one of the principal military architects of colonized Algeria. He determined the configuration of many Algerian towns. Pervasive urban formations to designate and separate native Algerian enclaves, a hallmark racial ordering of the settler colony, were his too: "Natural segregation was increased by the decision to delimit (*cantonner*) the Arabs into isolated neighborhoods that later become the 'Negro villages' (*villages nègres*)"[59]

French imperialists using the pejorative *nègre* intended to underscore the racial debasement of the predominantly Muslim segregated enclaves. Monumentalizing Bugeaud in nineteenth-century colonial Algeria and then memorializing his transferred statue in twentieth-century France show how colonialism can be an ongoing project of monument-making and colonial propaganda even if the original historical link was the segregation of Indigenous villages from settler town centers.

FIGURE 31. "Statue du Duc d'Orléans, Place du Gouvernement," postcard and stamp of General Bugeaud's statue. Cancellation stamp on the recto side reproduces the postcard image. Éditions Jomone, Algiers, no. 10. Author's collection.

NOSTALGERIA IN FRANCE

Postcard photographs have become iconic in the Pied-Noir community of France. They are also vectors of nostalgeria, the portmanteau term for displaced former settler yearnings for a lost French Algeria and colonial society. Credit for the neologism coined from "nostalgia" and "Algeria," *nostalgérie* in French, is attributed to Henry de Montherlant, who uses the word to capture the hidden, contradictory, and impossible longings for the lost homeland, the shame of losing the colony, and the formation of selective, often politicized former settler memories in his anti-colonialist novel *Le sable de rose* (*The Sand Rose*). Written in the 1930s but published decades later, Montherlant's novel and his version of nostalgeria were revisited by Jacques Derrida (1930–2004), a native Algerian Jew, who became a Pied-Noir when he moved permanently to France.

> But perhaps one should begin by repeating "return" and "to return." The movement, the temporality, the speed of the film, its kinematics obey memory first, the drive to anamnesis and nostalgic retrospection. One must first return to cherished landscapes, above all, to deserted spaces—sea or ocean or dry land; coastlines and beaches; places known or dreamed (Algeria, which the Actor calls his "nostalgeria"—El Biar, Algiers, and Kabylie—his childhood home, the schools, the houses of worship . . .)[60]

The novel by Algerian writer Yasmina Khadra (b. 1955, pseudonym of Mohammed Moulessehoul) *Ce que le jour doit à la nuit* (*What the Day Owes the Night*) recounts a reunion in Aix-en-Provence near Marseille decades after the 1962 departures. André, formerly of Rio Salado, explains to his Algerian Muslim childhood friend the distinctions between ordinary nostalgia and the particularity of the strong sense of loss for Algeria, or nostalgeria, a sentiment that the mayor of El Maleh believed he recognized in me when he mistook me for a returning Pied-Noir:

> Here, we don't say nostalgia . . . we say nostalgeria [*nostalgérie*]. . . . Algeria sticks to my skin. . . . Sometimes it gnaws at me like the shirt of Nessus, sometimes its delicate fragrance surrounds me. I try to lose it but can't manage. How to forget? I wanted to shout out my early memories, to move on, to start from scratch. No go. I'm not a cat, I have only one life, and my life stayed there, in the *bled* . . . It's useless to try and collect all the horrors to vomit it up, nothing works. The sun, the beaches, our streets, our cuisine, our good old times getting drunk, and our happy days supplanting anger

> and I surprise myself by smiling where I was getting ready to bite. I never forgot Rio . . . Not for a single night, not for a moment.[61]

In France, wrenching removals of colonial monuments from Algeria accompany settlers' memories of safekeeping. Yet nostalgeria is subject to historical revisions. In 1962, the French military removed the statue of General Thomas Robert Bugeaud, conqueror of Algeria, from downtown Algiers to France because it feared Algerian depredations. As global commemorative landscapes evolve, there have been recent attempts to topple the general's statue in France. For historian Olivier Le Cour Grandmaison, statues and streets in France named for Bugeaud, "executioner of Algerian 'natives' and enemy of the Republic . . . [are] permanent insults to the emancipation of peoples and to Algerians in particular."[62] In 2021, Marseille's socialist mayor Benoît Payan renamed the Bugeaud School for an Algerian infantryman, Ahmed Litim, who was killed in World War II liberating the city from Nazi occupation.[63] Instead of renaming and removing, some heritage workers argue for adding explanatory plaques, supplementary statues, and removing only damaged monuments to museums.

Times have changed. French historian Alain Ruscio recalled an attempt during the interwar years to erect a statue to the Emir Abdelkader in Paris when an eponymous square was inaugurated in 2006 near the Paris Mosque.[64] We might see resemblances in how statues of the Emir Abdelkader and those of Martin Luther King Jr. in the United States are being managed. Architectural historian Dell Upton believes that memorializing civil rights and the legacy of slavery has just begun to become something more than erecting the statue of the great man. Like the Emir, who was assimilated into France as a symbol of pacification and conciliation, Martin Luther King has been assimilated and "whitened" as a figure of reconciliation, Upton concludes, because "King statues are unthreatening and demand no uncomfortable thought."[65]

Assimilation, in colonial parlance, meant inclusion in French society by eradicating Algerian Muslim identity. Algerian resistance fighters therefore opposed having a statue dedicated to the Emir in French Algeria because they considered it to be another example of colonial assimilation.[66] In October 1949, they attempted to destroy a thirty-three-foot column, erected that same month at Cacherou (now Sidi-Kada) near the Emir's birthplace in western Algeria, dedicated to Franco-Algerian friendship. The words inscribed on the monument are attributed to the Emir: "If Muslims and

Christians listened to me, I would put an end to their differences and they would become brothers inside and out."[67] Later, during the Algerian War of Independence, commandos from the Special Organization (OS, Organisation spéciale), a precursor entity to independent Algeria's ruling FLN party, tried to dynamite the monument. Recontextualized after independence, it has become a modest tourist destination for Algerians.

AN ALGERIAN GAZE IN FRANCE: MEMORIALIZING THE STATUE OF BLANDAN

The colonial statue of Sergeant Blandan, the foot-soldier hero in accounts of France's conquest of Algeria, stood in Boufarik, eighteen miles southwest of Algiers. As a child, Malek Kellou, who grew up in Mansourah, regularly passed through Boufarik en route to Algiers. He saw the dark bronze statue, a frightening reminder of the napalm bombs and the soldiers occupying his village during the independence war. Kellou settled in Nancy, France in the 1990s where he unexpectedly came upon the statue of Blandan that he had often seen as a child. Unbeknownst to him, it had been removed at independence and placed in Nancy where the army headquarters of Blandan's unit was located. Later it was moved again to a street in Nancy where Kellou saw it.[68] For Kellou, the sight of the statue brought back painful memories of his childhood internment in a French regroupment camp, outdoor prison camps created by the French military to house forcibly relocated Algerian rural inhabitants during the independence war. As a filmmaker, Kellou wanted to produce a documentary *Lettre à mes filles* (*A Letter to My Daughters*) about his Algerian childhood. He returned to Mansourah with one of his daughters to document the painful experiences of forcible internment by the French. He never made his film but did help his daughter, Dorothée Myriam Kellou, complete her film, *À Mansourah, tu nous as séparés* (*In Mansourah, You Separated Us*) about the massive rural displacements.[69]

Pierre Hippolyte Blandan (1819–1842) joined the French army in Algeria in 1837. In 1842, while leading twenty men from Boufarik, he was attacked at Beni-Mered by an Algerian cavalry contingent of 250 to 300 men. An anonymous account published in 1887 to support efforts to commission a statue states that Blandan reputedly shouted, "Courage my friends, defend yourselves to the death!"[70] Outnumbered and mortally wounded by Algerian fighters, Blandan died defending the army mail service. The legend of his heroism circulated widely thanks to an order written by General Thomas-Robert Bugeaud, who called for a monument to commemorate him:

> Which heart could be cold enough not to feel electrified while passing in front of a monument erected on the site of combat, and where the action and the names of the heroes who were involved are remembered! This memorable combat, having taken place on our main communication route, and the entire army and all the colonists will parade frequently in front of the glorious monument; we will stop and bow. Who can calculate feelings experienced by all will produce glory for the Fatherland![71]

Bugeaud was responsible for advancing the French occupation of Algeria and settling the Mitidja plain where he created Beni Mered in 1843 as a European agricultural colony. He placed two memorials to Blandan in two towns. The first was a fifty-six-foot cut stone column erected in Beni-Mered that was dismantled stone by stone during the colonial era with only a postcard image to record its existence (figure 32).

The second, a figurative statue of Blandan, was sculpted by Charles Gauthier (1831–1891) from stone quarried in Algeria. Inaugurated on May

FIGURE 32. Column of Beni Mered. Postcard, J. Geiser, Algiers, no. 14. Author's collection.

1, 1887, for the town of Boufarik, the statue was expensive. The unusually large sum of over 66,000 francs was raised to pay to send Gauthier to Boufarik and to cover the costs of the Thiébaut Frères foundry in Paris, which is famous for casting New York City's Statue of Liberty. Blandan stands alert and upright, even as the statue was intended to commemorate the instant when the third fatal bullet entered his body. The statue and emplacement gained in gravitas when his remains were exhumed from the nearby military cemetery and interred inside the pedestal (figure 33).

Bugeaud placed monuments in Algeria for different purposes: to con-

FIGURE 33. Sergent Blandan monument in Boufarik, Algeria. Postcard, no publisher. Author's collection.

firm that land had been appropriated, and to assuage settler anxieties, and to threaten native Algerians. They became part of the rituals supporting the French conquest. For example, native troops were obliged to participate in military ceremonies and pay homage to the military men who had butchered other Algerians: "There were also the commemorative celebrations in which the 'Moslem' veterans would be invited to place a wreath at the foot of the statue of General Bugeaud or of Sergent Blandan, both heroes of the conquest and liquidators of thousands of Algerian patriots."[72]

The increasing numbers of war memorials of "statuefied" French soldiers often made the Algerian native into a participant, however unwilling, in military obligations such as the performances in France's colonial commemorative calendar. Thus, the Algerian landscape of sculptures became a "taskscape," defined by Tim Ingold as "a pattern of activities 'collapsed' into an array of features."[73] A statue was a familiar element in the pattern of activities of the colonial and postindependence landscape, a landmark, a meeting point, the focal point of a plaza, a player in the vast spectacle of French military might and forced Algerian conscription.

Like the figurative statue of Blandan removed from Boufarik at Algerian independence to the French provincial city of Nancy, the statue of Cecil Rhodes is an apparition of the "living dead," according to Simukai Chigudu, designating statues and institutions named for Cecil Rhodes that found their way from South Africa to the colonizer's homeland in England:

> [Colonialism] wasn't a period that had passed, but a historical mass that bent everything around its gravity. . . . We at least recognized that the statue of Rhodes did not actually exist in the past. It is not a sterile historical relic, or some accurate record of prior events. It is a piece of self-conscious propaganda designed to present an ennobled image of Rhodes for as long as it stands. . . . [Critics] couldn't fathom the ways in which colonialism had never really ended.[74]

Memories of colonization, Chigudu tells us, are not static but rather constantly altered by objects and forms. Evolving Algerian and French anthropologies of how the living abide near and through the dead of French Algeria are replete with the descriptions of removals, repatriation, destruction, and sacralization of tombs, monuments, statues, and memorialized graves.

Being with the Dead, Hans Ruin's evocative book title, concerns the living and encompasses the demolition, preservation, and installation of new forms of memorialization to the dead.[75] Depending on the moment and perspective, Algerians might destroy and the French might conserve colonial monuments, but these roles are reversed when Algerians preserve as the French spoliate. French and Algerian cultural battles over vestiges and remains continue even after the end of settler colonialism. Historian Benjamin Stora famously described an endless "war of memories" (*la guerre de mémoires*).[76] The battles also play out on monuments. The massive postindependence transfers from Algeria of statues and colonial archives raise many issues of heritage and law.[77] The object histories detailed in the next three chapters describe statues and monuments dispatched to French provincial towns that are emblematic of the vast numbers of artifacts that moved back and forth between the northern and southern shores of the Mediterranean Sea. Since 1962, statues and plaques have been repaired, changed, and created in Algeria. Algerian state funding continues to subsidize the effort to place growing numbers of war memorials and statues to replace French ones, while local initiatives often safeguarded colonial monuments, especially those bearing the names of Algerian and French soldiers killed defending France during the two world wars. The claim that a monument is being saved or showcased by moving it to France—Lyon's Oran war memorial—or protecting it in an Algerian compound in Misserghin transforms the objects and changes public perceptions of them.

CHAPTER TWO

MOVING WAR MONUMENTS

From Oran Province to France

ORAN IN ALGERIA AND LYON in France became twin cities in 1956 and remained so until Algerian independence in 1962. In 1967, the mayors and municipal representatives agreed to split a 1927 monument that had been erected in Oran to commemorate the troops from Algeria who fought for France in the two world wars. The sculpture of three standing soldiers at the top of the monument arrived in Lyon in December 1967 (see figure 2 in the introduction). The supporting plinth and column remained in Oran, where, in 1988, it was decorated with colorful ceramics and became a memorial for the Algerian Revolution. Covered, the silhouette and emplacement of the 1927 war memorial are still on display on Oran's seafront boulevard (see figure 3 in the introduction). This peripatetic memorial has commemorated different soldiers in various wars and touched different communities commemorating their different histories. It is emblematic of many French Algerian colonial statues and war memorials that were moved, stolen, modified, or destroyed and that continue to resonate; the colonial heritage still arouses disagreement, debate, and distress. The story of the war memorial erected in Oran in 1927 and moved to France in 1967 frames this chapter. Set in the context of wars and war memorials in Algeria, its story is atypical: this was the rare war memorial that was removed consensually and *legally* from Algeria after independence.

The Oran memorial was one of many commemorative monuments

erected in towns and cities throughout France and its colonies to honor the 1.4 million French war dead, including many conscripts from the French colonies who fought in both world wars. Universal military conscription became law in France on March 21, 1905, and was imposed in its overseas colonies by the decree of February 3, 1912. All men of military age in Algeria were eligible: the European settlers (*colons*) who were French citizens; Algeria's "native" Muslims (*indigènes*) who were not citizens but subjects; and Algeria's "native" Jews (*israélites*) who had been made citizens by the Crémieux Decree of 1870. A separate decree extended military obligation to France's sub-Saharan West African colonies and the "native troops of the black race" (*troupes indigènes de race noire*). The length of military service was not uniform. Muslim subjects in Algeria were conscripted for three years of service, and a census was taken to ascertain the number of eligible Muslims; this was one year more than that required of French citizens in the colony or in the metropole.[1]

During World War I, approximately 343,000 citizens and native subjects from French Algeria were mobilized for combat and an additional 120,000 Algerian Muslims were recruited to work in French factories for the national defense.[2] The 45th, 57th, and 58th divisions of colonial infantry comprised 173,000 native Algerian Muslim soldiers of whom 26,000 were killed in the Great War. Of the 73,000 French citizens of Algeria (European settlers and enfranchised native Algerian Jews), between 12,000 and 22,000 died. France's minister in charge of war pensions, Louis Antériou (1887–1931), estimated that 47,000 men from Oran Province had been killed or were missing in action, 126,000 had been wounded, and 16,000 were maimed and disabled. [3] Upon their return from World War I combat, many Algerian Muslim veterans challenged the racialized religious and social formations in the settler colony that distinguished Muslim, Jewish, and settler soldiers. Historian Dónal Hassett points out that Muslim soldiers who had defended France demanded change in status and created the League of Muslim Veterans of Oran Province (Ligue des anciens combattants musulmans d'Oranie, or LACMO) in 1930.[4] After all, hadn't they gloriously defended and died for France? Even before World War I, an official military report of 1912 spoke to their prowess: "Our native troops are superb. For fifty years, they have asserted their legendary value, their endurance at every test in all campaigns in Europe and the colonies."[5] Algerian Muslims had never enjoyed the rights granted to Indigenous Jews in 1870.[6] The Senatus-Consulte of July 18, 1865, barred them from French citizenship on the basis of reductive legal definitions of religion, which historian James McDougall calls the colonial creation of an "Islamic personality" for North African Muslims.[7] The 1875 Native Code (Code de l'indigénat) maintained the status of Muslims. And while the 1919 Jonnart Law was one of various meager efforts to give more rights to natives, the right to vote granted Algerian Muslim males was limited to municipal elections.[8]

The deaths of so many soldiers in World War I provoked France, in a rare effort, to fund and build commemorations of all soldiers, including those from Algeria who were buried on European battlefields. Government subsidies for World War I war memorials were granted by the law of October 1, 1919; the law of July 31, 1920, stipulated that their numbers were to be proportional to the numbers of war dead.[9] Subsidies covered between 5 to 25 percent of a monument's cost, which depended on its materials—1,800–2,400 francs for cement, 3,500–4,500 for a coat of bronze, and 8,000–12,000 for marble. The funds were organized by the Souvenir Français, a nongovernmental association established in 1887 after the Franco-Prussian War of 1870–72 to oversee the maintenance of war monuments, build military cemeteries, and preserve the memory of soldiers from the metropole and overseas colonies who died fighting for France. By 1918, the Souvenir Français was working closely with the state through the Ministry of Veterans. Various government entities put in place the *Tomb of the Unknown Soldier* beneath the Arc de Triomphe in Paris in 1920, an annual Armistice Day was established on November 11 by the law of October 24, 1922, and in 1923, a national ossuary was created in Verdun to house the remains of unidentified soldiers.[10]

Between the two world wars, approximately 36,000 war memorials were erected in France, in Algeria (integrated as France's southern departments or provinces), and in its other overseas colonies.[11] Historian Antoine Prost classified war memorials from the Franco-Prussian War to World War II based on commemorative discourses, placement, location of headstones and stelae, and analyses of their shape, the figures on them, and their facades. He inventoried ninety-one *poilus,* mustachioed foot soldiers, one of the most popular of the statues that could be selected from catalogs. Nine hundred statues of the victorious soldier (*poilu victorieux*) by Eugène Benet (1863–1942) were purchased and 400 memorials were adorned with a sculpture by Étienne Camus (1867–1955) of the soldier at rest (*poilu en repos*).[12]

By 1922, the process for selecting and erecting monuments to the World War I dead was well established. In Algeria, this involved selecting a jury, a sculptor, and a design for the monument. In Oran, a committee of local settler dignitaries guided by the Souvenir Français had been formed as of 1921 to create a war memorial.[13] The committee determined the site and conditions for a "victory monument" (*monument de la victoire*), required a model, plans, and capped costs at a substantial 200,000 francs.[14] An appeal for financial contributions was published in the local francophone newspaper of record *L'Echo d'Oran*, targeting veterans' associations and families of the dead. The appeal was couched in terms of national piety, Algerian valor, and Oran provincial solidarity.

> An artwork of Oranian solidarity, because bronze must materialize in a grandiose work of art the resplendent glory of all Oranian children [*enfants*], regardless of race, origins, or religion, who were *poilus*, soldiers of noble France. . . . All of Orania must commemorate France's prestigious Victory and the role her children played in it with a superb monument that bears witness to admiration and recognition of all of them together, again regardless of race, origin or religion.[15]

By 1924, sufficient funds had been collected to open a national competition to French artists. French sculptor Albert Pommier (1880–1943) submitted the winning design; local architects Paul Dordet and Paul Pinet (1869–1834) were named as project coordinators. Pommier's model showed a group of mustachioed *poilus*, citizen infantrymen of Republican France. Two of them face forward, one holds a rifle at rest, while a third Senegalese infantryman-sharpshooter (*tirailleur*) with pronounced Negroid features wearing a barely visible *chéchia* cap faces the other direction. Hasset concludes that a "clear sculptural hierarchy, reflecting the social hierarchy of colonial society, is established in a monument which barely pays lip service to the fraternity of arms, while simultaneously highlighting the imperative of safeguarding the dominance of the European community" (figure 34).[16]

Pommier had studied at the École des Beaux-Arts in Paris and joined a group of artists formed during the interwar period to look for solemn, classically oriented monumental styles to enhance the role of public sculpture. In 1919, after his wartime service, Pommier went to Algeria on a resident fellowship at the Villa Abd-el-Tif, a prominent artists' colony in Algiers. Modeled on the French Academy at the Villa Medici in Rome, the Algiers establishment sought to nurture aesthetic productions overseas by importing and hiring metropolitan artists.[17] Pommier's stay in Algiers changed him. He became an Orientalist artist who produced expensive bronze me-

FIGURE 34. Albert Pommier's model (*maquette*) with two of three soldiers. The proposed model appeared on the cover of *L'Afrique du Nord Illustrée* 171, 30 August 30, 1924,1; and in Darot, "Les sacrifices de l'Oranie durant la Grande Guerre," 74.

dallions, brass plates, and busts depicting the lives of Algerian Muslim natives for European buyers. His newer visual themes often corresponded to images from the vast output of the "scenes and types" postcard stereotypes of native Algerian women, the Arab horsemen, and more.[18] He also entered the parallel upscale international art market for colonial fantasies fashioned into expensive medals and intricate bas-reliefs.

Pommier's service as an infantry medical corpsman and stretcher-bearer (*brancardier*) informed his affecting renditions of the *poilu*. Influenced by sculptor and stretcher-bearer Gaston Broquet's (1880–1947) famous 1922 bronze in Paris, Pommier added a relief of two soldiers carrying a wounded soldier for his second commissioned Algerian war memorial in Oran Province (figure 35).

FIGURE 35. Pommier, *Le monument de Hammam Bou Hadjar*, in Rey, "Le Monument de Hammam-Bou-Hadjar," 160.

On the basis of Pommier's sculpture for Oran, the municipal committee in Hammam Bou Hadjar, a thermal spa town forty-four miles southwest of Oran, chose him to design their war memorial, which was installed on the town's main square in 1931. The *poilu* was a solitary soldier whose uniform and stance resembled his Oran counterpart. Pommier used unpolished Carrara marble to achieve a dull, rough finish. Oran-born art historian Robert Rey (1888–1964) describes Pommier's sculpted soldiers in Oran and Hammam Bou Hadjar:

> A few steps form a plinth, an almost cubic rectangle rises whose four sides are bordered by a flat band bearing a bas relief. A simple column soars from this squared section, where the fateful years 1914–1918 will be legible on one side and the names of the dead on the other. The large, sober square figure of a man of war wrapped in his hood weighted down with mud and rain stands atop the column over the entire surface of the section. He takes some refuge in his thick muffler, his face hardened by fatigue on which a strong spirit beats. The man holds the straps of a buckled bag between his feet and knees, on the ground, a symbol of the exhausting war that forced

> us to lift an ever-faltering hope to the height of our souls and which made us into an army of Sisyphus for four years. The bas-reliefs on the base are no less simple.[19]

The only records of the dedication of the Oran monument are found in contemporary newspaper articles and postcards on "the province of Oran to its children, who died for the homeland 1914–1918" (*le département d'Oran à ses enfants morts pour la Patrie 1914–1918*). The names of the dead, too numerous to be listed individually on the memorial, were nonetheless differentiated by listing the names of French citizens and colonized subjects separately in the city's newspapers; in France they are ordered alphabetically. Indeed, many colonial war memorials such as the one in Misserghin separated the names of *indigènes* from European names by engraving them on different sides of monuments, where they remain to this day, carving colonial discrimination in stone (see figure 19 in chapter 1).

The names of Algerian Muslims incised on war memorials reflect a French colonial practice of deliberately changing surnames, or onomasticide.[20] Precolonial North African names consist, at a minimum, of a first name followed by the names of a father and a grandfather and often a string of names describing the holder's moral, physical, or social qualities, place of birth or ancestry, and tribal affiliation or membership in religious orders. An Arab-Berber name traditionally functioned as an individual's biography that is unique to the individual and disappears with death. France forced a change on the names of their native subjects in North Africa, beginning with Algeria, its first North African colony: The law of March 23, 1882, on the civil status of Muslim natives in Algeria imposed patronymic surnames on all Algerian heads of households and French identity cards recording that name. If someone refused to choose a surname, French civil servants had the right to create one, according to article 5.[21] Already transformed by French law, then, the names of dead Muslims soldiers were segregated on war memorials, just as the Muslim soldier was segregated in combat units, and Muslims were generally segregated in colonial towns and villages. Colonial war monuments thus inscribed Algerian names in stone epitaphs written in French orthography.

Pommier's 1927 Oran monument commemorated famous battle sites in Europe and in the eastern Mediterranean: Charleroi, Marne, Aisne, Flandre, Artois, Lorraine, Somme, Champagne, Verdun, Argonne, Dardanelles, and Orient. On the fourth side of the monument facing the Mediterranean was the command to remember (*Souvenez-vous*). *L'Echo d'Oran* reported the numbers of the war dead arranged by colonial subdistrict, that is, by the towns and villages of Oran Province. In the absence of the names of soldiers on the monument, aggregate numbers, not individual names of the war dead from Oran Province were published in *L'Echo d'Oran* under separate colonial rubrics of French and native. The monument reads: "Oran: 3,208; Sidi-Bel-Abbès: 1,217; Mostaganem: 3,439; Tlemcen: 1,136; Mascara: 2,257; and Sud-Oranais: 1,252."[22] These names of each subdistrict recorded on the Oran monument reflected the history of French colonization of western Algeria. Many of the towns and villages from which the soldiers had come had been established in waves to produce wine, grains, alfa, and fruit for export. As of the French occupation of Oran in 1831, the native population was subjected to "legal" expropriations as French laws granted ownership to European settlers who could then use the land titles and associated legal practices to identify, buy, and transmit allotments, or sell and create concessions of "free" plots of land.

The sequential construction of towns and villages was initiated by General Thomas Robert Bugeaud (1784–1849) in his decree of April 18, 1941. Each town served as a jumping off point for the next one.[23] As they became self-governing "full-fledged communes" or *commune de plein exercice,* the Algerian Muslims were segregated in rural hamlets or *douars* (French spelling for Arabic *duwwār),* known as "Arab villages," *faubourg indigènes* and *villages nègres,* providing sources of cheap labor to the nearby *commune mixte.* The *commune mixte* was a rural area where the majority of the population was colonized but where French government appointees ran the administration. The colonial town cordoned the semistructured douar-commune that often devolved into a *bidonville* or shantytown. Spatial segregation was omnipresent in the prototypical provincial colonial town center. Of some 600 new colonial towns and villages built during the French occupation, many were planned around a central square that reassuringly reproduced the metropolitan spaces of the war memorial flanked by a church, a town hall, and a gendarmerie. Each settlement would later send men to war to defend the French homeland and raise war memorials to them. Some memorials were modest columns with plaques purchased through catalogs and shipped from France, while others were supported by successful local fundraising and created by commissioned sculptors. Pommier's three soldiers of Oran was one of the most memorable of these in western Algeria (figure 36).

FIGURE 36. The 1927 Oran war memorial showing two of the three soldiers who face south toward the heart of the city. Postcard, Éditions Alexander Sirecky (EAS), Oran. Author's collection.

INAUGURATION OF THE 1927 ORAN WAR MEMORIAL AND WORLD WAR II MILITARY SERVICE

Oran's monument to the 12,000 dead of World War I was inaugurated on May 26, 1927, by Maurice Viollette (1870–1960), a member of the Socialist party who served briefly as governor-general of Algeria (May 12, 1925–November 20, 1927). The description of the ceremony published in *L'Echo d'Oran* lists the attending grandees and religious leaders, including the Bishop of Oran Monsignor Léon-Auguste-Marie-Joseph Durand (1878–1945), the Chief Rabbi Jonas Weill (b. 1869), and the Protestant Pastor Brunet. The Muslim community was represented by the Mufti of Oran—who goes nameless in the account—and by Bachaga Sahraoui, who received the medal of "Grand

Chancelier de l'Ordre National de la Legion d'Honneur" for his exemplary military service as a cavalry officer.[24] Troops from Oran were assembled and paraded. The following day, the newspaper account of the inauguration included the official speeches. General Stanislas Naulin (1870–1932) of the 19th Army Corps that included the 45th Algerian Division of *zouaves* (Europeans) and *tirailleurs* (Algerian Muslims) was the only speaker to praise the heroism of the colonial troops: "It was the division, the 45th Algerian, one of those beautiful khaki divisions like the 37th, 38th and Division of Morocco, shock troops that would be in every battle and would rank everywhere among the finest units of the French army during 1914–18."[25] Naulin was referring to the horrific combat experiences of the colonial troops under his command who were ill-equipped and maskless in the face of poison gas used against them.[26]

During World War II, about half the 550,000-strong French army originated in the colonies: 134,000 Algerians, 73,000 Moroccans, 26,000 Tunisians, and 92,000 from French West Africa.[27] Their service was commemorated with monuments and military parades honoring their exploits. But some commemorative parades turned violent as veterans demanded equality for Muslims of French Algeria. On May 8, 1945, in Algeria, military parades in the Sétif region for Victory-in-Europe Day heralded what many consider to be the opening salvo of Algeria's War of Independence. Members of the Algerian People's Party (Parti du peuple algérien, PPA) raised the Algerian flag, which had first been brandished (and banned) during the July 14, 1937, Bastille Day celebration in Algiers.[28] When marchers headed toward Sétif's elaborate World War I monument sculpted by Algerian-born Joseph Ebstein (1881–1961) and inaugurated on November 11, 1922, the French army started shooting into the crowd. Widespread violence ensued: over a hundred Europeans were killed by Algerians, while the French army led incursions and bombarded the region killing between 6,000 and 20,000 Algerians as the towns of Guelma, Kherrata, and additional villages, were torched and extrajudicial executions carried out.[29] It would take sixty years for the French to acknowledge this as a "massacre," an "inexcusable tragedy," and a French "error."[30]

A less well-known French military repression had occurred during a patriotic parade in Oran held a week earlier on May Day 1945. Houari Souiah (1915–1990), the city's first postindependence prefect, led uniformed Algerian combat veterans displaying the banned national flag and calling for an independent Algeria through Oran's streets. A large contingent of marchers left from Faubourg Lamur on Oran's periphery (the native sector of El Hamri) heading to the town's central "native village" Mdina Jdida (Arabic for *ville nouvelle,* the "new city"), one of the many Muslim enclaves established to keep Muslims out of sight.[31] The protesters marched from Mdina Jdida, El Hamri, and Village Les Planteurs, neighborhoods that Algerians saw as crucibles of revolutionary activism.[32] Crossing the Boulevard Sebastopol, they entered the invisible gateway to the predominantly European city. Souiah and thirty party members and other associated groups were swiftly rounded up, imprisoned, and tortured; some were killed. A year later many were released, thanks to the general amnesties of March 1946.[33] The marchers of May 1945 had served in the wartime military service or been involved in clandestine nationalist organizations during World War I and under Algeria's Vichy-era during World War II. They later became regional leaders of the armed revolution launched in 1954 and prominent officials in Oran's political life after independence. These post-1962 Oran municipality officials made decisions about colonial-era monuments and the creation of new ones. They erected in Tahtaha Plaza of Mdina Jdida a monument complex that lists the names of those who died defending national self-determination in Oran (figure 37). As with many monuments built in the 1990s to the martyrs of the Algerian War, its shape evokes the iconic 1982 Martyrs' Memorial of Algiers.[34] Oran is symbolized by two lions, one

FIGURE 37. Memorial sculpture complex to Algerian independence in Tahtaha, the main square of Mdina Jdida (former "native quarter"). Photo by author, May 16, 2014.

meaning of the city's name Wahran in Arabic. Each lion flanks the central sculpture, echoing the two lions at the entrance to Oran's colonial theater. Another decision that is salient to the afterlives of Pommier's 1927 Oran war memorial was the response by the Oran municipality to an official request from a delegation of European settlers formerly from Oran Province who had relocated to Lyon, France, after 1962.

ORAN-LYON: TWIN CITIES

Between 1956 and 1962, official exchanges were organized during which delegates from Lyon paid homage to Oran's war memorial. Shortly after 1962 and Algerian independence, officials from Lyon came to Oran seeking the repatriation of the Oran monument to Lyon and the removal of the bodies of the parents of longtime Lyon mayor Edouard Herriot. The historical, personal, and commercial connections between the two cities and their respective mayors facilitated these negotiations.

Francois-Nicolas Herriot, father of Edouard Herriot (1872–1957), served as an infantry officer in western Algeria. His wife, Jeanne-Eugénie Collon, was born in Mostaganem in 1852, her father an army officer stationed in western Algeria. The couple was buried in Algeria. Their son, Edouard Herriot, served as Lyon's mayor for 35 years (1905–1940) and "liked to say that his parents were based in the Oran cemetery."[35] Demoted for his opposition to Vichy, Herriot returned to office in 1945 and served until his death on March 26, 1957. According to Alain Amato, chronicler of French Algeria's war memorials in France, just before his death, Herriot made a last-ditch colonial attempt to link Oran and Lyon—by "enriching . . . mutual differences" and signing an agreement on November 11, 1956, to make French colonial Oran and Lyon twin cities; the arrangement was made all the easier because Oran's French mayor Henri Fouques-Duparc (1903-1976) was proud to have been born in Lyon.[36] During his tenure as Oran's mayor from 1948 until his departure in 1962, Fouques-Duparc, like Herriot, was active in his city with significant construction projects, parks, and a promenade.

The Algerian graves of Herriot's parents provided an opportunity to manage and reimagine material exchanges between France and newly independent Algeria. Louis Pradel (1906–1976), who succeeded Herriot as mayor of Lyon (1956–1976), arranged for the bodies of Herriot's parents to be exhumed from the Oran cemetery and reinterred in the Herriot family mausoleum in Lyon's Loyasse cemetery on June 24, 1967. Whether Lyon's municipal leaders were fulfilling a wish of Lyon's revered mayor by exhuming his parents' bodies is unclear, but they exceeded Herriot's imagined wishes.[37] Exhuming the dead was part of a process that historian Michael Kammen calls "the constructedness of the past":

> Were [those responsible for reburying] always and unambiguously seeking to do justice to the dearly departed? Were they dutiful deeds more beneficial to themselves than to the deceased? Did they recognize or acknowledge a difference between the two motives—or perhaps see any symbiotic relationship between them? To what extent were exhumations acts of devotional fantasy, sometimes even a delusion?[38]

Kammen suggests that reburials are a literal form of historical revisionism, "setting the record straight in some sense."[39] The large-scale movement of human remains between Algeria and France began after Algeria's independence. The buried bodies of settler ancestors in Algeria, the cemeteries where they lie, and the war memorials that symbolically represent their sacrifices to a French state that they believed had abandoned them elicited strong emotions. Even before attempting any monument removal, Lyon's leaders and their constituents from Algeria agitated politically about the fate of Christian cemeteries in Algeria. Those at Tamashouet or El-Maleh in Oran Province, for example, still provided safe repositories for European settlers' graves, statues, monuments, and war memorials. Franco-Algerian bilateral negotiations through diplomatic channels only began in 1967, a year *after* Herriot's body was removed.[40] But it took fifty years to resolve the emotionally charged issue of managing settler and Algerian Jewish bodies and their monuments in Algeria's Christian and Jewish cemeteries: the removal of the remains of Edouard Herriot's parents from their Algerian graves was well in advance of legislation finalized only in 2011.

The movement of settler remains to France from cemeteries in Algeria peaked in 2011 and again in 2016. But two generations after independence, there was less desire or ability to move settler remains, which were being aggregated to make way for the exponential expansion of Algeria's urban population. French consular services in Algeria had some 7,500 bodies exhumed from the cemeteries of colonial villages and towns throughout Oran Province and reburied in Oran's large Christian cemetery of Tamashouet and in other Christian cemeteries in Relizane, Mascara, and Saïda, which were designated for settlers from former agricultural villages in western Algeria (figure 38).[41]

FIGURE 38. Aggregated human remains from the cemeteries of Sidi Chami, Hassi-Ameur, Hassi-Mefsoukh (Renan) and Gdyel (Saint-Cloud) listed by their Algerian names, bracketed by former French colonial names. Tamashouet Christian cemetery, Oran. Photo by author, May 6, 2017.

In some cases, exhumation and reburial made it also possible for Algerians to appropriately revere the dead. In 1966, Emir Abdelkader's remains were brought from Damascus, his final place of exile, and ceremoniously reburied in the national cemetery of Algiers alongside heroes of Algerian independence.[42] The Catholic priest Father Alfred Bérenguer (1915–1996) was also given a state burial. I had met him in 1990, when he was living at Dar Essalam, a former Benedictine monastery reallocated to a spiritual society of lay people and priests founded by Italians. Bérenguer had been vilified by the settler community in Algeria for fighting for an independent Algeria and for adopting Algerian nationality. He and members of various Catholic orders were forced to leave Algeria during the Dark Decade.[43] Father Alain Feuvrier, a Jesuit priest who had headed the library in Tlemcen, and a friend from my 1990–92 sojourns with whom I reconnected in Aix and Lyon through Algerian friends, had also been exiled from Oran to France during the Dark Decade. He explained that he and Bérenguer had been physically threatened by local Islamist groups and therefore moved to the monastery in Aix-en-Provence after a lifetime in Algeria. When Bérenguer died, Feuvrier informed the Algerian consulate in Marseille and arrangements were quickly made to repatriate the remains to the Christian cemetery in Tlemcen. Feuvrier accompanied his casket.[44]

The link with the former colony is not fully severed so long as new memorials honor the French dead buried in Christian cemeteries in Algeria. In 2013, an ornate cross was placed in front of the circa 1885 war memorial in Oran's Christian cemetery of Tamashouet dedicated to "our dear departed" (*à nos chers disparus*). The French *disparus* ("disappeared," "dead," and "missing in action") makes a discreet reference to the events of Algeria's first independence-day celebrations, July 5, 1962, when settlers and Algerians were killed. The identities and numbers of those killed and the numbers of perpetrators are fiercely debated between Algeria and France.[45] Many bodies from the event were never recovered, but an artifact commemorates the mournful occasion. In the Tamashouet cemetery, the burial sites of Europeans from Oran are managed by the French consulate in Algeria and Pied-Noir associations, including Collectif sauveguarde des cimetières d'Oranie (CSCO) that was founded in 2004 in France (figure 39).[46]

FIGURE 39. In May 2013, Collectif sauveguarde des cimetières d'Oranie (CSCO) erected a cross next to the base of the World War I monument for those without burial places. Photo by author, October 2019.

THE MONUMENT FOLLOWS THE BODIES

Their visits to independent Algeria to repatriate the bodies of Herriot's parents gave the Lyon delegates the opportunity to pay their respects at the war memorial and to initiate contacts with Oran's municipal councilors.[47] The Lyon Municipal Archives, folders, maps, and architectural plans trace three convergent stories: the story of the linkages between colonial Oran and Lyon; the story of the reburial of Herriot's parent's; and the removal of the Oran monument to Lyon.[48] A letter dated February 19, 1964, written by World War II veteran Pierre Padovani, who lived in Oran, to the Lyon municipality gives some idea of the situation. On his own, Padovani had gone to place flowers at the memorial on the occasion of independent Algeria's second Armistice Day, November 11, 1963, and observed that there were no commemorative ceremonies and only a few other wreaths. But if the monument was not attracting people to it, he noted that it was still intact, as was the square around it except for minor discolorations from Organisation de l'armée secrète (OAS) terrorist activities in the summer of 1962. He urged the Lyon council to act immediately and remove it.[49]

Believing that to preserve the monument required its removal from Algeria, a delegation of former European settlers from Oran Province made an official request of the Lyon municipal council to retrieve Oran's 1927 war memorial. The records and correspondence in Lyon's municipal archives date from after the city council had made its decision, so few details are available about the process. But according to Luc Demarchi, moderator of the Lyon Pied-Noir organization's Cercle algérianiste de Lyon website, Lyon's municipal councilors, among them Gilbert Prudhomme, Louis Bonnardel, and Napoléon Bullukian, negotiated with the Algerian authorities.[50] They were aware that the French army and navy could no longer help remove French Algeria's war memorials or statues (*opération d'enlèvement*) as of June 15, 1964, and that without French military support, the costs of shipping the monument to Lyon would be exorbitant. Bullukian (1905–1984), a wealthy local builder, philanthropist, and survivor of the Armenian Genocide, would help fund the legal move of the war memorial from the port of Oran, controlled by Algerian authorities, to Marseille.[51] They therefore needed to meet officially with their counterparts in Oran.

As one solution to the cost issue, Lyon's city architect proposed removing only the top part of the memorial—the sculpture of the three soldiers—

along with a section of the upper column and attaching a new appropriately inscribed pedestal once in Lyon (figure 40).[52]

But the city of Oran insisted on keeping the entire twenty-seven-foot stone column, although it was willing to part with the three soldiers (figures 2, 3, 40, and 41). In July 1967, Ben Ali Seghier, mayor of Oran, wrote to the mayor of Lyon, "I gladly grant you the authorization to transfer Oran's monument to the dead to Lyon, but the stone base must remain in place." [53] Lyon's architect reported that, "For technical reasons, as well as at the request of the Algerian Services, only the upper part of the monument was moved, the base remaining on site in Oran"; the three sculpted soldiers would stand on a new appropriately inscribed pedestal in Lyon.[54]

My two interviews with participants from each side shed some light on the question of why Oran let the monument go to Lyon. Mohammed Benguesmia-Chadly (1943–2020), an elected Oran municipal councilor between 1984 and 1989, who founded CIVIC or Comité d'initiative et de vigilance citoyennes d'Oran, was on the negotiating team in the 1960s. I

FIGURE 40. Photo of the 1927 inauguration including the Lyon architect's markup of the proposed cut for the monument's removal. Ville de Lyon, Archives municipals (AML), ANFANOMA, cote 425 WP 14

asked him to explain why Oran parted with the monument: "We were all so young, most of the municipal council in our twenties immediately after independence. Our priorities were education, rebuilding a newly independent Algeria. We didn't know any better. I personally regret it."[55]

My second interlocutor, Émile Azoulay (1929–2018), was a Maghrebi Jewish businessman originally from Oujda, Morocco, and Mostaganem, Algeria, who resettled in Lyon in 1962. A municipal councilor during Louis Pradel's mayoralty, he was part of the team negotiating to bring the Oran war memorial to Lyon. When I asked him why the Lyon municipality chose to remove Oran's monument, Azoulay answered only that he passed by it often before 1962 and missed it. His comment seems to suggest that statues in public spaces are essential parts of a landscape.[56]

Prudhomme, a Lyon municipal councilor, may have photographed the dismantling process of the three soldiers. In figure 41, we see them hoisted by crane from the pediment and the wooden packing case on a flatbed truck in which they will be packed.[57] Nouba Bouledras was fifteen when the photo was taken. He recalled helping his father, Mohamed Bouledras (known as Hamani) and another marble worker, Houari Bekkay, remove the figures

FIGURE 41. Three busts lowered into a crate, Oran, 1967. Photographer unconfirmed, attributed to Gilles Prudhomme. Image courtesy of Émile Azoulay, also posted on the Association des Algérianistes de Lyon website.

from their stone base.[58] When I showed Nouba the photo from my research in Lyon in 2014, he identified himself as the boy in the truck and his father as the man standing on the top left of the column who was overseeing the removal process.

1967: THE ORAN MONUMENT COMES TO LA DUCHÈRE

Lyon's mayor Pradel had decided to create a place for a war memorial in the heart of La Duchère to remind inhabitants of their lost Algeria. In 1966, the choice was the World War I memorial of Oran with which the newly relocated repatriates from western Algeria were familiar. The three soldiers left Oran aboard the cargo ship *Maguelone* bound for Marseille on December 15, 1967, and then to Lyon on December 26.[59] The removal left a paper trail.[60] Oran's mayor, Ben Ali Seghier, the schoolteacher heading Oran's newly installed municipal council (Assemblée populaire communale, APC) was the first elected APC president or mayor, and he served for a decade from 1965 to 1975. The Oran newspaper *La République*, (the former *L'Echo d'Oran*) reported that the municipal councils of Lyon and Oran respected all administrative protocols.

> It should be noted that this operation follows a transfer procedure filed with the People's Communal Assembly (APC) of Oran by the Lyon municipality. Studied and adopted in deliberation by the APC of Oran, the request was also approved by the prefect of the department. Note also that the delegation of municipal councilors of Lyon was received on Thursday by Mr. Ben Ali Seghier, president of the Oran APC. During a cordial interview, the French delegation expressed the wish to see a delegation from the Oran APC attend the ceremony in Lyon to mark the installation work of the monument.[61]

The request for an official Algerian delegation from Oran to attend Lyon's inauguration of the monument a mere five years after independence was unlikely since the event was organized under the auspices of General Edmond Jouhaud (1905–1995). Jouhaud was an unrepentant supporter of French Algeria who had advocated the use of violence against an independent Algeria. Born west of Oran in Bou-Sfer, Jouhaud had been a leader of the notorious paramilitary OAS and was one of four French generals who were responsible for the failed 1961 putsch of De Gaulle. Condemned to death, Jouhaud was absolved, released, and ultimately amnestied.[62]

The inauguration date was July 15 to avoid coinciding with the festivities of July 14, France's national holiday.[63] The soldiers from the original memorial would be placed on a new concrete pedestal to which additional stone plaques had been added. Roger Fenech, the Tunisian-born mayor of La Duchère and later the president of the Front national des rapatriés (National Front of the Repatriates, renamed the National Federation of the Repatriates), spoke on behalf of the settlers from Oran Province:

> [The war memorial of Oran] recalls our land of Oranie and the fight of two generations of its sons so that France could live. It will be the place of meditation, contemplation, a place of recollection where the repatriates, who lost their graves, can evoke the memory of their dead.[64]

To the enduring dismay of many repatriates, however, the monument measured barely ten feet tall, much less than the original monument that measured twenty-seven feet (figure 42).

A second inaugural ceremony took place on November 9, 1968, in the presence of General Edmond Jouhaud, who had been released recently from

FIGURE 42. Back of the Lyon war memorial from Oran depicting a Senegalese infantryman (not visible in the colonial postcard). Photo by author, November 11, 2013.

prison. Saïd Benaissa Boualam (1906–1982), known as Bachaga Boualam, stood at his side; Boualam was a politician and former colonel in the French army and the Algerian leader of the Harkis.[65] Depending on who does the telling, Boualam symbolizes Muslim support for French Algeria through stellar military service or is the arch-collaborator who betrayed independent Algeria. The square in which the monument stands was named for him as are many streets in French towns that have dense repatriate or Harki populations.

THE 1927 MONUMENT IN ORAN AFTER 1967

The afterlives of the sundered Oran war memorial diverged in 1967. The 1927 war memorial column that remained in Oran evolved after its original statue of World War I soldiers was removed to Lyon. The European settler and native Jewish populations left their monuments, and the question was what to do with them after independence. A variety of meanings in the Algerian postcolony have been attached to Oran's colonial monuments, figurative statues of soldiers and female nudes, busts of great men (*grands hommes*), or somber war memorials.[66] After 1962, the Oran war memorial had become a monument to the martyrs of the Algerian Revolution, and a plaque with their names was attached to it. According to Mohammed Freha, a founding member, historian and curator of the city's private memorial museum to the Algerian Revolution, the plaque was removed and placed in Oran's Civil Prison around 1987.[67] Every year on July 5, Algeria's official independence day, a diminishing delegation of veterans of the War of Independence visited the plaque until its removal.[68]

In the 1980s, the monument underwent major stylistic changes that were symbolic as much as aesthetic (figure 43).

These included a revetment of multicolored Spanish-imported faience tiles known as *zillīj* (polychrome mosaic tilework from inlaid glazed pottery). Tilework was common in the precolonial Maghreb, and colonial art historians even compared ceramic wall decorations to colorful vertical carpets. After independence, the Algerian state used faience increasingly, adding ceramics and imported Spanish tiles to the mihrab and columns of Oran's 1795 Hassan el-Pacha mosque, which was renovated in the late 1980s.[69] Abstract faience gave way to ceramic figurative art to decorate Oran's urban landscape notably in areas marked off as commemorative spaces and sites of heritage. Tiles were used to remold urban heritage in-

FIGURE 43. Oran's 1927 World War I colonial war memorial transformed into an Algerian monument to the martyrs of the revolution. Photo by author, May 12, 2014.

cluding the cover of Oran's twentieth-century war monument and the city's eighteenth-century mosque. The French colonial monument and the Ottoman era mosque, separated by two centuries, are joined stylistically, as if the state were creating a uniform heritage palette through tilework. On the façade are verses in black calligraphy by Moufdi Zakaria (pseud., 1908–1977), the author of Algeria's national anthem "Qasaman" ("We Pledge"). According to Mohamed Benguesmia-Chadly, president of the Association Culturel de la Ville d'Oran and elected Oran municipal councilor between 1984 and 1989, Oran's governor Abdelmalek Sellal called upon artists from Algiers around 1988 to decorate and cover the colonial war memorial in ceramic to celebrate the conference of the Arab Maghreb Union (Ittiḥād al-Maghrib al-ʿArabī) which was convened for Oran. Benguesmia-Chadly was among those who protested—not against having the monument tiled, but in the name of local Oran artists who should have received the artistic commission.[70]

For each generation born after Algeria's 1962 independence, the 1927 monument has become incrementally illegible. The sacrifices of colonial troops and their storied French military career are pre-independence history not to be celebrated. By 1987–88, twenty years after the three sculpted soldiers were removed, the project to resurface the war memorial with colorful tiles and Arabic script aligned the monument's exterior with Algeria's heroic fight for independence. Within a few generations, the sculptural record of Algerian soldiers who had fought for France in two world wars had disappeared.[71] The monument marks a double absence and currently appears as a cenotaph, empty of bodies:

> No more arresting emblems of the modern culture of nationalism exist than cenotaphs and tombs of Unknown Soldiers. The public ceremonial reverence accorded these monuments precisely because they are either deliberately empty or no one knows who lies inside them, has no true precedents in earlier times. To feel the force of this modernity one has only to imagine the general reaction to the busy-body who "discovered" the Unknown Soldier's name or insisted on filling the cenotaph with some real bones. Sacrilege of a strange, contemporary kind! Yet void as these tombs are of identifiable mortal remains or immortal souls, they are nonetheless saturated with ghostly national imaginings. (This is why so many different nations have such tombs without feeling any need to specify the nationality of their absent occupants. What else could they be but Germans, Americans, Argentinians . . . ?)[72]

ORAN IN LYON: URBAN PLANNING AND THE REPATRIATES

During my 2013–14 stay in Lyon, I was able to appreciate the historic center preserved thanks to the city's heritage work. Lyon suffered war damage both by retreating German armies strategically dynamiting the city's bridges in May 1944 and by Allied aircraft bombardments. After World War II, the industrious Lyonnais rebuilt their city preserving the core of "Old Lyon" (Vieux Lyon).[73] The moment was propitious for preservationists. France's first minister of cultural affairs, André Malraux, enshrined the principle of "protected sectors" (*secteurs sauvegardés*) as early as 1962, expanding the protection of single architectural units to encompass entire neighborhoods. The category of a central single monument worth preserving was extended to the surrounding site, thereby acknowledging the atmosphere of a neighborhood in the emotions and feelings a district's ensemble exerts.[74] The "Malraux law" 62-903 of August 1962 gave rise to three heritage projects in different parts of France: preserving the Marais section of Paris, protecting the medieval Dordogne town of Sarlat, and safeguarding Old Lyon.[75] The 1962 Malraux law thwarted Lyon's mayor, Louis Pradel whose plans to modernize the city included the construction of a pass-through highway that would have destroyed the Renaissance city center. Pradel, called "the demolisher" (*démolisseur*), failed to get his highway built and Old Lyon was saved. Instead, he devoted three mayoral mandates modernizing Lyon, building extensively in new suburban neighborhoods, adding new highways there, and establishing commemorations to France's various wars.

Mayor Edouard Herriot had planned housing in Lyon, and Pradel, his successor, launched the project for La Duchère, one of Lyon's four major city projects (*grands projets de ville*, or GVP) and one of fifty government-funded urbanization projects.[76] With national and municipal subsidies, urban planners could produce exemplary modern housing for a post–World War II society. La Duchère was located within the city limits, although it was somewhat isolated on a high plateau overlooking Lyon. François-Régis Cottin (1920–2013), the area's principal architect, originally intended to provide housing for residents living in Lyon's insalubrious working-class neighborhoods. He designed five edifices between 1960 and 1962 (often with associates such as Franck Grimal).

A government order (*ordonnance*) of August 18, 1962 was issued during this era of modernization to provide housing for repatriates. The government required that French provinces that had received funds for special construction programs to reserve 30 percent of their housing stock for the returnees of North Africa, the economic basis for European settlers from Algeria to resettle in France. Nearly half of all the new constructions in La Duchère was earmarked for the repatriate exodus from western Algeria, including Oran.[77] Thousands of housing units were built by 1962 and made available to the 25,000 repatriates who moved to Lyon and whose numbers grew to 100,000 in the surrounding region.[78] These were European settlers in the main with some native Jews (400 families were established in 1963 according to the census by the Rav Hida Synagogue, or around 15 percent of La Duchère).[79] They accounted for between 6 percent to more than 52 percent of the various neighborhoods of La Duchère, which locals dubbed the "Pied-Noir district." Between 1962 and 1968, a total of 37,276 repatriates moved to Lyon, a city with one million inhabitants.[80] For historian Yann Scioldo-Zürcher, these mass housing projects for repatriates after 1962 were social peace programs after the brutal Algerian War.[81] Housing on a grand scale was seen as a balm for the traumatic military experience of young

Frenchmen and for the brutality of the metropolitan police force that had imprisoned and occasionally deported Algerians from France.

As Lyon expanded after World War II, monuments were preserved, replaced if destroyed, and new ones erected. According to historian Antoine Prost, few new war memorials were built between the 1960s and late 1980s, but Prost did not count the community memorials to the Algerian War.[82] He ignored the million plus settlers of French Algeria and their offspring and the memorials and monuments that migrated from Algeria primarily to France.[83] Pieds-Noirs and Algerian Muslim Harki soldiers were only officially acknowledged in 1999 when France officially acknowledged the Algerian War. Nearly forty years of official silence may have accounted for the proliferation of associations, statuary, war memorials, and organizations by both communities, argues historian Claire Eldridge; she notes that scholars overlooked the period before the hypermemory culture wars when Harkis and Pieds-Noirs created memory narratives through local associations and incorporated war memorial rituals into municipal events and Catholic celebrations.[84] Activist Pied-Noir memorializations fervently embraced repatriated monuments, such as Lyon's Oran monument, along with associated commemorative days and pilgrimages (figure 44).[85]

FIGURE 44. Oran war memorial relocated to La Duchère, Lyon, France. Postcard, Éditions La Cigogne. ca. 1970. Author's collection.

THE EVOLUTION OF LA DUCHÈRE, LYON

Commemorative plaques on Lyon's Oran monument changed over the years to honor the soldiers of the African army under General De Lattre de Tassigny who liberated Lyon during World War II, while other plaques on the same monument designate the sacrifices of European and Harki victims of the Algerian War of Independence ("formations supplétives et assimilées pour leurs sacrifices"). At the request of the Association nationale des français d'Afrique de Nord, d'outre-mer et de leurs amis (ANFANOMA), the most prominent inscription is written in gold and expresses gratitude to the city of Lyon for welcoming the repatriates ("En souvenir de leur terre natale, la Ville de Lyon à ses enfants d'Afrique du Nord qu'elle a accueillis").[86] When I conducted interviews in Lyon in 2013–14, residents explained Pradel's generous housing policies for repatriates. They described themselves to me as "pioneers" settling and constructing anew in virgin rural territory in France just as they had heroically tamed Algeria. As they prospered, many left the neighborhood for wealthier areas and made way for a population of newer immigrants. During my stay, a new mosque was under construction in 2014 rising next to Cottin's church and the Algerian Jewish synagogue to accommodate the growing population of Muslims in the La Duchère neighborhood affectionately and ironically called "little Jerusalem."[87] By 1987, a local Muslim association, the Association des Musulmans de La Duchère, was founded with a growing membership of 2,500 that prayed in the mosque during major holidays.

In the 1990s, La Duchère reached a tipping point. Riots had broken out in greater Lyon in 1997, and Gérard Collomb, La Duchère's mayor, redesigned housing projects for his district which he implemented in 2001 after becoming mayor of Lyon. Since 1962, publicly subsidized housing (*logements locatifs sociaux*) in La Duchère had hovered around 80 percent, an economic marker of socioeconomic deprivation and discrimination, but these descriptors were never applied to the repatriates. La Duchère came to resemble the ghettoized suburban enclaves of *grand ensembles* with their devalued building complexes, high numbers of subsidized units, and an impoverished population who could never be considered as French repatriates.

Many of Cottin's buildings in La Duchère would earn protected status in 2007 under France's newer twentieth-century heritage preservation classification law of 1999 (known as patrimoine du XXe siècle), such as the district's Church of Notre Dame du Monde-Entier.[88] Also included was the landmark residential Panoramic Tower rising 220 feet, still standing at a time when seventeen other monumental social housing towers in the greater Lyon region were knocked down in the twenty-first century. Although three large slab blocks (*barres des milles*) of apartments were spectacularly demolished in 2005, 2010, and 2015, other *barres* by Cottin and his team remain in La Duchère, evidence of the thousands of housing units erected between 1960 and 1962 coincidentally in time to welcome the repatriate exodus from Algeria. The Lyon municipality did demolish some buildings including one squat structure next to the Panoramic Tower formerly housing public services. For the local branch of European settlers of Algeria, the Fédération nationale des rapatriés (FNR) de Lyon, this meant losing free space for meetings and administrative offices (figure 45).

Since the 1990s, the repatriates from Algeria no longer live near the Oran war memorial. The army veterans (draftees, career military, and Harkis) whose history was commemorated by the war memorial and its changing inscriptions, do however still travel to it on days relevant to their Algerian

FIGURE 45. The Plateau of La Duchère: Panoramic Tower (left) and, in the center, the squat building that housed the headquarters of the repatriate organization of Lyon was demolished. A residential *barre* is on the right. Photo by author, February 15, 2014.

past. The concentrated population of repatriates had created dozens of associations with roots in French Algeria that were and remain centered around synagogues, churches, a local soccer team, and hometown clubs representing their places of origin in Algeria. Historian Jean-Jacques Jordi sees changes in each decade: he considers that the robust community of Pieds-Noirs spent their first decade organizing around successful claims for indemnification and liberating their political detainees, including Jouhaud, and that after the 1970s, the hometown associations linked to Algeria's settler towns proliferated along with religious and athletic associations. By the 1990s, however, the themes and activities shifted as associations organized discussions about identity, the fate of their cemeteries in Algeria, and the creation of museums.[89]

By the end of 2013, the government agency responsible for reparations and indemnifications for the repatriated, that had been created on July 15, 1970, was phased out.[90] The various institutions for repatriates created under President Chirac—Mission interministérielle aux rapatriés, known as MIR and created by decree of May 27, 2002; the Agence nationale pour l'indemnisation des français d'outre-mer; and the Service central des rapatriés—were eliminated and their activities put under the vast umbrella of the National Office for Veterans and Victims of War (Office national des anciens combattants et victimes de guerre, ONAC-VG). It had a new mission:

> Strengthen the mission of memory: take on the role to strengthen the link army-nation.
>
> . . . ONAC-VG must be reoriented beyond its nationals towards the national community and to citizens. It is through the action of memory that this work is best done. A first reorganization of the Office intervened in the framework of the policy of memory with the creation of the missions, memory and communication.[91]

The French government's decisions were predicated on a mission accomplished assumption. The Pied-Noir community was considered successfully integrated into French society. What did ensue were appeals to memory in the forms of more statues, monuments, official national days, museums, and exhibitions.

PROTECTIVE DISPOSSESSION

During the early postindependent years, two Algerian interwar monuments by Albert Pommier were brought to France. One was brought legally from Oran to Lyon, while the other—Pommier's *poilu* sculpted for a town fifty miles southwest of Oran, Hammam Bou Hadjar—came illegally. They characterize two different trajectories for war memorials. Pommier's soldier from Hammam Bou Hadjar was among the first colonial war monuments removed from Algeria to France, a year after Algerian independence (figure 46).

FIGURE 46. Pommier's pedestal reproduced in Rey, "Le Monument de Hammam-Bou-Hadjar," 1922, p. 15.

Like the Oran memorial, it was transferred without its towering pedestal and base, but unlike the case of the three Oran soldiers, this removal was carried out by the French military that was still entrenched in the naval base of Mers-el-Kebir near Oran. On April 19, 1964, it was ceremoniously installed in Fréjus in the south of France where it sits on a low, simple replacement base on the seafront boulevard facing Algeria. New inscriptions for a new pedestal reference the monument's trans-Mediterranean trajectory and multiple losses, conflating the colonial dead of World Wars I and II scattered on Europe's battlefields with settler ancestors buried in Algeria: "To our cherished dead who remained in Hammam Bou Hadjar, a plaque is dedicated by the City of Fréjus to the memory of the offspring of Algeria who died for France, 1914–1918, 1939–1945."[92]

Fréjus is located in the southeastern Var and includes nearby Saint-Aygulf and Saint-Raphaël, towns linked to France's colonies in North Africa and Indochina. Fréjus had been a departure point for troops garrisoned at Camp Gallieni, sailing to the colonies. The camp was named after General Joseph Gallieni (1849–1916), who is buried in Saint-Raphaël. During World War I, military barracks, depots, training grounds, and hospitals in Fréjus-Saint-Raphaël housed thousands of colonial troops who were to be acclimated to European winters before being dispatched north to the front. The region's economy was tied to the military bases and lucrative attractions for the large transient population of soldiers and the sizeable number of troops that reflected the reach of France's empire. Many camps remained in active use until 1960, when many of France's overseas colonies became independent.[93]

Fréjus is replete with architectural reminders of France's colonial history. A massive war memorial to France's Vietnam war was erected in 1993; additional memorials include the Hông Hiên Tu Buddhist pagoda of 1917 built by Indochinese troops and the Missiri mosque-like structure of 1928–30 resembling the mosque in Djenné, Mali.[94] The garrison of the 21st marine regiment (Régiment d'infanterie de marine) is still in use alongside the naval museum (Musée des Troupes de Marine). A bronze sculpture from 1994 is dedicated to Africa's Black Army (*Mémorial de l'Armée Noire*) by Yvon Guidez. The region is also home to three spoliated war memorials, including the Hammam Bou Hadjar monument by Albert Pommier.[95]

A confluence of geopolitical changes framed the ways in which these three west Algerian monuments were installed in Fréjus: the contribution of the war in Algeria to the downfall of the French Fourth Republic in 1958, the return of Charles de Gaulle to power, and the election of a former Vichy bureaucrat, André Léotard, as mayor of Fréjus. Alain Amato, the chronicler of "repatriated" statues from Algeria to France, named Gaston Montamat (1894-1986), a French war veteran who moved to Hammam Bou Hadjar, as the force behind all three removals. The story goes that in 1963, Montamat was living in the Oran region and was alerted by an unnamed Muslim war veteran about potential attacks on Pommier's war monument in Hammam Bou Hadjar. During these early years of independence, Montamat could still call on the French army and engineering corps to transport the statue, which he himself helped dismantle into three parts and crate in order to bring it to Mers-el-Kebir. Also, according to Amato, the Algerian mayor of Hammam Bou Hadjar intervened physically to retain at least the twenty-six-foot column and plaques.[96]

Montamat's activities, supported by repatriate groups in southern France, can be understood as Pied-Noir theft. They set up possibilities for accumulating monuments from Algeria that created modified artworks in France and then in Algeria by leaving the space of a removed monument empty. Three of Montamat's Algerian monuments decorate the seafront boulevard of Fréjus. In Algeria, new, refurbished or transformed monuments replaced Pommier's sculpted soldier. One of these has two large marble panels inscribed with the names of the dead commemorating the martyrs of the Algerian Revolution from Hammam Bou Hadjar. Between a thin marble, arcade-like structure edged in the red, white, and green of the Algerian flag, a central brown marble, screen-like cut-out suggests the shape of a gravestone that frames a lone armed Algerian combatant on the move (figure 47).

Art historian June Hargove proposes that "the shuffling of monuments was a gentle form of iconoclasm."[97] In the main square of Hammam Bou Hadjar, new postindependence Algerian war memorials are surrounded by colonial-era buildings, many such as the Protestant and Catholic churches become mosques or cultural centers. However, the French-built city hall in the background of figures 47 and 48 continues to carry out city administrative functions.

Montamat's exploits did not end with relocating Pommier's *poilu* of Hammam Bou Hadjar to Fréjus. Another repatriate group, relocated to France's southern Var region, dispatched the intrepid Montamat to two more sites. Pied-Noir accounts obscure how he seized his next prize: a bronze soldier from Mascara that he brought to his adopted hometown of Saint-Raphaël (figure 49).[98]

The Mascara war memorial, erected by noted architect Charles

FIGURE 47. New monument to the martyrs of the Algerian revolution in the main square of Hammam Bou Hadjar. Photo by author, May 2018.

FIGURE 48. View of the square: Pommier's *poilu* replaced by an ensemble of monuments to the dead of the Algerian War of Independence in front of the colonial-era city hall in Hammam Bou Hadjar. Photo by author, May 2018.

FIGURE 49. Charles Montaland's colonial war memorial, Mascara. Postcard, Éditions Photo-Africaines (EPA) no. 4. Author's collection.

Montaland (1871–1946), remains in Algeria where it has been repurposed with a large, suspended scroll replacing the French infantryman with the names of Algerians martyred during the War of Independence. These removals and pairings of statues that talk to each other across the Mediterranean raise questions about the power of living with colonial artworks. One response is found in the reconfigured Charles Montaland colonial war memorial in Algeria. Montaland's original plaques naming the colonial world-war dead were relegated to the plinth while the statue of the *poilu* was the sculptural centerpiece. In contrast, the roll call of the Algerian dead from Mascara was aesthetically foregrounded through enlargement and aniconism to replace the stolen soldier.[99] Algerian replacements for missing colonial war memorials (or for parts of them spoliated to France) are widespread; they are dynamic palimpsests that communicate decolonized history.

Mascara's current iteration of the war memorial draws attention to the monumental colonial past offering a formal solution to decolonization that lies in renewed Algerian appearances. Colonial architect Charles Montaland could not have envisioned this revised monument that emerged from the entwined processes of French removal and Algerian replacement, but his buildings are valued and preserved in Algeria where they are part of national patrimony. Montaland's magnificent city hall, the *hôtel de ville*, national theater, and Palace of Meriem Azza with its gardens and sculpture are among the architectural glories of central Skikda (formerly colonial Philippeville). His neo-Mauresque train station, which lost its clock tower on February 1962 in a bombing engineered by OAS partisans of French Algeria, still stands. Montaland's structures and sculptures are the pride of Skikda and Algeria, with renovated exteriors and interiors repurposed by Algerians who now control their architectural destiny.[100]

Gaston Montamat continued after he removed Pommier's *poilu* from Hammam Bou Hadjar and Montaland's statue from Mascara. In 1965, he removed the Tlemcen war memorial to the southern French city of Saint Aygulf, sculpted by Joseph Ebstein (born in Batna, Algeria, 1881–1961), who also made the Sétif war memorial (the locus of the 1945 Sétif massacres) and the *Winged Victory* statue on top of the Constantine war memorial (see chapter 4).[101] Erected in 1924, Ebstein's Tlemcen monument depicts a female *Winged Victory* leading a helmeted French *poilu* and colonial soldier wearing a *chéchia* of the Army of Africa (figure 50). Approximately 500

FIGURE 50. Colonial war memorial of Tlemcen sculpted by Joseph Ebstein, inaugurated in 1925. Postcard, Éditions Photo-Africaines (EAP). Author's collection.

soldiers from Tlemcen died in the two world wars. On behalf of the Pied-Noir veterans of Saint-Aygulf next to Saint-Raphaël, Montamat called on the French military still stationed at Mers-el-Kebir and relocated it in 1965 to southern France to serve as a repatriate pilgrimage site.[102] Gaston Montamat retired to Saint-Raphaël. In 1975, he helped erect a national memorial to the Army of Africa.[103]

Montamat's early removals contrast starkly with legal transfer negotiations between Oran and Lyon, but the prevailing discourse in Lyon and Montamat's self-representation is one of saviors rather than pillagers. In fact, for the community of former settlers who relocated to southern France, the sole possibility for preserving beloved monuments was to take them.

In nineteenth-century Algeria, European settlers were defined by their displacement, their settling on lands across the Mediterranean, and their encounter with Indigenous collectives; after 1962 in France, the Pied-Noir collectivity were resettlers, defined by their displacement and their encounter with the metropolitan community.[104] On both occasions, the settlers benefited with rights, social structures, and erected statues: these were sovereign displacements. The history of the 1927 war memorial of Oran raises issues of place and urban sites during periods of colonization and decolonization and the important technical and esthetic innovations around new war memorial installations. The Oran war memorial represents, dramatizes, and concretizes how we think about monuments in our present environment.

CHAPTER THREE

DISMANTLING A WORLD

Sidi-Bel-Abbès and the French Foreign Legion

"But it's a little Paris!" (Mais c'est un petit Paris!)

NAPOLEON III ON SEEING SIDI-BEL-ABBÈS[1]

THE TRAJECTORIES OF TWO FRENCH colonial-era war memorials after 1962 in Sidi-Bel-Abbès, a military garrison town fifty-six miles south of Oran, reflect Algerian and French decisions about what Algerians would see, commemorate, and steward after decolonization. The first is a war memorial by sculptor Charles Sarrabezolles erected in 1928; the second, a French Foreign Legion war memorial by Charles-Henri Pourquet erected in 1931. Both are numbered among the monuments raised during the interwar period in the main square and traffic circles of most towns and villages in metropolitan France to embellish neighborhoods and memorialize World War I losses and in French Algeria, a period replete with commemorations of one hundred years of French rule. The two statues in Sidi-Bel-Abbès reflect the starkly opposed roles played by "natives" in French Algeria's settler-military complex: the men were subjected to French military rule at home on the one hand and drafted into the French military to fight for France abroad on the other. One statue reflects the violence done to soldiers killed for France in World War I and the other the violence inflicted on Algeria by the French Foreign Legion.

FOUNDATIONS OF SIDI-BEL-ABBÈS

On March 10, 1831, less than a year after the French invaded Algeria, King Louis-Phillipe decreed the creation of a French Foreign Legion (Légion étrangère). Legionnaires were to be foreign nationals recruited to fight for the empire as engineers and soldier-builders (*soldat-bâtisseurs*). Bearded Legionnaires would later lead military parades equipped with the tools of their mission: laborer axes, gloves, and leather aprons enabling them to conquer *ense et aratro* (by sword and plow). Marshal Thomas-Robert Bugeaud (1784–1849), who later became governor-general of Algeria used this Latin motto in reference to imperial Rome and looked to the earlier empire in other ways as well.[2]

In western Algeria near Morocco, the French military and the Legion designed what would later become the town of Sidi-Bel-Abbès as of 1849. The story of Sidi-Bel-Abbès and the Legion are so deeply intertwined in the colonial imagination that the town is sometimes described as emerging for the Legion ex nihilo. General Raoul-Marie Donop (1841–1910) gave the most common account of the origins of Sidi-Bel-Abbès:

> Founded only in 1849 on the site of a small redoubt that had been built near the marabout dedicated to Sidi-Bel-Abbès, this town has the particularity of showing, in a very special way, the French aptitude to colonize, because it is the only one of all the cities of Algeria to have no historical past. Everything here was created by the French with the help of foreign labor.[3]

Like the histories of many French colonial sites, this founding settler myth portrayed Algeria as a *terra nullius*, "the land of no one" or "unowned land." As of January 5, 1849, it was possible to invent a town in this land without people by decree. Léon Bastide (1844–1921), town historian and mayor (1874 and 1892–1907) of Sidi-Bel-Abbès, describes the clusters of commercial enterprises barely emerging from the shadows of a core of strategically located military "barracks facing a canteen" (*casernes doublées d'une cantine*).[4] Captain Hugues-Eugène Prudon (1809–1891), a trained engineer assigned to serve under Generals Bugeaud and Pélissier, is credited with breaking the first ground. The thirty-five-year-old Prudon arrived in Algeria in 1844 where he laid out a grid or checkerboard (*plan en damier*) typical of colonial military projects.[5] This was one of many infrastructural accomplishments for which Prudon was celebrated:

> Sidi-bel-Abbès, Prudon, two inseparable names. For seven consecutive years, the indefatigable chief engineer carried out a considerable variety of works, fortifications, military and civil buildings, roads, water conduits, irrigation, etc., with admirable intelligence and energy. In the middle of the scrub-covered plain, an entire city emerged from the ground, rich, populous, flourishing today as it will remain for a long time. Surrounded by superb gardens, the city itself disappears under magnificent shade, an imperishable creation to which Prudon's name will always be attached.[6]

Prudon carefully designed a world on western Algeria's Mekerra Plain at the convergence of army supply routes essential for the military's southward expansion. He divided some forty-two hectares for different purposes: military buildings and fortifications covered twenty-one hectares, ten hectares were designated for civilian structures like those in a French town—a central square around which a church, courthouse, post office, schools, and a town hall stood. The remaining land was demarcated into settler housing. French Algerian nineteenth-century military-settler towns of Algeria such as Blida, Batna, Saïda, Bedeau, and Bossuet would have similar urban designs and administrative structures.

Prudon modeled Sidi-Bel-Abbès in western Algeria on a Roman fortress-camp located in eastern Algeria at Lambaesis near Constantine. Built around 120 CE by the Third Augustan Legion (Legio III Augusta), Lambaesis followed a topographical map, or centuriation, of the Hadrianic Roman rectangular *castrum*.[7] This era of "new Roman centurions" was to be organized by a "centuriation" for which Sidi-Bel-Abbès was the "model of regularity":[8]

> At least for the origins of colonization, Rome started anew [*tabula rasa*] ignoring the past by imposing a new framework on its conquests. Indifferent or disdainful, it ignored the previous administrative organization and marked its rights of eminent domain by perspectives of conquest: taking possession as if engraved in the soil. Following the eternal political principle of "divide and conquer," centuriation isolates zones of resistance, especially mountainous regions, even insinuated into valleys and divides mountain ranges eroding the lower slopes.[9]

Explicit references to the Roman empire and North Africa legions were significant for the French empire. The monthly review of the French engineering corps mapped Sidi-Bel-Abbès onto Lambaesis to show a clear genealogy (figure 51):

> History shows us that the Ancients worked the same way in similar countries as well as in present-day Algeria. Arrive at a point, establish a camp that becomes a colony: this is what our predecessors, the Romans, did. With history book in hand, an ordinary tourist visiting these two military camps that became colonial towns will quickly realize that identical methods were used to build these two towns, the one in the first century AD and the second in the nineteenth.[10]

The engineering, or castrametation analogy was echoed by the similarities of the two military designers in the two imperial legions, French General

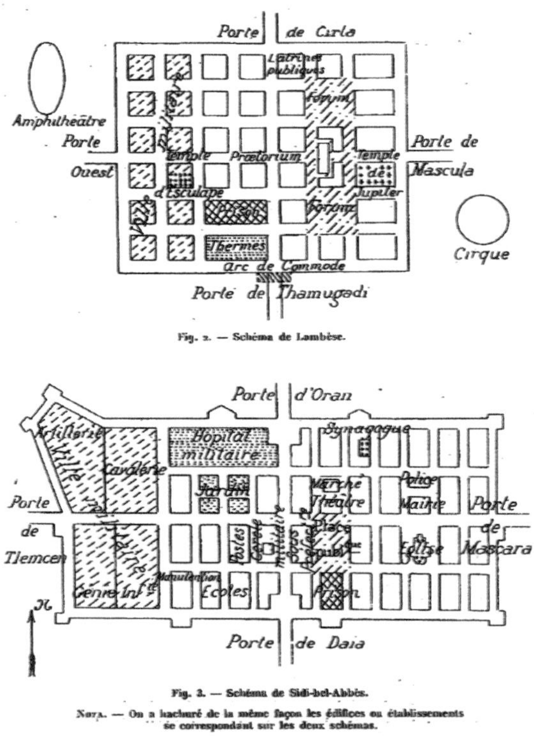

FIGURE 51. **[Étienne-Philippe-Jules] Gauzence de Lastours, "L'Algérie et le service en campagne algérienne,"** ***Revue du génie militaire*** **42, no. 2 (1911): figures 2 and 3, p. 385. Bibliothèque nationale de France (BnF).**

Marie-Alphonse Bedeau and Roman legionnaire General Quintus Flavius, creators and defenders of empire.

> The enclosure is flanked on the side, but the arrangement is the same here, with the four gates at the cardinal points, the overall rectangular measuring 350m by 800m, the prefecture located like the praetorium, the hospital like the thermal baths, the church and the synagogue like temples, the theater, the public square, with the military town distinctly separated; in a word, all the grouping needed for the civilization that follows the army. Would not Quintus Flavius, the legate of the Third Legion, buried near Lambèse have recognized his colleague and imitator General Bedeau? This simple glance brings out the two successive roles of the army as creator role and defender.[11]

The work of Algerian historians Ammara Bekkouche, Daho Djerbal, Karim Ouldennebia, and Redouane Ainad-Tabet cited throughout reclaim other histories of the Indigenous region of Sidi-Bel-Abbès that do not celebrate a town built ex nihilo, but rather examine overlooked archaeological sites, medieval Arab historiography, oral traditions, and the landscape itself, which all attest to the presence of people and habitations that were ignored by the colonial military. The Neolithic sites, Roman ruins and milestones, Arab and Berber habitations and wells provide ample evidence that the region was long inhabited.[12] In the eleventh century, the Béni Amer tribal confederation arrived in conquering waves from the east and settled in the Mekerra Valley, part of the invasions of the greater Bedouin Hilali tribes from Mascara to Tlemcen into the vastness of western Algeria.[13] In the eighteenth century, a mausoleum for Sidi-Bel-Abbès el-Bouzidi, who gave his name to the town, was erected to honor the holy man, who claimed lineal descent from the Prophet Muhammad. Many local legends recounted to me by interlocutors attest to the saint's long-standing presence and miraculous resistance. He transformed himself into a dove, so the story goes, to put an end to quarrels between two tribal fractions, thereby ensuring that peace reigned between the disputatious Amarna and Ouled Brahim tribes. At his death, Sidi-Bel-Abbès el-Bouzidi is said to have been buried on the site where a dove alighted to symbolize the alliance. A variant tale has it that the saint transformed himself into a dove to escape the warring tribes to whom he was to minister. A second local etiological miracle still circulates accrediting him with *baraka*, miraculous capacities that guaranteed that the town's Arabic name would be preserved despite attempts to rename it "Napoléonville," in honor of Emperor Napoleon III (1808–1873).

An elected settler official is said to have informed Napoleon that local sentiment protested the proposed name change: "They say, 'you take our land,' if you attack their saint's name, they will rise."[14]

Notwithstanding the town's saintly name and inhabitants, Prudon ordered its conquest, expropriating and expelling the native populace for settlers and soldiers. The common French military practice in the towns established in Algeria relegated the native Muslim population to segregated enclaves.[15] Residents interviewed in 1993 by historian Redouane Ainad-Tabet gave accounts about the town center and the exclusion of the local population: "You don't walk about the European town, you're immediately pushed back. It was more spatial discrimination. (On ne tourne pas en ville [europèene]; on était immédiatement refoulé. C'était une autre discrimination spatiale)."[16]

Men worked as low-wage laborers for Europeans while many of the women worked in the notorious bars and brothels of the disreputable districts of Sidi-Bel-Abbès. Much later, by World War I, the scandal of mobile field bordellos (BMC, *bordel mobile campagne*) and spatially restricted "red light" districts (*quartiers réservés*) provoked the same police and health surveillance being carried out throughout North Africa by and for the military just as they were done in metropolitan France:[17]

> Wherever Legionnaires have regular barracks, prostitution festers. Sidi-Bel-Abbès, for instance has been named the Brothel of the Legion. There along the rue Mansard, the Rue Verte, and of course the rue d'Ambulance—which got its name from the many ambulances that picked up knifing victims—almost every house is a "crib," with revealingly dressed, or undressed, *filles de joie* enticing passing soldiers from doorways and windows.[18]

Such streets attached to the colonial native enclave of El Graba such as Rue Verte were demolished in 2010 (figure 52).[19]

The Legionnaires called the racialized urban organization of colonial towns the "Casbah," although in Sidi-Bel-Abbès and other Algerian towns, "El Graba" was used more commonly to describe native rural construction of packed earth. The name El Graba comes from the plural of *gourbi*, a French colonial term adapted from Algerian Arabic to conjure urban informality, haphazard construction, illegal street vendors, and a precarious existence. These native sections were called *ville* or *village nègre* (Negrotown), *villes musulmanes* (Muslim towns), and *villes arabes* (Arab towns) through-

FIGURE 52. **Entrance to the demolished Rue Verte. Photo by author, November 2019.**

out French Algeria.[20] A toponymic war was waged over the central Indigenous square—the 1873 French name for the native district, the Faubourg Bugeaud for the general against the Algerian name Tahtaha (esplanade).

Topography and military walls concretized the long-standing divisions and tensions between colonizers and colonized in Sidi-Bel-Abbès. El Graba was starved of infrastructure and amenities and hemmed in by the town's Jewish cemetery and the mosque of el-Aadam built in 1892.[21] It was only under the short-lived administration of René Justrabo (1917–2013), Algeria's only elected Communist mayor (1947–1953), who was supported by such eminent municipal councilors as Dr. Abdelkader Azza, that paved roads, a post office, a music rotunda, and the Tahtaha esplanade were built. Electricity was brought soon after to Seneclauze, the second native enclave or "island" (*îlot*) on the town's periphery where the population was most dense.[22] Frantz Fanon call this mobilization of topography, architecture, and infrastructure to regulate individual spaces and respiration "occupied breathing . . . combat breathing":

> There is not an occupation of territory, on the one hand, and the independence of persons on the other. It is the country as a whole, its history, its daily pulsation that are contested and disfigured, in the hope of a final destruction. Under these conditions, the individual's breathing is observed, it is occupied breathing. It is a combat breathing.[23]

The Legion's conquest and occupation of Sidi-Bel-Abbès from 1846 to 1962 was stamped on the colonial architecture, a visceral exercise of sensorial domination. Even the local calendar was structured by the Legion's ceremonies and commemorations. As it paraded around the city, the Legion's marching band declared its domination sonically over the cacophony of church bells each Sunday afternoon.[24]

CARLO SARRABEZOLLES: THE 1928 WAR MEMORIAL OF SIDI-BEL-ABBÈS

On December 9, 1928, a war memorial was unveiled in Sidi-Bel-Abbès's central square and traffic roundabout Place Georges Clémenceau, designed by Carlo Sarrabezolles (1888–1971). Its costs had been covered by municipal and national subsidies and local veteran associations among others. The original design for the memorial can be reconstructed from the archives of the Sarrabezolles Foundation in Paris where photographs and notes about North African troops, as well as plaster models and studies, document Sarrabezolles effort to accurately portray the soldiers on the monument. Sarrabezolles drew on his war memories as he had served in the French army during World War I, mostly incarcerated in a German prisoner-of-war camp (figure 53).[25]

The dedication took place before a large group of dignitaries, members of the French Foreign Legion, schoolchildren, and veterans of World War I from local associations who stood at the crowd's forefront. Prominent visiting military and colonial authorities had alighted at the train station and made their way in a procession to be officially welcomed in the rain. A crowd of townspeople walked through the town's public gardens to the main square to hear the speeches and watch the ceremonial placing of flowers and garlands at the memorial's base accompanied by a children's choir.[26] Town poet and chronicler Léon Adoue explained the symbolism in Sarrabezolles's sculpture:

> [The war memorial's] principal motif represents victory leading in her wake of glory, infantrymen, Zouaves, Spahis, Legionnaires, components of that

FIGURE 53. Carlos Sarrabezolles, colonial war memorial, Sidi-Bel-Abbès. Postcard, Neurdein et Levy, ca. 1930, Compagnie Alsacienne des Arts Photomécaniques-Strasbourg (CAP: 1924–1932). Courtesy of Fondation Sarrabezolles.

> beautiful Army of Africa of which our war dead were a part. The names of the dead are engraved the length of the base. Two women—France and Sidi-Bel-Abbès—spill tears over the pain of the great and small homeland on these names.[27]

A dynamic group of colonial and French soldiers stands atop the memorial's high base behind a nine-foot figure of Victory whose legs face forward while twisting her torso to look back at the troops behind. The soldiers following closely on her heels, appearing to be hurling themselves into battle from their twelve-foot pedestal positioned to align with the town's grand avenues as if it were forging the way to battlefield carnage (figure 54).

Sarrabezolles's method of swiftly sculpting fresh concrete, a process he invented and perfected, produces an effect that has been described as a "petrified motion picture that grips the spectator's imagination."[28] He adeptly conveys the intense crush and forward motion in the heat of the battlefield.

The names of the town's war dead—native Algerian subjects and French settler-citizens—were listed alphabetically on the memorial. This was a political gesture that contrasted with the general practice of segregating the names of war dead on French Algeria's monuments (figure 55).

The base of the war memorial functioned as a high wall with two free-

FIGURE 54. Photo of Sarrabezolles's plaster model for the top of the monument. Courtesy of Fondation Sarrabezolles.

FIGURE 55. Sarrabezolles colonial war memorial of 1938. *Monument aux morts,* Postcard, Éditions La Cigogne, Algiers, no. 512. Author's collection.

standing female figures symmetrically placed on its sides. The native woman of Sidi-Bel-Abbès is cloaked with a head scarf, her head bowed with grief. France's Marianne is draped in Roman style and wears a Phrygian liberty cap; she holds her head high as she looks upward, supplicating or triumphant arms upraised (figure 56).

In 1931, Sarrabezolles reprised a similar female figure in a bas-relief placed in the Paris metro station at Richelieu-Drouot to honor the employees of the Metropolitan Railway (Compagnie du chemin de fer métropolitain), who had fought and died for France in World War I. This black marble caryatid stands with arms upraised in a semicircle framed by the names of the war dead below and the names of the battlefields where they fought (figure 57).

FIGURE 56. Photo of Sarrabezolles's plaster model of the entire monument. Courtesy of Fondation Sarrabezolles.

FIGURE 57. **Sarrabezolles, Paris metro war memorial, 1931. Photo by author, September 2019.**

RECOGNIZABLE ERASURES

During the first decade of Algerian independence, the two female sculptures and soldiers were removed from Sarrabezolles's monument. Historian Karim Ouldennebia dates the transformation to the first municipal elections of 1967 when Dr. Abdelkader Hassani (1920–1985), a physician and nationalist hero, was elected between 1967 and 1971. These dates were confirmed by Mohamed Zenaidi, mayor of Sidi-Bel-Abbès from 1976 to 1979.[29] A memorial to Algerian martyrs now stands on the same site where traces of the 1928 Sarrabezolles World War I monument remain. The original base still stands in the center of the busy downtown traffic circle with the same steps. The original alphabetical list of the names of native and European settler war dead is covered by a thin square marble panel that makes the memorial somber and bare. A new list naming Algerian martyrs lies between the original wall and the steps.[30] This imposing martyrs' monument in a very public location confronts viewers with references to two world wars and the Algerian War of Independence in ways that preserve the partly destroyed, perhaps salvaged, but in all cases appropriated, colonial past for the Algerian present (figure 58).

The reconfigured base and steps of the 1928 Sarrabezolles memorial that remained in Sidi-Bel-Abbès had a different meaning and served a different purpose (compare figures 55 and 58) after independence: to commemorate the *shahīd*, the Algerian martyr for independence. Architectural historian Adrian Forty explores the process of repurposing, which is

> not carried out in the spirit of iconoclasm, of getting rid of something, but more in recovery. It's a forgetting of the process of forgetting in order to recover a memory that had been there initially. One cannot assume that simple iconoclasm removes a memory; it leaves a gap. What stands on these objects, plinths, what is striking is the emptiness of these plinths, which is not an act of forgetfulness: you are left wondering what was there before. Precisely through the void that is above them.[31]

Many memorials to the martyrs of the Algerian Revolution, which is itself a cultural memorializing form that emerged from a violent war for

FIGURE 58. Monument to the martyrs of the Algerian revolution ca. 1968, Sidi-Bel-Abbès. Photo by author, May 22, 2017.

independence, provide examples of recoverable traces and recognizable erasures. Algerians after independence confront French memorializations of their conscription, their military service for France during two world wars, and their deaths far from home. French war memorials are sometimes preserved by a remodel. Art historian Nabila Oulebsir refers to a "mirror reading" for many such equipoised changes that took place during the presidency of Houari Boumédiène (1965–1978). She proposes a model of spatial decolonization to better comprehend the monuments, their inhabited spaces, and the ways that Algerians relate to urban centers and monuments:

> A statue or monument collapses, so one hundred thirty years of colonization therefore suddenly disappear. The "cleansing" of the artistic heritage seeks to purify an urban space overloaded with traces and signs of an abolished history, the history of French Algeria. It began on the first Independence Day in the capital by recuperating former places of power and urban centers. In that brief breath of freedom granted to the Algerian population, one of its first acts in response to the proclamation of independence, on the very day that it was proclaimed, was to march and demonstrate at strategic points in Algiers, the capital. In public spaces and squares . . . that were hardly neutral, and which constituted the urban and architectural scene of freedom regained.[32]

Many postindependence alterations—a change of form, of names, of individuals being commemorated—appear to be both symbolic and synecdochic, a part standing for the whole of the struggle for independence. For Oulebsir, the first decade of independence was a time of "cleansing," when Algerians and former European soldiers and settlers made numerous attempts to remove and destroy major French civic and religious monuments. But where the monuments were changed and differently charged with meaning, the central squares and wide colonial-era avenues leading to them were barely modified. Apparently, they did not carry the same symbolic power: they were not writing history.

The second example in this discussion is the French Foreign Legion monument of 1931 of Sidi-Bel-Abbès, an entirely French project to remove monuments to France by the French military and the Legionnaires themselves.

THE FRENCH FOREIGN LEGION WAR MEMORIAL (1931–1962)

The monument to the glory of the French Foreign Legion was erected in Sidi-Bel-Abbès in 1931 at the height of the massive countrywide centennial celebration of colonial rule in French Algeria.[33] Well-known sculptor Charles-Henri Pourquet (1877–1943) was commissioned for the project and designed a grandiose monument to the dead of World War I and of French imperial adventures beyond Algeria. The French interwar monthly *L'art funéraire et décoratif* (1919–1924), devoted to funerary statues that connected localities and sponsored artists, promoted him assiduously, describing his work as actively producing "statuary of pain" (*statuaire de douleur*).[34] Their catalogs advertised Pourquet's models for the *poilu* and especially of the infantryman barring the enemy's passage with his rifle, which appeared in several hundred sites throughout France in tributes to battlefield valor. A second *poilu sentinelle* (soldier-sentinel) carried his rifle upright. Versions of both models appeared in Pourquet's depictions of the four Legionnaires that were added to the Sidi-Bel-Abbès Legionnaire monument (figure 59).

In 1929, after finishing the molds for the globe and the four soldiers, Pourquet and his wife traveled to Sidi-Bel-Abbès to oversee the installation and participate in the monument's inaugural festivities in 1931 (figure 60).[35]

The impressive rectangular granite base measuring approximately thirty feet by twenty-three feet supports a twenty-foot-high bronze globe on which gilded patches designate countries where the Legion was or remained actively engaged. Four bronze legionnaires are stationed like sentinels at the four corners of the pedestal that is covered in thin layers of onyx, each representing one of the Legion's four emblematic expeditions: the 1830–1840 conquest of Algeria, the Mexican campaigns, the colonial battles of 1885–1910, and World War I. Given the monument's exorbitant cost—600,000 francs—the salaries of the Legion units were docked by decision of Colonel Paul-Frédéric Rollet (1875–1941). Not only did individual soldiers contribute to the costs for the monument, they also excavated and hand carried the onyx quarried at Sidi-Hamza near Tlemcen. In the emblematic soldier-builder-pioneer worker of Pourquet's monument, Legionnaire laborers and stonemasons were depicted in a symbolic fusion with the stones they quarried and hauled, rooting themselves in Algerian soil and toil.[36] The local *pierre de Chanzy* that was used for parts of the monument came from the quarry of the colonial village of Chanzy, twenty-five miles south of Sidi-Bel-Abbès. Known in the third century CE as the Roman cavalry fort

FIGURE 59. Monument models for sale depicting Charles-Henri Pourquet's soldiers. *L'art funéraire et décoratif* 30 (1921): 1.

FIGURE 60. Side view of the 1931 Legionnaire monument, Sidi-Bel-Abbès. Postcard, Éditions Alexandre Sirecky, Oran, no. 43. Author's collection.

(*castra*) of Kaputtasaccura, Chanzy had once been part of a lengthy frontier defense road (the *nova praetentura*) established by Septimius Severus to maintain the boundaries (*limes*) between Roman and so-called barbarian territory.[37] In their subjugation of the region, French military leadership saw a parallel with the history of the nomadic Berber tribes resisting Romanized parts of Mauretania Caesariensis. Both the quarry and the town of Sidi Ali Ben Youb were renamed after General Antoine Alfred Chanzy (1823–1883), commander of a Legion subdivision and later governor-general of Algeria (1873–1879).

The marble and onyx from these quarries were famously exported throughout the Mediterranean basin. Marble sourced from Sidi Hamza and Aïn Tekbalet was used in medieval mosques in western Algeria, some examples of which are housed in the Tlemcen museum.[38] In colonial Algeria, quarries were exploited for export by European investors who extracted onyx industrially, with a preference for Sidi Hamza stone:

> Let's say right off the bat that by their deposit, their color and their shape, these onyx-marbles are unlike those that were and are still exploited in Algeria, however famous and appreciated they might be, like those of Ain-Tekbalet that we were recently discussing. Nor do they resemble the onyxes of Mexico and California. They have something distinctive from every viewpoint.[39]

Historian David Prochaska considers that settler colonial symbols and language are crucial for replacing and erasing native geographic signifiers with French names.[40] The monument was to convey "monumentality in architecture . . . defined as a quality, a spiritual quality inherent in a structure which conveys the feeling of its eternity, that it cannot be added to or changed."[41] Charles Pourquet's sculpture was to remain permanently on this site as a visual representation of the Legion's storied combat crowned by an imposing three-dimensional globe.

The Évian Accords stipulated that the French army had to leave most of independent Algeria by July 5, 1962. The French Foreign Legion was required to leave its "mother" base, the Maison Mère at Sidi-Bel-Abbès in 1962. There were exceptions to this order: the 1st régiment étranger de cavalerie (REC, Foreign Cavalry Regiment) which stayed until 1967, the 2nd Régiment Étranger d'Infanterie (REI, Foreign Infantry Regiment) that remained in Colomb-Bechar until 1968, and the 4th régiment étranger (4th RE) that stayed until 1964.[42] The manpower of those regiments helped dismantle the monument in Sidi-Bel-Abbès for shipping to a new Legion headquarters in Aubagne, southern France. On September 29, 1962, more than two months after Algerian independence, the last of the carefully numbered and labeled stones were loaded onto trucks to board ships to cross the Mediterranean.[43] Recalling the Legion's last days in Sidi-Bel-Abbès, former Legionnaire colonel Albéric Vaillant, described the dismemberment of their cherished structures: "the Legion left nothing in its wake" (*la Légion ne laissa rien derrière elle*). He describes the removal and the revelry that culminated in a funeral pyre. Vaillant and the remaining 700 Legionnaires drank, gave speeches, and mourned on the emptied monument platform:

> All the war memorials were recovered, including "the ball" [*boule*] of course. That was the most difficult part. The concrete base was incredibly hard. It took the brave pioneers ten days, and many hammer-pickaxes to make a clean sweep. The last salute was given for the departure of the three coffins of General Rollet, Prince Aage and Legionnaire Zimmermann. . . . The evening before, we heaped old wood on the site where the monument had stood and set it on fire. Lieutenant Selosse declaimed Borelli's entire poem and threw his pennant into the blaze, as Borelli had wanted: it was not to leave Bel-Abbès. Then we danced all night long and donned battle dress at dawn. General Lefort's orders were announced in front of the last square. With the Colonel's jeep in the rear, the trucks drove into what had been "the sacred way," and the convoy rolled to Oran where Arnaud de Foïard, the battalion chief of the 2nd REP [*Régiment étranger de parachutistes*], and the [ship] *Sidi-Bel-Abbès* awaited. Admiral Lorrain had added two clandestine boat trips to the allotted tonnage; the Legion left nothing behind.[44]

Djelloul Talha, founder and president of a local association dedicated to preserving the colonial heritage of Sidi-Bel-Abbès, Espace (Association pour la protection du patrimoine archéologique, architectural, culturel et environnemental), recalls the Legion's departure from his hometown and evokes the bright nocturnal bonfires.

> We Algerians were *indigènes*, in colonial terms, and assumed the Legion was burning and destroying its barracks. The town center was the most segregated place, and we rarely went there. Sometimes a progressive French teacher brought us on a school trip to visit. We were happy to see the Legion go. It was a garrison town [*ville garnison*], a military town [*ville à vocation militaire*], and automatically an occupation of Algerians.[45]

The globe counts among the many monuments, war memorials, and statues that were shipped to France with the help of the French navy. It joined other Legion artifacts including the Legion war memorial formerly located in the main square of the garrison town of Saïda, some fifty miles southeast of Sidi-Bel-Abbès. Dedicated to Legionnaires killed during the so-called colonial pacification campaigns of Algeria's southern territories of Oran Province, it was swiftly dismantled on June 23, 1962, just days before the official date of Algerian independence of July 5, 1962, and relocated to Bonifacio, Corsica, to the site of the former French Foreign Legion garrison. Sculpted by Robert Delandre (1878–1961) and inaugurated in 1910, the statue has a single soldier on a pedestal wearing a colonial pith helmet and brandishing a flag and a sword aimed at the "lion of Africa" below him (figure 61).[46] It commemorates the French Foreign Legion's role in subjugating Algerian resistance along the Algerian-Moroccan border in the 1880s under Sheikh Bou-Amama that threatened French colonial interests in the region for decades.[47]

FIGURE 61. Monument removed from Saïda, Algeria, to Bonifacio, Corsica, France, to commemorate the French Foreign Legionnaires killed during the South Oran campaigns of pacification (1897–1902). Photo by Jean-Pol Grandmont, Wikipedia Commons: https://commons.wikimedia.org/wiki/File:Bonifacio_L%C3%A9gion_JPG1.jpg.

A NEW MUSEUM FOR THE FRENCH FOREIGN LEGION IN AUBAGNE, FRANCE

The dissolution of the French Foreign Legion was being considered by the French government because of its losses. A failed April 1961 putsch against Charles de Gaulle's Fifth Republic had lowered morale, and the Legion's involvement in the last violent throes of French Algeria was seen as a betrayal by de Gaulle.[48] However, the Legion managed to regroup in France in new headquarters in Aubagne where their war memorial and a museum with associated military ceremonies became indispensable for restoring the regimental spirit. In 1966, the Musée de la Légion Étrangère was established adjacent to Legion headquarters in Aubagne. Among the museums items displayed behind glass are a model of the Sidi-Bel-Abbès globe made from Sidi Hamza onyx (figure 62).

I visited the museum on November 26, 2019. Museumgoers are barred from the central parade grounds except on special commemorative occasions, and the globe monument (*boule*) is barely discernable through the narrow window from inside the exhibition (figure 63).

FIGURE 62. The onyx-marble model of Pourquet's globe on exhibit, French Foreign Legion Museum, Aubagne. Photo by author, November 26, 2019.

FIGURE 63. View of the Legion's globe from a museum window on the parade grounds. Photo by author, November 26, 2019.

Pourquet's Sidi-Bel-Abbès monument stands on the Legion's parade and mustering ground in Aubagne visible only from within the museum. In the exhibition rooms and on the wall, texts, photographs, military uniforms, and artifacts laud the heroic highpoints of the Legion's history.

Two important rooms that were formerly in Algeria—the Hall of Honor (Salle d'Honneur) for the 1st Foreign Legion Regiment (1er Régiment étranger, 1er RE) and the Temple of Heroes—were recreated. The Hall of Honor was installed between 1888 and 1892 in Sidi-Bel-Abbès and refurbished in the 1930s, during the decade of centennial French colonial activities (figure 64).

The Legion participated in French Algeria's festivities by transforming the original hall into an embryonic military museum named the Musée du Souvenir de la Légion Étrangère.[49] The museum's design was influenced by the elaborate museums in Algiers (Musée des Beaux Arts, the Bardo,

FIGURE 64. **"La Salle d'Honneur de la Légion Étrangère." Postcard Éditions Alexander Sirecky (EAS), Oran, no. 35. Author's collection.**

Stéphane Gsell Museum), in Oran (Demaeght Museum), in Constantine (Gustave Mercier Museum), and the colonial archaeology museums on-site at Timgad, Tipasa, Guelma, Lambèse, and Djemila among other provincial cities.[50] In 1961 in Algeria, the Temple of Heroes was a last addition to accommodate the Legion's Algerian War losses, but independence put an end to the plans for an enlarged ceremonial edifice. In its move from Sidi-Bel-Abbès to Aubagne, the Legion's command headquarters conceded key ceremonial functions to the new museum, which became a temple of esprit de corps where enlistment and veneration rituals are enacted in the recreated crypt (figure 65).

These heroes of the French Foreign Legion's numerous military campaigns were celebrated in Sidi-Bel-Abbès until 1962 and in Aubagne after Algerian independence in various ceremonies. General Paul-Frédéric Rollet (1875–1941), the acknowledged "father" of the Legion, is credited with having created these ceremonies. He rehabilitated Legion traditions and established new institutions and practices in Algeria, including object veneration during the interwar years. The wooden prosthetic hand of Captain Jean Danjou (1828–1863), an historical fake, was one such fetishized object.[51] Wounded in Algeria, Danjou died fighting in France's failed Mex-

FIGURE 65. **Recreated Hall of Honor (Salle d'Honneur), Aubagne Museum. Photo by author, November 26, 2019.**

ican expeditions (1863–1867). His wooden hand nestles among regimental colors stored in the Aubagne museum crypt and is paraded annually to commemorate the "Camerone Day" losses in Mexico on April 30, 1863.

Regimental museums under the aegis of the armed forces honor war achievements in displays that lean toward propaganda. The Aubagne museum houses decontextualized place markers of conquest and bears witness to war plunder.[52] Many museum objects evoke the early decades of Algeria's military occupation. A fourteen-foot column stands behind protective glass flanked by cannons used in French Indochina, all on a bed of pebbles. The inscription reads: "Route de l'Edough—Randon—Général—Artillerie—10e Rgt de Génie—3e Rgt—31e Léger—Zouaves—Légion étrangère—1842" (figure 66). There is no information about how and when these objects were removed.

The column was erected by General Jacques Louis Randon (1795–1871) in 1842 (*colonne Randon*) to represent his expansion of territorial conquest through military infrastructure projects. It stood on a new route, the thirteen-mile road built in three months by the labor of 1,000 men to connect Bône (now Annaba), where Randon was commander (1841–1847) to the cork oak forests of Edough in Kabylia. Later Randon was named

FIGURE 66. General Randon's column, removed from colonial Bône (currently Annaba) to the Aubagne Museum. Photo by author, November 26, 2019.

governor-general of Algeria (1851–1858). The Randon column spoke to many accomplishments: the repression of local resistance made Bône's periphery secure for settler farmers. the European city was extended, and the commercial exploitation of Algeria's cork oak forests for the nascent colonial wine industry advanced. All of this came at a cost to the Indigenous Kabyle agriculturists and pastoralists. They were displaced and suffered from the environmental changes wrought by overharvesting the trees and setting wildfires rather than practicing the small, controlled burns used by Kabyles to enrich forest pasturage.[53] Randon continued his infrastructural work elsewhere in Algeria. He oversaw the construction of 9,000 miles of roads, railway tracks, and bridges to effectively control the native population and access the colony's mineral and forest riches.

THE LEGION'S LEGACY: MUSEUMS, PRISONS, ARTIFACTS, AND CEREMONIES

The Aubagne museum also houses a Corinthian capital, labeled "probably from Lambèse excavations" attributing provenance to the Legion's 2nd Regiment (figure 67).

The settler town of Lambèse (Arabic-Berber Tazoult now) is located near Batna and 100 miles south of Constantine. Like Sidi-Bel-Abbès, the town of Lambèse grew around the nineteenth-century French Foreign Legion camp; soon after, the colonial-era prison of Lambèse was established in 1852. The French camp and the prison were archaeologically associated by the French military with the Third Augustan Legion and its Roman prison camp (*carcer castrensis*) of Lambaesis (figure 68).[54]

FIGURE 67. Corinthian capital on display at the Aubagne Museum. Photo by author, November 26, 2019.

FIGURE 68. Ruins of the Praetorium of Roman Lambaesis with colonial-era Lambèse Prison in the background. Photo by author, June 12, 2022.

Today the ruins of Lambaesis stand not far from the museum in Tazoult whose collection includes archaeological vestiges, artifacts, mosaics, and fragments from Roman North Africa. A Roman stone, incised with the year 1861, is stored in the Tazoult/Lambèse Museum attesting to the archaeological pursuits of the Legion (figure 69).

The French Foreign Legion's archaeological excavations, appropriations, and spoliations were carried out by "incidental archaeologists" or inexperienced soldiers overseen by Legionnaire Colonel (later General) Jean-Luc Carbuccia (1808–1854), who commanded the Legion's 2nd Regiment.[55] Carbuccia was notorious for removing and defacing a Roman column and adding an inscription to honor Henri d'Orléans, the Duke of Aumale (1822–1897), an officer in the military campaigns of Algerian conquest who became governor-general of French Algeria. Carbuccia also intervened to rebuild and de-sacralize the derelict tomb of a Roman military leader, Titus Flavius Maximus. Carbuccia's added inscription makes an explicit link with his imagined forebear, "Colonel Carbuccia to his colleague of the III Roman Legion."[56] This inscription suggests the imaginary genealogy connecting the Roman empire and its Legion with the French empire and its Legionnaires.

Algerian independence may have put an end to the Legion's claims of following in the footsteps of imperial Rome. After everything, the Legion pursued an identity of being the legacy of imperial Rome by pillaging. Lam-

FIGURE 69. French Foreign Legion year incised on a Roman-era stone, Tazoult Museum, Tazoult, Algeria. Photo by author, June 12, 2022.

baesis is a rich archaeological resource for architecture, artifacts, mosaics, and antique fragments from Roman North Africa, many of which found their way into French collections and museums: "deported" according to Algerian archaeologist Nacéra Benseddik.[57] The Legion's excavation and distribution of Roman antiquities to French museums and private collections has yet to be fully reckoned with.[58]

"REPATRIATION" AND SPOLIATION?

"To the victor go the spoils" is a general condition of war and a recurrent feature of revolutionary war: "to destroy a society the conquerors and revolutionaries destroy monuments."[59] During the French Revolution, many statues of figures of the old order at odds with the rhetoric of revolutionary political rupture were the objects of notable iconoclastic acts. Abbé Henri Grégoire (1750–1831) designated as "revolutionary vandalism" the widespread de-sacralizing of churches and the transformation of libraries and monuments.[60] Monuments were looted, sold for profit, demolished, melted down, and moved around. Plunder, *butin* in French, English *booty*, Hindi *lut*, American English *loot*: the term applies to the prize of theft culled during a state-run enterprise.[61] During the Napoleonic wars, the plunder from European countries, and famously from Egypt, was significant and never fully restituted by the 1815 Treaty of Vienna. The 1830 conquest of Algeria was the beginning of successive waves of plunder during 132 years of occupation.[62] During World War II, Vichy leaders removed, destroyed, and melted thousands of selected statues to produce more bullets for Germany.[63] The collection in the Aubagne Museum and in the Lambèse/Tazoult Museum (established in the colonial period) are more examples of imperial military plunder. The question is what to do with the loot.

"How does a city and a nation deal with a legacy of atrocity? How are contemporary identities negotiated and shaped when concrete reminders stand of a past that most wish they did not have?"[64] Culturally significant monuments, no less than buildings and sites, count among the casualties of war and regime change. The array of postwar responses includes removing, repairing, restoring, or reconstructing. On both sides of the Mediterranean Sea between Algeria and France, "difficult" or "dissonant heritage" defines the many war memorials removed and relocated to France, including the Legionnaire globe, the Randon column, and the Lambaesis capital, while the formerly colonized Algerians are addressing the material presence of statues, statuettes, stelae, monuments, military cemeteries, and other effigies of the French colonial past that remain on their soil.

We can consider the afterlife of monuments in a settler colonial military town by looking at Sidi-Bel-Abbès where the Legion's globe is one among many pieces of moveable military property to have been relocated. Although the municipality leveled the town's prostitute district, it maintained many other immoveable properties and buildings—churches, synagogues, military installations, and cemeteries—which sometimes benefited from extended bilateral negotiations.[65] In post-1962 Algeria, certain Catholic diocesan buildings were gifted by the Catholic Church to the fledging independent state, notably Oran's Catholic cathedral and Tlemcen's Church of Saint Michel that have since been transformed into spacious central public libraries by Algerian architects. In turn, the Algerian state granted the church the continued use of some properties stipulating non-proselytism and the elimination of church education.

The ownership of moveable objects, by contrast, is in question, as the processes are subsumed under the rubrics of "repatriation" and "recuperation." Were statues smuggled illegally? Do they, as special objects that often resemble human beings, fall into the category of repatriate? Whose laws determine how they are handled? Why were they being repatriated and was their original home in France? Former settlers answered my questions in different ways, with some indicating support for transporting *their* statues out of Algeria but agreeing that this was smuggling and claiming that French protection was essential for the statue's survival. Others asserted that the French Foreign Legion owned its statues, just as the numerous Catholic churches and parishes established by settler communities owned their churches, bells, and statues of the Virgin Mary in the reestablished settler communities across the Mediterranean.[66]

The settlers, in their lawsuits, claim lost property and reject Algerian laws about "vacated property" (*biens vacants*) left behind by the colonizers.[67] The Évian Accords provided for property transfers from French colonial state institutions to Algerian institutions.[68] But when is removal of a colonial artifact a form of spoliation? Are the timing of the act and the status of the colony any indicators? If postindependence removals from Algeria to France are acts of looting or pillage abetted by the French military and by individual settlers without consulting the officially recognized Provisional Government of the Algerian Republic (Gouvernement provisoire de la République algérienne, or GPRA), does the date of the act matter? How is the removal of statues, monuments, and other artifacts defined? How is ownership defined? To whom does a significant work of art belong? The objects from colonial Algeria that made their way to France are claimed by those who desired them the most and were willing and able to pay the costs for transporting and reinstalling them. Settler accounts describing the movements of statues from Algeria attribute agency to objects in this frequent formulation I heard about monument arrivals to a new place: "During the exodus of Algeria, the statue followed a group of repatriates who settled in x" (Lors de l'exode d'Algérie, la statue suivit un groupe de rapatriés qui s'installèrent à x). Repatriation, according to the repatriated? For European settlers, this means that their mountain of objects has a personality, signaling that these demands are a result of lost sovereignty and bygone settler claims to indigeneity in French Algeria.

Political treaties such as the Évian Accords lay out a bilateral state-to-state framework for disengagement and decolonization. Cultural material studies from anthropology and folklore encompass notions about the agency of an object, asking whether statues, monuments, and artifacts are "spolia," defined by art historians as elements of sculpture and architecture taken from one location and reused in another place to demonstrate dominance or control. Practiced famously throughout the ancient Mediterranean when ancient Greek or Roman artifacts were incorporated into medieval structures, it continues to the present. In his pioneering work on spolia, Arnold Esch describes the artistic "reuse" of objects whereby transformation is "not death but rather new life, new agency, a new adventure."[69] His argument is akin to the equation that moving objects saves them. Dale Kinney, by contrast, looks at the motivation for removal: if it is ideologically driven, requires considerable effort, and involves violence, we are talking about spolia:

> Spoliation entails a forcible transfer of ownership. The spoliated object (animal, person, monument, or culture) is denuded of its portable assets (skin, wealth, ornament, artistic patrimony) and the assets—the spolia—are taken as booty or salvaged. Spolia are survivors of violence, about which they might be mute (if they bear no visible signs of it) or eloquent.[70]

The removal and retention of statues must be considered in the context of the imperial drive to colonize the Maghreb and the exodus of the European population from newly independent countries in North Africa. To define spoliation in the French-Algerian case, I return to the initial French conquest and occupation of Algeria and the nineteenth-century French spoliations that are the "memory" behind the 1962 bilateral Franco-Algerian agreements.

On July 5, 1830, a French amphibious landing on the shore near Algiers at Sidi Ferruch of approximately 37,000 soldiers, 27,000 sailors, and 567 ships equipped with their guns and stores occurred in in a single day. Prominent personalities followed the successful invasion and conquest. In 1833, Alexis de Tocqueville described the destruction, which he witnessed firsthand. He expressed his appreciation for the Ottoman Algiers Regency, which was a functioning state possessed of property and taxation regimes and endowed with religious institutions and traditions of higher learning, libraries, and manuscripts. He celebrated the Algerian conquest in a letter of 1837 in which he was also attentive to the vanquished:

> [T]he entire civil and military government of the [Algiers] regency was in Turkish hands. Hardly were we [French] masters of Algiers than we hastened to gather up every single Turk, from the dey to the last soldier of his militia and transported the lot of them to the coast of Asia. In order to make the vestiges of the enemy domination disappear, we first took care to tear up and burn all written documentation, administrative records, and papers, authentic or otherwise, that could have perpetuated any trace of what had been done before us. The conquest was a new era, and from fear of mixing the past with the present in an irrational way, we even destroyed a large number of streets in Algiers so as to rebuild them according to our own method, and we gave French names to all those we consented to leave alone.[71]

Tocqueville provides an insight into contemporary concepts about settler colonialism, describing the conquest as an erasure. Both colonialism and settler colonialism are premised on domination, but only setter colonialism, according to Patrick Wolfe, seeks to replace the original population of the colonized territory with a new society of settlers that usually comes from the colonial metropole.[72] The process involves destroying records of ownership, among others, and seizing lands. The rich coastal beylical lands of the Algiers Regency were appropriated while the inland areas were considered to lack inhabitants. This made it possible for the French Foreign Legion in Sidi-Bel-Abbès to claim sovereignty over "unoccupied" semipastoral lands during their military incursions into the interior. The intersecting history of colonization and decolonization followed by displacement and exile is told through the movement of statues and monuments during which French colonial stuff crossed the Mediterranean. This historical-geographic axis of objects traverses the sea between France and Algeria along the "French Mediterraneans" corridor, the phrase by historians Patricia Lorcin and Todd Shepard for the north-to-south colonial expansion and the south-to-north decolonizing exodus.[73]

SIDI-BEL-ABBÈS AFTER INDEPENDENCE

What is the relationship between the residents of Sidi-Bel-Abbès and the legacies of the French colonial and military-built environment after 1962, specifically the sculptural reminders of that past? After the Legion's globe was displaced, the space it occupied at the center of Sidi-Bel-Abbès's French military complex became a parade ground for the Algerian gendarmerie school that took over the Legion's buildings. In the decades after 1962, the Legion's war memorials, monuments, statues, and pleasure district that remained were destroyed outright, fell into ruin, or disappeared without a trace, while others were replaced, preserved, and moved. A significant number of French colonial monuments and statues remain intact or in partial recognizable forms of erasure in Algeria, such as the Sarrabezolles war memorial.

Some sculptures captured in postcards from Sidi-Bel-Abbès are gone. *The Fall of Icarus* (*La chute d'Icare*), a marble statue by French sculptor Auguste Maillard (1864–1944), first presented at the Paris Universal Exposition of 1900, was installed in the public garden in 1929. According to Djelloul Talha of the town preservation society, the municipality removed the statue in 2005 for restoration, but it has since disappeared (compare 70 and 71).[74] *Orphée expirante* (*Dying Orpheus*, 1888 or 1881) by Alphonse Eugène Guilloux (1852–1939) and *La caresse du fauve* (*Léda et Zeus*) by an unknown sculptor were donated to the colonial-era municipality to adorn the central public garden. For now, their emptied plinths for the missing sculptures remain.

The public garden has new Algerian monuments including a war memorial commemorating a particularly bloody skirmish on July 7, 1961, when two Algerian soldiers ambushed over twenty Legionnaires. The site also marks a mass grave discovered when the garden was replanted of more than forty Algerians killed during the war.

The colonial architecture of Sidi-Bel-Abbès's center has been restored.

FIGURE 70. Emptied plinth of *La caresse du fauve* (Léda et Zeus) in the public gardens. Photo by author, May 22, 2017.

FIGURE 71. *Orphée expirante* (*Dying Orpheus*, 1888 or 1881) by Alphonse Eugène Guilloux (1852–1939). Postcard, ND Phot., no. 10. Author's collection.

The town hall built by settlers to endure has been maintained by Algerians. Brahim Hasnaoui, a native son from nearby Sidi Ali Ben Youb (formerly colonial Chanzy named for the general), oversaw the rehabilitation of the city hall façade built in 1876 with its slate roofs (*toitures en ardoise*) that were introduced by Alsatian settlers to Sidi-Bel-Abbès and still dot the town. He invited Spanish Basque specialists to make the repairs, reprising a history of imported architectural techniques.[75] Two museums in the town, one part of a national network of martyr museums throughout Algeria and a second devoted to local history, also preserve and present Algerian views of the colonial past through artifacts.

THE AGRICULTURAL SCHOOL AND THE MUSEUM TO ALGERIAN *MUJĀHIDĪN*

The agricultural school of Sidi-Bel-Abbès was created in 1926 and officially opened on November 3, 1930. It became the largest school for agricultural science in Africa. Since 2005, it has been integrated into degree programs at the University of Sidi-Bel-Abbès. When the Algerian state ended viniculture, Abdelkader Ghalem-Sardi, a 1977 graduate and passionate curator of local farm conditions, rescued the colonial wine cellar (*cave*) from demolition. He converted storage space and made a museum of agricultural history, recognized by international museum associations, within a working farm, workshops, and stables of the school.[76]

I visited the farm on May 22, 2017, well after a April 2008 group tour by a Pied-Noir repatriate association of former students and their families. Like numerous repatriate associations in France, the alumni of the agricultural school published a richly illustrated volume on colonial agricultural infrastructures—the creation of farming villages, the reach of viniculture underpinning French Algeria's wine industry, and the myriad dams, reservoirs, and irrigation projects.[77] Even though our respective museum tours were separated by decades, we both appreciated the well-maintained condition of Sidi-Bel Abbès's colonial buildings, including the city hall, post office, theater, central covered market, and especially the amphitheater, frescos, and cafeteria and various building belonging to the agriculture school. In their association newsletter, former students wrote with emotion about the ways in which Ghalem-Sardi preserves their school's documentation, photos, and artifacts: "tous çela a échappé à l'oubli" (it has all escaped oblivion).[78] Ghalem-Sardi salvaged the marble memorial plaque listing the names of students who died in World War II after it was removed from the rectory's outer wall (figure 72).

The memory of the settler past is partially preserved. Ghalem-Sardi is the custodian of the colonial past, able to preserve more than the museum can tell.[79] According to him, he rejected the request of repatriate tourists for the marble memorial plaque and provided souvenir photographs instead. He told me that the plaque belonged to Algeria and that it was an artifact needing a tour guide's interpretation because museum artifacts do not recount the violent history of the colonial agricultural school. He felt that it was his responsibility to remind visitors about the minority of native students who were admitted only after 1936 but were barred from dormitories and forced to bunk in the stables with the animals until 1940, and that Algerian Jewish students were banned during the Vichy years. He presented that intact local memory of being dispossessed of tribal lands (93 percent were in settler hands) and the system of native sharecropping that ensured the exploitative exportation of a colonial agricultural system based on the monocultures of alfa and grapes.[80] Ghalem-Sardi's acts of artifactual salvage and discourses about the objects in his collection reflect pride in native agricultural history as well as anger.

During my visit that same day to the town's state-run Mujāhidīn Museum to combatants, several preserved church bells of Sidi-Bel-Abbès

FIGURE 72. Marble memorial plaque of the war dead, Agricultural Museum of Sidi-Bel-Abbès. Photo by author, May 22, 2017.

stood at the entrance in a space devoted to French atrocities and Algerian resistance during the War of Independence (figure 73).[81] Military and religious colonial objects in these two museums memorialize and recall a difficult heritage. On display is the productive role in which new contexts decolonize the settler worlds of Sidi-Bel-Abbès through objects.

In the Aubagne museum, the by-now familiar processes of transferal and object repatriation recreate spaces for reviewing a relinquished French military venture in Algeria. In Sidi-Bel-Abbès, the decolonization process involves the transformation of French Algeria's war memorials into Algerian martyr memorials and creates monuments and sites for the narratives of the colonized, while also preserving and salvaging colonial artifacts and architecture. The circulation of these statues and monuments between Algeria and France is a salutary reminder of the unfinished Algerian conversation with the departed French other. Moreover, in the case of Sarrabezolles's war memorial, the principle of reversibility, key to architectural renovation, is operative if the new Algerian martyrs' memorial replacement is indeed a palimpsest as I conjectured.

Colonialism may have ended, but it left complex questions about decolonization regarding the difficult, dark heritage of French fortified settlements and monuments that influence the evolving postindependence heritage of Algerian memorials to the martyrs and combatants of the revolution.

FIGURE 73. Church bells on display in the Mujāhidīn Museum, Sidi-Bel-Abbès. Photo by author, May 22, 2017.

CHAPTER FOUR

CREATING PROVENANCE

Ahmed Benyahia and Public Sculptures in the Constantine Region

HOW HAVE ALGERIAN ARTISTS TRANSLATED and transformed the difficult heritage of French settlements and monuments after decolonization? How has Algeria created and defined its own heritage? This chapter explores the emptied sites of French Algeria and Algeria's appropriation of space and renewal of the colonial sculptural heritage in Constantine, Algeria's third largest city.[1] It focuses on an individual artist, Ahmed Benyahia (b. 1943) who has reused, repurposed, and replaced colonial-era public art since 1962. In the region of Constantine, he has created public statues for many villages and towns—among them, Zighoud Youcef, Guelma, Medaghri Belgimouze, and Salah Bey—that he sees as being in dialogue with their social and political contexts (figure 74). He also serves as president of the city's preservation association and in that capacity has also considered questions of provenance, political activism, and the selection of French colonial artifacts to be safeguarded in Constantine. He asks what has replaced and should replace the repatriated colonial patrimony, which artists should make the statues for a newly independent Algeria to honor its revolution, where the statues should stand, and how they can create a synthesis between the colonial past and future aspirations. At the same time, Benyahia's art is a challenge to the former French colonial arbiters of artistic taste and to their successors in postindependent Algerian ministries. He provokes Algerian cultural brokers and state bureaucrats to consider what constitutes an object of beauty, a monument, a memorial.

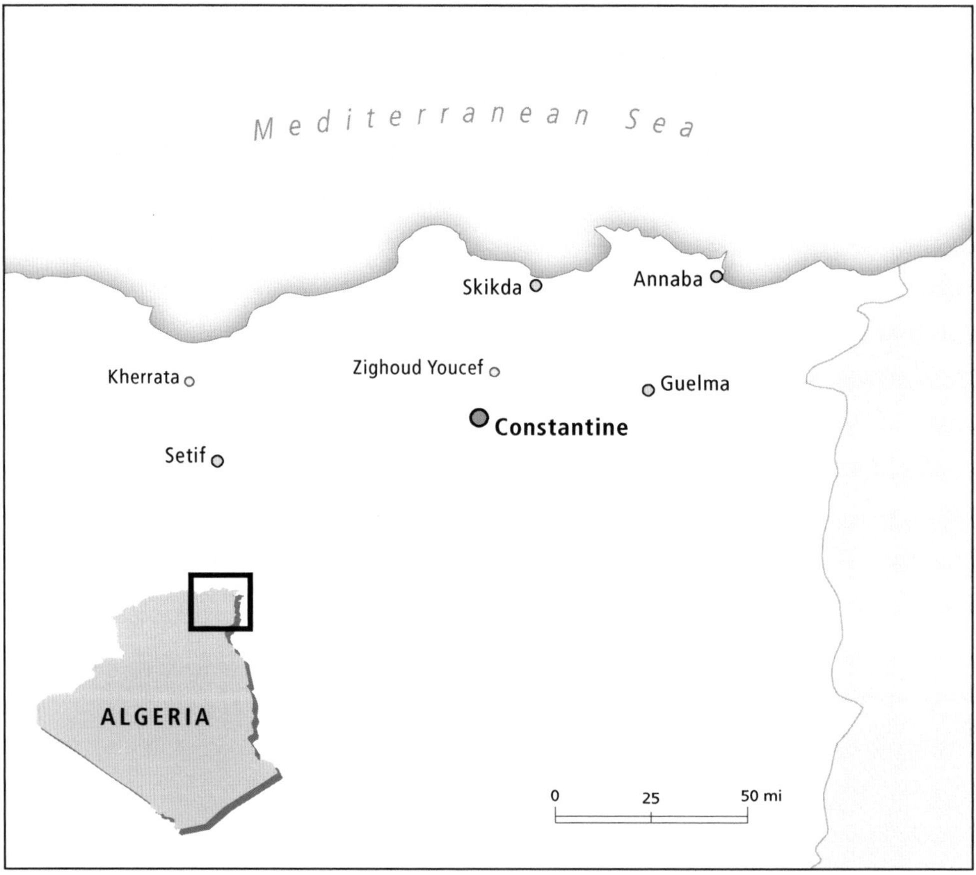

FIGURE 74. **Map of Ahmed Benyahia's public sculptures in Constantine, Guelma, and Zighoud Youcef. Map by Erin Greb Cartography.**

Ahmed Benyahia was the first and only "native" Algerian (i.e., non-European and Muslim) student in the art school of Constantine (École Municipale des Beaux-Arts de Constantine) which he entered in 1956 at age thirteen; in 1962 at Algerian independence, he became its director. He is part of the first postindependence class to graduate from the Algiers's School of Fine Arts (École des Beaux-Arts d'Alger) that was founded in 1843 and officially installed in its spacious building in 1881. There, Benyahia enrolled in the atelier of M'hamed Issiakhem, well known for his approach to modernist social realism.[2] While still a student, he designed the third Algerian postal stamp issued to commemorate the country's first international trade fair in 1964. The stamp depicts a large traditional water jug overlaid with the vertical outlines of an electricity pylon and a minaret against a vibrant blue background (figure 75). As of 1963, philately was deemed Algeria's "ambassador to the world," and postage stamps are often seen as a nation's site of memory: major Algerian artists such as Ali Ali-Khodja and Choukri Mesli all designed postage stamps.[3]

For a time after independence, Algiers was a "mecca" for European radicals, American Black Power exiles, and international anti-colonial militants,

FIGURE 75. Third Algerian stamp issued after independence, design by Ahmed Benyahia, 1964. Author's collection and Benyahia Archives. Reproduced by permission of Ahmed Benyahia.

who, unlike local dissidents, escaped state arrest.[4] On June 19, 1965, while still a student, Benyahia was forcibly disappeared and tortured for five months for his opposition to the 1965 military coup d'état against Ahmed Ben Bella, Algeria's first president. Expelled from art school, he graduated as an external student and eventually left for Paris to study at the École des Beaux-Arts, graduating in 1969. From 1970 to 1975, he continued in the atelier of César Baldaccini (1921–1998), a professor of sculpture at the art school from 1970 to 1986, noted for his ties to the post-1960 Nouveau Réalisme (New Realism). César's monumental abstract castings, ready-made appropriations, and writing on art and provenance were important influences for Benyahia who drew on the sculptural series *Empreintes Humaines* (*Human Imprints*) featuring the artist's enlarged bronze thumb (*Pouce,* 1965). Benyahia also benefited from studying artwork by Ossip Zadkine (1888–1967), whose *Torse de la Ville Détruite* (*Torso from a City Destroyed,* 1953) commemorates Germany's carpet bombing of Rotterdam, anti-imperial internationalism, and war memories. During the years he spent moving between Constantine, Algiers, and Paris, Benyahia had these works in mind as he sought to make Algerian artwork express solidarity with global artistic mobilizations. In his art practice, he would later subvert colonial practices and legacies.

ZIGHOUD YOUCEF (1921–1956): A HERO, A SCULPTURE, A TOWN

In the late 1960s, Benyahia set about creating a statue of Zighoud Youcef, a resistance fighter, hero, and martyr known and admired as Colonel Si Ahmed, who died fighting in the Constantine region in 1956. Zighoud was active in the initial revolutionary political party formations and subsequent clandestine organizations as well as the congresses that spearheaded the struggle in the north Constantine region for the FLN (Front de libération nationale, National Liberation Front). He was also known as "the man of 20 August 1955" for attacking European settlers in the Constantine region that garnered widespread support and led to French army reprisals and collective punishments of the surrounding Algerian Muslim population.[5] On September 25, 1956, Zighoud and his fellow combatants were caught in a French army ambush in Sidi Mezghiche, twenty miles north of the village of Condé-Smendou. They were captured and killed, and their corpses were dumped in the main square. French soldiers forced the town's inhabitants to view and identify the corpses aligned in the square, a military strategy of enforced humiliation. The story goes that everyone remained mute, except for one inebriated villager who drew himself upright and saluted his fallen leader, identifying Zighoud Youcef's body to colonial authorities. For Benyahia, the Zighoud statue is a dialogue with time and suffering that includes the effervescence and hope of independent Algeria's first decades. He saw Zighoud, the forgotten regional hero as a symbol of marginalization, someone who launched an irreversible revolution yet proved that decolonization did not bring liberty.[6]

My interest in Benyahia was piqued in 2019 when I heard a riveting online video interview, "The Long History of a Short-Lived Statue" by historian Natalya Vince and filmmaker Walid Benkhaled posted on YouTube to launch an online series documenting Algeria's "Generation Independence" (*Jīl al-istiqlāl*).[7] I began interviewing him in 2020 in person and by phone about the Zighoud statue. Benyahia explained that he had gone to FLN headquarters in Constantine seeking support for a statue of Zighoud. Rebuffed, he headed to the eponymous village of Zighoud Youcef, where he gained the trust of the local resistance fighters and combat veterans. While amassing the requisite clay, he met Zighoud's wife, sister, and military comrades, including Lakhdar Ben Tobbal, to get descriptions of the hero's face since few photos of him existed (figure 76).

Zighoud's statue was a Benyahia family project including Benyahia's cousin Abderrezak Benyahia who provided photo documentation (figure 77). Born in Souk Naâmane (formerly Rouget-de-L'Isle) in 1929,

FIGURE 76. Photo of Youcef Zighoud, original sepia-toned, date unknown. Wikipedia Commons: https://fr.wikipedia.org/wiki/Zighoud_Youcef#/media/Fichier:Zighout_Youcef.jpg.

FIGURE 77. Clockwise: Nasreddine Benyahia, Abdelaziz Benyahia (artist's brother assassinated in 1998 during the Dark Decade), and Ahmed Benyahia crouching. Photo by Abderrezak Benyahia, summer 1972. Reproduced by permission.

Abderrezak began working in 1947 as an assistant developing pictures for another cousin, Ahmed Taieb, a Lyon-trained photographer, who owned a studio and shop in colonial Châteaudun-du-Rhumel (now Chelghoum el Aid), Ahmed Benyahia's birthplace. In 1957, Abderrezak escaped his hamlet for Constantine where he joined Ahmed Benyahia in the city center FLN guerrilla cell (Wilaya II, zone 5, region 2). In 1963, entranced by images in darkroom developing solutions, Abderrezak obtained a Rolleiflex camera and joined the newspaper *La Dépêche de Constantine*, renamed *al-Nasr* (*Victory*) after independence, where he worked as staff photographer until he retired in 1989.

As the Zighoud statue was taking shape, the local FLN official informed the regional hierarchy about the project. Benyahia was summoned before various representatives of Algeria's Office of Mujāhidīn, which was responsible for memorializing former combat veterans. Its committee concluded that the village of Zighoud Youcef was too small for the statue, "too small even for Constantine, he is a national figure," Benyahia recalled. The matter ended badly. The mayor of the town of Zighoud Youcef was briefly imprisoned on what seemed to be spurious charges, and Benyahia was obliged to continue work under the close supervision of FLN higher-ups in Constantine.

In 1969, the statue was completed and inaugurated to great fanfare and ceremony on August 20, the fourteenth anniversary of Zighoud's daring 1955 military attack and the seventh anniversary of Algeria's independence. Military officers in parade dress and Zighoud's former comrades-in-arms dressed in traditional robes and bearing wartime firearms escorted the statue. Benyahia estimates that 10,000 people watched it be placed inside the FLN party headquarters in Constantine (figure 78).

To make his statue, Benyahia used parts of a French colonial monument to the war dead of 1914–1918 that had been officially inaugurated October

FIGURE 78. Anniversary parade to inaugurate the statue of Youcef Zighoud, Constantine, August 10, 1969. Photo by Abderrezak Benyahia. Reproduced by permission.

7, 1922, in the Place de la Brèche with speeches by General Valentin surrounded by a contingent of French soldiers, by the city's long-serving mayor Émile Morinaud (1865–1952), the bishop of Constantine, and various colonial municipal officials and dignitaries orating amidst the local viewing population.[8] The monument had the traditional decorated plinth and a tall column topped by a Gallic cockerel whose massive wings became pivotal for the Zighoud statue (figure 79).[9] The decorative plinth still stands at the Place de la Brèche in downtown Constantine (figure 80).

Benyahia explains in the Vince and Benkhaled video interview how the French World War I memorial became the victim of warring factions within the Algerian army in the summer of 1962.

> When I started to do the bronze part of the statue . . . someone said to me, "There are the wings of the Gallic cockerel that have been impounded." And I remembered that in 1962, there had been clashes opposing the army of the frontiers supported by the Wilaya 1 [of the National Liberation Army] against the Wilaya II in Constantine—basically it was a race to take power, and they started killing each other in the city of Constantine. The frontier army won, they were well equipped and well organized, and they occupied Constantine. There was a huge crowd, and there was the Gallic cockerel, and they started shooting at it. Except the Gallic cockerel did not abdicate, it refused to fall! [Laughs] So they brought in a 10-ton truck, ropes and cables and they pulled. The column broke into pieces and the Gallic cockerel fell. The wings and the body were separated. They were picked up and taken to the pound in the Bardo area of Constantine. When I went there, I only found the wings, I didn't find the body of the cockerel. Because I would have kept it with all I know now about the importance of memory. But there were only the wings, so I melted them down to mold part of Zighoud Youcef because I wanted to put the statue where the Gallic cockerel had been [at the Place de la Brèche]. So in some way there is this fusion of history—the past via the Gallic cockerel and the future by the statue of Zighoud. I made the statue with the index finger pointing[10]

Benyahia's description of his own statue to me as an "act of witness" and a "fusion of history" implies a blend of past and future battles. Algerian independence did not spare the country further battles among Algeria's military leadership. During the war, the country had been carved into six interior zones (*wilāyāt*) of resistance in addition to the autonomous zone of Algiers. Constantine was the capital of Wilaya II where Benyahia witnessed the clashes that erupted on July 25, 1962, between the forces of Wilaya I under commander Tahar Zbiri who was allied with the powerful, better-equipped Algerian army

FIGURE 79. The 1922 colonial war memorial (*monument aux morts*) of Constantine, Algeria. Postcard, Photo Agence Jomone, Algiers. Author's collection.

FIGURE 80. Ahmed Benyahia in front of the empty plinth, Place de la Brèche, Constantine. Photo by author, May 29, 2022.

positioned on the Moroccan and Tunisian borders *(armée des frontières)*, and the fighters of Wilaya II from the interior forces under the Provisional Government of the Algerian Republic (GPRA), the diplomatic political government-in-exile.[11] Twenty-five people were killed and thirty wounded. A second series of clashes that took place in Constantine on August 15 and 16, 1962, claimed another one hundred lives. That fall, Constantine came under the sway of the army of the frontiers. Many local resistance fighters were sidelined while others, such as Colonel Chaabani of Wilaya VI, as Benyahia noted, rallied to the army of the frontiers. The battle led to the destruction and disappearance of the column of the World War I memorial at the Place de la Brèche. Internecine battles devolved into an attack on the crowing cockerel, symbol of the departed French military that had made the sacrifices of conscripted Algerian soldiers during two world wars virtually invisible.

The pointing index finger of Benyahia's Zighoud Youcef statue was a source of confusion, variously interpreted as an admonition or accusation: "if an index can be translated into sentence form, that sentence would be in the imperative, *Look over there!* or *Watch out!*"[12] Benyahia told me that veterans had asked him why he created it on the statue. He explained, the finger indicated French colonialism, then the *mujāhidīn*, then the contested political legitimacy of the divisive armies. It points to colonialism, independence, anti-regionalism, the persistence of revolutionary hero worship, and the ups and downs of his career in Algeria.

The question of the index finger had also come up in his meeting with Algerian President Houari Boumédiène (nom de guerre of Mohamed Ben Brahim Boukharouba,1932–1978). "And I said, 'It's a composition, it's just like that.' And they said, 'No, we think that you wanted to say to us "You've betrayed the Algerian revolution, the fighters of independent Algeria, or independent Algeria has betrayed the martyrs." ' I said, 'That's your reading!' "[13]

The conversation with President Boumédiène also clarified the reasons for his stance against art forms representing regionalism (*jihawiyya*) and commemorations of local heroes:

> And I think that's one of the reasons—but President Boumédiène himself gave me the fundamental reason, because I met him in 1975 at the Cherchell Military Academy. He said to me, "*Yā fannān*, artist, France has left for us traps and mines. One of them is regionalism and tribalism. If we erect the statue of Zighoud now, the Kabyles are going to say, why didn't you do Amirouche ["Colonel" Amirouche Aït Hamouda, 1926–1959]? And the Chaouia, why didn't you do Ben Boulaïd [Mostefa Ben Boulaïd, 1917–1956]?[14]

Ultimately, despite his wariness of igniting regional jealousies and factional fighting, President Boumédiène supported and sponsored the statue. To keep it out of sight, the president's entourage intervened using state directives against depicting regional heroes in three-dimensional forms.[15]

Benyahia returned to Paris after his statue of Zighoud Youcef was finished and safely installed in 1969, but its installation was short-lived. Colonel Mohamed Ben Ahmed (1927–1996), known by his nom de guerre Abdelghani and commander of Wilaya II responsible for Constantine, had it removed.[16] Nicknamed locally the Bey of Constantine, the imperious Abdelghani gave a directive leading to the statue's disappearance one midnight in 1972, when it vanished into trucks and was not seen again until 1986.[17] A delegation of academic administrators preparing for a university conference on historiography in Constantine requested in 1986 that the statue be reinstalled for a twentieth anniversary commemoration of Youcef Zighoud.[18] Benyahia informed them it was up to them to find it:

> And when they found it, surprise! The statue of Zighoud Youcef, his symbol, had been guillotined! The body on one side, the head on the other. We didn't know what happened. They found it in a garage somewhere, they didn't tell me where. So it had to be restored. I got in touch with an old welder from the Bardo area and we did what we could to restore it. Just as we were going to install it, where the cockerel had been, a telegram arrived from the offices of President Chadli Bendjedid stating: "Any public installation of the statue of Zighoud Youcef postponed." And so for a second time we couldn't install it. It stayed like that. We restored it, and we took it back to its starting point at the headquarters of the party. And it stayed there. Two years later, there was the revolution of '88, multipartyism, the FLN disappeared. This huge building before becoming the headquarters of the party had been the Constantine Chamber of Commerce and Industry during the colonial period. It's a very beautiful building and the FLN did not want to give it back for political reasons. They decided to give it to Justice, to make it a court. So they had to get rid of the statue.[19]

In the video interview, Benyahia continues his account of the statue's peripeties:

> For a good while, the building [where the statue was housed] was empty. I met a friend who was director of the land registry and I said to him that the statue has been abandoned and he said to me, "I'm going to make it public property [*bien public*], so no one can touch it anymore." It came into

> public ownership [*propriété publique*] with a legal existence. It was given an identity. Apparently Zighoud Youcef on his own wasn't enough! Then one day they decided to decommission the building and reallocate it. I went to see the FLN, the administration and I said to them, "Listen, this story, this statue has really had its ups and downs. Either Zighoud Youcef is a hero of the revolution as we've been told and the statue should be installed in public, or Zighoud Youcef is a traitor and I'm ready to melt down the statue. There is a third solution, you give it to me, and I'll put it in my garden." And we left things like that. Then one day I was at home, and I heard my children say, "Dad, Dad, your statue." It was on the news, the Minister of Mujāhidīn, Mr. Abadou, without asking my opinion or anything, had decided to install it in the Martyrs' Cemetery. . . . And they made a pathetic plinth, and they installed it any old way and it's there in the Martyrs' Cemetery until today.[20]

Until 2021, the statue of Zighoud Youcef was entombed in Aïn Smara Martyr's Cemetery, Constantine's official resting place for Algerian war heroes and heroines (figure 81). The cemetery was designed by Ahmed Benyahia.

In 2021, Benyahia was contacted indirectly by a family foundation dedi-

FIGURE 81. Benyahia statue of Zighoud Youcef in Martyrs' Cemetery, Constantine. Photo by Ahmed Benyahia, ca. 2019. Reproduced by permission.

cated to Zighoud Youcef and headed by Zighoud's only daughter Chamma. She wanted to install Benyahia's statue in the main Martyrs' Square of the town of Zighoud Youcef, which had lost 1,200 people during the war—enormous for a small town whose main square is linked to Zighoud Youcef's demise. On February 18, 2021, on the centennial of Zighoud's birthday and during the COVID pandemic, Benyahia's statue—sculpted when he was twenty-five—was installed in the town. Forty-five years later, the war hero with the pointing finger took his place as an Algerian commemorative public sculpture in the town that had been renamed for him.[21] Since 2021, it stands bronze head reattached and finger pointing at the center of a traffic circle at the intersection of roads, a highway, and a mosque (figure 82).

The village of Zighoud Youcef, formerly colonial Condé-Smendou, like many in French Algeria, already had an interwar memorial (figure 83). Its bronze rooster was illegally removed by French forces at independence and brought to a military educational training camp in Coëtquidan, Brittany, where it was set up on a new pedestal on July 25, 1969. A plaque dated Sep-

FIGURE 82. Ahmed Benyahia at the inauguration of his statue in the town of Zighoud Youcef. Photo by Arris Mohamed Benyahia, February 18, 2021. Reproduced by permission.

tember 2012 was added to refer to the statue's Algerian provenance, naming a certain Lieutenant Vola, curator of the memorial museum, who confected a new monument from Condé-Mendou's cockerel for new metropolitan military parades, ceremonies, and rituals.[22]

Stripped of its rooster, the pedestal and column in former Condé-Smendou were transformed into a monument to the martyrs of the Algerian War of Independence whose names surround the base (figure 84).

FIGURE 83. **Condé-Smendou, colonial war memorial. Postcard. Author's collection. Open access, https://fr.geneawiki.com/index.php?title=Alg%C3%A9rie_-_Cond%C3%A9-Smendou&action=info.**

FIGURE 84. Colonial *monument aux morts* converted to an Algerian monument to the martyrs of independence, town of Zighoud Youcef (colonial Condé-Smendou). Photo by author, June 6, 2022.

COLONIAL PLACE DE LA BRÈCHE

Constantine's Place de la Brèche commemorates the breach in Constantine's walls during France's 1837 conquest of the city. There, the interwar colonial war memorial with plinth, column, and cockerel was inaugurated in 1922. The early period of monument decolonization that began at independence in 1962 was eventful. Days after Algerian independence, the French army removed one memorial to the colony's "great men" that stood where the city walls had been breached (see chapter 1). It commemorated Lieutenant-Colonel Louis Juchault de Lamoricière (1806–1865) who had defeated the city in 1837 in a battle that had taken two years.[23] A first French assault in 1835 was repelled by Algerian troops and city-dwellers under Ahmed Bey ben Mohamed Cherif of Constantine (ca. 1784–1850).[24] But the massive artillery bombardments commanded by General Sylvain-Charles Valée (1773–1846) breached Constantine's fortress and defensive walls in 1837, and Lamoricière entered Constantine on October 13 at the head of French troops. At the time, there were some fifty-nine mosques, thirty-five *zaouias* (buildings housing Sufi confraternities), four *medersas* (school-mosques), and nine *marabouts* (saint shrines) in Constantine, but its conquest led to a massive reorganization of Constantine's urban space into upper European and lower "native" quarters.[25] The eighteenth-century Mosque of Souk el Ghzel (market of spun wool) was transformed into the Catholic church of Notre-Dame-des-Sept-Douleurs in 1839, which was consecrated a cathedral in 1876, and after independence, reverted to the mosque of Hassan Bey, the name of its founder-builder. The twelfth-century Sidi Makhlouf Mosque was destroyed and replaced between 1849 and 1854 with the seat of the newly built neoclassical style prefecture and town hall.[26]

Between 1840 and 1870, Constantine was remade into a French colonial city. The central Place de la Brèche was created and enlarged with three straight main arteries bored through the curvilinear streets of the medina, the precolonial Muslim city. Following patterns of transformations to Algiers, the urban fabric of Constantine's dramatic destruction and construction was a colonial Haussmannization that preceded and was concurrent with the renovation of Parisian streets by Georges-Eugène Haussmann (1809–1891). Haussmann renovated Paris streets to make it easier for the army to move en masse in the city; this involved penetrating (*percement*), regularizing, and opening the city. Fear of the urban underclass and of epidemics eliminated old neighborhoods in favor of boulevards and squares; in

Algiers and Constantine, massive urban clearance and demolitions cleared the way for armies and settlers.[27]

The French state also had a monopoly over names and place names as of 1779 that was pursued in Algeria after 1830.[28] The Overseas Archives in Aix-en-Provence (ANOM) include records of Constantine's legal place name changes filed under *hommages publics* (public tributes). Minutes of city council deliberations describe how a colonial municipality honored the European war dead, but rarely the Algerian Muslim dead of World War I. Archival documentation of name changes based on the "Ordonnance du 10 juillet 1816" originally required metropolitan ministerial oversight. As of 1920, the colonial prefecture or local city council became responsible for naming, accounting for the interwar frenzy of new names in the colony.[29] Towns, streets, schools, and squares were named for prominent settlers, army divisions, generals of the Algerian conquest, and famous French historical figures, such as Joan of Arc. In turn, colonial history was reversed with the return of precolonial Arab-Berber names or new toponyms and Muslim names of holy men. The story of the Zighoud statue recalls the endless name changes of streets, towns, and schools employed after regime changes: conquest, destruction, expropriation, and reappropriation all speak to dominion.

The name Zighoud Youcef frequently replaced the names of French colonists and generals.[30] In Constantine, the Boulevard Joly de Brésillon is a sweeping street-cum-promenade, overlooking the valleys as it drops to the Place de la Brèche and skirts the 1922 cockerel monument. According to a nostalgic post by a former European settler of Constantine, Joly de Brésillon was an 1850s colonist who was allotted land for a cotton concession that never materialized. [31] After independence, the avenue was renamed Boulevard Zighoud Youcef and Condé-Smendou, the town where Zighoud was born, was also renamed Zighoud Youcef. The Place de la Brèche was renamed the First of November Square to commemorate the launch date of the Algerian Revolution in 1954.

As with many new names for central city squares throughout Algeria, the colonial name Place de la Brèche remained to recall the population's resilience in assimilating and repopulating the former European quarter built on destroyed parts of their medina. Former French colonial names often endure because of habit or because new cumbersome decolonizing rubrics are rejected.[32] The local population was well aware of the signification of Place de la Brèche, that the open square was a second breach to separate the new European city from the Algerian medina.[33] The square, its name, and the built French colonial architecture over the ruins of the former Arab-Berber-Muslim-Ottoman town reflect the sequence of empire and violence in Constantine. Entire streets and homes were razed to make way for settler colonial architectural structures. The interwar colonial administration chose to erect the elongated war memorial, a phallic shaft plus cockerel, on the site of the ramparts' breach that signaled the fall of the city in 1837.

The destruction of the column and winged rooster on the Place de la Brèche created a new situation that emptied out, an act of freedom, a toppling of a statue, indeed a Situationist "positive hole" in which Benyahia's refashioning of the Gallic cockerel is a precursor to his heritage projects appropriating French colonial material culture. I derive the concept from the Situationist International:

> All space is already occupied by the enemy, who has domesticated it for its own use down to the elementary rules of this space (beyond legal authority to geometry itself). The moment of authentic urbanism's appearance will be the creation, in certain areas, of the absence of this occupation. What we call construction starts there. It can be understood with the help of the concept of the "positive hole" [*trou positif*] invented by modern physics. Materializing liberty means first shielding from a domesticated planet a few small fragments of its surface.[34]

Benyahia prefers the Situationist term *détournement* (rerouting or hijacking) to describe a method for weakening the power of old cultural spheres:

> *Détournement* [hijacking] of prefabricated aesthetic elements. The integration of present or past artistic productions into a superior construction of a milieu. In this sense there can be no situationist painting or music, but only a Situationist use of those means. In a more elementary sense, *détournement* within the old cultural spheres is a method of propaganda, a method that reveals how these spheres wear out and lose importance.[35]

A colonial war memorial, once melted down, became palatable in the Algerian public sphere, although not fully acceptable to the state for its first forty years.

THE POLITICS OF COMMEMORATIVE STATUES AFTER INDEPENDENCE

Lamoricière's statue was removed from Constantine by the French military at independence. In its place, a traffic circle with flowers was placed. By 2001, a large clock was installed. In 2014, it was replaced by another statue that came to be seen as resembling a coronavirus after the onset of the epidemic in 2020 (see chapter 1). These latest Algerian government commissions are often kitsch sculptures and speedy implantations of statues in traffic circles to fill emptied spaces.[36]

During the Dark Decade of the 1990s, government officials began glorifying local heroes of the Algerian Revolution. In the face of terrorism often directed against state institutions, patriotism was expressed by making statues to memorialize revolutionary martyrs who were no longer relegated to forgettable roles as regional actors. Benyahia was prescient with his Zighoud Youcef statue long before local countermonuments to Boumédiène's state monopoly on martyrdom began to appear with frequency. Often in consultation with political actors such as the hero's descendants in family foundations, for example, local authorities erected Mostefa Ben Boulaïd's busts in his birthplace of Arris and a second one along Batna's eponymously named main boulevard (see chapter 1).[37] Amirouche Aït Hamouda (1926–1959) statues are found in several sites including his birthplace Tassaft Ouguemoune where it was inaugurated in 2020. In 2016, a statue of Ahmed Ben Bella (1916–1995), Algeria's first president (1963–1965) was erected in the colonial-era main square of Tlemcen, rather than his birthplace Maghnia, to celebrate the centenary of his birth.[38] A statue to Krim Belkacem (1922–1970) stands in Tadmait, Tizi Ouzou, and a bust of Maurice Audin (1932–1957) in Algiers.

Boumédiène's reluctance to commemorate regional revolutionary actors in sculptures set in prominent public places (while promoting place-name replacements) is no longer an obstacle. Since his death in 1978, countless statues of Algeria's heroes have been commissioned and are displayed prominently. Often a statue is placed in a traffic roundabout, whose numbers increase as cities grow, the product of state partnerships with municipalities and governorates to decorate newer districts and redecorate colonial urban cores with public art. Despite Boumédiène's opposition to statues and portraits of him in public, a statue burnished with patinated bronze resin, which produces a fake bronze effect, was prominently elevated in the central traffic circle near Guelma's city hall in 2002 (figure 85).[39]

For Benyahia, his Zighoud Youcef statue functioned to divert the population's rage into an acceptable cultural artifact that embodies preservation and destruction. The French form changed but the essential act of monument-making did not. Similar provenance examples of reusing sculptural material by settlers (including the army and the Catholic Church) also date to the nineteenth-century occupation of Algeria.[40] Statues erected in Algeria were made in Algeria, some by colonial authorities from melted down Ottoman cannons, such as the Saint-Augustine statue of Annaba and the Duke of Orleans equestrian statue from central Algiers removed by the military at independence and positioned in Neuilly, France. The cycle of recycled materials—Ottoman cannon to colonial Christian statue or colonial war memorial to Algerian hero statue—embellishes the city. Benyahia's Zighoud Youcef statue reproduces and represents local anti-colonial ways of knowledge unacceptable to Algeria's leadership in the early decades

FIGURE 85. Gilded statue of Houari Boumédiène, Guelma, sculpted by Djanet Dahel (b. 1950), 2002. Photo by Billel Benguedouar, June 9, 2022. Reproduced by permission.

of independence. Not only did he destructure unequal relations between colonizer and colonized, but he also acknowledged the colonizers while physically subsuming them into his sculpture.

To some extent, the story of the Zighoud statue is anything but straightforward with the endless deferral. Since 2021, it stands at the center of a traffic circle where the town of Zighoud Youcef's roads and highways converge. The traffic circle was perfected in and for Paris. It was the city with the earliest traffic circles first constructed at Place de l'Étoile, then renamed for President Charles de Gaulle (1890–1970) on his death. Architect Eugène Hénard (1849–1923) created the *carrefour à gyrations* at the Place de l'Étoile, comprising twelve linear avenues and adjacent pedestrian walkways transformed into an aesthetically pleasing, modern metropolitan urban space. The ubiquitous "roundabout" or "traffic circle" in English and *rond-point* (in both French and Algerian Arabic) arrived to Algeria, where French colonial urban planners deployed its possibilities as another disciplinary architectural tool to police so-called chaotic North African cities through the central traffic island. Infrastructure became paired with ornamental civic art projects because the traffic circle, protected from heavy pedestrian traffic, seems to call forth monumental sculpture, greenery, and fountains illuminated by night. In colonial Algeria, the traffic circle was a reference point but also signaled, indexically so to speak, one more place to demonstrate the power to populate European settler sites with familiar monuments and statues.[41]

Postindependent Algerian towns and cities expanded exponentially after independence, and traffic circles entered the stream of new avenues and highways. Examples are in Oran, Algeria's second largest city, where the statue of the town's resistance hero, Ahmed Zabana, graces a traffic circle that marks major eastward extensions to the colonial seaside boardwalk. Unlike Benyahia's statue infused with genuine French colonial bronze, the Zabana statue is burnished with patinated bronze resin or fake bronze.[42] Numerous versions of the Emir Abdelkader on horseback with sword aloft, which replaced the statue of General Bugeaud in Algiers, populate new urban neighborhoods throughout the country.[43] While the emplacement of Benyahia's Zighoud Youcef statue at the juncture of roads, a highway, and a mosque created the new traffic circle, it reversed the normal order of town development with the statue preceding and inviting the *rond-point*. Moveable French colonial art in public spaces, built over razed Algerian spaces, has been subjected to more violence in its disassembly by the French (spoliation for the purpose of repatriation), Algerian disassembly (partial demolition), Algerian replacement, and ultimately by Benyahia who reuses it.

WHAT PUBLIC SCULPTURE FOR ALGERIA?: SOCIALIST VILLAGES (1973 AND 1978)

President Houari Boumédiène had advocated for new architecture for a new nation. He commissioned important architects, among them Brazil's Oscar Niemayer, Egypt's Mustafa Moussa, and France's Fernand Pouillon.[44] Architects built new Algerian universities, mosques, resort and sport complexes, and student and urban housing; as well, designers and more architects were hired for the 1970s projects to construct new agricultural villages.[45] For Benyahia, the question of which statues fell after independence became what might replace them. He aimed to make sculptures that acknowledged colonial rural expropriations and camp internments while looking to the future by marking sites of postindependent land redistributions. The opportunity to create new public art came in 1971 when Boumédiène called for one thousand "socialist villages." Boumédiène's Agrarian Revolution of 1971 sought to remake the brutal colonial heritage of massive land dispossessions magnified by the French military program of forcibly displacing wide swaths of the rural population into regroupment camps first set up in 1957 during the independence war.[46] Socialist villages were built for and often on land allocated to former inhabitants of those regroupment camps. Benyahia recounted that 1,000 socialist villages and 1,000 mosques were considered; a few villages had commissioned sculptures.[47] In 1973, the Ministry of Agriculture commissioned two sculptures from him. The first was located in Medeghri Belgimouze, a socialist village attached to the commune of El Anceur, sixty miles northwest of Constantine. It received much media and scholarly attention in the 1970s and '80s. Boumédiène's land reform program uniquely targeted benefits to the women's cooperative. Anthropologist Willy Jansen's 1980s fieldwork in a pseudonymous village in the region led her to conclude that "women without men"—widows, divorcées, spouses of disabled husbands—were the actual beneficiaries in contrast to the limited impact on married women who were "veiled, secluded and without land."[48]

Benyahia's sculpture was influenced by Boumédiène's rhetoric of redistributing agrarian land to landless agricultural laborers and by César, his mentor and proponent of New Realism, who assigned new beauty to useless discarded materials in European capitalist society. Benyahia amassed agricultural implements abandoned by the departed European settler farm-owners and used them. Remaking found detritus, the sculpture questioned the organization of colonial agricultural practices through a new regard for the material ways in which implements were assembled. At Medeghri Belgimouze, he positioned found rakes, scythes, plows, shovels, picks, and wheels on the earth like upright sentinels in a row. To this lineup, he added new sculpted bronze forms of the sun and sheaves of wheat. He named the sculpture after global revolutionary slogans adopted to the call for the Agrarian Revolution: *La terre à qui la travaille* (the land to those who work it).[49] These agricultural tools were brought together as an exercise in remembrance; his sculpture catalogs and conserves a material archive that attests to Algerian presence, ingenuity, and cocreation of colonial rural farm worlds. Preserving fragments of tools used by former colonized laborers produces a material relation with the colonial period in Medaghri-Belghimouze and connects with the sought after, self-reliant future of Algerian agriculture. On site, Benyahia worked in tandem with Makhloufi Laïfa, his architecture classmate from the Algiers School of Fine Arts, who was also assigned to the village. They planted the sculpture at the foot of the hill near the mosque to adapt to the village's topography. It was installed in 1973 but has since disappeared, except in photos taken by his photographer cousin, Abderrezak Benyahia (figures 86 and 87).[50]

A second sculpture in the village of Salah Bey still stands. Benyahia attributes its dilapidation to the general abandonment of public spaces since the Dark Decade. Approximately 200 hectares of land that were once the summer palace of Salah Bey ben Mostefa, the bey of Constantine from 1771–1792, with well-watered orchards and gardens, are a different starting point for a socialist village.[51] Boumédiène's Agrarian Revolution nationalized the lands of the Bendjelloul family, the descendants of Salah Bey, which they managed to regain in the early 1990s. Installed in 1978, Benyahia's Salah Bey sculpture reuses colonial-era farm materials elevated on top of three posts festooned with large plant fronds as the plow, rakes, and other implements reach skyward. He addresses themes of accumulating and recuperating found colonial objects, reversing colonial histories by highlighting Algerian rural labor and reformulating new postindependence futures (figures 88 and 89).

FIGURE 86. Ahmed Benyahia, Medaghri-Belghimouze sculpture erected in 1973. Photo by Abderrezak Benyahia, 1973. Reproduced by permission.

FIGURE 87. Worker posing in front of a hollowed-out circle of the sun for Medaghri-Belghimouze sculpture. Photo by Abderrezak Benyahia. Reproduced by permission.

FIGURE 88. Benyahia sculpture, socialist village of Salah Bey, 1978. Photo by Ahmed Benyahia. Reproduced by permission.

FIGURE 89. Salah Bey sculpture on January 8, 2023. Photo by Ahmed Benyahia. Reproduced by permission.

GUELMA (1976)

Benyahia's sculpture for the city of Guelma commemorates the French army massacres of May 8, 1945. In Guelma as in Sétif and Kherrata, colonial forces fired on Algerian demonstrators during the celebratory marches for Victory in Europe Day making May 8 a day of mourning for Algerians.[52] To celebrate their military service under the French flag, Algerian marchers including World War II conscripts demanded equal rights, given French "aphasia" about the massive roles played by colonial troops in the liberation of France.[53] During the demonstration, an estimated 102 European settlers died. In response, the French retaliated throughout the region and between 6,000 and 8,000 Algerian Muslims were killed. Some sixty years later, the "massacre" was acknowledged as such by France in 2008 (see chapter 1).

Benyahia's monument for Guelma was inaugurated in 1976 and set at the crossroads of the town's Roman theater and the French colonial-era military barracks near the boulevard taken by Algerian demonstrators in the march to mark the end of World War II.[54] His initial three-foot plaster model was completed in Paris between 1971 and 1972, inspired by the Black September conflict between the armed forces of Jordan and Palestine Liberation Organization fighters which concluded with the PLO's expulsion from Jordan. Benyahia observed that political resistance embodied in the Palestinian struggle and art have long inspired Algerian artists.[55] Influenced by his garden, Benyahia transformed abstract images of upright and destroyed flowers into contorted human arms reaching skyward. In Paris, he modeled the Guelma statue in plaster, then shipped it to Algiers for display. The actual statue was made from artificial marble, a combination of white cement added to powdered marble fragments, remnants from the Emir Abdelkader Mosque that was under construction in Constantine as of 1968 (figure 90).

When new fences were built around the archaeological garden and a second set of enclosures was built to protect Guelma's surviving antique wall and Roman theater, his Guelma sculpture was moved without Benyahia's knowledge or permission to the square known as Place du 8 Mai 1945 around the year 2000. Comparing figures 90 of 1976 and 91 of 2022, it becomes clear why Benyahia objected to the relocation: the original heavy black chains encircling the plinth were lost; the tall base (that forced spectators to look up) was replaced with an unimpressive two-step foundation; new marble slabs covered the iridescent cement-cum-marble fragments;

FIGURE 90. Inauguration of Ahmed Benyahia's *Monument to May 8, 1945 Massacre*, Guelma, May 8, 1976. Photo by Abderrazak Benyahia. Reproduced by permission.

and an ugly label was put in place. For all that, Benyahia's sculpture now stands and is admired in a central square with a park and convivial spaces filled with cafés. During our June 9, 2022, visit, bystanders repeatedly expressed their admiration for the statue and their pleasure in meeting the artist (figure 91).

FIGURE 91. Ahmed Benyahia gestures toward his sculpture in Guelma. Photo by Billel Benguedouar, June 9, 2022. Reproduced by permission.

CONSTANTINE'S *MONUMENT AUX MORTS* (1968–PRESENT)

Constantine is considered the first colonial Algerian municipality to have begun the project for a World War I monument by placing a cornerstone on the outcropping of Sidi M'Cid on November 18, 1918. On May 7, 1930, the monument was inaugurated as part of French Algeria's centenary celebrations (figure 92).

Algeria-based architects Marcel Dumoulin and Maurice de La Chapelle drew on the widely appropriated symbols of the French conquest of Algeria for their sixty-foot memorial inspired by the Roman Arch of Trajan in Timgad (Latin Thamugadi) (figure 93), seventy-four miles south of Constantine, the site of a successful military camp originally planned for the legendary Third Augustan Legion by the Roman Emperor Trajan. Here a town was built ex nihilo at the foothills of the Aurès mountains to subdue the "savage" tribes of the hinterland and display the wealth and grandeur of Rome in North Africa.[56]

FIGURE 92. Constantine's *monument aux morts* (note empty spaces that once displayed reliefs in the niches under two outer arches). Photo by author, June 6, 2022.

FIGURE 93. **Trajan's Arch (late 2nd-early 3rd CE), height: 40 feet, Timgad, Algeria. Photo by the author, June 11, 2022**

Still perched atop of Constantine's war memorial, a copy of Trajan's Arch, is another *Winged Victory* (*Victoire ailée*), sculpted by Joseph Ebstein, (1881–1961).[57] Born in Batna, Ebstein was an Algerian Jewish sculptor noted for his war monuments throughout the colony, many of which integrated large-scaled *Winged Victory* figures. As a citizen, he was able to attend the Algiers École des Beaux-Arts where he studied with Victor Fulconis (1851–1913) and Léon Fourquet (1841–1938), two sculptors in French Algeria, before moving to the École des Beaux-Arts in Paris to work under Louis-Ernest Barrias (1841–1905) and Jules Coutan (1848–1939), preeminent Second Empire academic monument makers.[58] For Constantine's *Winged Victory*, Ebstein enlarged a nine-inch bronze Roman statuette that had been unearthed in 1858 by Colonel M. Ribot, the French engineering officer who was responsible for razing the city's Ottoman fortress walls to accommodate new colonial structures (figure 94). The original was deposited and remains in Constantine's Cirta Museum.[59]

FIGURE 94. Scale of the *Winged Victory* sculpture in photo of Ebstein. "Le monument aux morts de Constantine," *L'Afrique du Nord Illustrée* 443 (October 26, 1929): 5.

PRESERVATION

Benyahia spent more than sixty years working to preserve the Arch and *Winged Victory*, Algeria's most spectacular colonial war memorial. He told me a story about something that happened in 1968, giving a variant of other stories I heard throughout Algeria during my fieldwork, each time with a different monument and a different cast of municipal actors and outcomes (see chapter 2 on Oran's war memorial removal to Lyon, France). European settlers from the Constantine Pied-Noir association based in Marseille approached Constantine's first elected Algerian mayor, Ahcène Boudjenana, who had been a resistance fighter during the war and the long-time activist head of the railway workers' union.[60] The former European settlers requested that *their* war memorial be moved to France. Benyahia begged Boudjenana to refuse. He argued that decolonization was complex, layered, and involved refusing to remove the traces of the Phoenicians, Romans, Vandals, Arabs, Turks, and the French. He reminded the mayor of his nickname, Monsieur Peugeot, for his admiration for French products and pointed out that the monument was part of the Algerian heritage, an important urban landmark, and a point of reference comparable to the Eiffel Tower.

Last but not least, according to an argument that Benyahia cites about other colonial artifacts, the war memorial was material proof that Algerians who had died in two wars had been used as cannon fodder to defend France. Men from Benyahia's family were conscripted, fought, and died for France at Verdun and Ypres, and their names were engraved on the war memorial's inner wall of bronze plaques among the 844 soldiers from Constantine who died during World War I (figure 95). During World War II, two uncles, Hafsi and Salah Benyahia, the artist's paternal uncles, had survived the bloody battles of Monte Cassino in Italy (January–May 1944); his uncle Ali was dispatched to the Syrian front, and his father, Mohamed, served as an infantryman in the Constantine contingent. The Algerian Muslim soldiers from Constantine defended the Château de Versailles, where Mohamed Benyahia was taken prisoner in 1940 by the German army.[61]

FIGURE 95. Benyahia family members' names on the Constantine memorial. Photo courtesy of Ahmed Benyahia. Reproduced by permission.

In 1968, the municipal council voted unanimously to legally dispatch Constantine's war memorial to Marseille, but Boudjenana vetoed the decision following Benyahia's advice. The magnificent French colonial war monument, what Benyahia terms a visual dialogue with time and suffering, remained in Constantine, but needed to be rescued again in the ensuing decades. In the 1980s, incremental neglect, vandalism, and municipal distaste led to another attempt to remove the monument. Four bas-reliefs of French generals Foch, Joffre, Franchet D'Espèrey, and Pétain (which was removed in 1944) placed in the niches in 1930 were stolen. One of four bronze plaques listing the names of the war dead was vandalized with an electric chainsaw and subsequently replaced with a marble version in 2014 during an official celebration marking the centenary of World War I.

Three generations of the Benzarti family served as municipal guards after the grandfather was hired by the French and provided with a residence near the monument. The last guardian was fired in the 1980s after the municipality asked why it should pay to preserve a monument to colonialism. One proposal was to topple Ebstein's *Winged Victory* and all other French symbols and write "Allah" and "Muhammad" in Arabic calligraphy in the emptied niches of the bas-reliefs.[62] Other suggestions included a replacement statue in the shape of an open book like many postindependence memorials erected elsewhere (in Sidi-Bel-Abbès, see chapter 3) and El-Maleh (see chapter 1). The Wali of Constantine, Chaaban Aït Abderrahim rejected both the calligraphy and the partial destruction. Benyahia resurrected the project of a monument in the shape of a book and proposed a sculpture as part of Constantine's Martyrs' Cemetery, off the highway to Aïn Smara. For Benyahia, saving Constantine's colonial war memorial is thus intimately related to his subsequent Algerian martyrs' monument; both projects are owed to his work as a creative sculptor but also as a vigilant partisan of preservation.

MARTYRS' CEMETERY, AÏN SMARA: *MONUMENT DES DEUX LIVRES* (*MONUMENT OF THE TWO BOOKS*, 1982)

Benyahia designed the layout, the war monument, and a building in the cemetery that the municipality subsequently modified. He also designed a large gate for vehicles framed by pointed pedestrian gates resembling the triangles in the meeting hall (figure 96). The white concrete cubes with triangular apertures are repeated in the nearby hall designated for meetings, lectures, and reflection (figure 97).

FIGURE 96. Entrance to the Martyrs' Cemetery, Aïn Smara, designed by Ahmed Benyahia in 1982. Photo by author, June 24, 2022.

FIGURE 97. Martyrs' Cemetery, Aïn Smara, meeting hall designed by Ahmed Benyahia in 1982. Photo by author, June 24, 2022.

An elegant concrete monument to the Algerian martyrs of the independence war is an integral sculptural component of Benyahia's cemetery design. It sits at the top of a flight of flagstone stairs on the steep hill from which the surrounding verdant countryside is visible. For the stairway, he worked closely with masons to cut, dress, and lay his intricate designs, a craft still alive in the 1980s. From the magnificent setting with stone pathway and trees, his sculpture of abstract elongated shapes emerges, representing two open books inscribed in raised black letters with the names of battles and visible from afar (figure 98).

The monument has gone through removals and additions (figure 99). Benyahia pointed out that it was once covered with bullet holes, cartridges, and machine guns, which the Algerian army removed during the Dark Decade so that terrorists would not reuse them. Between Benyahia's sculpted forms at ground level, a third open book is perched on top of a small

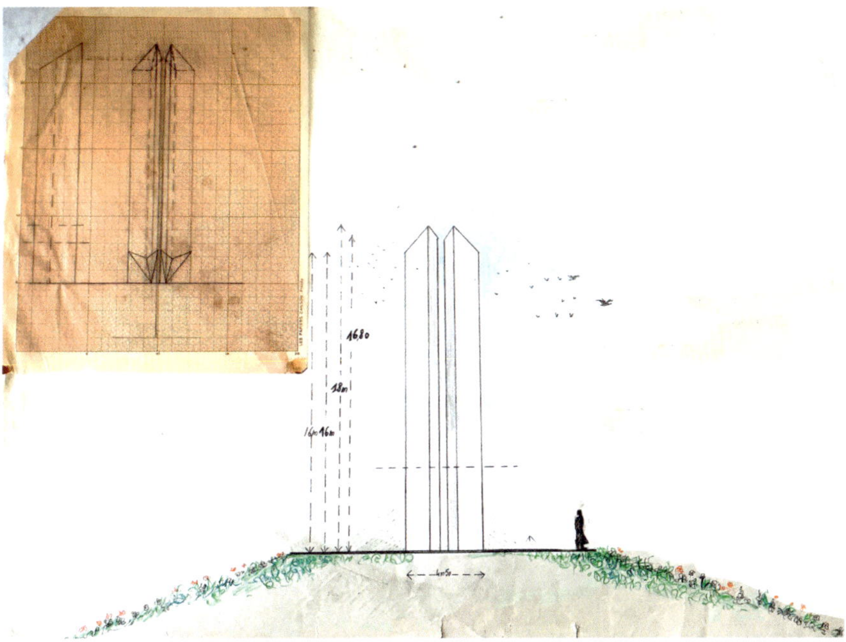

FIGURE 98. Sketch for the *Monument to the Martyrs of the Algerian Revolution* by Ahmed Benyahia. Reproduced by permission.

FIGURE 99. Ahmed Benyahia, *Martyrs' Monument of Two Books,* Aïn Smara cemetery. Photo by author, June 24, 2022.

stubby podium. It is unclear who added the mini-book and when, although the intention is to ensure the familiar stone presence of an open book, well-known to Algerian viewers from numerous martyrs' monuments.

PLACE DE LA PYRAMIDE (1980)

Constantine's former Place de la Pyramide (now Place Colonel Amirouche) is composed of a traffic circle whose star-shaped pathways simulate the eight streets that converge on it. In 1866, a pyramid was erected to mark the area where General Charles-Marie de Damrémont (1783–1837) was mortally wounded by Ottoman cannon fire during the invasion of Constantine. Demolished in 1914, it was replaced by an obelisk and statue of the general brandishing his sword. An Ebstein *Winged Victory* hovered over Damrémont's right shoulder (figure 100).

In the 1950s, the statues of Damrémont, Ebstein's *Winged Victory,* and the fountain were removed leaving the obelisk. Constantine's public squares changed again at independence in 1962. The statue of General Sylvain Charles Valée (1773–1846), who succeeded Damrémont as commander of occupied Constantine, had embellished the Garden of the Mercantiles

FIGURE 100. ***Winged Victory*** **and General Damrémont by Joseph Ebstein. Postcard, LL (Léon et Lévy, no. 239), undated. Author's collection.**

next to the municipal casino. An artillery expert, Valée was famed for the "Valée system" that deployed lighter, swifter, longer-range, and standardized bronze cannons in warfare, which he first tested successfully in Algeria against Algiers (1830), then Constantine (1837).[63] Although they are not visible in the postcard photo, six cannons surrounded his statue (figure 101).

At independence, Commandant Larbi Berredjem, associated with Lakhdar Ben Tobbal and the Army of the Interior,[64] one of many with viscerally negative responses to colonial artifacts, sternly refused even a trace of French material domination and declared that all colonial statues were to be destroyed immediately. He also declared, moreover, that he himself would burn those that were not removed. According to Benyahia, Berredjem attributed the guilt of colonialism to inanimate objects. Valée's statue had been removed by the French military to France by January 1963.[65] Years later, Benyahia discovered four of the six original cannons that had been transferred on Berredjem's orders to the municipal depot in the Chalet des Pins neighborhood (today's Cité des Pins) and planned a new statue using them. As he did so often, he began with drawings that captured the actual site and surrounding buildings. Figure 102 shows his sketch for the monu-

FIGURE 101. Statue of General Valée, postcard, ca. 1910. Constantine gardens. Collection Idéale. P.S., CC BY-SA 4.0 https://creativecommons.org/licenses/by-sa/4.0 via Wikimedia Commons.

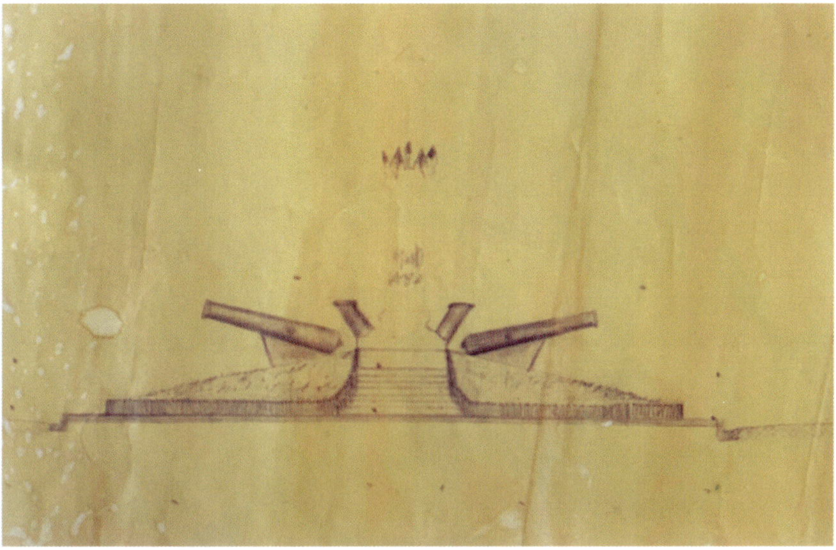

FIGURE 102. Sketch for Constantine's obelisk and four cannons by Ahmed Benyahia. Reproduced by permission.

ment with flagpole holders at mid-obelisk, which were never installed; the municipality planted trees to obscure clear sight lines for his repurposed cannon and obelisk ensemble. In 1980, the four cannons were placed around the obelisk at the Place de la Pyramide as a Situationist *détournement*, Benyahia's "occupation of the occupation."[66]

Benyahia's transparent politics and aesthetics clash with Algerian state projects to control public art, but sometimes slide through due to pragmatic calculations by involved parties. Cannons were transformed from murderous weapons glorifying the statue of a French artillery general to valorizing independent Algeria's takeover and reuse of remnants with the colonial tribunal and gendarmerie in the background repurposed for Algerian administration (figure 103). Adding to Algeria's complex ecology of toponyms—unchanged or Arabized French names or new names—for many city dwellers, the square is both Place de la Pyramide and Place des Canons, anchoring Benyahia's salvage and preservation in urban memory. Many of Benyahia's individual acts of Situationist *détournement* improvise on the possibilities of preserving and reusing the remains of French colonial statues and monuments. In late 1980, new state laws enabled him to step up his projects, add more public artworks, and form new associative networks.

FIGURE 103. Four cannons placed at the Place de la Pyramide in 1980 designed by Ahmed Benyahia. Photo by author, June 5, 2022.

ASSOCIATION DE DÉFENSE DU VIEUX ROCHER / JAMʿIYYA AL-DIFĀʿ ʿAN AL-ṢAKHR AL-ʿATĪQ / ASSOCIATION TO PRESERVE THE "OLD ROCK" (ADDVRC), 1992

The 1987 law of associations consolidated new freedoms including constituting nongovernmental associations unaffiliated with the single ruling FLN party during the presidency of Chadli Bendjedid (1979–1992).[67] This was the culmination of a long history of associations in French Algeria. In 1901, the French law of associations touched the lives of associations in settler society. Algerian Muslim members were rarely included in settler social events, so as of the 1920s, many communally distinct clubs and societies (*nādī*) became spaces for Algerian cultural and nationalist activities.[68] On December 31, 1962, the new nation promulgated a law regarding the freedom of association and reinstated the 1901 law of associations. Over time, laws functioned to restrict state-approved societies.[69]

Associations were among the earliest preservation and heritage societies in Constantine. In the summer of 1989, Ahmed Benyahia and some fifty prominent figures of Constantine created the Association de défense du Vieux Rocher (Association to Preserve the "Old Rock," ADDVRC). Abdelkrim Badjadja (1945–2022), director of the archives for Constantine, was its first president. When he resigned six weeks later, Ahmed Benyahia replaced him and remains president to this day. Benyahia is among a handful of social actors, occasionally with government allies and more often without, who have grasped the potential of associative life against hegemonic discourses on public art and statuary. Hoping for the emergence of a strong civil society, he saw the association as another tool to intervene and protect Constantine's patrimony against rapacious real estate development, insensitive urban planning, and entrenched bureaucratic interests. State laws could be instrumentalized against the state apparatus. The association's first assembly was announced by Benyahia's widely disseminated poster in which graphic design and an eye-catching calligram evoke the city's signature Roman aqueduct (figure 104).

FIGURE 104. Ahmed Benyahia, poster, watercolor on paper, 63 cm × 50 cm, 1989. Reproduced by permission.

TANGIBLE HERITAGE

Since Algeria's policies are oriented toward legislating tangible heritage, the Association de défense du Vieux Rocher, under Benyahia's leadership, sought to intervene in centralized laws on architecture and access to public space.[70] As of 1990, the tasks of safeguarding heritage and supervising rehabilitation, restoration, and renovation operations devolved to the wilaya and commune (i.e., the state and municipality of Constantine). Controversially, Benyahia with Badjadja began by attempting to preserve not only the precolonial Ottoman walled city, a perennial patrimonial priority in Algeria, but also the French colonial built environment. The association forwarded detailed dossiers to the municipality to classify as protected heritage not only the medina or *vieille-ville* but also the Prison of El Koudia (Coudiat Aty), built in 1853 by the French military.[71] Although they successfully saw to the first steps by listing and publishing both sites in the official government journal, local authorities were required to publicize and inscribe all new initiatives for these measures to have legal force and be applied.[72] They have yet to do so.[73] Prior to 1989, the same government tactics that made civil society initiatives difficult to organize were redeployed to hamstring associations and disband them for inactivity. To forestall these outcomes, Benyahia maintains the annual re-registration requirement and spends his own money, never drawing down the association's treasury, to avoid a state audit shutting down activist associations for supposed fiduciary malfeasance.

Constantine's Association to Preserve the "Old Rock" has won some environmental and heritage battles, often by mobilizing the media and public opinion. It was able to valorize urban history by affixing educational plaques to honor deserving, forgotten local heroes associated with a specific site. On June 10, 1990, for example, it placed a commemorative plaque in the medina at the house of a leader of the anti-colonial resistance, Mohamed Benelbedjaoui, killed in the battle of Constantine during the French siege of 1837 (figures 105 and 106).[74]

As president of the association to preserve Constantine's heritage, Benyahia was instrumental in organizing the renovation and repair of Constantine's colonial war memorial. In 2015, for Europe's centennial commemorations of 1914 and the outbreak of World War I, the ambassadors from France, Bernard Emie, and Germany, Ger Gotz Lingenthal, former enemies as Benyahia notes, participated in jointly laying wreaths at Constantine's *monument aux morts,* a first for Algeria.

FIGURE 105. Marble plaque commemorating Benelbedjaoui's martyrdom of 1837 defending Constantine, affixed June 17, 1999. Photo by Ahmed Benyahia, June 19, 2022. Reproduced by permission.

FIGURE 106. Plaque site in interior courtyard, Benelbedjaoui house, Constantine medina. Photo by Ahmed Benyahia, June 19, 2022. Reproduced by permission.

The association has also lost battles against numerous, ever-changing local and state administrations. Victories can be defined as delays and diversions to city plans for demolishing the medina and evicting inhabitants of the Souika neighborhood by forcing the tramway line to reroute, a stellar Benyahia Situationist *détournement*.[75] By contrast, real estate interests successfully eliminated the central gardens and municipal casino opened in the interwar period. This was a beloved gathering place before and after independence that acquired a café-brasserie, auditorium, dancehall, a cinema—Le Colisée—and sports amenities (figure 107).[76]

Before the municipal casino was demolished in the 1980s, Benyahia proposed extensive renovations for a cultural complex to maintain the colonial architectural imprint and trademark tall column. His numerous sketches (two of which are reproduced here) outline new garden paths and a refurbished green environment. The colonial casino urban garden had been divided between green shady areas (*jnān markantiyya*) and areas for the poor (*jnān zawaliyya*) with lesser amenities, mirroring settler and native urban divides, but Benyahia's plans revitalized extensive green spaces adjacent to the casino for everyone (figures 108 and 109).

A multistory Novotel and Ibis hotels surrounded with high, spiked fences and manned police guard posts replaced the destroyed gardens when

FIGURE 107. Constantine's municipal casino, ca. 1930s. Postcard, "Real-Photo" C.A.P. no. 38. Author's collection.

FIGURE 108. Ahmed Benyahia's designs for his proposed rehabilitation of the municipal casino. Reproduced by permission.

FIGURE 109. Ahmed Benyahia's sketches for gardens, pond, and casino. Reproduced by permission.

construction began in 2012. The appropriation of green spaces assured the high fortress-like walls blocking the magnificent panorama to the Hamma Valley below.

THE UNIVERSAL MUSEUM OF COLONIALISM'S CRIMES AGAINST HUMANITY (LE MUSÉE UNIVERSEL DU COLONIALISME, CRIME CONTRE L'HUMANITÉ)

Benyahia's heritage projects target the ubiquitous colonial prisons in Algeria, the architectural legacy of French Algeria as a carceral state.[77] He has long wanted to transform Constantine's 1853 El Koudia Prison and the adjacent gendarmerie that served as a colonial military court with its underground tunnel to the prison. He seeks to forestall further urban demolitions by creating a museum of colonial art and artifacts. He envisages a complex museum to the memory of colonialism and crimes against humanity. Supported by the preservation association he heads, they were able to list the prison buildings as part of the national patrimony in 1992. In 2013, the local authorities agreed to the museum project, which was ideally timed for Constantine's award as the "Arab cultural capital" of 2015. ALECSO (the Arab League Educational, Cultural, and Scientific Organization) had launched the project in Arab countries patterned on Europe's "capitals of culture" that began in 1983. But the prison remained open and simply got a fresh coat of paint for the occasion.[78] For now, a plaque affixed to its outer stone walls lists the Algerians guillotined in the prison during the Algerian War.

For Benyahia, the question is how a colonial penal institution becomes a space that rehistoricizes and reappropriates its building. He plans to appeal to memory to make this a national souvenir, laboratory, art museum, and memorial to carceral colonialism for future generations of Algerians lacking any experience of life before 1962. He intends to evacuate the current prison population and create exhibitions about storied detainees such as Cheikh Mohamed El-Mokrani, the leader of the 1871 popular uprising against the French occupation, and his comrade Muhand Amezyan Aheddad known as Cheikh El Haddad, who died in the prison in 1873, as well as the legendary 1956 prison escape of Mostefa Ben-Boulaïd, the resistance leader of the Aurès region, and thirty inmates. The museum will include exhibition spaces, archives, a library, conference halls, and a restaurant and teahouse specializing in Constantine gastronomy.[79]

Museums dedicated to the French-Algerian past have fared poorly thus far. In Montpellier, France, the Musée de Montpellier sur l'Histoire de la France et de l'Algérie, proposed by historian and Constantine native Benjamin Stora and his colleagues, failed to materialize.[80] In Bou Saada, Algeria, anthropologist Barkahom Ferhati, a native of Bou Saada, established Le Musée National Nasr Ed-din Etienne Dinet de Bou Saada in the former home of the painter Etienne Dinet, a convert to Islam. The museum was torched during the Dark Decade. Both museums are failed efforts (*avorté*).[81] Lyon's Montluc Prison Museum struggles to acknowledge its murderous role as a detention site for Algerian militants in France including eleven who were guillotined.[82] As it happens, even museum plans for the Serkadji Prison in the Casbah of Algiers, the formerly colonial Barberousse Prison built over an Ottoman fortress in 1856, experienced reversals. Closed at independence by President Ahmed Ben Bella and reopened as a high security prison after the coup d'état of President Houari Boumédiène, it was emptied of inmates in 2014 and officially converted in 2018 to a national museum in memory of colonialism.[83] Article 3 of the Decree of 2014 defines its mission:

> The national public museum "Prison Serkadji" reflects the struggle and sacrifices of the Algerian people to recover their freedom and attests to the inhuman, cruel and degrading prison practices and different forms of physical and psychological torture of colonialism. The museum includes detention areas, cells and other spaces as well as historical museum collections, objects, ethnographic documents, photographs and audiovisual recordings about colonial penitentiary practices. It is responsible for their conservation, enhancement, and public display.[84]

As of this writing, it remains closed to the public. Benyahia's museum is aspirational, curated only in his imagination and among his personal archives. He evokes in his comments to me aspects of Édouard Glissant's unrealized "Art Museum of the Americas" and André Malraux's *musée imaginaire,* if the English translation is "a museum without walls" as a "collection of works with the power to help us live."[85] Unlike Malraux's project of decontextualized images, Benyahia deploys colonial-era postcards to prove loss, absence, spoliation, and transformations in Constantine. He envisions collecting an array of colonial monuments slated for recuperation and repatriation to counter the outflow of statues "repatriated" in 1962. He demands the return of monuments to colonial generals—*à nos grands hommes* (to our great men)—that the French army removed, such as Constantine's statue of Lamoricière. His museum would be filled with colonial artwork, statuary removed to France or badly preserved, decaying sculptures in Algeria. While historical and aesthetic parameters matter for Benyahia, to love a French colonial statue requires that it be part of the fabric of urban daily life or be displayed in the El Koudia Prison Museum as an object of repression and part of the vestiges of settler colonialism:

> Tools of repression must be preserved. We can reconstruct evidence with objects, removing them is being an accomplice. Statues speak, prison walls speak. If statues are in France, they speak differently or are silent. Statues, objects of colonialism such as postcards should fill the museum. Colonial objects are key elements of a crime that needs to be proven. We can reconstitute our history with French objects, including the things they took that we Algerians do not always value. Otherwise, we are accomplices to removing traces of the crime since we can only reconstitute the crime with the objects of the crime. Objects of crime revive emotions of course.[86]

Benyahia's museum would combat the erasures of colonial objects removed from Algerian landscapes.

In *The First Man,* Albert Camus describes settler efforts to leave nothing behind: before leaving Algeria, settler-farmer Veillard pours his wine on the ground and ploughs up his vines: "Since what we made here is a crime, it has to be wiped out."[87] Algeria has often treated the French colonial heritage that was not poured out or ploughed up as Algerian patrimony. Historian Andrew Bellisari chronicles the successful Algerian negotiations for the return in 1970 of over 300 French paintings taken from the Museum of Fine Arts in Algiers to the Louvre Museum just before the war's end.[88] The 2018 "Sarr-Savoy Report" coauthored by French and Senegalese academics Bénédicte Savoy and Felwine Sarr advocated for restituting sub-Saharan artifacts held in Euro-American museums, but in a footnote Algeria was ruled out as a special case, one that required its own commission:

> On the African continent, the case of Algeria (which has been made the object of intensive negotiations since the 1960s that resulted in important movements of restitution or long-term deposits after independence) and the case of Egypt (which has been inscribed in a logic of multilateral exploitation of the country's rich cultural resources by several Western nations), whose cultural heritage are both present in the public French collections, result from very different contexts of appropriation and therefore imply legislative contexts very different than the cases concerning sub-Saharan Africa. These cases should be the object of a more specific reflection and mission.[89]

A second report commissioned by President Macron was released on January 29, 2021: *Les questions mémorielles portant sur la colonisation et la guerre d'Algérie*. It departs from the precisions of the Sarr-Savoy inventory of artifacts instead seeking to reconcile memories between France and Algeria.[90]

Benyahia's museum collection must also rescue and repurpose some vestiges to account for anti-colonial Algerian removals and destruction of everything with French ties. He also proposes that Constantine's Orientalist paintings be housed in this museum, including Gustave Guillamet's *La famine en Algérie*, which was restored as a condition of its loan to a Guillamet exhibition in Bordeaux. The copy of a Horace Vernet painting *La Prise de Constantine* (*The Taking of Constantine*) still molders in the Cirta Museum's storage. In 1962, when Benyahia was director of Constantine's Municipal École des Beaux-Arts, he salvaged the large canvas that was displayed in the municipal buildings from Larbi Berredjem's order to destroy colonial artwork. The original is in the Salle de Constantine of the Château de Versailles in a room that was part of Louis-Philippe's plan, between 1837 and 1847, for a museum of French history commemorating the conquest of Algeria in a decorative, iconographic program.

Benyahia includes his own recent artworks that represent events from the colonial past. His grouping from a 2015 installation, the year Constantine was featured as the capital of Arab culture, takes as its subject the experience of Algerians imprisoned during the colonial period including those guillotined up to the year 1962. He has a vast archive of proposals for monuments and sculptures that were never actualized: for the Port of Algiers, a sculptural homage to the Battle of Algiers and the fourth forgotten martyr Mohamed Bouhamidi; at Sidi Fredj, where the French first landed in Algeria in 1830, he conjured a monument in homage to l'Étoile Nord Africaine, an early Algerian nationalist organization established in 1926. In his new sculpture and fierce acts of conservation, he remains rooted in his understanding of the complex meanings of colonial architecture and urban planning. His emotions about the senseless postindependence losses of the demolished casino and gardens draw inspiration from Les Esses, among other sources. He explained this to me during a trip we took together around the city. For Benyahia, linkages between love and settler colonialism are found in concrete matter. He notes that the role of emotions rather than measures for material restitution surely accounted for thematic repetitions of "settler love" in President Macron's pronouncement during his visit to Algeria in the summer of 2022 that the relationship between the two countries was *une histoire d'amour* (a history of love).[91]

LES ESSES: MORE SETTLER LOVE

"Les Esses" are spectacularly beautiful and functional passageways of exposed zigzagging stairs backed by steep walls. French engineers built many such dramatic staircases and switchbacks to traverse Constantine's sheer rocky sides. The ramps of Les Esses connect the city's upper Place de la Pyramide, refurbished by Benyahia, to the Avenue Aouati Mustapha (formerly La Rampe d'Italie), popularly known as Triq Sétif, the road to Sétif. Pedestrians walk, move about quickly, reach neighborhoods and each other climbing the steep straight stairs at the side or strolling along the gentle incline of the central ramp ways.[92] Both paths descend to the lower avenue, another urban balcony-like promenade offering breathtaking panoramas of the valley below (figure 110).

Two granite pyramid reliefs emerge from the high wall at a pedestrian

FIGURE 110. "Les Esses," Constantine. Photo by author, June 15, 2022.

resting spot in the middle of Les Esses, which lie directly below the Place de la Pyramide where General Damrémont fell in battle. The general's statue has been replaced by the obelisk and Benyahia's arrangement of four cannons. In June 2022, as we drove on the Triq Sétif passing alongside Les Esses, Benyahia commented, "The French really loved Constantine." He expanded on his phrase *amour colonial,* articulated in the Algerian saying "ils aiment l'Algérie sans les Algériens" (they love Algeria without Algerians), which I extrapolated to "settler love":

> Constantine does not leave you indifferent. Human beings, no matter how evil, when faced with something strong, magical, surprising like this place, compose buildings and structures in admiration of the natural site. The last conquerors, the French military, were defeated once and knew that if they did not vanquish the Constantine Beylik, the whole colonial enterprise would fail. Once they took possession, the French did everything to reduce the "rock" as an impregnable fortress and create an ensemble that would cut through the city, penetrate, wipe out resistance and connect it to the surrounding region with roads, traffic circles, and bridges for vehicles and passageways, staircases, footbridges and arcades for pedestrians. They did it for themselves, not for us, as if they were building their own country.[93]

Constantine has been continuously inhabited for at least two millennia. At 2,100 feet above sea level, it is a natural fortress city called the eagle's nest, the city of bridges, the old rock, and "city of air," or "city of love," if punned.[94] The spectacular site is a high flat-topped rock of limestone, roughly diamond-shaped, rising on three sides from the deep-sided ravines and steep gorges of the Rhummel River. Settler love meant domination and power over the gorges and ravines, and internally straightening out the labyrinthine medina. Indigenous inhabitants lived in the native quarters while a new European city extended beyond Constantine's natural site, an efficient strategy to ensure the settler colonial "non-encounter," or "the disavowal of both a founding violence and of indigenous presences."[95] These new colonial neighborhoods arose beyond the confines of the rock because settlers were there to transform the colony into their home.[96]

Settler love was lethal to the native. However, Benyahia believes that it must be remembered and acknowledged: memory emancipates because to maintain some symbols of colonial violence is to attribute humanity to the departing colonizers. His proposed conversion of a prison is "not a site of repentance or pardon, but a place of non-forgetting" (le musée n'est pas un lieu de repentance ou de pardon, mais un lieu de non-oubli).

When possible, part of the prison's beauty would be selectively preserved and acknowledged. For Benyahia, Algeria's postindependent possibilities for decolonizing public art must be rooted in real and lasting relationships with on-the-ground sculptural practices. For example, he could reimagine former emancipation struggles and express visually his solidarity with the dispossessed when he melted a French colonial war memorial to make a statue of a heroic Algerian fighter. As he tells it, he seeks to memorialize and bear witness visually to the historical embeddedness of genocidal colonial violence, the erased Algerian dead of two wars, and French Algeria's neocolonial ideologies.[97] Since French war memorials in Algeria included the French infantryman *poilu* often to represent colonial troops, his depictions are mindful of absent Algerian troops. Like many artists affected by Algerian revolutionary social reform and interested in French avant-garde art forms (installations, New Realism sculpture, Situationist *détournements*), Benyahia has always sought to use art to change minds, to be significant, to reimagine French destruction and harmoniously repurpose colonial buildings. This is his form of decolonizing art (elsewhere termed "decolonial aesthesis"), "at once the unveiling of the wound and the possibility of healing."[98] It gives him space to contemplate Constantine's makeover as a French colonial city while fighting ill-conceived postindependence transformations and depredations.

CONCLUSION

SETTLER REMAINS

FRENCH COLONIAL MONUMENTS ARE BROUGHT down in Algeria by actors with wildly opposing motives. On the French side, the army and engineering corps, the Catholic Church, and the departing European population bring what they think is theirs with them. In 1962, at the end of French Algeria, many statues and sections of statues were displaced and smuggled from Algeria to France. Since Algerian independence, claims and counterclaims have been made about ownership, provenance, and implantation of colonial monuments. Accusations have erupted about presumed or actual Algerian destructions that in turn confront the reality of French monument theft. Rarely has settler colonial memory embodied in monument removal been understood in terms of producing and reproducing colonial domination and reappropriation to the metropole.

In this book, I have never explicitly addressed why so much effort was expended by the French army, the European settlers, and the Catholic Church to "repatriate" their monuments. Individual settlers display their fierce psychological investment in remaking parts of their former colonial world in France, which obscures how European settler colonialism remains obscure to European settlers, and yet drives them. They told me that it was "because the monument is ours, it is French, we made it, and we're taking it back." These histories of monuments contribute to explaining a particular case of settler colonialism: that of the "returned" settlers of Algeria, a collective that benefited from the particular French law of return and repatriation, a law that gave them instant citizenship and property rights in a land they had often never visited. While bringing with them the statues and artifacts from an unnamable "over there" (*là-bas*), repatriates of Algeria in France evoke their nostalgeria—the traumatic loss of an Algerian homeland that most have refused to revisit.

Freud offers insight when he explains London's numerous monuments as conscious, neurotic symptoms of trauma; the capital city of the empire cannot let go:

> The monuments and memorials with which large cities are adorned are also mnemonic symbols. If you take a walk through the streets of London, you will find, in front of one of the great railway termini, a richly carved Gothic column—Charing Cross. One of the old Plantagenet kings of the thirteenth century ordered the body of his beloved Queen Eleanor to be carried to Westminster; and at every stage at which the coffin rested he erected a Gothic cross. Charing Cross is the last of the monuments that commemorate the funeral cortège. At another point in the same town, not far from London Bridge, you will find a towering, and more modern, column, which is simply known as "The Monument." It was designed as a memorial of the Great Fire, which broke out in that neighbourhood in 1666 and destroyed a large part of the city. These monuments, then, resemble the hysterical symptoms in being mnemic symbols; up to that point the comparison seems justifiable. But what should we think of a Londoner who sheds tears before the Monument that commemorates the reduction of his beloved metropolis to ashes although it has long since risen again in far greater brilliance? Yet every single hysteric and neurotic behaves like these two unpractical Londoners. Not only do they remember painful experiences of the remote past, but they still cling to them emotionally; they cannot get free of the past and for its sake they neglect what is real and immediate. This fixation of mental life to pathogenic traumas is one of the most significant and practically important characteristics of neurosis.[1]

European imperial capitals reflect a lost colony through statuary. Europeans in the colony rarely saw the Muslim majority population. Oral histories and memories of the French era note the invisibility of Algerian Muslims where Europeans dominated in colonial towns such as Oran. Sociologist André Akoun remembered his native Oran as a French town and Muslims as "inconsequential shadows." On a return visit in 1963, he wondered:

> "Where did they come from all these girls and boys . . . Were they from Oran? And, if so, where were they? Where had they been hidden?" The Oran he grew up in and remembers was "a French town through and through," in which Muslims were "inconsequential shadows," limited to a few women

> dressed in long white robes, their faces veiled and thus inscrutable, sometimes an old Arab in turban and gandoura, or the gangs of smiling Arab children who offered to shine your shoes.[2]

It was easy to take from those that one could not see, to become the owners in charge, to not see the new owners in charge. After many statues and monuments were illegally transported to France, they were seen as part of French Algeria's specific patrimony, an assertion of a settler community's distinct sovereign prerogative as Pieds-Noirs in France. Thus, settler collectives were constituted or reconstituted in displacements going in both directions: from the French metropole to the Algerian colony under the empire *and* back to the metropole from the colony after its independence.

The tenacity of repatriates to recuperate and display publicly a colonial French monument from Algeria is reflected by the most recently retrieved statue, that of Jerome Bertagna (1843–1903), sculpted by François-Léon Sicard (1862–1934). Bertagna was the colonial mayor of the eastern Algerian port city of Bône (now Annaba). His statue was inaugurated in 1907 and removed by the French army at Algerian independence. Minus its tall ornate pediment of an Algerian girl proffering a cornucopia of fruits and a young sailor in his skiff, the Bertagna statue was relocated to the Bertagna's Beaujolais wine domains in Burgundy. When the last Bertagna descendant died in the twenty-first century, the statue was donated and again moved at the behest of a Pied-Noir hometown association of repatriates from Bertagna's city of Bône (L'amicale des enfants de Bône). By 2019, funds were raised to transport and erect it in Aix-en-Provence in the courtyard of the Centre de documentation historique sur l'Algérie (CDHA), the Pied-Noir documentation center, library, and museum.[3] The by-now familiar process of French statue removal was complemented by an Algerian replacement memorial to the combatant-martyrs of Annaba who died in the war of independence.

On the Algerian side, the disappearances of statues or the remains of war memorials in Algeria were attributable to France and to Algeria whose disassembly and modifications sometimes implicated the Algerian state, the municipality, and the participation of well-known artists. Early iconoclastic acts by individuals and the state after 1962 resumed during the Dark Decade of the 1990s. Targeting statues for destruction, defacement, or removal is a highly performative act and one way to manage a difficult heritage. Then, the state and local associations defended French monuments and promoted new Algerian ones. Monuments in Algeria have differential rates of survival and creation even if they are not living organisms. They are metaphors in many ways. They celebrate an individual—for particular acts or events at a particular moment in time with particular stakes for specific balances of power—whose name is set in stone as if its story were forever cast. They celebrate events that have changed lives, usually by taking them. Once in place, a monument orders the world around it until that world changes and another story must be told, one statue destroyed and another erected.

In this book, these monuments have provided a lens on European settler spaces in Algeria, on colonizing power, destruction and preservation, on patrimony and presumed ownership, on memory and history writing. The French colonial monuments that remain standing in Algeria today often elicit care, memory, and community or state decision-making to preserve and repurpose. At play as well are the productive roles of destruction and replacement by another statue. Since 1962, Algerians have reflected on their French monumental heritage and how to decolonize it. The country adapted the material objects and institutions of colonial France to its needs by repurposing sculpture and monuments in a generative confrontation with European art.[4]

Many scholars address this knot of French-Algerian artistic influences and cross-cultural exchanges and contacts. Some like Fanon, in his essay "On National Culture," insist on looking to "the native intellectual who wishes to create an authentic work of art and must realize that the truths of a nation are in the first place its realities. He must go on until he has found the seething pot out of which the learning of the future will emerge."[5] Writer Abdelkebir Khatibi argues for a plural Maghreb (*Maghreb pluriel*) in which hybrid cultural spaces are mediated through a "third tongue" (*une langue tierce*) aware of the perspective of the Other.[6] Art historian François Pouillon notes Algerian receptivity to the art of the "colonizer Other" and suggests that Algerian art and art historical processes are attentive to "complicities," to the "internal fissures and the interaction processes that are part and parcel of all relations, including those between dominating and dominated." He goes on to say,

> that complicities do exist between them [is] the ransom to be paid for a history that is never truly heroic. . . . To put it another way, rather than considering the tautological art of identity lost and regained, we would instead be attending to real spaces filled with relational knots that are always difficult to untangle and that in any case cannot be reduced to a confrontation between self and other, past and present.[7]

Art historian Nadira Laggoune-Aklouche considers "appropriations, transfers, borrowings and graft" constitutive of postcolonial Algerian art, a "dialectic about identity and alterity."[8] Similarly, Virginie Rey describes as a catachresis when postcolonial Tunisians knowingly borrow, mix, and misuse Western concepts and models to achieve self-determination and reconceptualize the independent Tunisian self.[9]

French-Algerian aesthetic entanglements have been described in many ways.[10] French sociologist Pierre Bourdieu and Algerian sociologist Abdelmalek Sayad reflected on the cultural "sabir": "the alienating hybridity of those caught between two worlds condemned . . . to interferences and incoherences"; and draw on linguistic analogies of cultural infiltration derived from the lingua franca Mediterranean ports *sabir* language of North Africa.[11] For historian David Prochaska, state practices of replacement, repurposing, and recreation of war memorials to memorialize Algerian independence on the same site where a French statue once stood speak to a "clear-cut case of a cultural pattern which has been transferred to a different social and historical context and filled with a different but analogous content."[12] Other scholars point to mimesis, transvaluation, sedimentation, and appropriation with colonial monuments as found objects, "*objets trouvés* of the postcolony."[13] Andreas Huyssen finds the "memory art" of the Global South penetrated and transfixed by visual traces of political violence and trauma to produce a hybrid temporality that acts on and is animated by viewers.[14] Paul Basu's terms new postindependence monuments erected in Sierra Leone, a former British crown colony, "palimpsest memoryscapes" and the "postcolonial pastiche," in which "pastiche" is a "collage" never a postmodern mimesis or an act of "shallow imitation, forgery and travesty."[15] To concepts of doubling cultural patterns and their mirror images by the formerly colonized, anthropologist Anne Stoler modulates with analyses of "resilience" and "recursion":

> It's not that the postcolonial world mimics colonial norms, structures, and relations. We need to ask what forms are resilient. Are they embedded in habits of privilege or in those of acquiescence? Are they found in what is perceived as humiliation or in what counts as duress? What conditions the possibility of some elements becoming available and not others? I think of recursivity as refoldings that expose different (social) surfaces and historical planes. Recursion is neither a faithful copy nor a direct "translation" . . . Recursive histories include reworkings that neither look or feel quite the same.[16]

Each thinker has in mind new forms of thinking about art by mastering, assimilating, recombining, transforming, negotiating, absorbing, borrowing, and perhaps mimicking rather than rejecting. A sort of cross-pollinating *métissage*—the preferred term of Francophone Martinican writer Edouard Glissant—seizes material and symbolic contents, forms, and mechanisms of colonial violence. Many inherited French forms—and Algeria offers more examples than any other former French colony—have been adapted to Algeria in myriad ways. In a sense, if French colonial monuments in Algeria stood for the vast spatial appropriation by the colonizers that restrained the Algerian natives to the margins of the settler colony, they also generated something new: agency and creativity by the formerly colonized. Philosopher Bernard Stiegler calls this phenomenon the *pharmakon*, the pharmacological antithesis that demonstrates that each poison creates its own cure.[17] Statues and monuments became so powerfully omnipresent, so much part of an Algerian lived experience of place and environment that the formerly colonized could refashion these imperial objects for and by themselves for decolonizing ends.

The Algerian people sometimes formed an intimate connection with a French statue or a war memorial. In effect, the history of Algerian conscription and army service during two world wars are reflected in attachments to France's war memorials on the Algerian landscape which still evoke both national and local, colonial and postcolonial emotions on both sides. This complication involves counterintuitive perspectives about monument-making in postindependent Algeria. Public art and sculptures make tangible and visible the shift from colonial French presence to Algerian monument-making.[18] Generated from, and generative of, Algerian cultural decolonizing projects regarding French imperialism and colonialism, public art projects often add something to the experience of the present by never ignoring the past violence. Algerian decolonizing projects address the control over the redistribution of aesthetic resources in the same spaces, as defined by Lorenzo Veracini. His description is applicable to the vast heritage of the former colonial overseers: "Decolonisation also means committing to emplaced transformation—to changing the way we live without moving."[19]

Kouider Metair, an Algerian heritage worker, who founded Oran's preservation society of Bel Horizon in 2001, promotes the notion of a shared French-Algerian past (*patrimoine partagé*) in preservation projects.[20] The colonial war memorial in Algeria is no longer a provocation. Instead, Algerian state preservation projects of colonial art and architecture, according to architects Habib Benkoula and Larbi Marhoum, are synecdochic eruptions of Algerian nostalgia embedded in selective colonial-era built environments but are never to be equated with calls for a return to colonialism:

> The elite . . . wants to safeguard a European setting, a piece of colonization, while standing up as a block against colonization and its criminal character. Also, nostalgia for a European toponymy marks the spirits. Even sixty years after independence, the urban territory of the social imagination remains European and is taken as a reference. Many older people value themselves over Europeans they knew at "the time," if only to show their superiority over those who were not yet there. This shows the complexity of the definition of heritage in the case of the European territories of Algeria. The elite who defends this universal heritage cannot, in my opinion, see how the population that lives there does not feel concerned by the history it embodies.[21]

Ahmed Benyahia is emblematic of such a transformative process, creatively embracing the urge to seize and build upon materials from earlier violence, a sculptural equivalent of Fanon's understanding about which forms of violence could restore the humanity of the colonized. The colonial patrimony is an anticolonial resource. The conjuncture of artistic subjectivity and cross-fertilization between Algeria and France is striking in Benyahia's oil painting of an iconic French monument on the cover of this book. Napoleon's Arc de Triomphe in Paris incited Ahmed Benyahia's 1973 painting, which he repainted in 2013. Rows of gravestones flank a darkened road leading to the arch. His rendering refers to the Vichy era in France and in Algeria, a brutal epoch when colonialism met fascism during World War II: the Vel D'Hiv roundup of French Jews in Paris; the Nazi concentration camps of Dachau and Auschwitz; the graves of Algerian soldiers who died as cannon fodder defending France; and the French massacres in Guelma, Sétif, and Kherrata of May 8, 1945. The painting names the sites of Holocaust atrocities and commemorates colonial slaughter. In the space below the central archway of the triumphant arch, a cornucopia of types, iconic figures, and forms explodes in an homage to Che Guevara, to the French Resistance hero Jean Moulin, to the Algerian leader the Emir Abdelkader, to Gandhi, and to Mandela, who are tossed skyward where they are resized, reassembled, and brought into focus. Benyahia's cartoonish version of the French female standard bearer echoes the painting *Liberty Leading the People* (*La liberté guidant le peuple*) by Eugène Delacroix (1798–1863), completed in the fall of 1830, just months after France invaded Algiers. Delacroix's allegorical Liberty is shown emancipating her people by overthrowing the Bourbon monarchy of Charles X, but she also advances an imperial ideology that encompasses France's Algerian conquests of 1830.[22]

Benyahia's painterly commentary on Delacroix evolved over a period of forty years. He completed the first version while an art student in Paris in 1973. He learned from his mentor, the artist César Baldaccini about twentieth-century aesthetic impacts in which "starting over is not repeating." César asked, "Where do we contemporary sculptors come from? We come from Dada, we come from Duchamp, from the surrealists. No-one ever invented anything alone. We are each other's heirs."[23] Benyahia revisited his 1973 painting in 2013 when he was back home in Constantine. He painted over sections he deemed garish, muting vibrant reds with darker, more solemn crimsons while retaining a smooth surface. Both versions are inspired juxtapositions and amalgamations of monumental architecture of the Arc de Triomphe in France with Algeria's Arch of Trajan in Timgad and Constantine's war memorial arch. All of these iconic, majestic artifacts resonate powerfully in Algeria and France. His title draws from the famous inscription on the Pantheon façade, *Aux grands hommes la patrie reconnaissant* (To great men, the homeland is grateful) and changes it to *Aux libérateurs l'humanité reconnaissante* (To the liberators, humanity is grateful). This rewritten title is another in a long line of Situationist *détournements* that Benyahia uses, and it echoes the Situationist attack on titles and entitlement:

> The only historically justified tactic is extremist innovation. The literary and artistic heritage of humanity should be used for partisan propaganda purposes. It is, of course, necessary to go beyond any idea of scandal. Since opposition to the bourgeois notion of art and artistic genius has become pretty much old hat, [Duchamp's] drawing a mustache on the *Mona Lisa* is no more interesting than the original version of that painting. We must now push this process to the point of negating the negation. . . . Titles themselves, as we have already seen, are a basic element of *détournement*. This follows from two general observations: that all titles are interchangeable and that they have a decisive importance in several genres.[24]

The Situationist *détournements* in Benyahia's title highlight the gaping losses left by generations of Algerian war dead unacknowledged as liberators. Nor are they alone in the picture. His iconography is rich and evocative of communities of memory made multidirectionally salient following Michael Rothberg's approach to multiply, rather than selectively erase, inherited historical traumas. As if describing Benyahia's painting, Rothberg writes, "Contact—and even their conflict—produces more memory, not less. Memories—especially publicly articulated memories—echo each other, appropriate each other's forms and figures, and develop in dialogue with each other."[25] Benyahia's topics overlap and feed into each other yet resist easy syntheses in his attempt to incorporate French Algeria into a history of Algeria's present decolonization.

Algeria's place in settler colonial theory by virtue of decolonization seems to offer closure in settler colonial studies because the country presents a self-contained, neatly bracketed evolution from its 1830 colonization to its 1962 decolonization. Since the Algerian Revolution first defined itself by anti-colonialism, the emergence of newer Algerian sensitivities attests to a transition: colonialism ceases to be the foundation of the state (even if negatively) and becomes one part of a complex patrimony to be used, repurposed, mobilized, valorized, and reclaimed. When viewed through the lens of a reproducible transcultural memory and shared heritage on both sides of the Mediterranean, the presence of Algerian memories about France's places, beliefs, and ceremonial occasions, while saturated with painful violence and nostalgia, underscore how settler colonialism might end in the former colony. A post-settler passage into something else may be happening in Algeria, not in France.

ACKNOWLEDGMENTS

I first visited Algeria in the spring of 1990 as a conference participant invited by the current Centre national de recherches préhistoriques anthropologiques et historiques d'Alger (CNRPAH), thanks to then director, anthropologist Ahmed Benaoum. He encouraged me to begin my research project "Algérie Ailleurs" ("Algeria Elsewhere"), a study of two recreated pilgrimages in France by Oran Province's European Catholic settlers and native Algerian Jews, and he sent me to western Algeria. I am profoundly grateful for his generous introductions to colleagues, such as Mourad Yelles and Hadj Miliani, to what became the Centre de recherche en Anthropologie Sociale et Culturelle (CRASC) in Oran. Many more colleagues, such as Lamice El-Amari and Rachida Hasseni at the University of Oran Es-Senia's Institute of Translation gave me a welcoming home. Between 1990 and 1992, I received more grants to Algeria from the American Institute of Maghrib Studies (AIMS) and the American Philosophical Society (APS). During my first fieldwork period from 1990 to 1992, I am most grateful to have known Pierre Claverie (1938–1996), Bishop of Oran, whose counsel and presence continue to inspire me.

My heartfelt thanks to Robert Parks, Director, and Karim Ouaras, Associate Director of the Centre d'Études Maghrébines en Algérie (CEMA) in Oran, Algeria. In addition to his role as Warden of the West for Americans in Algeria, Bobby Parks has made CEMA my research base since he began serving as its founding director in 2006. There, he has given me an audience to present stages of my fieldwork, for example, on the Oran-Lyon war memorial on May 27, 2014, at a lecture jointly cosponsored by CRASC, and again by his organizing the AIMS-CEMA 2017 conference on historical preservation in North Africa. I am forever grateful for his friendship. My deepest gratitude goes to Kouider Metair and his remarkable group of heritage activists and advocates at the Association Belhorizon Oran for advice, feedback, support, urban tours, and access to their substantial visual archive.

The Collegium de Lyon residency of 2013–2014 supported my year of fieldwork in Lyon and a spring 2014 trip to Algeria. In Lyon, I thank Frédéric Abécassis from ENS-Lyon, and the librarians and archivists at Lyon's Municipal Archives. Émile Azoulay, Germaine Fabricatore, as well as Luc Demarchi and the members of the Cercle Algérianiste de Lyon were always available for research, interviews, books, and photographs.

For their company during numerous field trips over decades throughout Algeria as well as their knowledge of architecture, history, and heritage, I have been expertly mentored by Sidi Mohamed El Habib Benkoula, Robert Doisy, Abdelkader Ghalem-Sardi, Amine Kasmi, Abdennebi Mebtoul, Kouider Metair, Yassine Ouagueni, Karim Ouaras, Karim Ouldennebbia, Robert Parks, and Djelloul Talha. Donál Hassett remains a generous guide to the Archives of the Wilaya d'Oran and the history of the city.

Additional funding and research to Algeria were supported by the Fondation IMéRA, Aix-Marseille University under the directorship of Thierry Fabre during a fall semester 2019 residency in Marseille. IMéRA's vibrant intellectual atmosphere and weekly meetings guided by Thierry inspired my writing and research. My thanks to my UCLA colleague Aomar Boum for his friendship and constant support, most recently through the Maurice Amado Chair funds that helped support my fieldwork to Constantine in May/June 2022. UCLA's Faculty Research Grants (FRG) enabled more research visits to France and Algeria between 2017 and 2023. Additional generous UCLA book subventions came from the Renée and David Kaplan Fund of the Division of the Humanities thanks to support from UCLA's Department of Near Eastern Languages and Cultures ably chaired by Katherine Cooney as well as a second book subvention from the Center for European and Russian Studies (CERS) under the directorship of Laurie Kain Hart. I gratefully acknowledge the assistance of the Graham Foundation for the Arts for their substantial book subvention. I thank the Council on American Overseas Research Centers (CAORC) for awarding me a six-month CAORC-NEH fellowship to Algeria 2023–2024 that allowed me to complete this book.

In Constantine, I remain deeply grateful to Ahmed Benyahia and his extended family: to Rachida, Hichem, Arris, and Racim for their warm welcome and enduring friendship; to Arris and Racim Benyahia for sharing their photographs and computer art expertise; to Abderrezak Benyahia for permissions to his photo archive. I thank Hichem Benyahia for numerous critical readings, bibliographical items, and edits as well as his translations of my work into Arabic and French for further vetting (see his Arabic and French translations of my Yale lecture available on Facebook: https://www.facebook.com/benyahia.ahmed.94/videos/137191938589050). Most of all, I am grateful for the friendship of Ahmed Benyahia, who opened his home and personal archives. He is a constant inspiration and touchstone for our future projects. Also in Constantine, Hosni Kitouni, Monji Farid, and Yousra Salem were wonderful interlocutors. Natalya Vince and Walid Benkhaled generously commented and provided permission to reproduce materials from their videotaped interview with Ahmed Benyahia. Billel Benguedouar and Haroun Nemouchi expertly guided my research trips throughout the greater Constantine region. I thank them for their friendship, photographs, and intrepid navigation skills.

For multiple readings of the entire manuscript, I am indebted to Nadjib Berber, Zeynep Çelik, Mia Fuller, and Lorenzo Veracini. Deborah Glassman is my most valued critic, commenting on every page with her boundless encouragement, more edits, and rereadings. I thank Asma Sayeed for our joint Zoom writing "retreats" during the pandemic and her enthusiasm for the project. Additional thoughtful comments are by Ceren Abi, Can Açiksöz, Lahouari Addi, Marc André, Lamia Balafrej, Ali Behdad, Saddek Benkada, Habib Benkoula, Ahmed Benyahia, Hichem Benyahia, Rachida Benyahia, Chafika Berber, Anissa Bouayed, Aomar Boum, Sung-Eun Choi, Laryssa Chomiak, Daniel E. Coslett, Muriam Haleh Davis, Robert Doisy, Brahim El Guabli, Laurie Kain Hart, Jean Jackson, Idriss Jebari, Atika Mekki, Kouider Metair, Menouar Mrabtene ("Slim"), Jacob Mundy, Robert Parks, Gabrile Piterberg, Susan Ossman, Kashia Pierprzak, Jonah Flanagan Radding, Thomas Serres, Aparna Sharma, and Sarah Abrevaya Stein. Kate Wahl, Stanford University Press editor, offered extensive support, critical edits, and constant encouragement along with the Stanford series editors, Emily Benichou Gottreich and Daniel Zoghbie. With her able SUP staff, Kate Wahl guided this volume to publication. I thank my niece Farah Berber for transcribing interviews in French and Arabic, and Nadjib Berber, Skandar Berber, Aomar Boum, and Sevan Madadian for their talented computer skills with the book's images.

Portions of this text have been presented at several conferences. Editors such as David E. Kim, Mildred Mortimer, Valentina Rozas-Krause, Andrew Shanken, and Paul Silverstein provided illuminating feedback on early versions: parts of chapter 3 were published in the *Journal of North African Studies* (affiliated with the American Institute for Maghrib Studies), appearing in volume 25, number 5 (2020) as "Dismantling a World: France's Monumental Military Heritage in Sidi-Bel-Abbès, Algeria." Sections of chapter 4 appeared as "On the Wings of the Gallic Cockerel: Ahmed Benyahia and the Provenance of an Algerian Public Sculpture" in *Reframing Postcolonial Studies: Concepts—Methodologies—Scholarly Activisms,* edited by David D. Kim (London, Palgrave MacMillan, 2021), pp. 69–92. I thank both editors and publishers for permission to reprint selections.

I am grateful to Geneviève Appert-Sarrabezolles and the Sarrabezolles Foundation in Paris for opening the archives dedicated to her father, the sculptor Carlos Sarrabezolles including permissions granted to reproduce photos, documentation, and postcards. As a collector of postcards, I have made every effort to identify copyright holders and obtain permissions for the postcards in this publication. Many colonial postcards are out of copyright, or their current rights holders are unknown, or pirated images reprinted without attribution are available for online sales. Many postcard companies in French Algeria went out of business at Algerian independence in 1962, such as Éditions Alexander Sirecky (EAS of Oran), or were taken over by Algerians, such as Éditions Jomone, and rights holders to the colonial archive cannot be determined or are in dispute. Any rights holders who believe that illustrations have been reproduced without their knowledge are asked to contact the author. Notification of any additions or corrections that should be incorporated in future reprints or editions of this book would be greatly appreciated. Permission to use photographs and artwork is included in footnotes and captions. Unless otherwise noted, translations, postcards, and photographs are mine.

Finally, I extend my deepest gratitude and love to my in-laws and extended family—the Berber, Kahouadji, Tazi, Benyelles, and Hamdan families—for their boundless warmth and hospitality, promenades along the Oran corniche and the hills above Tlemcen, spectacular feasts and holiday gatherings, and endless food and care packages. I dedicate this book to my beloved husband Nadjib Berber (1952–2023).

NOTES

Introduction: Monuments After All

1. For the lyrics, music, and rise and fall of performances, see *Le Chant des Africains*, https://www.histoiredefrance-chansons.com/index.php?param1=MI0110.php.

2. Edward Gibbon, *Memoirs of My Life* (Hartnolls, UK: Ryburn Publications, [1796] 1994), 170. Quoted in Susan Stewart, *The Ruins Lesson* (Chicago: University of Chicago Press, 2020), 20.

3. I borrow "monuments after all" from Georges Didi-Huberman's title *Images malgré tout* (Paris: Minuit, 2003), on behalf of documenting the victim even through photography. His notion of *survivance* infuses my work to point to "the indestructibility of an imprint of time on our present life" alongside "the change of status, changing of meaning" (56, 59).

4. On French veteran commemorations, see Rémi Dalisson, *En mémoire du 11 novembre: Vie et mort d'une fête nationale des origines à nos jours* (Paris: Armand Colin, 2013); and Antoine Prost, *Les anciens combattants* (Paris: Gallimard, 1977).

5. The call for an anthropology of art for the MENA region is by Kirsten Scheid, "Start with Art: New Ways of Understanding the Political in the Middle East," in *Handbook for Political Science in the Middle East*, ed. Larbi Sadki (New York: Routledge, 2022), 432–444. Social approaches about art were espoused by Clifford Geertz, "Art as a Cultural System," *Modern Language Notes* 91 no. 6 (1976): 1473–1499. The role of colonialism in the creation of local art is beautifully analyzed in Hildred Geertz, *The Life of a Balinese Temple: Artistry, Imagination, and History in a Peasant Village* (Honolulu: University of Hawaii Press, 2004).

6. Eric Forcada, "Le monument de Sidi Ferruch d'Émile Gaudissard: Oeuvre de mémoires, mémoires d'une oeuvre (1830–2012)," *Mirmanda: Revista de cultura* 7

(2012): 78–88. A large scholarship exists on France's "mission to civilize" in Algeria including Osama W. AbiMershed, *Apostles of Modernity: Saint-Simonians and the Civilizing Mission in Algeria* (Stanford, CA: Stanford University Press, 2010); and Alice L. Conklin, *A Mission to Civilize: The Republican Idea of Empire in France and West Africa, 1895–1930* (Stanford, CA: Stanford University Press, 1997).

7. For witness testimony on the French army's monument removal on July 5, 1962, see Jean Puissegur, "Mémorial Sidi Ferruch," *Commando Guillaume* (blog), http://www.commandoguillaume.com/html/fra/page-42.html. For photographs of the Sidi-Ferruch monument and museum complex currently in France, see Fiona Barclay, "The Sidi-Ferruch Monument Revisited," August 30, 2022, https://www.pieds-noirs.stir.ac.uk/sidi-ferruch-revisited/.

8. Jérôme Duhamel and Réné Pétillon, *Grand inventaire du génie français en 365 objets* (Paris: Albin Michel, 1992), 196: "Between 1919 and 1925, a war memorial was erected in every community in France, with one exception: the village of Thierville in the department of the Eure, the only French village which had no dead to mourn, either in 1870 or in [19]14–18, nor in [19]39–45."

9. The literature is vast, but key texts recurring in this study are Maurice Agulhon, "La 'statuomanie' et l'histoire," *Ethnologie française*, 8, no. 2/3, (1978): 145–172; and June Hargrove, *The Statues of Paris: An Open-Air Pantheon* (Paris: Vendôme Press, 1990). For French statuomania in Algeria, see Jan C. Jansen, *Erobern und Erinnern. Symbolpolitik, öffentlicher Raum und französischer Kolonialismus in Algerien, 1830–1950* (Munich: Oldenbourg, 2013); and for postindependent Algerian statuomania, see Jan C. Jansen, "1880–1914; une statuomanie à l'algérienne," in *Histoire de l'Algérie à la période colonial: (1830—1962)*, ed. Abderrahmane Bouchène (Paris: Découverte, 2012), 261–265; Raphaëlle Branche, "The Martyr's Torch: Memory and Power in Algeria," *Journal of North African Studies* 16 (2011): 431–443; Emmanuel Alcaraz, *Les lieux de mémoire de la guerre d'indépendance algérienne* (Paris: Karthala, 2017); and Amar Mohand-Amer, "Les monuments aux martyrs en Algérie," in *Dictionnaire de la guerre d'Algérie*, ed. Tramor Quemeneur, Ouanassa Siari-Tengour, and Sylvie Thénault, 831–832 (Paris: Éditions Bouquins, 2023).

10. Peter Edwards, "'*Mort pour la France*': Conflict and Commemoration in France after the First World War," *Journal of Contemporary History* 1 (2000): 1–11: "The British ruled out repatriating their dead because of expense and prohibited individuals bringing bodies home for reasons of equality. The Americans had promised to bring home their dead if requested and 70 percent were repatriated. Conversely Germany was 'in no position' to exhume its dead from the areas it had occupied. However, the fact that the majority of the French dead had fallen on, and were buried in, their home soil raised other issues" (3). On names and absences, see Thomas W. Laqueur, *The Work of the Dead: A Cultural History of Mortal Remains* (Princeton, NJ: Princeton University Press, 2015), 417; Daniel J. Sherman, "Bodies and Names: The Emergence of Commemoration in Interwar France," *American*

Historical Review 103 (1998): 443–466; and Daniel J. Sherman, *The Construction of Memory in Interwar France* (Chicago: University of Chicago Press, 1999).

11. In Cara A. Finnegan, *Making Photography Matter: A Viewer's History from the Civil War to the Great Depression* (Urbana: University of Illinois Press, 2015), 131–132; she highlights viewer agency.

12. In Arthur Asseraf, *Electric News in Colonial Algeria* (Oxford: Oxford University Press, 2019), 41–42; he notes that the colonial surveillance system regulated publishers but not the viewing public. Nicholas Mirzoeff's term is "visuality," the sum of circulating images, or in this case French colonial ideas and information, against which he proposes a decolonial "right to look," a crucial historical moment for Algeria's production of monuments, see Nicholas Mirzoeff, *The Right to Look: A Counterhistory of Visuality* (Durham, NC: Duke University Press, 2011), 1–34.

13. Throughout the text, I draw on scholarship by Antoine Prost, "The Algerian War in French Collective Memory," in *War and Remembrance in the Twentieth Century*, ed. Jay Winter and Emmanuel Sivan (Cambridge: Cambridge University Press, 1999), 161–176; Annette Becker, *Les monuments aux morts: Patrimoine et mémoire de la Grande Guerre* (Paris: Éditions Errance, 1988); and Henry Rousso, *Face au passé: Essais sur la mémoire contemporaine* (Paris: Éditions Belin, 2016).

14. For the English translation of the Évian Accords, see "Algeria: France-Algeria Independence Agreements (Evian agreements)," *International Legal Materials* 1, no. 2 (1962): 214–230.

15. Post–World War II Germany and France hosted respectively former German-speaking settlers from lost settlements in the east and European settlers of Algeria as repatriates (although France was less welcoming to the Muslim Harkis), and provided numerous and successive state-sponsored resettlement and reparation programs, see Jan C. Jansen and Manuel Borutta, *Vertriebene and Pieds-Noirs in Postwar Germany and France: Comparative Perspectives* (Basingstoke: Palgrave-Macmillan, 2016). On Diefenbacher and French reparations to the category of the repatriated, see Sung-Eun Choi, *Decolonization and the French of Algeria: Bringing the Settler Colony Home* (Basingstoke: Palgrave Macmillan, 2016), 147–149.

16. Loi 61-1439 du 26 décembre 1961 relative à l'accueil et à la réinstallation des Français d'outre-mer (Law 61-1439 of December 26, 1961 on the reception and resettlement of overseas French) *JORF*, December 28, 1961, 11996: "Français ayant dû quitter ou estimé devoir quitter, par suite d'événements politiques, un territoire où ils étaient établis et qui était antérieurement placé sous la souveraineté, le protectorat ou la tutelle de la France"; and Michel Deifenbacher, *Rapport Parachever l'effort de solidarité nationale envers les rapatriés: Promouvoir l'oeuvre collective de la France outre-mer* (Paris: Documentation française, December 18, 2003). See the excellent discussion about terms for the French settlers of Algeria in Choi, *Decolonization and the French of Algeria*, 52–75.

17. See Susan Slyomovics, "'False Friends?': On Algeria, the Algerian Jewish Question, and Settler Colonial Studies," in *Race, Place, Trace: Essays in Honour of Patrick Wolfe*, eds. Lorenzo Veracini and Susan Slyomovics (London: Verso, 2022), 58–89.

18. Anglophone scholarly literature (and of course the French language as an orthographic principle) do not capitalize, but English italicizes *pied-noir.* For definitions based on "pioneer," see Pierre Bourdieu, *The Algerians* (Boston: Beacon Press, 1961), 130.

19. Benjamin Stora, "Pied noirs," in *Les mots de la colonisation*, ed. Sophie Dulucq et al. (Toulouse: Presses universitaires du Mirail, 2008), 91.

20. Pierre Bourdieu, *The Algerians*, 152; and Susan Slyomovics, "French Restitution, German Compensation: Algerian Jews and Vichy's Financial Legacy," *Journal of North African Studies* 17, no. 5 (2012): 881–901.

21. The aforementioned Law of December 26, 1961, applied to European settlers ("repatriates") holding French citizenship and returning from Algeria to France. Its purpose was to ease their economic and social integration into France, while a decree of March 10, 1962, set the conditions for allocating resettlement loans and grants. Neither law nor decree was applied to the Harkis.

22. Sung-Eun Choi, "The Muslim Veteran in Postcolonial France: The Politics of the Integration of Harkis after 1962," *French Politics, Culture, and Society* 29, no. 1 (2011): 24–45. On the five military groupings of Harkis serving in the French military, see Abderrahman Moumen, *Les Harkis* (Paris: Éditions Le Cavalier Bleu, 2008).

23. Lorenzo Veracini, "Settler Collective, Founding Violence and Disavowal: The Settler Colonial Situation," *Journal of Intercultural Studies* 29, no. 4 (2008): 363–379.

24. According to Andrea Smith, hundreds of thousands of Europeans, who arrived as settlers and colonists on North African shores as of the early nineteenth century, constituted an "invisible" migration; their decolonization became the story of an invisible return, of people coming "home" propelled by postindependence movements in Morocco, Algeria, Tunisia, and Libya, see Andrea L. Smith, "Introduction: Europe's Invisible Migrants," in *Europe's Invisible Migrants*, ed. Andrea L Smith (Amsterdam: University of Amsterdam Press, 2003), 9.

25. Patrick Wolfe, "Recuperating Binarism: A Heretical Introduction," *Settler Colonial Studies* 3, no. 3/4 (2013): 257. A double exposure and two images superimposed characterize nostalgia, according to Svetlana Boym, *The Future of Nostalgia* (New York: Basic Books, 2002). On distinctions between colonial nostalgia (France) and imperial nostalgia (Britain), see Patricia M. E. Lorcin, "The Nostalgias for Empire," *History and Theory* 57, no. 2 (2018): 269–285.

26. Andrea L. Smith, *Colonial Memory and Postcolonial Europe: Maltese Settlers in Algeria and France* (Bloomington: Indiana University Press, 2006).

27. Alain Amato, *Monuments en exil* (Versailles: Éditions de Atlanthrope, 1979),

11–21. See SHD 1R 368. On archive removals, see Todd Shepard, "'Of Sovereignty': Disputed Archives, 'Wholly Modern' Archives, and the Post-Decolonization French and Algerian Republics, 1962–2012," *American Historical Review* 120, no. 3 (2015): 869–883; and Susan Slyomovics, "Repairing Colonial Symmetry: Algerian Archive Restitution as Reparation for Crimes of Colonialism?" In *Time for Reparations: A Global Perspective*, ed. Jacqueline Bhabha, Margareta Matache, and Caroline Elkins (Philadelphia: University of Pennsylvania Press, 2021), 201–218.

28. The remarkable story of the return of French paintings to Algiers after their removal from the Algiers Musée National des Beaux Arts (National Museum of Fine Arts) at independence is described by former settlers Élisabeth Cazenave and Jean Christian Serna, *Le patrimoine artistique français de l'Algérie: Les oeuvres du Musée nationale des Beaux-arts d'Alger de la constitution à la restitution* (Chire-en-Montreuil, France: Éditions Abd-el-Tif, 2017), 26–47. Cazenave, an art historian, provides an inventory of the returned objects, deemed "repatriated" when returned to Algeria. See also Andrew Bellisari, "The Art of Decolonization: The Battle for Algeria's French Art, 1962–70," *Journal of Contemporary History* 52, no. 3 (2017): 625–645.

29. Conquest enforced by laws brought Algeria under various French civil and military authorities by the ordinance of July 22, 1834, which officially annexed Algeria's Ottoman territories; the ordinance of March 4, 1848, which granted the northern provinces of Algiers, Constantine, and Oran departmental status; and the law of December 24, 1902, placed the Sahara (Southern Territories) under military administration.

30. On monuments, see Alois Riegl, "The Modern Cult of Monuments: Its Character and Its Origin," *Oppositions* 25: (1982 [1903]): 20–51. For the notion of the ensemble, see Tilmann Breuer, "Ensemble: Konzeption und Problematik eines Begriffes des Bayrischen Denkmalschutzgesetzes," *Deutsche Kunst und Denkmalpflege* 34 (1976): 21–38.

31. See English and French texts available at the Icomos site: https://www.icomos.org/en/179-articles-en-francais/ressources/charters-and-standards/167-the-athens-charter-for-the-restoration-of-historic-monuments.

32. Regina F. Bendix, Aditya Eggert, and Arnika Peselmann, *Heritage Regimes and the State* (Göttingen: Universitätsverlag Göttingen, 2012), 11.

33. Robert Shannan Peckham, "Introduction to the Politics of Heritage and Public Culture," in *Rethinking Heritage, Politics, and Culture in Europe*, ed. Robert Shannan Peckham (London, I. B. Tauris 2003), 1.

34. Nasser Rabbat, "Identity, Modernity, and the Destruction of Heritage," *International Journal of Middle East Studies* 49 (2017): 740. Although *turāth* often fills the slot of tangible architectural "heritage" in many contemporary preservation projects, the Arabic term extends to spiritual and textual Islamic culture, see Nabila Oulebsir, *Les usages de patrimoine: Monuments, musées et politique coloniale en Algérie (1830–1930)* (Paris: Édition de la Maison des sciences de l'homme, 2004), 14.

35. National Council of the Algerian Revolution (Conseil National de la Révolution Algérienne, CNRA), 1962, Tripoli Program, available at: http://www.el-mouradia.dz/francais/symbole/textes/tripoli.htm: "Sa prospérité économique, la vigueur exceptionnelle de son people, ses traditions de lutte, son appartenance à une culture et à une civilisation communes au Maghreb et au monde arabe, ce sont là autant de facteurs qui ont longtemps soutenu la résistance nationale...... La nécessité de créer une pensée politique et sociale nourrie de principes scientifiques et prémunie contre les habitudes d'esprit erronées, nous fait saisir l'importance d'une conception nouvelle de la culture. La culture algérienne sera nationale, révolutionnaire et scientifique. Son rôle de culture nationale consistera, en premier lieu, à rendre à la langue arabe, expression même des valeurs culturelles de notre pays, sa dignité et son efficacité en tant que langue de civilisation. Pour cela, elle s'appliquera à reconstituer à revaloriser et à faire connaître le patrimoine national et son double humanisme classique et moderne afin de les réintroduire dans la vie intellectuelle et l'éducation de la sensibilité populaire."

36. Susan Slyomovics, "'The Ethnologist-Spy Was Hanged, At That Time We Were a Little Savage': Anthropology in Algeria with Habib Tengour." *Boundary 20: An online journal* 3 (2018), https://www.boundary2.org/2018/12/susan-slyomovics-the-ethnologist-spy-was-hanged-at-that-time-we-were-a-little-savage-anthropology-in-algeria-with-habib-tengour/.

37. Loi 98-04 du 20 Safar 1419 correspondant au 15 juin 1998 relative à la protection du patrimoine culturel (Law 98-04 of 20 Safar 1419 corresponding to June 15, 1998 on cultural heritage) *JORA*, June 17, 1998, 3–15.

38. Loi 99-07 du 19 Dhou El Hidja 1419 correspondant au 5 avril 1999 relative au moudjahid et au chahid (Law 99-07 of 19 Dhou El Hidja 1419 corresponding to April 5, 1999 on moudjahid and chahid), *JORA*, April 12, 1999, 3–9.

39. Yassine Ouagueni, "The Birth of the Notion of *Patrimoine* (through the Generations) in Algeria," *Journal of North African Studies* 25, no. 5 (2020): 753–770; Nora Gueliane and Kaouther Bouchemal, "Algeria and Its Heritage: Inventory of the Various Heritage Policies, from the Pre-colonial to Colonial and Post-colonial Times," in *Transcultural Diplomacy and International Law in Heritage Conservation*, ed. O. Niglio and E. Y. J. Lee, 257-272 (Springer: Singapore, 2021); and Nabila Oulebsir, *Les usages de patrimoine*.

40. Charles-André Julien, *Histoire de l'Algérie contemporaine* (Paris: PUF, 1979), 255.

41. The city plans of the Danger family of architects are cited in Jean-Pierre Frey, "Figures et plans d'Oran 1931–1936, ou les années de tous les Danger," *Insaniyat* 23–24 (2004): 111–134.

42. Henri Auguste Jouin, "About the Genius of Statuary," *Sculpture Journal* 27, no. 1 (2018): 117.

43. Rosalind Krauss, "Sculpture in the Expanded Field," *October* 8 (1979): 33.

44. Ann L. Stoler, *Duress: Imperial Durabilities in Our Times* (Durham, NC: Duke University Press, 2016), 4.

45. On biographies of monuments in relation to the art of public memory, see James L. Young, *The Texture of Memory: Holocaust Memorials and Meaning* (New Haven, CT: Yale University Press, 1992); and Igor Kopytoff, "The Cultural Biography of Things: Commoditization as Process," in *The Social Life of Things*, ed. Arjun Appadurai (Cambridge: Cambridge University Press, 1986), 64–92.

46. Frantz Fanon, *The Wretched of the Earth* (New York: Grove Press, 1963), 38.

47. Françoise Choay, *The Invention of the Historic Monument* (Cambridge: Cambridge University Press, 2001), x.

48. "Monuments as Monsters: Michael Rakowitz and Erin L. Thompson in Conversation," *Art Journal Open* (June 16, 2022), http://artjournal.collegeart.org/?p=16895.

49. Fanon, *The Wretched of the Earth*, 51–52.

50. On several *Winged Victory* (*Victoire ailée*) statues in Algeria, see chapters 1 and 4. The Blida statue was inaugurated on July 7, 1925, according to local newspaper accounts, see "Cérémonie patriotique: Inauguration du monument aux morts," *Le Tell: Journal politique et des intérêts coloniaux* 63, no. 6163 (July 8, 1925): 1–2.

51. On colonial legal violence and dispossession, see Isabelle Merle, "De la 'légalisation' de la violence en contexte colonial: Le régime de l'indigénat en question," *Politix* 17, no. 66 (2004): 137–162; and Didier Guignard, *L'abus de pouvoir dans l'Algérie coloniale* (Nanterre: Presses universitaires de Paris-Ouest, 2010).

52. Michael Fried, *Absorption and Theatricality: Painting and Beholder in the Age of Diderot* (Berkeley: University of California Press, 1980) highlights the spectacular, performative nature of sculpture in which presence is always linked to aggression intrinsic to literalist works. See also Michael Fried's "Art and Objecthood," *Artforum* 5, no. 10 (1967): 12–23; and Patrick Wolfe, "Settler Colonialism and the Elimination of the Native," *Journal of Genocide Research* 8, no. 4 (2006): 387–409.

53. First published in 1836, Henri Fonfrède, "De la décolonisation d'Alger," in *Oeuvres de Henri Fonfrède: Recueillies et mises en ordre par Charles-Alcée Campan, son collaborateur* (Bordeaux: Chaumas-Gayet, 1846), vol. 8: 233, 240. Historian Charles-Robert Ageron first recorded Fonfrède's use in his "Décolonisation," *Encyclopaedia Universalis*, https://www.universalis.fr/encyclopedie/decolonisation/.

54. Todd Shepard, *The Invention of Decolonization: The Algerian War and the Remaking of France* (Ithaca, NY: Cornell University Press, 2006); and Philip Naylor, *France and Algeria: A History of Decolonization and Transformation* (Gainesville: University Press of Florida, 2000). On ruptures and continuities of 1962, see Malika Rahal, *Algérie 1962: Une histoire populaire* (Paris: La Découverte, 2022).

55. Ariella Aïsha Azoulay, *Potential History: Unlearning Imperialism* (London: Verso, 2019), 10.

56. Fanon, *The Wretched of the Earth*, 36.

57. For the first decades of the conquest, demographer Kamel Kateb estimates 875,000 native Algerians deaths, see Kamel Kateb, *Européen, "indigènes," et juifs en Algérie (1830–1962)* (Paris: Éditions de l'Institut National d'Études Démographiques, 2001).

58. Anissa Bouayed, "Histoire de la peinture en Algérie: continuum et ruptures," *Confluences Méditerranée* 81 (2012): 163–79.

59. Finbarr Barry Flood, "Refiguring Iconoclasm in the Early Indian Mosque," in *Negating the Image: Case Studies in Iconoclasm*, ed. Anne L. McClanan and Jeffrey Johnson (Aldershot: Ashgate, 2005), 15; and Finbarr Barry Flood, "Lost Histories of a Licit Figural Art," *International Journal of Middle East Studies* 45, no. 3 (2013): 566. For example, art historian Christiane Gruber's extensive research demonstrates that Islamic prohibitions on depicting the Prophet Muhammad, or the human figure, vary across historical eras and among clerics whenever it comes to an absolute ban, see *The Praiseworthy One: The Prophet Muhammad in Islamic Texts and Images* (Bloomington: Indiana University Press, 2019). According to Gruber, "the Qur'anic verse on Solomon's *tamathil* allowed Muslim monarchs (from the first century of Islam until the present day) the possibility of expressing their royal pedigree and power through figural images, including three-dimensional statuary"; see her "Idols and Figural Images in Islam: A Brief Dive into a Perennial Debate," in *The Image Debate: Figural Representation in Islam and across the World*, ed. Christiane Gruber (London: Gingko Press, 2019), 12. See also Mika Natif, "The Painter's Breath and Concepts of Idol Anxiety," in *Idol Anxiety*, ed. Josh Ellenbogen and Aaron Tugenhaft, 41–55 (Stanford, CA: Stanford University Press, 2011).

60. Andrea Brazzoduro, "Towards a Postmodern National Narrative? The Algerian War Memorial and Contemporary French Landscapes of Memory," *Memory Studies* 15, no. 4 (2022): 863. He counts merely ten *départements* out of ninety-eight in France that did not erect their own monument by 2018.

61. Etienne Balibar, "Algérie, France: une ou deux nations?" *Lignes* 30 (1997) 16. To address existing paradigms in art theory, global history, colonialism, and decolonization, this particular biography of the Oran-Lyon war memorial studies colony and metropole as a single analytical frame following Frederick Cooper and Ann Stoler, *Tensions of Empire: Colonial Cultures in a Bourgeois World*, ed. Frederick Cooper and Ann Laura Stoler (Berkeley: University of California Press, 1997).

62. Nabila Skander, "Pour M. Tebboune, l'histoire n'est qu'un enjeu politique (Hosni Kitouni, historien)," *Algérie Cultures*, May 9, 2020, https://algeriecultures.com/actualite-culturelle/pour-m-tebboune-lhistoire-nest-quun-enjeu-politique-hosni-kitouni-historien/: "Nous sommes encore dans un terrible tête-à-tête névrotique avec les Français, comme pris dans le drame d'un divorce interminable et où aucune des parties ne veut vraiment s'en aller sans avoir pris avec elle tous les biens de la maison."

63. Patricia M. E. Lorcin, "France and Rome in Africa: Recovering Algeria's Latin Past," *French Historical Studies* 35, no. 2 (2002): 295–329.

64. Gregory John Ashworth and John E. Tunbridge, *Dissonant Heritage: The Management of the Past as a Resource in Conflict* (New York: Wiley, 1996). On dissonant versus difficult heritage, see Mia Fuller, "Difficult How? Italy's *Inertia Memoriae* of Fascism," in *Difficult Heritage? The Afterlife of Colonial and Fascist Architecture, Monuments, and Works of Art in Contemporary Italy*, ed. Carmen Belmonte (Milan: Silvano, 2023), 15–23.

65. Kamal Daoud, *Meurseult, contre-enquête* (Arles: Actes Sud, 2014); and Albert Camus, *L'étranger* (Paris: Gallimard, 1942).

66. Mohammed Aîssaoui, "L'hommage émouvant de Régis Debray à Kamel Daoud," *Le Figaro*, May 5, 2015, https://www.lefigaro.fr/livres/2015/05/05/03005-20150505ARTFIG00249-l-hommage-emouvant-de-regis-debray-a-kamel-daoud.php: "Vous avez fait rapatrié l'*Étranger* dans votre culture. Vous avez fait d'Albert Camus, un auteur français qui parle de vous, à vous. Eh bien nous, le jury Goncourt, nous rapatrions votre *Meursault, contre-enquête* dans le trésor de la littérature françcais, de la littérature tout court."

Chapter 1: Encountering Monuments

1. Elizabeth Edwards, "Material Beings: The Objecthood of Ethnographic Photographs," *Visual Studies* 17, no. 1 (2002): 69–75.

2. As Smith notes, photography cannot disclose worlds yet "makes us aware of its invisibility," for example of colonial structures of domination, see Shawn Michelle Smith, *At the Edge of Sight: Photography and the Unseen* (Durham, NC: Duke University Press, 2013), 6. See also Mechtild Widrich, *Performative Monuments: The Rematerialisation of Public Art* (Manchester: Manchester University Press, 2014), 27 on photography's "dual capacity of acting as quasi-legal document of the past (a convention applicable even when the photographs are staged) and of offering an experiential re-enactment for the viewer in the present." On frontality as a culturally specific form of seeing and posing, see Pierre and Marie-Claire Bourdieu, "The Peasant and Photography" *Ethnography* 5, no. 4 (2004): 601–616.

3. On colonial ideology, cartography, and administrative oversight of the Commission des Monuments Historiques in Algeria by the Ministry of War, see Nabila Oulebsir, *Les usages du patrimoine: Monuments, musées et politiques coloniale en Algérie (1830–1930)* (Paris: Éditions de la Maison des sciences de l'homme, 2004), 14, 19–20, 98–102. On the beginnings of architectural photography in France through the commission, see Micheline Nilsen, *Architecture in Nineteenth-Century Photographs: Essays on Reading a Collection* (Farnham: Ashgate, 2011).

4. Ariella Aïsha Azoulay, *Potential History, Unlearning Imperialism* (London: Verso, 2019), 2; and Daniel Foliard, *The Violence of Colonial Photography* (Manchester: Manchester University Press, 2022).

5. Ségolène Le Men, "La statuaire publique en images: une pédagogie civique

par le manuel scolaire et par la carte postale," in *La statuaire publique XIXe siècle*, ed. Ségolène Le Men and Aline Magnien (Paris: Centre des monuments nationaux / Monument Éditions du Patrimoine, 2004), 32–55.

6. Malek Alloula, *The Colonial Harem* (Minneapolis: University of Minnesota Press, 1986), 4. For Alloula, colonial French postcards are as pervasive as bird shit, an expensive commodity used for fertilizer in the nineteenth century that he too recirculates. His emphasis, not mine, is the archive of Algerian *scènes et types*, a genre of exotic scenes matched to erotic physical types of Algerian natives, notably the staged harems of native women. See also, François Pouillon and Michel Mégnin, "Le miroir aux alouettes: destin sociologique des images du nu indigène," *L'Année du Maghreb* 6 (2010): 19–45; David Prochaska, "The Archive of *Algérie imaginaire*," *History and Anthropology* 4, no. 2 (1990): 373–420; Susan Slyomovics, "Visual Ethnography, Stereotypes, and Photographing Algeria," in *Orientalism Revisited: Art, Land, and Voyage*, ed. Ian Richard Netton, 128–150 (London: Routledge, 2012); and Zeynep Çelik, "A Lingering Obsession: The Houses of Algiers in French Colonial Discourse," in *The Walls of Algiers*, ed. Zeynep Çelik, Julia Clancy-Smith and Frances Terpak, 134–160 (Seattle: University of Washington Press, 2009).

7. On the infrastructure of postcards, see Jacques Derrida, *La carte postale* (Paris: Flammarion, 1980), 7. Postal service came late to rural Algerians according to Annick Lacroix, "La poste au douar: Usagers non citoyens et État colonial dans les campagnes algériennes de la fin du xixe siècle à la Seconde Guerre Mondiale," *Annales: Histoire, Sciences Sociales* 71, no. 3 (2016): 709–740. See instructions to the postal service laws of 1872 that included an amendment attached to the budget, permitting the creation of postcards with special low tariffs in France and between France and Algeria, https://fr.wikisource.org/wiki/Instruction_n%C2%B072_de_l%27Administration_des_postes.

8. Ariella Azoulay, *The Civil Contract of Photography* (New York: Zone Books, 2008), 13.

9. Elizabeth Edwards, "Objects of Affect: Photography beyond the Image," *Annual Review of Anthropology* 41, no. 1 (2012): 221–234.

10. On explanatory captions as necessary to photography, see Walter Benjamin, "The Work of Art in the Age of Its Technological Reproducibility," in *The Work of Art in the Age of Its Technological Reproducibility, and Other Writings on Media* (Cambridge, MA: Harvard University Press, 2008), 27.

11. See Tina Campt, *Listening to Images* (Durham, NC: Duke University Press, 2017); Emmanuel Alloa, "Seeing-as, Seeing-in, Seeing-with: Looking through Images," in *Handbook of Image Studies*, ed. K. Purgar, 483–499 (London: Palgrave Macmillan, 2021); and Lydia Pyne, *Postcards: The Rise and Fall of the World's First Social Network* (London: Reaktion Books, 2021). On postcard collecting, see Naomi Schor, "*Cartes Postales*: Representing Paris 1900," *Critical Inquiry* 18, no. 2 (1992): 188–244; Rebecca J. DeRoo, "Colonial Collecting: French Women and Al-

gerian *Cartes Postales*," in *Postcards: Ephemeral Histories of Modernity*, ed. David Prochaska and Jordana Mendelson, 85–92 (University Park: Pennsylvania State University Press, 2010); and Beatrice Ivey, "Virtual Returns: Colonial Postcards Online and Digital 'Nostalgérie' among the Former European Settlers of Algeria, *Humanities and Social Science Communications* 9, no. 112 (2022): DOI: 10.1057/s41599-022-01134-3.

12. Abdo Shanan, "The Right to Memory," *Flare*, September 4, 2020, https://medium.com/flare-photoforum/the-right-to-a-memory-d7bb72a5a731. On nostalgia through postcards, Paul Azoulay, *La nostalgérie française (Collections "Les cartes postales de l'histoire")* (Paris: Eric Baschet Editions, 1980). On nostalgia about the state-produced Algerian postcards of the 1970s after the takeover of Éditions Jomone, see Ed McAllister, "Algeria's Belle Epoque (1) Postcards and Nostalgia: Images of Algiers in the 1970s," *Texture du temps*, 2012, https://texturesdutemps.hypotheses.org/414.

13. Focusing on the lived experiences of monuments as sites of traumatic experiences, see Dylan Trigg, *The Memory of Place: A Phenomenology of the Uncanny* (Columbus: Ohio University Press, 2012).

14. Claude Mouton, *Lamoricière: De l'Algérie française aux zouaves pontificaux: Vendéen, africain, romain, un grand soldat de la chrétienté* (Montsurs, France: Résiac, 1990).

15. Alain Amato, *Monuments en exil* (Versailles: Éditions de Atlanthrope, 1979). See Leïla Sebbar, *Mes Algéries en France* (Saint-Pourçain-sur-Sioule, France: Éditions Bleu Autour, 2005), which is a part of a three-volume series on Algerian sites of memory and monuments in France. Sebbar's book juxtaposes monuments, cemeteries, personal history, landscapes, and a rich portfolio of photographs of her encounters and travels through France in search of Algeria in France. On colonial wonder, see Stephen Greenblatt, *Marvelous Possessions: The Wonder of the New World* (New York: Clarendon Press, 1991), 14.

16. Amato, *Monuments en exil*, 20: "Les années passant, ces souvenirs évoquent maintenant avec beaucoup d'acuité le symbole du pays natal perdu. Si j'emploie pour eux le qualificatif 'd'exilés' c'est parce que je pense que les monuments et les statues sont toujours crées en fonction du lieu et de l'espace qu'ils vont occuper et que par suite de l'indépendance de l'Algérie ils sont été reinstallés très loin de ces lieux et de ces espaces pour lesquels ils avaient été primitivement conçus." Statues removed by the military are listed in SHD 1H 1091–4881. On exile versus exodus, see Lorenzo Veracini, *The World Turned Inside Out* (London: Verso, 2021), 104. Algerian artist Amina Menia reprises Amato's title "Monuments in Exile" for emptied plinths on the Algerian landscape in her installation, "Monuments in Exile," https://aminamenia.com/works/monuments-in-exile/: "These marble 'stumps' thus regenerate by trying to take root in another soil of memory."

17. Amato, *Monuments en exil*, 186. "Puis vint l'indépendance et, en une nuit, celle du 8 au 9 juillet 1962, la statue fut déboulonnée et embarquée pour Marseille

par le Génie de l'Armée française. Elle séjourna sur les quais de Marseille jusqu'en juin 1963. Elle fut transférée à Nantes, le ministre des Armées l'ayant attribuée à la ville natale de Lamoricière. Dès son arrivée elle fut remisée en pièces détachées au dépôt de la Moutonnerie. Environ un an plus tard Me Pennetier, maire de Saint-Philbert-de-Grand-Lieu et conseiller général de la Loire-Atlantique, apprit son existence et eut l'idée de la réclamer pour sa commune. C'est en effet du lieu dit 'La Moricière,' à deux kilomètres de Saint-Philbert, que la famille tient son nom. Cinq années s'écouleront où Me Pennetier multiplia les démarches et, le 29 juin 1969, récompensé de sa ténacité, il inaugura la statue devant deux mille personnes. Le corps du général Lamoricière repose à la chapelle du cimetière de Saint-Philbert."

18. By 1963, the first Algerian government regulations for name changes and toponyms were placed under the aegis of the Ministry of the Interior, see Décret 63-105 du 4 Avril 1963 relatif aux hommages publics (Decree 65-105 of April 4, 1963 on public commemorations) *JORA*, April 12, 1963, 339. Currently this ministry along with elected municipal officials of the APC are responsible for name changes.

19. Ahmed Benyahia, interview with author, May 31, 2022, Constantine. Berredjem's acts of substitution and replacement exemplify philosopher Michel Serres's argument that a statue often marks the place of the dead body, which turns an object into cause, see Michel Serres, *Statues: The Second Book of Foundations*, trans. Randolph Burks (London: Bloomsbury, 2015).

20. On "before and after" photography, see Kate Palmer Albers and Jordan Bear, "Photography's Time Zones," in *Before-and-After Photography: Histories and Contexts*, ed. Jordan Bear and Kate Palmer Albers, 1–11 (London: Bloomsbury, 2017).

21. Mark Sealy, *Decolonising the Camera: Photography in Racial Time* (London: Lawrence and Whishart, 2019).

22. Richard Wrigley, "Breaking the Code: Interpreting French Revolutionary Iconoclasm," in *Reflections of Revolution: Images of Romanticism*, ed. Alison Yarrington and Kelvin Everest, 182–195 (London: Routledge, 1993).

23. To this day, in the central city square of Padua, Italy, there are several vacant pedestals to mark the destruction of statues by Napoleon's Army in 1797. Commemorating the importance of this historical moment was given as justification for emptied plinths when replacements with significant female figures to the all-male pantheon were suggested.

24. For additional sculptures by Dugaret, see Claire Viala, "Oeuvre d'un artiste marbrier Oranais: Sainte-Germaine veille sur le cimetière de Mers-El-Kebir, *L'Echo d'Oran*, November 2, 1950, http://www.merselkebir.org/annonces_1950.htm. More photos of the pre-1962 Oran train station war memorial are available at the Pied-Noir website Popodoran, http://popodoran.canalblog.com/archives/2012/12/24/25988908.html.

25. Samir Slama, *Arbres et paysages remarquables* (Oran: Bel Horizon Editions, 2019).

26. See "Déplacement du monuments aux morts Promenade de Letang," *Travaux nord-africains,* February 22, 1939, 2. The verso side of figure 11 postcard has no photography company name as many pirated postcard images also circulated.

27. Tony [pseud.], "La vraie figure du meeting de Dimanche," *Oran-Spectacles* 230, October 14, 1933, 7. According to the Pied-Noir website "Arzew Mémoire," the model was by Cassar for the sculptor Isaac Sarraude, http://www.arzew.fr/page18/page26/page26.html.

28. Marina Warner, *Monuments and Maidens: The Allegory of the Female Form* (London: Weidenfeld and Nicolson, 1985), xix–xxi; and Annette Becker, *Les monuments au morts: Patrimoine et mémoire de la Grande Guerre* (Paris: Errance, 1988), 59–64, 73–75.

29. See the description on the Louvre Museum site, https://www.louvre.fr/oeuvre-notices/victoire-de-samothrace and Sophie Basch, "La postérité littéraire et artistique de la Victoire de Samothrace: Petite anthologie," *Revue d'histoire littéraire de la France* 3 (2019): 615–627. The stamp's placement on the postcard in figure 14 places two female allegorical representations in playful conversation.

30. Maurice Dreyfous, *Dalou: Sa vie et son oeuvre* (Paris: Librairie Renouard, 1903), 194–195. The architect is identified as M. Formigé: "Au sommet se dresse une statue de *Victoire* et au niveau de la petite base, une femme, vue de dos, symbolisant la *France* entièrement drapée, un genou enterre, achève d'écrire au bas de l'obélisque les derniers noms des soldats qui se sont illustrés à l'affaire de Sidi Brahim, et dont la liste couvre déjà la face tout entière du monument. Sa main gauche tient un drapeau, dont la hampe dressée et les plis retenus, épousent la ligne oblique de l'obélisque. A côté d'elle reposent, sur le piédestal, le haut shako et le gros fusil des vieilles troupes d'Algérie. Là-haut, la Victoire, étendant les bras, fait planer dans l'espace la palme et la couronne de laurier. La tête, au geste souple, légèrement infléchie vers l'épaule gauche, semble chanter. Une draperie qui entoure le corps, au-dessous des reins, s'appuyant aux hanches et découvrant le bas-ventre et l'aine gauche, rappelle, par l'ensemble de sa disposition à cette place, la draperie de la Vénus de Milo ; elle serre ensuite le contour des jambes et s'échappe à gauche en un pli flottant. La nudité du torse, droit et très souple, émergeant de ses plis, attire à soi de la sorte, toute la lumière. Par derrière, deux petites ailes d'aigle, étendues et battantes, en modèrent et en harmonisent le Ion; elles emprègnent la marche des pieds nus, posés à la cime de l'obélisque, d'un sentiment de vol; leurs lignes équilibrent celle de la draperie qui, auprès d'eux, palpite au souffle du vent. Les statues sont de bronze, l'obélisque est de marbre algérien. Un vaste cartouche, lauré d'une guirlande courante et retombante, en décore la façade; la dédicace du monument y est entaillée."

31. Beatrice Ivey, "The Monument of Sidi-Brahim," *Narratives of French Algeria* (blog), December 10, 2018, https://www.pieds-noirs.stir.ac.uk/the-sidi-brahim-monument/: and Amato, "Périssac," in *Monuments en exil,* 63–172. The French military removal from Algeria according to files at Château Vincennes archives

was confirmed on April 1, 1963, see SHD 1R368-2, "Souvenir Militaires," Dossier "Souvenir de la Sidi Brahim: [4eme Div.] Affaire reglée le 1 avril 1963."

32. Mohamed Cherfaoui, interview with author, June 21, 2018, Oran.

33. Albert Memmi, *The Colonizer and the Colonized*, trans. Howard Greenfeld (New York: Orion Press, 1965), 172–173.

34. Paul Landowski, *Journal*, November 5, 1926, http://journal.paul-landowski.com/node/363. "[J'ai] complètement chamboulé le groupe arrière du *monument d'Alger*. Deux arabes formeront l'arrière plan. Une sorte de guerrier du sud. Le groupe principal sera formé d'une femme française et d'une femme arabe dans les bras l'une de l'autre. Effet commence à être excellent. Le mort est moulé." Image, reproduced by permission, is available at: http://www.paul-landowski.com/en/portfolio/monument-aux-morts-dalger-ou-le-pavois/.

35. Zeynep Çelik, "Colonial Statues and Their Afterlives," *Journal of North African Studies* 25, no. 5 (2020): 711–726. See also Beatrice Ivey, "The Landowski-Issiakhem Pavois," Narratives and Representations of the French of Algeria, Stirling University (blog), November 28, 2018, https://www.pieds-noirs.stir.ac.uk/the-landowski-issiakhem-pavois/; and Claire Garcia, "Migrations, transferts et réécritures: Le destin des monuments publics d'Algérie après l'Indépendance," *Les Cahiers de l'École du Louvre*, 12 (2018), https://journals.openedition.org/cel/920.

36. Fanny Gillet, "'Il suffira d'ouvrir la coquille pour le récupérer': Histoires développées du Monument aux Morts d'Alger de Paul Landowski," in *L'Algérie au présent: Entre résistances et changements*, ed. Karima Dirèche (Paris: Karthala, 2019), 559–560.

37. Amina Menia, "Enclosed @Mosaic Rooms," https://aminamenia.com/works/enclosed-at-mosaic-rooms/. When Issiakhem's exterior cracked revealing Landowski's monument, two other artists took the event as subjects for museum installations: Katia Kameli, *Trou de mémoire*, 2018, https://www.katiakameli.com/photos/trou-de-memoire/; and Neïl Beloufa, "L'ennemi de mon ennemi," 2018, https://www.paul-landowski.com/en/2018/04/02/algiers-war-memorial-palais-de-tokyo/.

38. Thomas W. Laqueur, *The Work of the Dead: A Cultural History of Mortal Remains* (Princeton, NJ: Princeton University Press, 2015), 414.

39. Michael Taussig, *Defacement: Public Secrecy and the Labor of the Negative* (Stanford, CA: Stanford University Press, 1999); and Lamia Balafrej, "Islamic Iconoclasm, Visual Communication and the Persistence of the Image," *Interiors* 6, no. 3 (2015): 351–366.

40. Alaphilippe created war memorials for the Algeria towns of Tipasa, Ain-Temouchent, Saida, Mostaganem, Bougie, Bourj Bou-Arreridj, Batna, Tebessa, Guelma, Philippeville, and Fedj Mzala. On Camille Alaphilippe, see M. Michel, "Alaphilippe," *Notre rive: Revue nord-africaine illustrée*, January 1, 1927, 20. On female representations of Marianne embodying the French Republic (wearing a Phrygian cap, laurel wreath, or helmet), see Maurice Agulhon, *Marianne au combat*

(Paris: Flammarion, 1979); and Maurice Agulhon, *Les metamorphoses de Marianne: L'imagerie et la symboliques républicaines de 1914 à nos jours* (Paris: Flammarion, 2001).

41. On histories of multiple violence and dispossession of Algerians in Rio Salado, see Messaoud Benyoucef, "L'été meurtrier: Rio Salado, Août 1962," *Socialgerie*, April 27, 2013, https://socialgerie.net/spip.php?article1168.

42. Mohamed Hirreche Baghdad, "Les inscriptions funéraires au cimetière d'Aïn El-Beida (Oran): État des lieux," *Insaniyat* 62 (2013): note 54, http://journals.openedition.org/insaniyat/14376.

43. Since medieval times, church bells are named and dedicated to a saint, blessed, and consecrated by the clergy. Jean Rodhain, "Les cloches d'Algérie," *Messages du Secours Catholique* 163 (1966), https://fondationjeanrodhain.org/jean-rodhain-textes-de-jean-rodhain/1966/les-cloches-dalgerie.

44. Benyoucef, "L'été meurtrier: Rio Salado."

45. On the history of the war memorial, see the Pied-Noir website devoted to the pre-1962 village of Trois Marabouts, https://troismarabouts.jimdofree.com/le-village/monuments-aux-morts/.

46. Cherif and Abdelhak Ben-Boulaïd, and Abdefettah Chenni, WhatsApp interviews with the author during the month of July 2021. Photos of the 2014 inauguration by Cherif Ben-Boulaïd are available on the Facebook page dedicated to Mostefa Ben-Boulaïd. On Joseph Ebstein's colonial war memorial, see Susan Slyomovics, "Female Winged Victory Statues of North Africa: Roman Provenance, French Colonial Appropriations, and Algerian Preservation," in *Breaking the Bronze Ceiling: Women, Memory, and Public Space*, ed. Valentina Rozas-Krause and Andrew M. Shanken (New York: Fordham University Press, 2024), 230–252. See also, Centre Pompidou/MNAM-CCI/Bibliothèque Kandinsky, Fonds Joseph Ebstein.

47. Some analytic histories of the period (which refer to the dirty war, the civil war, or the Black Decade) are Luis Martinez, *La guerre civile en Algerie* (Paris: Karthala, 1998); James D. Le Sueur, *Between Terror and Democracy: Algeria since 1989* (London: Zed Books, 2010); Abderrahmane Moussaoui, *De la violence en Algérie: Les lois du chaos* (Arles: Actes Sud/MMSH, 2006); Hugh Roberts, *The Battlefield Algeria 1988–2002: Studies in Broken Polity* (London: Verso, 2003); H. Souaidia, *La sale guerre* (Paris: La Découverte, 2012); and Jacob Mundy, *Imaginative Geographies of Algerian Violence: Conflict Science, Conflict Management, Antipolitics* (Stanford, CA: Stanford University Press, 2015).

48. Prosper Bouniceau-Guesmon, *M.F. de Saint-Vidal et sa fontaine: Étude critique* (Paris: A. Lemerre, 1889), 31: "L'Asie, sous la figure d'une ondoyante odalisque mollement couchée dans une attitude sensuelle, ayant à sa gauche le narghileh, n'est-ce pas la pensée s'absorbant dans la recherche des raffinements du plaisir et voilée par la langueur des voluptés ainsi que le sybaritisme des pays de polygamie et des harems embaumés des enivrants parfums de l'Orient?" On visualizing con-

tinents through the female body, see Maryanne Cline Horowitz, "Rival Interpretations of Continent Personifications," in *Bodies and Maps: Early Modern Personifications of the Continents*, ed. Maryanne Cline Horowitz and Louise Arrizoli, 1–24 (Leiden: Brill, 2020). Renaissance and Baroque versions of continent personifications traditionally counted four continents. Late nineteenth-century French statues added a fifth, Oceania, to include overseas French colonies in the Pacific Ocean.

49. See Adrien Berbrugger, *La Bibliothèque-musée d'Alger: Livret explicative des collections diverses de ces deux établissements* (Algiers: Imprimerie Bastide, Libraire Editeur, 1860), 102–103; and Nicolas Lamare, *Les fontaines monumentales en Afrique romaine* (Rome: École française de Rome, 2019).

50. Video recordings documenting his actions circulated globally, e.g., YouTube clip: https://www.youtube.com/watch?v=C1BpG7ZzfBQ. On public art as a provocation for violence, see W. J. T. Mitchell, "The Violence of Public Art: Do the Right Thing," *Critical Inquiry* 16, no. 4 (1990): 880–899.

51. On the necessity of protecting the fountain as patrimony during the tramway's planning stages between Sétif and the Franco-Belgian company, see Said Madani, "Le tramway de Sétif: Projet urbain ou simple projet de transport," *Cahiers Géographiques de l'Ouest* 12/13 (2017): 173. He confirmed that, "Le Wali avait également mis l'accent sur la nécessité d'éviter la fontaine de Aïn El-Fouara qui fait partie du patrimoine bâti de la ville."

52. Idir Benaidja, "Le rapport ordinaire à l'héritage bâti de l'époque de la colonisation française en Algérie: L'exemple de l'hôtel de ville de Kherrata (Bejaia)," *L'Année du Maghreb* 19 (2018): 81–98; and S. Chouadra et al., "Le patrimoine colonial entre la problématique du renouvellement urbain et la préservation de la mémoire des lieux, cas de la ville de Sétif, Algérie," *Sciences & Technologie D* 42 (2015): 9–19. On Algerian appreciation of colonial architecture, see also Jean-Jacques Deluz, *Le tout et le fragment* (Algiers: Barzakh, 2010).

53. Ann Laura Stoler, "'The Rot Remains': From Ruins to Ruination," in *Imperial Debris: On Ruins and Ruination*, ed. Ann Laura Stoler, 1–37 (Durham, NC: Duke University Press, 2013).

54. Monument Lab, *National Monument Audit*, 2021, 4, https://monumentlab.com/projects/national-monument-audit.

55. The 2022 vandalism of Sétif's statue circulated widely on social media. On the rich variety of iconoclasm as political acts, see Dario Gamboni, *The Destruction of Art: Iconoclasm and Vandalism since the French Revolution* (New Haven, CT: Yale University Press, 1997). See also Bertrand Tillier, *La disgrâce de statues: Essai sur les conflits de mémoire, de la Révolution française à Black Lives Matter* (Paris: Payot, 2022), who opposes a history of "statuoclastie" to "statuomanie."

56. A photo of Mascara's equestrian statue of the Emir is available at: https://commons.wikimedia.org/wiki/File:Mascara_Emir_AEK.jpg.

57. Amato, *Monuments en exil*, 20: "Si les objets ont une âme, Bugeaud dans son

enveloppe de bronze doit sentir bien seul dans sa retraite d'Exideuil, lui qui connut pendant cent dix ans la vie trépidante de la rue d'Isly à Alger." (If objects have a soul, Bugeaud enveloped in bronze must feel very alone in his retirement of Exideuil, he who knew for a hundred and ten years the bustling life of Rue d'Isly in Algiers.)

58. For detailed histories of Bugeaud's statue, see Alison McQueen, "Politics and Public Sculpture in Nineteenth-Century Colonial French Algeria," *Sculpture Journal* 28, no. 1 (2019): 7–34; Çelik, "Colonial Statues and Their Afterlives."; Natasha Marie Llorens, "The Other Battle of Algiers: Overcoming an Architecture of Oppression," *World Policy Journal* 35, no. 2 (2018): 63–69.

59. Charles-André Julien, *Histoire de l'Algérie contemporaine, la conquête et le début de la colonisation (1827–1871)* (Paris: Presses universitaires françaises, 1964), 255: "La ségrégation naturelle fut accrue par la décision de Lamoricière de cantonner les Arabes dans des quartiers isolés qui deviennent, plus tard, les villages nègres." Many authors add quotations marks to "Negro villages" as do I, although elsewhere I translate *villages nègres* as "Negrotowns."

60. Jacques Derrida and Safaa Fathy, "Contre-jour," trans. Max Cavitch, *PMLA* 131, no. 2 (2016), 548. Another history is provided by Amy Hubbell, who attributes the term *nostalgérie* to the poem of the same title by Marcello Fabri, see Amy L. Hubbell, "(Re)turning to Ruins: *Pied-Noir* Visual Returns to Algeria," *Modern & Contemporary France* 19, no. 2 (2011): 147–161.

61. Yasmina Khadra, *Ce que le jour doit à la nuit* (Paris: Julliard, 2008), 400; *What the Day Owes the Night*, trans. Frank Wynne (London: Vintage, 2011). "Ici, nous ne disons pas nostalgie . . . nous disons nostalgérie. . . . L'Algérie me colle à la peau . . . Des fois, elle me ronge comme une tunique de Nessus, des fois elle m'embaume comme un parfum délicat. J'essaye de la semer et n'y arrive pas. Comment oublier? J'ai voulu mettre une croix sur mes souvenirs de jeunesse, passer à autre chose, repartir à zéro. Peines perdues. Je ne suis pas un chat et je n'ai qu'une vie, et ma vie est restée là-bas, au bled . . . J'ai beau essayer de rassembler toutes les horreurs pour le vomir, rien à faire. Le soleil, les plages, nos rues, notre cuisine, nos bonnes vieilles cuites et nos jours heureux supplantant mes colères et je me surprends à sourire là où je me prépare à mordre. Je n'ai jamais oublié Rio . . . Pas une nuit, pas un instant."

62. Olivier Le Cour Grandmaison, "Bugeaud: Bourreau des 'indigènes' algériens et ennemi de la République," *Blog de Olivier Le Cour Grandmaison*, Mediapart, September 4, 2017, https://blogs.mediapart.fr/olivier-le-cour-grandmaison/blog/040917/bugeaud-bourreau-des-indigenes-algeriens-et-ennemi-de-la-republique. The call for the removal from schools and streets of the name of Jean-Baptiste Colbert, author of the Code Noir of slavery in the French colonies is by Louis-Georges Tin, "Mémoire de l'esclavage: 'Débaptisons les collèges et les lycées Colbert!'" *Le Monde*, Sept 17, 2017, https://www.lemonde.fr/idees/article/2017/09/17/debaptisons-les-colleges-et-les-lycees-colbert_5186813_3232.html.

63. Gilles Rof, "À Marseille, l'école Bugeaud bientôt rebaptisée du nom d'un tirailleur algérien," *Le Monde,* May 10, 2021, https://www.lemonde.fr/politique/article/2021/05/11/a-marseille-l-ecole-bugeaud-debaptisee-pour-porter-le-nom-d-un-tirailleur-algerien_6079825_823448.html.

64. Alain Ruscio, "Pour une statue à la gloire de l'Émir Abd El-Kader à Paris," *Orient XXI,* September 6, 2017, https://orientxxi.info/magazine/pour-une-statue-a-la-gloire-de-l-emir-abd-el-kader-a-paris,1985. On the prior colonial history of erecting a statue to the Emir in Algeria beginning with Ferhat Abbas writing pseudonymously, see Jan C. Jansen. "Creating National Heroes: Colonial Rule, Anticolonial Politics and Conflicting Memories of Emir ʿAbd Al-Qadir in Algeria, 1900–1960s," *History and Memory* 28, no. 2 (2016): 3–46.

65. Dell Upton, *What Can and Can't Be Said: Race, Uplift, and Monument Building in the Contemporary South* (New Haven, CT: Yale University Press, 2015).

66. See Saliha Belmessous, *Assimilation and Empire: Uniformity in French and British Colonies, 1541–1954* (Oxford: Oxford University Press, 2013), 117–204.

67. *Si les musulmans et les chrétiens me prêtaient l'oreille, je ferais cesser leurs divergences et ils deviendraient frères à l'intérieur et à l'extérieur.* See the 1949 dedication ceremony at https://www.youtube.com/watch?v=W7B6_Krt_nA; and Jan C. Jansen, *Erobern und Erinnern: Symbolpolitik, öffentlicher Raum und französischer Kolonialismus in Algerien, 1830–1950* (Munich: Oldenbourg, 2013), 453–454. On the complex iconography of the Emir, see François Pouillon, *Abdelkader, l'émir de la resistance* (Ghent, Belgium: Snoeck, 2019).

68. The French military removal date from Algeria, according to files at Château Vincennes archives, is confirmed as March 20, 1963, see SHD 1R368–2, "Souvenir Militaires," dossier on "Statue Sgt Blandan: [20eme Div.] Affaire reglée le 20 mars 1963."

69. Dorothée Myriam Kellou, *À Mansourah, tu nous a séparés,* film, 2019, 1 hour 11 min; and Dorothée Myriam Kellou, "Algérie coloniale: Le silence de nos pères," *Orient XXI,* October 25, 2019, https://orientxxi.info/lu-vu-entendu/algerie-coloniale-le-silence-de-nos-peres,3367.

70. *"Courage mes amis, défendez-vous jusqu'à la mort!"* in *Le Sergent Blandan et le combat d'El-Mechdoufa (près de Beni-Mered)* (Algiers: Adolphe Jourdan, 1887), 16. See Amato, *Monuments en exil,* 136–142.

71. *Le Sergent Blandan,* 27: "Quel serait le coeur assez froid pour ne pas se sentir électrisé en passant devant un monument élevé sur le lieu du combat, et où seraient retracés l'action et les noms des héros qui en furent les acteurs! Ce mémorable combat ayant eu lieu sur notre principale communication, toute l'armée, tous les colons défileront fréquemment devant le glorieux monument; on s'arrêtera, on s'inclinera. Qui pourrait calculer ce que le sentiment éprouvé par tous produira de gloire pour la Patrie!" Historian William Gallois refers to Bugeaud's "instant historicizing" as a hallmark of colonial values reliant on the immediacy of the moment,

see Gallois, *A History of Violence in the Early Algerian Colony* (New York: Palgrave Macmillan, 2013), 46.

72. Frantz Fanon, *A Dying Colonialism* (New York: Grove Press, 1965).

73. Tim Ingold, "Temporality of Landscape," *World Archaeology* 25, no. 2 (1992): 162.

74. Simukai Chigudu, "'Colonialism Had Never Really Ended': My Life in the Shadow of Cecil Rhodes," *The Guardian,* January 14, 2021, https://www.theguardian.com/news/2021/jan/14/rhodes-must-fall-oxford-colonialism-zimbabwe-simukai-chigudu.

75. Hans Ruin, *Being with the Dead: Burial, Ancestral Politics, and the Roots of Historical Consciousness* (Stanford, CA: Stanford University Press, 2019).

76. Benjamin Stora, *La guerre des mémoires: La France face à son passé colonial (entretiens avec Thierry Leclere)* (La Tour d'Aigues: Éditions de l'Aube, 2007).

77. Slyomovics, "Repairing Colonial Symmetry, 201–218.

Chapter 2: Moving War Monuments

1. Adolphe Messimy, "Le service militaire des indigènes algériens," *Bulletin de la réunion d'études algériennes* 10, nos. 2/3 (1908): 79-93. See Décret 3668 du 3 février 1912 relatif au recrutement des indigènes algériens (Decree 3668 of February 3, 1912 for the Recruitment of Algerian Natives) *JORF,* February 7, 1912, 1208 which mandated three years for Algerian Muslims plus seven years as a reservist.

2. Gilbert Meynier, *L'Algérie révélée: La guerre de 1914–1918 et le premier quart du XXe siècle* (Geneva: Droz, 1981), x; and Charles-Robert Ageron, *Les Algériens musulmans et la France (1871–1919)* (Paris: Presses universitaires de France, 1968), 2 vols.

3. Antériou cited these statistics during the 1927 inauguration of the monument, "L'inauguration du monument départemental de la Victoire," *L'Echo d'Oran,* May 23, 1927, 2. On settler soldiers, see Claire Eldridge, "'The Forgotten of This Tribute': Settler Soldiers, Colonial Categories and the Centenary of the First World War," *History and Memory* 31, no. 2 (2019): 3–44. The 2014 centenary of World War I produced extensive scholarship on colonial military service (settler support and native conscription), including for the English-speaking viewer; David Olusoga, *The World's War: Forgotten Soldiers of Empire* (London, Head of Zeus, 2014) linked to a BBC TV series.

4. Dónal Hassett, *Mobilizing Memory: The Great War and the Language of Politics in Colonial Algeria, 1918–39* (Oxford: Oxford University Press, 2019), 156–162.

5. See the decree in footnote 1 of this chapter, which summarizes prior conscription laws, pp. 1208–1210; Richard S. Fogarty, *Race and War in France: Colonial Subjects in the French Army, 1914–1918* (Baltimore, MD: Johns Hopkins University Press, 2008); and Belkacem Recham, *Les musulmans algériens dans l'armée française, 1919–1945* (Paris: L'Harmattan, 1996).

6. Michelle Mann, "The Young Algerians and the Question of the Muslim Draft, 1900–1914," in *Algeria Revisited: History, Culture and Identity*, ed. Rabah Aissaoui and Claire Eldridge, 39–54 (London: Bloomsbury, 2017). Parallel demands by returning African American soldiers recount similar denials of equal rights, see W. E. B. DuBois, "Returning Soldier," *The Crisis*, 1919, https://glc.yale.edu/returning-soldiers.

7. James McDougall, *History and the Culture of Nationalism in Algeria* (Cambridge: Cambridge University Press, 2006), 93–94.

8. Olivier Le Cour Grandmaison, *De l'indigénat, anatomie d'un "monster" juridique: Le droit colonial en Algérie et dans l'empire français* (Paris: La Découverte. 2010).

9. Jan C. Jansen, "Une autre 'Union Sacrée'? Commémorer la Grande Guerre dans l'Algérie colonisée (1918–1939)," *Revue d'histoire moderne et contemporaine* 2, no.2 (2014): 32–60. See Loi du du 25 octobre 1919 relative à la commémoration et à la Glorification pour la France au cours de la Grande Guerre (Law of October 26, 1919 for the commemoration and glorification of France during the Great War) *JORF*, October 26, 1919, 11910. Note especially article 4 on monument placement, article 5 on state subventions rated according to individual deaths per commune, article 6 on the dates of November 1 or 2 to commemorate the war dead, and article 7 that these laws apply to Algeria and the colonies. On the history of the Souvenir Français, Jean-Christophe Denis, *Le Souvenir Français à travers les siècles, 1887–2017* (Paris, Éditions Bernard Giovanangeli, 2017).

10. Nicolas Offenstadt, "(Hi)stories and Memories of the Great War in France (1914–2018)," in *Writing the Great War: The Historiography of World War I from 1918 to the Present*, ed. Christoph Cornelissen and Arndt Weinrich, 11–49 (Berghahn Books, 2021).

11. Jérôme Duhamel and Réné Pétillon, *Grand inventaire du génie français en 365 objets* (Paris: Albin Michel, 1992), 196: "Between 1919 and 1925, a war memorial was erected in every community in France, with one single exception: the village of Thierville in the department of the Eure, the only French village which had no dead to mourn, not in 1870, nor in [19]14–18, nor in [19]39–45."

12. Antoine Prost, "Monuments to the Dead," in Pierre Nora, *Realms of Memory: Rethinking the French Past* (New York: Columbia University Press, 1996), vol 3: 307–330. Prost also listed 224 plain columns or stelae, 19 of which were adorned with a simple urn or a funerary torch, and 30 decorated with the Croix de Guerre, the French military cross.

13. Joseph Darot, "Les sacrifices de l'Oranie durant la Grande Guerre 1914–1918," *Le livre d'or de l'Oranie* (Algiers: Éditions de *l'Afrique du Nord Illustrée*, 1925), 74. The committee was headed by a local lawyer, M. Boluix-Bassel.

14. "Un Monument aux Morts de l'Oranie," *Art et Décoration* 45 (1924): 5–6. On the system of subscription, funding, and juried contests in France, see Chantal Martinet, "La Souscription" and "Le Concours" in *La sculpture française au xixe*

siècle (Paris: Éditions de la Réunion des musées nationaux, 1986), 231–238 and 216–217. This system was transferred to Algeria.

15. "Une Œuvre patriotique Départementale: Le monument commémoratif de la victoire (Hommage aux morts de la Grande Guerre), Un Appel aux Populations de l'Oranie," *L'Echo d'Oran*, January 8, 1922, 2: "Œuvre de solidarité oranienne, parce que l'airain doit matérialiser dans une œuvre d'art grandiose la gloire resplendissante de tous les enfants de l'Oranie, sans distinction de race, d'origine, ni de religion qui furent des 'poilus' qui furent les soldats de la noble France. . . . Il est indispensable que l'Oranie commémore par un monument superbe la Victoire prestigieuse remportée par la France et la part que ses enfants ont prise à cette Victoire tous confondus dans le même témoignage d'admiration et de reconnaissance encore une fois quelle que soit leur race, quelle que soit leur origine quelle que soit leur religion."

16. Donál Hassett, "A Tale of Two Monuments: The War Memorials of Oran and Algiers and Commemorative Culture in Colonial and Post-Colonial Algeria," in *Commemorating Race and Empire in the Great War Centenary*, ed. Shanti Sumartojo and Ben Wellings (Liverpool: Liverpool University Press, 2018), 157.

17. On the importance of the Algiers' Villa Abd el-Tif residency for artists primarily from France in the creation of an Algerian artistic scene, see Élisabeth Cazenave, *La villa Abd-el-Tif: Un demi-siècle de vie artistique en Algérie, 1907–1962* (Saint Raphael, France: Association Abd-el-Tif, 1998); and Roger Benjamin, *Orientalist Aesthetics: Art, Colonialism, and French North Africa, 1880–1930* (Berkeley: University of California Press, 2002), 143–157. On Pommier and his Algerian sojourn, see Jean Alazard, "Le sculpteur Albert Pommier," *L'Art et les artistes* 31, new series no. 160 (1935): 89–94.

18. See Malek Alloula, *The Colonial Harem* (Minneapolis: University of Minnesota Press, 1986); and Susan Slyomovics, "Visual Ethnography, Stereotypes, and Photographing Algeria," in *Orientalism Revisited: Art, Land, and Voyages*, ed. Ian Richard Netton, 128–150 (London: Routledge, 2012).

19. Robert Rey, "Le Monument de Hammam-Bou-Hadjar," *Art et Décoration* 42 (July-December 1922): 159: "Sur un socle, formé de quelques marches, s'élève une base, une sorte de parallélépipède presque cubique dont les quatres faces latérales, bordée d'un bandeau plat porte un bas-relief. De cette base monte une colonne toute unie, de section carrée, où se liront, d'un côté, les années fatidiques 1914–1918, de l'autre les noms des morts. Et sommant cette colonne, pose sur toute la surface de la section, la grande figure, sobrement équarrie, d'un homme de la guerre. Il est engoncé dans sa capote alourdie de boue et de pluie. Il réfugie à demi, dans son cache-nez épais, un visage durci par les fatigues mais où palpite beaucoup d'esprit. Entre ses pieds et ses genoux, repose, à terre, le sac bouclèe don't l'homme tient les courroies; le sac pesant, symbole de cette guerre harassante qui nous obligeait à remonter au sommet de nos âmes un espoir sans cesse basculant et qui fit de nous tous, pendant quatre année, une armée de Sisyphes. Les bas-reliefs de la

base n'ont pas moins de simplicité." See also, Eldridge, "'The Forgotten of This Tribute'"; and *À nos grands hommes: La sculpture publique française jusqu'à la seconde guerre mondiale à travers la carte postale* (Paris: Musée d'Orsay et l'Institut National d'Histoire de l'Art, 2004), CD-ROM.

20. Farid Benramdane, "'Qui es-tu? J'ai été dit': De la destruction de la filiation dans l'état civil d'Algérie ou éléments d'un onomacide sémantique," *Insaniyat* 10 (2000): 79–87.

21. See decree in Robert Estoublon and Adolphe Lefébure, *Code de l'Algérie annoté: Recueil chronologique des lois, ordonnances, décrets, arrêtés, circulaires, etc., formant la législation algérienne actuellement en vigueur, avec les travaux préparatoires et l'indication de la jurisprudence* (Algiers: A. Jourdan, 1896), 500. Article 5 appears on p. 574.

22. "L'inauguration du monument départemental de la Victoire," *L'Echo d'Oran*, May 23, 1927, 2.

23. A. Bussière, "Le Maréchal Bugeaud et la colonization de l'Algérie: Souvenirs et récits de la vie colonial en Afrique," *Revue des Deux Mondes (1829–1971)* 4, no. 3 (1853): 449–506. In 1847, the European settler population of Algeria was estimated at 100,000 inhabitants, see Jacques Frémeaux, *La France et l'Algérie en guerre, 1830–1870, 1954–1962* (Paris: Economica et Institut de Stratégie Comparée, 2002), 24. On the colonial commune, see Jacques Berque, *Le Maghreb entre deux guerres* (Paris: Seuil, 1962), 13: "une timide amorce d'une commune."

24. Bachagha Belhadj Sahraoui known as "Si Sahraoui" (1856?–1937) of the Ouled Sidi Khaled tribe, was elected representative to the region of Trezel as "Membre du Conseil Superieur du Gouvernement" for Djebel Amour, Tousnina, Sougueur, Ouled Sidi Khaled, Department of Oran. His military prowess and political appointments are discussed in Charles-Robert Ageron, "Enquête sur les origines du nationalisme algérien: L'émir Khaled, petit-fils d'Abd El-Kader, fut-il le premier nationaliste algérien?" *Revue de l'Occident musulman et de la Méditerranée* 2 (1966): 29n54.

25. *L'Echo d'Oran*, May 27, 1927, 2: "C'était la division oranaise, le 45e algérienne, une de ces magnifiques divisions kaki, comme le 37e, le 38e et la division du Maroc, troupes de choc qui de 1914–18 allaient être de toutes les batailles et qui partout allaient se classer parmi les belles unités de l'armée française." See also, "M. Violette à Oran," *L'Afrique du Nord Illustrée* 318, June 4, 1927, 3–4.

26. On April 22, 1915, the 45th Division from Oran suffered the first and most significant chemical gas attack in World War I when Germany released 165 tons of lethal chlorine gas over the battle trenches of Ypres, Belgium. Poison gas would eventual be banned in international treaties because of its horrifically high mortality rates. Naulin's "shock troops" were the colonial infantry used as cannon fodder against the latest combat threat of chemical warfare.

27. Dominique Lormier, *C'est nous les Africains: L'épopée de l'armée française d'Afrique (1940–1945)* (Paris: Calmann-Lévy, 2006); and Eric T. Jennings, *Free*

French Africa in World War II: The African Resistance (Cambridge: Cambridge University Press, 2015).

28. Jan C. Jansen, "Celebrating the Nation in a Colonial Context: Bastille Day and the Contested Public Space in Algeria, 1880–1939," *Journal of Modern History* 85, no. 1 (2013): 36–68.

29. Redouane Ainad Tabet, *Le 8 mai 1945 en Algérie* (Algiers: OPU, 1987); Boucif Mekhaled, *Chroniques d'un massacre: 8 Mai 1945, Sétif, Guelma, Kherrata* (Paris: Syros/Au Nom de la Mémoire, 1995); and James McDougall, "The Impossible Republic: The Reconquest of Algeria and the Decolonization of France, 1945–1962," *Journal of Modern History* (2011): 790–811.

30. On February 27, 2005, Hubert Colin de Verdière, French ambassador to Algeria, publicly acknowledged that the events at Sétif after VE Day to be a French error, see Florence Beaugé, "Paris reconnaît que le massacre de Sétif en 1945 était 'inexcusable,'" *Le Monde*, March 9, 2005, https://www.lemonde.fr/international/article/2005/03/09/paris-reconnait-que-le-massacre-de-setif-en-1945-etait-inexcusable_400904_3210.html.

31. Saddek Benkada, "La création de Médina Jdida, Oran (1845): un exemple de la politique coloniale de regroupement urbain," *Insaniyat* 5 (1998): 103–111; and Fadila Kettaf, *La fabrique des espaces publics en Algérie* (Paris: L'Harmattan, 2019), 317–323.

32. On Oran's "native villages," see René Lespès, *Oran: Étude de géographie et d'histoire urbaines* (Paris: F. Alcan, 1938), and for the 1940s, see René Emsalem, "Les villages indigènes d'Oran," *Revue de géographie jointe au Bulletin de la Société de géographie de Lyon et de la région lyonnaise* 25, no. 4 (1950): 289–299; and Ammara Bekkouche, "Un quartier nommé Ville Nouvelle: Du village nègre colonial à la Medina J'dida des Oranais," *Les Annales de la recherche urbaine* 98 (2005): 114–121

33. On Souiah's life, see Omar Carlier, "'Homme fétiche' ou 'Homme-symbole'? Un notable-militant: Houari Souiah, Premier préfet d'Oran (1915–1990)," *Cahiers de la Méditerranée* 46/47, no. 1 (1993): 203–247; and Mohamed Freha, *Oran: Une ville témoine* (Oran: Enadar, 2017), 20–24.

34. For images and site plan of the Algiers Martyrs' Memorial (known as "Maqam Echahid" in Arabic), see https://www.alger-city.com/tourisme/que-visiter/memorial-du-martyr.

35. Alain Amato, *Monuments en exil* (Versailles: Éditions de Atlanthrope, 1979), 112; and Gérard Bourdin, "Les ambiguïtés d'un rapprochement: Parrainages et jumelages, 1956–1962," in *La France en guerre 1954–1962: Expériences métropolitaines de la guerre d'indépendance algérienne*, ed. Raphaëlle Branche and Sylvie Thenault, 82–100 (Paris, Autrement, 2008).

36. "Projet de jumelage regional," SHD 1H 2462/1, Annexe 2, p. 4.

37. This initiative was at the behest of the local Lyon "Edouard Herriot Committee" after his death, see http://www.mdemoblog.fr/edouard-herriot-lyon-oran/.

38. Michael G. Kammen, *Digging Up the Dead* (Chicago: University of Chicago Press, 2010), ix–x.

39. Ibid.

40. Décret 68-728 du 7 août 1968 portant publication de l'échange de lettres entre la France et l'Algerie des 29 avril et 30 juin 1968 concernant le regroupement des sepultures civiles françaises situées dans certains cimetières d'Algérie (Decree 68-728 on the publication of letters exchanged between France and Algeria concerning regrouping civilian French tombs situated in certain Algerian cemeteries), *JORF*, August 7, 1968, 7799.

41. Oran-Tamashouet, Mascara, Relizane, and Saïda, the four designated large urban cemeteries, regrouped 22 local cemeteries of western Oran Province. By 2009, Tamashouet had integrated close to 7,500 graves financed by the French government and coordinated by the French consulate of Oran that reopened in 2007 after the end of Algeria's Dark Decade. See Arrêté 21 octobre 2011 modifiant l'arrêté du 23 juin 2011 relatif au regroupement de sépultures civiles françaises en Algérie (Order October 21, 2011 modifying the order of June 23, 2011 on regrouping civilian French tombs in Algeria) *JORF*, October 27, 2011, https://www.legifrance.gouv.fr/jorf/id/JORFTEXT000024717650.

From the large literature on settler mourning and memorial practices in France, see Andrea L. Smith, "Settler Sites of Memory and the Work of Mourning," *French Politics, Culture & Society* 31, no. 3 (2013): 65–92; and Natalya Vince, *The Algerian War, the Algerian Revolution* (London: Palgrave Macmillan, 2020).

42. On the restitution of the remains of nineteenth-century Algerian resistance fighters from a Paris museum to reburial in the Algiers' Martyrs' Cemetery, see Constant Méheut, "France Returned 24 Skulls to Algeria. They Weren't What They Seemed," *New York Times*, October 18, 2022, https://www.nytimes.com/2022/10/17/world/europe/france-algeria-restitution-skulls.html.The counterexample is the disgraced non-repatriable body of French Admiral François Darlan (1881–1942), the Vichy head of all French forces in North Africa, who surrendered to American troops in Algiers. He was assassinated by an anti-Vichy pro-monarchist, who in turn was immediately executed. Darlan's body is discreetly buried, if not forgotten, in the French naval cemetery of Mers el-Kebir near Oran.

43. Alfred Bérenguer, *Un curé en Amérique latine (1959–1960)* (Algiers: SNED, 1966); and Alfred Bérenguer, *En toute liberté: Entretiens avec Geneviève Dermenjian* (Paris: Centurion, 1994).

44. Father Alain Feuvrier, interview with author, Lyon, March 2014.

45. The literature on what took place in Oran during the last months of French Algeria, especially during the summer of 1962, is vast and contentious with disputed numbers of Algerian and French killed, why, and how. An overview in English is Amy L. Hubbell, "Remembering the 5 July 1962 Massacre in Oran, Algeria," in *Places of Traumatic Memory: A Global Context*, ed. Amy L. Hubbell, Natsuko

Akagawa, Sol Rojas-Lizana, and Annie Pohlman, 219–240 (Cham, Switzerland: Springer International Publishing, 2020).

46. See their website, Collectif sauveguarde des cimetières d'Oranie (CSCO), http://csco.e-monsite.com/ which is attempting to recreate a virtual crowd-sourced cemetery.

47. "Le Monument aux Morts d'Oran rapatrié à Lyon dans le quartier de la Duchère," Le Cercle Algérianiste de Lyon website, https://www.cerclealgerianiste-lyon.org/le-monument-aux-morts-doran-rapatrie-a-la-duchere/; and Jean Luc Pinol, "Le monument aux morts d'Oran transporté à La Duchère," Fresques INA, https://fresques.ina.fr/rhone-alpes/fiche-media/Rhonal00121/le-monument-aux-morts-d-oran-transporte-a-la-duchere.html.

48. AML 425 WP 14: Letter dated March 5, 1964 from Brun de la Valette, Secretary General of the Association nationale des français d'Afrique de Nord, d'outre-mer et de leurs amis (ANFANOMA) to Mayor Luis Pradel.

49. Ibid., Letter to Michel G. Villiere, municipal councilor, Lyon, from Pierre Padovani, February 19, 1964. Padovani's remarks help researchers date the end of organized military monument transfers.

50. Luc Demarchi, interviews with the author, Lyon, spring 2014.

51. See his self-published autobiography, Napoléon Bullukian, *De l'Ararat à Napoléon* (Lyon: Éditions La Pensée Universelle, 1975).

52. AML 425 WP 14, Letter of chief architect to the mayor of Lyon, March 31, 1964: "on pourrait se contenter du Groupe Sculptural terminal qui pourrait être placé sur un socle assez haut, ce qui permettrait de graver les inscriptions lapidaires nécessaires."

53. AML 425 WP 14: Letter of July 12, 1967 from Benali Seghier, mayor of Oran to the Mayor of Lyon. "Je vous accorde bien volontiers l'autorisation de transférer à Lyon le monument aux Morts d'Oran en précisant toutefois que le socle en pierre doit demeurer en place." The architect's report in the same file: "Pour des raisons techniques, ainsi qu'à la demande des Services algériens, seule la partie supérieure du monument fut déplacée, le socle restant sur place à Oran," Région Rhône-Alpes website, https://patrimoine.auvergnerhonealpes.fr/dossier/monument-aux-morts-d-oran/2f0a2558-1574-498b-ac0d-c61012cbc8aa.

54. Ibid.

55. Mohammed Benguesmia-Chadly, interview with author, May 16, 2014, Oran.

56. Émile Azoulay, interviews with author during March 2014, Lyon. See Paul Veyne, "Conduites sans croyances et oeuvres d'art sans spectateurs," *Diogène* 143 (1988): 3–22. Both Azoulay and Benguesmia-Chadly remained actively engaged in heritage initiatives in their respective cities: Azoulay was instrumental in having a synagogue built for Algerian Jews in La Duchère in Lyon where many repatriates initially settled. In Oran, Benguesmia-Chadly led historical walking tours of pre-

independent, revolutionary Oran tracing the perimeters of Oran's besieged native quarter with its barbed wire enclosures that was under military surveillance and endured daily sniper fire throughout 1962. On May 16, 2014, I attended his tour of the former "native quarter" of Medina Jdida that he brought to life through walking paired with oral testimony at key buildings especially by women actors from that period. For example, Fatiha Zemmouchi, daughter of the founder of the school Madrassat al-Falah, recounted the struggle for literacy in Oran's colonial native quarter. See Malika Rahal, "Oran 1962: Des trois dimensions du souvenir," *Textures du temps*, July 16, 2018, https://texturesdutemps.hypotheses.org/2731.

57. Émile Azoulay possessed color Polaroid images of the removal which he allowed me to rephotograph on my cellphone with oral permission to reproduce. A full set was posted by Luc Demarchi, "Le Monument aux Morts d'Oran," Cercle algérianiste de Lyon, August 9, 2007, http://www.cerclealgerianiste-lyon.org/mamo.html.

58. Nouba Bouledras, interviews with author, June 27 and July 1, 2018, Oran. He told me that he owed his workshop and metier to Isaac Sarraude, the Algerian Jewish marble-maker, who had made the Arzew naval memorial (figure 12), and who left his workshop to the Bouledras family when he left Oran at independence.

59. AML 425 WP 14, http://www.patrimoine.rhonealpes.fr/dossier/monument-aux-morts-d-oran/2f0a2558-1574-498b-ac0d-c61012cbc8aa.

60. Hassett, "A Tale of Two Monuments," 151–168.

61. "Le Monument aux Morts transféré à Lyon," *La Republique*, December 9, 1967, 14: "Il est à signaler que cette operation fait suite à une demarche de transfert déposé auprès de l'Assemblée Populaire Communale d'Oran par la municipalité lyonnaise. Etudié et adopté en deliberation par le APC d'Oran cette demande a également été approuvé par le préfet du département. Notons par ailleurs que la déléegation des conseillers municipaux de Lyon a été reçue jeudi par M. Seghir Benali president de l'APC d'Oran. Au cours d'un cordial entretien, la délégation française a formulé le voeu de voir une delegation de l'APC d'Oran assister à Lyon à la cérémonie qui marquera les travaux d'installation du monument."

62. French law granted amnesties for criminal acts committed before the official French-Algerian cease-fire of March 19, 1962, and therefore did not absolve Edmond Jouhaud for crimes committed after that date. His sentence was commuted to life imprisonment in 1964. However, he was released in 1967 and in 1969 was named president of the Front national des rapatriés, one of the largest and earliest settler associations in France. In 1982, he was amnestied by President François Mitterand and reintegrated into the army where he retained his former rank and prerogatives. On President François Mitterand's rehabilitation of the putsch's four generals, see Jean Guisnel, *Les généraux: Enquête sur le pouvoir militaire en France* (Paris: Édition de La Découverte, 1990), 66–78. See also justifications by Edmond Jouhaud, *O mon pays perdu: Mémoires de Bou-Sfer à Tulle* (Paris: Fayard, 1969). Jouhaud's grave in Champniers cemetery in southwest France is a

tourist site for settlers. Other graves of supporters of French Algeria also became sites of settler pilgrimages, for example the grave in Bourg-la-Reine of Jean Bastien-Thiry, DeGaulle's failed assassin, see https://commons.wikimedia.org/wiki/File:Bourg-la-Reine_(s%C3%A9pulture_Bastien-Thiry).JPG.

63. Institut National de l'Audiovisuel (INA), Video Archive, "*L'inauguration du monument aux morts d'Oran transporté à La Duchère*," Rhône Alpes actualités, ORTF, July 16, 1968, http://www.ina.fr/video/LXF04042372.

64. Voice over: "Toujours à Lyon, la veille de ce 14 juillet, avait eu lieu à 11h sur le plateau de La Duchère l'inauguration du monument aux morts d'Oran. Ce quartier lyonnais, dont la moitié des habitants sont des rapatriés, conservera désormais le souvenir des morts des deux dernières guerres, tombés en Oranie. En présence des personnalités civiles et militaires de Lyon et d'une nombreuse assistance, trois allocutions étaient prononcées successivement par messieurs Fenech, Pradel, et Thierry. Cette émouvante cérémonie devait se terminer par plusieurs dépôts de gerbes au pied du monument." Archive Video, INA, Emission Région, "L'inauguration du monument aux morts d'Oran transporté à La Duchère," Rhône Alpes actualités, July 16, 1968: "Il rappelle notre terre d'Oranie et le combat de deux générations de ses fils pour que vive la France. Il sera le lieu de recueillement où les rapatriés, qui ont perdu leur tombe, pourront évoquer la mémoire de leurs morts," https://fresques.ina.fr/rhone-alpes/fiche-media/Rhonal00121. See "Le Monument aux Morts d'Oran rapatrié à Lyon dans le quartier de La Duchère," Le Cercle Algérianiste de Lyon, https://www.cerclealgerianiste-lyon.org/le-monument-aux-morts-doran-rapatrie-a-la-duchere/.

65. Among his books are Bachaga Boualam, *Mon pays, la France* (Paris: Édition, 1962); and Bachaga Boualam, *Les Harkis au service de la France* (Paris: Édition, 1963).

66. Myriam Bacha, *Architectures au Maghreb (XIXe–XXe siècles): Réinvention du patrimoine* (Tours, France: Presses universitaire François Rabelais, 2011); and Reinhart Kosseleck, *L'expérience de l'histoire* (Paris, Gallimard/Le Seuil, 1997), 135–160.

67. Mohamed Freha, interview with author, October 28, 2019, Oran. After the plaque was removed, a list of the martyrs of the Algerian Revolution from the Oran region—thirteen shot and twenty-nine guillotined in Oran Civil Prison—is currently posted on the wall of the Oran museum, Espace d'Histoire et de Mémoire de la Ville d'Oran, established by Freha. Mohamed Freha, interview with author, September 26, 2023, Oran.

68. Ary Renan, "Les Arts arabes dans le Maghreb, Tlemcen," *Gazette des Beaux-Arts* (1892): 383–401.

69. On the mosque, see Amine Kasmi, "Masjid Hassan el-Pacha, Oran, Algeria," Archnet, https://archnet.org/sites/6350/media_contents/136299.

70. Mohamed Benguesmia-Chadly, interview with author, May 16, 2014, Oran.

71. On contemporary Oran, see Habib Benkoula, "La question de la ville ou la

ville en question," *Le Quotidien d'Oran,* October 25, 2020, http://www.lequotidien-oran.com/index.php?news=5294953; Diana Wylie, "'Part of Who We Are': Using Old Buildings to Foster Citizenship in North Africa (Oran, Algeria, and Casablanca, Morocco)," *Buildings & Landscapes: Journal of the Vernacular Architecture Forum* 25, no. 1 (2018): 44–63; Nabila Metair, "Twentieth Century Architecture in Oran: Its Contemporary Heritage-Value," *Journal of North African Studies* 26, no. 3 (2021): 404–425; and Jack Goody, *The Myth of the Bagre* (Oxford: Clarendon Press, 1972).

72. Benedict Anderson, *Imagined Communities: Reflections on the Origins and Spread of Nationalism* (London: Verso, 1983), 50.

73. See Françoise Choay on the invention of the concept of the historic city center in *L'Allégorie du patrimoine* (Paris: Seuil, 1992). On December 5, 1998, Vieux Lyon was inscribed in UNESCO's list as a World Heritage site because it exemplified a coherent model of urbanity from the medieval age to the nineteenth century, https://whc.unesco.org/en/list/872/.

74. On monuments, see Alois Riegl, "The Modern Cult of Monuments: Its Character and its Origin," *Oppositions* 25 (1982 [1903]): 20–51. For the notion of the ensemble, see Tilmann Breuer, "Ensemble: Konzeption und Problematik eines Begriffes des Bayrischen Denkmalschutzgesetzes," *Deutsche Kunst und Denkmalpflege* 34 (1976): 21–38.

75. The first so-called Malraux law concerned monuments, see Loi 62-880 du 31 juillet 1962 relative à la restauration de grands monuments historiques (Law 62-880 of July 11, 1962 on restoring great historical monuments), *JORF,* August 2, 1962, 7651. On Malraux and the French heritage regime, see Herman Lebovics, "Cultural Policy," in *The French Republic: History, Values, Debates,* ed. Edward Berenson, Vincent Duclert and Christophe Prochasson (Ithaca, NY: Cornell University Press, 2011), 344–335; and Herman Lebovics, *Mona Lisa's Escort: André Malraux and the Reinvention of French Culture* (Ithaca, NY: Cornell University Press, 1999.)

76. See Kenny Cupers, *The Social Project: Housing Postwar France* (Minneapolis: University of Minnesota Press, 2014); and Sarah Rojon, "La renovation de l'habiter dans le grand ensemble de la Duchère: Pour en finir avec la figure des nouveaux habitants," *Recherches sociologiques et anthropologiques* 1 (2014): 47–67.

77. Michel Paulin, "François-Régis Cottin: L'oeuvre," *Bulletin de la société academique d'architecture de Lyon* 21 (2013): 26–37; Jacques Rey, *Lyon, cité radieuse: Une aventure du Mouvement moderne international* (Lyon: Libel, 2010), 120–125; and the special issue of the *Bulletin de la société académique d'architecture de Lyon* 17–18 (2009): *La Duchère 1948–2014.* See also Guy de Longeaux, "Naissance d'un grand ensemble: Genèse d'une société nouvelle," *Études* (1964): 375–392.

78. Marc André, "Les rapatriés d'Algérie et la presse: Le cas lyonnais," *Outremers* 97, no. 368/369 (2010): 421–438.

79. Annie Schwartz, *La Duchère, 40 ans* (Lyon: Audacce, 2003), 88–106. "Hida," an acronym for Haim Yosef David Azulai, was an important eighteenth-century

Jerusalem-born rabbi and thinker sent to North African Jewish communities between 1773 and 1777 to gather funds.

80. G. Desplanques, "Les migrations extérieures, les rapatriés d'Algérie," *Les collections des de l'Institut national de la statistique et des études économiques* 39 (June 1975): 72.

81. Yann Scioldo-Zürcher, *Devenir métropolitain, parcours et politique d'intégration de rapatriés d'Algérie en métropole, de 1954 au début du XXI° siècle* (Paris: Éditions de l'École des hautes études en sciences sociales, 2010).

82. On relevant monument scholarship, see chapter 1, footnote 30.

83. Michel Deifenbacher, *Rapport Parachever l'effort de solidarité nationale envers les rapatriés: Promouvoir l'oeuvre collective de la France outre-mer* (Paris: Documentation française, December 18, 2003); and Richard L. Derderian, "Algeria as a *lieu de memoire*: Ethnic Minority Memory and National Identity in Contemporary France," *Radical History Review* (2002): 28–43.

84. Claire Eldridge, *From Empire to Exile: History and Memory Within the Pied-Noir and Harki Communities* (Manchester: Manchester University Press, 2016). See also Derderian, "Algeria as a *lieu de memoire*."

85. For an example of a recreated Pied-Noir Catholic pilgrimage and statue brought from Oran, see Susan Slyomovics, "The Virgin Mary of Algeria: French Mediterraneans *En Miroir*," *History and Anthropology* 31 (2020): 22–42.

86. AML 425 WP 14: Séance de Commission Generale du 26 Fevrier 1968, minutes approving added inscription.

87. Groupe interreligieux Abraham de la Duchère, "Déclaration," May 28, 2012, http://www.christianismesocial.org/Declaration-du-Groupe.html.

88. The official label "Patrimoine du XXe siècle" (heritage of the twentieth century) was created in 1999 by France's Ministry of Culture and Communication. For further protection of these buildings, an additional inscription as a UNESCO's World Heritage site was called for. This was replaced by the Décret 2017-433 du 28 mars 2017 relatif au label "Architecture contemporaine remarquable" pris en application de l'article L. 650-1 du code du patrimoine (Decree 2017-433 of March 28, 2017 on the label "remarkable contemporary architecture" issued pursuant to article L. 650-1 of the heritage code), *JORF*, March 31, 2017, https://www.legifrance.gouv.fr/loda/id/JORFTEXT000034308019/?isSuggest=true. In addition, a listing as a UNESCO's World Heritage site strengthens a building's protection.

89. Jean-Jacques Jordi, *De l'exode à l'exil: Rapatriés et Pieds Noirs en France* (Paris: L'Harmattan, 1993). See also studies of Pied-Noir associations by the Oran-born Maurice Calmein, founder of the Cercle des Algérianistes on November 1, 1973, with the Lyon branch created in the mid-1980s. See Maurice Calmein, *Les associations pied- noirs, 1962–1994* (Carcassonne: SOS Outre Mer, 1994) updated to Maurice Calmein and Thierry Rolando, *Les français d'Algérie de 1962 à 2014* (Friedberg: Atlantis, 2014).

90. This refers to Agence nationale d'indemnisation des français d'outre-mer

(ANIFOM) and the Agence de défense des biens et intérêts des rapatriés (established by the ordonnance of September 19, 1962). Indemnification and reparations are ongoing disputes between France and Algeria. Briefly, the director Mohamed Himour declared an inventory of 24,300 property items in dispute and deemed still the property of foreigners who left the country (*propriété d'étrangers ayant quitté le pays.*) Algeria's position is only those persons regardless of nationality, who did not leave Algeria at independence or during the 1960s can claim restitution or indemnification for their property, otherwise all *biens vacants* (abandoned properties) belong to the Algerian state, see Robert P. Parks, "Claiming Bits and Pieces of the State: Squatting and Appropriation of Public Domain in Algeria," *Middle East Law and Governance* 11 (2019): 103–135. Since 2000, over 600 court cases have been filed by Pieds-Noirs in France before the United Nations Human Rights Commission demanding restitution or indemnities, see Yann Scioldo-Zürcher, "The Cost of Decolonization: Compensating the Pieds-Noirs," in *France Since the 1970s: History, Politics and Memory in an Age of Uncertainty*, ed. Emile Chabal, 99–114 (London: Bloomsbury, 2015).

91. Senate, Office national des anciens combattants et victimes de guerre, ONACVG, http://www.senat.fr/rap/r13-132/r13-1329.html: "Renforcer la mission mémoire: aller vers un rôle assumé dans le renforcement du lien armée-Nation. . . . L'ONAC-VG doit également être réorienté, au-delà de ses ressortissants, vers la communauté nationale et vers les citoyens. C'est au travers de l'action de mémoire que ce travail peut le mieux se faire. Une première réorganisation de l'Office est intervenue dans la cadre de la politique de mémoire avec la création des missions mémoire et communication."

92. "A nos chers morts restés à Hammam-Bou-Hadjar. Une plaque est dédiée par la Ville de Fréjus à la mémoire des enfants d'Algérie morts pour la France, 1914–1918, 1939–1945." See Amato, *Monuments en exil*, 107–109; Andrea L. Smith, "Settler Sites of Memory and the Work of Mourning," *French Politics, Culture & Society* 31, no. 3 (2013): 65–92; and extracts posted on Pied-Noir website from Georges-Emile Paul, *Hammam-Bou-Hadjar 1874–1962: Petite chronique de mon village algérien et de son environnement* (Montpellier: Transcomp Éditions, 1988), http://hammambouhadjar.free.fr/le_village.htm.

93. Spencer Segalla, *Empire and Catastrophe: Decolonization and Environmental Disaster in North Africa and Mediterranean France since 1954* (Lincoln: University of Nebraska Press, 2020); and Gregory Mann, "Locating Colonial Histories: Between France and West Africa," *American Historical Review* (2005): 409–434.

94. Christiane Gruber, "The Missiri of Fréjus as Healing Memorial: Mosque Metaphors and the French Colonial Army (1928–64)," *International Journal of Islamic Architecture* 1, no. 1 (2012): 25–60.

95. For official images of the Pommier monument in Fréjus, see the website of the Var department, http://memoires-de-guerres.var.fr/article.php?laref=3485.

96. Amato, "Fréjus," in *Monuments en exil*, 107–109.

97. June Hargrove, *The Statues of Paris: An Open-Air Pantheon* (Antwerp: Mercatorfonds, 1989), 194. She notes that artworks no longer deemed worthy of display are parked in the Depot of Auteil located in Ivry, photo on p. 195.

98. See Amato, "Saint-Raphaël," in *Monuments en exile*, 189–190 for the account of Montamat's removal of the Mascara colonial war memorial and figure 49 postcard.

99. For Mascara's postindependence memorial to the martyrs of the Algerian War, see the Pied-Noir website, "Mascara Algérie de ma jeunesse," http://p-rubira.com/galerie/picture.php?/912.

100. Montaland's remarkable Skikda city hall is made of reinforced concrete in the "neo-Mauresque" style and is inscribed in *JORA*, no. 57, October 12, 2017, 29–31, along with his post office, town hall, and train station as national immoveable cultural property (*biens culturels immobiliers*), preceded by similar 2007 classification of his Dar Meriem Azza Palace.

101. Élisabeth Cazenave, *Les artistes de l'Algérie: Dictionnaire des peintres, sculpteurs, graveurs, 1830–1962* (Paris: Association Abd-el-Tif, 2001), 233.

102. Amato, "Saint-Aygulf," in *Monuments en exil*, 177–179.

103. For a detailed account of the protagonists, the settler who wanted the statue and the mayor who kept the plinth, see Amato, *Monuments en exil*, 112–116.

104. On communities of resettlers elsewhere in the world such as the Acadians or Scotch-Irish, see Lorenzo Veracini, *The World Inside Out* (London: Verso, 2021).

Chapter 3: Dismantling a World

1. Hadjer Merbouh, "Toponymes urbains à Sidi Bel Abbès-ville (Algérie): Usages, représentations et identités sociolinguistiques," *Nouvelle revue d'onomastique* 53 (2011): 128; and Annie Rey-Goldzeiguer, *Le royaume arabe: La politique algérienne de Napoléon III, 1861–1870* (Algiers: SNED, 1977).

2. Monique Dondin-Payre, "*L'exercitus Africae* inspiratrice de l'armée française d'Afrique: *Ense et aratro*," *Antiquités africaines* 27 (1991): 141–149. See also Gustave Boissièr, *L'Algérie romaine* (Paris: Librairie Hachette, 1883), vol. 2: 333–480.

3. Raoul-Marie Donop, *Lettres sur l'Algérie (1907–1908)* (Paris: Plon, 1908), 131: "Fondée seulement en 1849, sur l'emplacement d'une petite redoute qui avait été construite près du marabout consacré à Sidi-bel-Abbès, la ville offre cette particularité qu'elle montre, d'une façon toute spéciale, l'aptitude que les Français possèdent à coloniser, puisque, seule de toutes les villes de l'Algérie, elle n'a aucun passé historique, et que tout y a été créé par des Français, avec l'aide de la main-d'oeuvre étrangère."

4. Léon Bastide, *Bel Abbés et son arrondissement: Histoire administrative* (Oran: Imprimerie Perrier, 1880), 301–315; and Léon Adoue, *La ville de Sidi-Bel-Abbès: Histoire, légende, anecdotes* (Sidi-Bel-Abbès: René Roidot, Imprimeur-Editeur, 1927).

5. Amine Kasmi, "The Plan as a Colonization Project: The Medina of Tlemcen under French Rule, 1842–1920," *Planning Perspectives* 34, no. 1 (2019): 25–42.

6. "Nécrologie: Le Général Prudon," *Revue du génie militaire* (January 1, 1892): 267. "Sidi-bel-Abbès, Prudon, deux noms inséparables. Pendant sept années consécutives, l'infatigable chef du génie, avec une intelligence et une énergie admirables, y fût exécuter des travaux considérables de toute nature, fortifications, bâtiments militaires et civils, routes, conduits d'eau, irrigations, etc., faisant sortir de terre, au milieu d'une plaine couverte de broussailles, une ville tout entière, aujourd'hui et depuis longtemps déjà riche, populeuse, florissante, entourée de superbes jardins et disparaissant elle-même sous de magnifiques ombrages-, création impérissable à laquelle restera toujours attaché le nom de Prudon." See also Xavier Malverti, "Les officiers du Génie et le dessin de villes en Algérie (1830–1870)," *Revue du monde musulman et de la Méditerranée* 73/74 (1994): 229–244.

7. On the camp of the III Augustan Legion in Lambaesis, see Louis Leschi, *Etudes d'épigraphie, d'archéologie et d'histoire africaines* (Paris: Arts et Métiers graphiques, 1957); and Michel Janon, *Lambèse: Capitale militaire de l'Afrique romaine* (Ollioules: Nerthe, 2005).

8. Xavier Malverti and Aleth Picard, "Algeria: Military Genius and Civic Design (1830–70)," *Planning Perspective* 6, no. 2 (1991): 215.

9. "[À] l'origine au moins de la colonisation, Rome fit table rase du passé en imposant à ses conquêtes un cadre nouveau: soit par indifférence, soit par mépris, elle ignorait l'organisation administrative préexistante et marquait ses droits de propriété éminente en toisant sa conquête: la prise de possession est comme gravée dans le sol ; selon le principe politique éternel: 'diviser pour régner', on voit la centuriation isoler les zones de résistance, c'est-à-dire surtout les régions montagneuses, s'insinuer même dans les vallées et morceler les massifs dont elle ronge les premières pentes," in R. Chevallier, "La centuriation et les problèmes de la colonisation Romaine," *Études rurales* 3 (1961): 64. See also Michael Greenhalgh, "The New Centurions: French Reliance on the Roman Past during the Conquest of Algeria," *War & Society* 16, no. 1 (1998): 1–28.

10. "L'histoire nous montre que les Anciens n'ont pas opéré autrement, dans les contrées analogues aussi bien que dans l'Algérie actuelle. Arriver sur un point, y établir un camp qui se transforme ensuite en colonie: c'est ainsi qu'ont fait là les Romains nos prédécesseurs. Le simple touriste se rendra facilement compte de l'identité des méthodes en visitant, l'histoire en main, deux camps militaires devenus villes de colonisation, l'un au premier siècle de notre ère, l'autre au dix-neuvième," Gauzence de Lastours, "L'Algérie et le service en campagne algérienne," *Revue du génie militaire* 42, no. 2 (1911). On the "trivalent significance . . . for French domination: justification, admiration, and emulation " see also, Patricia M. E. Lorcin, "France and Rome in Africa: Recovering Colonial Algeria's Latin Past," *French Historical Studies* 25, no. 2 (2002): 295.

11. Gauzence de Lastours, "L'Algérie et le service en campagne algérienne," 387: "L'enceinte a un flanquement latéral; mais voici la même disposition, les quatre portes aux points cardi-naux, la forme d'ensemble rectangulaire de 350 m sur 800

m, la préfecture placée comme le praetorium, l'hôpital comme thermes, l'église et la synagogue comme temples, le théâtre, la place publique, avec la ville militaire bien séparée; en un mot tout le groupement nécessaire à la civilisation qui suit l'armée. Quintus Flavius, le légat de la 3e légion, dont le tombeau se voit près de Lambèse, n'aurait-il pas reconnu pour son collègue et imitateur le général Bedeau? Ce simple coup d'oeil fait ressortir en même temps les deux rôles successifs de l'armée: rôle créateur, role défensif."

12. Native Berber villages, isolated houses, and fortified enclosures before the Arab invasions were archaeologically recorded in Bossuet and north to the plain of Sidi-Bel-Abbès at the limits of the Roman *limes* by Stephane Gsell, *Atlas archéologique de I'Algérie* (Algiers: Adolphe Jourdan, 1911); and B. H. Warmington, *The North African Provinces from Diocletian to the Vandal Conquest* (Cambridge: Cambridge University Press, 1954), 8–19.

13. On tribal histories, see Pierre Boyer, "Historique des Béni Amer d'Oranie, des origines au Senatus Consulte," *Revue de l'Occident musulman et de la Méditerranée* 24 (1977): 39–85. On the Roman fort, see Cap. D., "Le Tessala (Actacilis?) et ses ruines," *Revue Africaine* 8, no. 2 (1857): 81–85.

14. Toufik Adda Bou Djellal, mayor of Sidi-Bel-Abbès, interview with the author, June 25, 2018. See also legends of the marabout collected in Adoue, *La ville de Sidi-Bel-Abbès.*

15. Ammara Bekkouche, "Enjeux coloniaux et projection urbaine en Algérie: Le cas de Sidi-Bel-Abbès," *Insaniyat* 13 (2001): 45–59; Redouane Ainad-Tabet, "Sidi-Bel-Abbès: Des mythes fondateurs de la colonisation à la libération," *Insaniyat* 3 (1998): 7–24; and Daho Djerbal, "Processus de colonisation et évolution de la propriété foncière dans les plaines intérieures de l'Oranie (subdivisions de Mascara et Sidi-bel-Abbès, 1850–1920)," (PhD thesis, Université Paris-VII, 1979); and Karim Ouldennebia, *Histoire de Sidi-Bel-Abbès: Le face à face Koubba-Redoute* (Oran: Edition Dar AlQods, 2022).

16. Ainad-Tabet, "Sidi-Bel-Abbès," 378; and Karim Ouldennebbia [al-Mecherfi, pseud.], "La commune mixte de la Mekerra (1874–1962)," 2014, http://bel-abbes.info/les-lundis-de-lhistoire-la-commune-mixte-de-la-mekerra-1874-1962/.

17. On the BMCs, see Raphaëlle Branche, "La sexualité des appelés en Algérie," in *Des hommes et des femmes en guerre d'Algérie*, ed. Jean-Charles Jauffret, 402–415 (Paris: Autrement, 2003). For an overview of the prostitution industry in North Africa, see Christelle Taraud, *La prostitution coloniale: Algérie, Maroc, Tunisie (1830–1962)* (Paris, Éditions Payot, 2003); on "ghettos of vice," see Aurelie Evengeline Perrier, "Intimate Matters: Negotiating Sex, Gender and the Home in Colonial Algeria," (PhD diss. Georgetown University, 2014), 200–207; a chapter by Judith Surkis, "Special Moeurs and Military Exceptions,"152–180, in *Sex, Law, and Sovereignty in French Algeria, 1830–1930* (Ithaca, NY: Cornell University Press, 2019); and for Sidi-Bel-Abbès, see Ouldennebia, *Histoire*, 255–259.

18. There are vast numbers of movies, memoirs, and literature about the sexual

life of Legionnaires. This quote appears in an American men's pulp magazine, see Vincent Peters, "Legion of Violent Lovers," *Whisper,* May 1950, 10–11: https://monlegionnaire.files.wordpress.com/2012/02/legion-of-violent-lovers.jpg.

19. Abdelkrim Mammeri, "Sidi Bel Abbes: Début de la démolition des anciennes maisons closes," *El Watan,* December 20, 2010, https://www.elwatan.com/regions/ouest/bel-abes/sidi-bel-abbes-debut-de-la-demolition-des-anciennes-maisons-closes-20-12-2010.

20. Samia Henni, "Black Color and 'Negro Village': Why Skin Color Still Matters in Architecture?" *Trans Magazin: Farbe* 30 (2017): 158–161. For Sidi-Bel-Abbès, see ANOM 92 2M 168 A6: "Le village indigène dit 'village nègre.' "

21. Photo of the mosque by Neurdein Frères, photographer, *Sidi-Bel-Abbès. La Mosquée / ND Photo,* Sidi Bel Abbès Algeria, 1860–1890, Library of Congress, https://www.loc.gov/item/2004665046/.

22. On Justrabo's life, internment in Camp Lodi, and attachment to Algeria, see Georges Vayrou, "Sur la route de Dijon: Parcours croisés de deux militants anticolonialistes," *Cahiers d'histoire: Revue d'histoire critique* 123 (2014): 157–162. On Azza's political trajectory, see Malika Rahal, "A Local Approach to the UDMA: Local-Level Politics during the Decade of Political Parties, 1946–56," *Journal of North African Studies* 18, no. 5 (2013): 703–724.

23. Frantz Fanon, *A Dying Colonialism* (New York: Grove Press, 1965), 65.

24. Jan C. Jansen, "Celebrating the Nation in a Colonial Context," *Journal of Modern History* 85, no. 1 (2013): 36–68. The pageantry of flags, military parades, and uniforms characterize ceremonies of dictatorships to publicly perform continuity and history, according to Giorgio Agamben, *The Kingdom and the Glory: For a Theological Genealogy of Economy and Government* (Stanford, CA: Stanford University Press, 2011).

25. I thank his daughter, Geneviève Appert-Sarrabezolles for providing me with postcards, images of the plaster models, and Sarrabezolles's archival correspondence with his wife to arrange his spring 1928 boat passage to Algeria. Also known as Charles Marie Louis Sarrabezolles, he was much in demand during the interwar period to design monumental buildings such as churches and war memorials. For his list of works, prizes, and accomplishments, see his website at http://sarrabezolles.chez-alice.fr/. Additional bibliography on Sarrabezolles includes Geneviève Appert-Sarrabezolles, Marie Odile Lefèvre, et al., *Carlo Sarrabezolles, sculpteur et statuaire 1888–1971* (Paris: Somogy Éditions d'Art, 2003); and Carlo Sarrabezolles, *De l'esquisse au colossal* (Montreuil, France: Éditions Gourcuff-Gradenigo, 2008).

26. "Inauguration du monument aux morts à Sidi Bel Abbès," *Le Progrès de Sidi-Bel-Abbès* 2550, December 11, 1928, 1.

27. "Son motif principal représente la victoire entraînant dans un sillage de gloire, des tirailleurs, des zouaves, des spahis, des légionnaires, éléments de cette belle armée d'Afrique dont firent partie nos morts de guerre. Le long de socle on a gravé les noms de ces morts. Deux femmes en larmes—la France et Sidi-bel-

Abbès–répandent sur ces noms la douleur de la grande et de la petite patrie." Adoue's speech was reproduced in "Inauguration du monument aux morts à Sidi-Bel-Abbès," *L'Echo d'Oran*, December 10, 1928, 2–3.

28. F. S. Onderdonk, *The Ferro-concrete Style: Reinforced Concrete in Modern Architecture* (New York: Architectural Book Publishing, 1928), 128. For descriptions of his techniques, see Carlo Sarrabezolles, *La sculpture sans maquette par taille directe du béton en prise* (Paris: Société d'Encouragement pour l'Industrie Nationale, 1933).

29. Karim Ouldennebia and Mohamed Zenaidi, email correspondence with author, January 28, 2019.

30. The marble additions were made by well-known local European marble-makers (*marbliers*) who continued their business along the Christian cemetery road after independence. The town mayor informed me that Roger and André Aubert, who designed the town's mausoleums and sculptures for the Christian community, were the local artisans for the replacement monument and that André Aubert converted to Islam and remained in Sidi-Bel-Abbès throughout Algeria's Dark Decade. He died around 2018 and was buried in the Muslim cemetery.

31. Adrian Forty, *The Art of Forgetting* (New York: Berg, 1999), 10.

32. Nabila Oulebsir, *Les usages du patrimoine: Monuments, musées et politiques coloniale en Algérie (1830–1930)* (Paris: Éditions de la Maison des sciences de l'homme, 2004), 310: "Une statue ou un monument s'écroule et cent trente ans de colonisation s'effacent donc subitement. Ce 'nettoyage' du patrimoine artistique vise la purification de l'espace urbain surencombré de traces et de signes d'une histoire abolie, celle de l'Algérie française. Il est amorcé dès le premier jour de l'Indépendance, dans la capitale, par la récupération des anciens lieux de pouvoir et des centres urbains. Dans le bref soufflé de liberté accordée à la population algérienne, l'un des premiers gestes exprimés par cette dernière à la proclamation de l'Indépendance a été de défiler et de manifester le jour même au niveau des points stratégiques de la capitale Alger. Des espaces et des lieux qui ne sont pas neutres comme la place du Gouvernement ou le boulevard de la République, des édifices publics comme l'hôtel des Postes, ont constitué la scène urbaine et architecturale de la liberté recouvrée."

33. Jan C. Jansen, "Fête et ordre colonial: Centenaires et résistance anticolonialiste en Algérie pendant les années 1930," *Vingtième Siècle* 1, no 121 (2014): 61–76.

34. Daniel J. Sherman, *The Construction of Memory in Interwar France* (Chicago: University of Chicago Press, 1999), 172–175.

35. "Le monument aux morts de la légion étrangère a Sidi-Bel-Abbès: Le sculpteur Henri Pourquet presidera à la mise en place du monument," *L'Echo d'Alger* 7831, March 19, 1931, 1.

36. Alain Amato, *Monuments en exil* (Versailles: Éditions de Atlanthrope, 1979), 36–37; H. Héraut, "Charles-Henri-Pourquet, statuaire de la Légion étrangère,"

Légion étrangère 38, no. 6 (1938): 22–23. See the special memorial issue of the Legion's journal *Képi blanc* no. 382bis (September 1979), especially pp. 9–11 with contemporary photos of soldiers excavating stones from the quarry.

37. Kh. Mansouri, "Hammam-bou-Hannifa," *Encyclopédie berbère*, 22 (2000): 3345–3349.

38. See John J. Herrmann Jr., Donato Attanasio, Robert H. Tykot, and Annewies van den Hoek, "Aspects of the Trade in Colored Marbles in Algeria," *L'Africa romana* XIX, Sassari 2010, Roma (2012): 1331–1342. On Tlemcen onyx-marble, see Rachid Bourouiba, *L'art religieux en Algérie* (Algiers: SNED, 1973), 174. For the French colonial period, Jean-Baptiste Del Monte, born in Carrara from a family involved in marble extraction for generations, is considered the early developer of the Aïn Tekbalet quarries.

39. J-O. Tournier, "Nouveau marbre onyx d'Algerie à Sidi Hamza près Tlemcen," *Le monde du travail de l'Afrique française, L'économiste algérien-tunisien technique et scientifique. Bulletin officiel des adjudications,* January 10, 1897, 2: "Disons de suite que par leur gisement, leur coloration et leur forme, ces marbres-onyx ne ressemblent en rien à ceux qui ont été et sont encore exploités en Algérie, tant célèbres et tant estimés qu'ils soient, comme ceux de Ain-Tekbalet dont nous parlions il n'y a pas longtemps. Il ne ressemblent pas davantage aux onyx du Mexique et de la Californie; ils ont un caractère personnel à tous les points de vue."

40. David Prochaska, *Making Algeria French: Colonialism in Bône, 1870–1920* (New York: Cambridge University Press, 1990).

41. Louis Kahn, "Monumentality," in *New Architecture and City Planning: A Symposium*, ed. Paul Zucker, 577–588 (New York: Philosophical Library, 1944).

42. Jean-Denis G. G. Lepage, *The French Foreign Legion: An Illustrated History* (London: McFarland, 2008), 219–221.

43. Jean Michon, "Sidi-bel-Abbès: Capitale légionnaire," *Guerres mondiales et conflits contemporains* 237, no. 1 (2010): 25–38.

44. Albéric Vaillant, "Récit des anciens: De Bel Abbès à Aubagne et à la Corse," *Le Trait d'union: Journal de l'Amicale des anciens de la Légion Etrangère de Paris*, 84 (2012): 7–8. "On récupéra tous les monuments aux Morts dont, bien entendu, '*la boule*' Ce fut le plus difficile. Le socle de béton était d'une dureté incroyable. Il fallut dix jours et combien de marteaux-piqueurs, aux braves pionniers, pour faire table rase. La dernière prise d'armes fut celle du départ des trois cercueils du Général Rollet, du Prince Aage et du Légionnaire Zimmermann. . . . La veille au soir, on entassa du vieux bois sur l'emplacement du monument disparu. On y mit le feu. Le Lieutenant Selosse déclama tout le poème de Borelli et jeta son fanion dans le brasier. Tel était le vœu de Borelli: son fanion ne devait pas quitter Bel-Abbès. Après quoi, on dansa toute la nuit et revêtit la tenue de combat au petit jour. Devant le dernier carré fut lu l'ordre du jour du Général Lefort. Les camions s'avancèrent dans ce qui avait été la voie sacrée, jeep du colonel en queue et le convoi roula vers Oran où l'attendait le chef- de-bataillon Arnaud de Foïard et le 2ème R.E.P., et le

Sidi-Bel-Abbès, pour la traversée. Grâce à l'Amiral Lorrain, qui avait ajouté au tonnage prescrit deux voyages de bateau clandestins, la Légion ne laissa rien derrière elle."

45. Djelloul Talha, interview with author, May 22, 2017, Sidi-Bel-Abbès.

46. Amato, *Monuments en exil*, 49–51. On the Legion's description of the monument, see http://monumentsmorts.univ-lille3.fr/monument/26206/bonifacio-place/.

47. Peter Von Sivers, "Secular Anxieties and Religious Righteousness: The Origins of the Insurrection of 1881 in the Nomadic and Sedentary Communities of the Algerian Southwest," *Peuples Méditerranéens* 18 (1982): 145–162; and E. Graulle, *Insurrection de Bou-Amama (avril 1881)* (Paris: H. Charles-Lavauzelle, 1905).

48. Eckard Michels, "From One Crisis to Another: The Morale of the French Foreign Legion during the Algerian War," in *The Algerian War and the French Army: Experiences, Images, Testimonies*, ed. Martin S. Alexander, Martin Evans, and J. F. V. Keiger, 88–100 (New York: Palgrave Macmillan, 2002).

49. Serge Andolenko, *Une visite aux Salles D'Honneur et au Musee du Souvenir de la Légion Etrangère* (Sidi-Bel-Abbès: Presse Régimentaire, 1938). The epitome of the French military museum remains the national Army Museum (Musée de l'Armée) at Invalides, see Caroline Barcellini, *Le Musée de l'Armée et la fabrique de la nation: Histoire militaire, histoire nationale et enjeux muséographiques* (Paris: L'Harmattan, 2010).

50. Élisabeth Cazenave and Jean Christian Serna, *Le patrimoine artistique français de l'Algérie: Les oeuvres du Musée nationale des Beaux-arts d'Alger de la constitution à la restitution* (Chire-en-Montreuil, France: Éditions Abd-el-Tif, 2017), 45–47. French Algeria's centenary encouraged Algeria's second military museum, the Musée Franchet d'Esperey, also established in 1930 in the Algiers Casbah and moved to the Palace of the Dey to house artifacts from the conquest. At independence and similar to the creation of the Aubagne museum, most of the collection in the Franchet d'Esperey museum was transferred to the Infanterie established in Montpellier, France. The transfer process is documented in "Musés Franchet d'Esperey," 1962, SHD H 2116/2. Artifacts from former museum displays are the "Salle des Maréchaux" with uniforms, weapons, portraits, busts, toiletry, correspondence, flags and banners of military units, but also sabers and daggers gifted to France's generals by the Bey of Tunis and Sultan Moulay Hafid. In addition to the military archives' list of items (most removed to France), a museum visitor's guide was published, see Musée Franchet d'Espérey Alger (Casbah), *Livre-guide pour la visite du musée* (Algiers: Baconnier-Hélio, ca. 1941).

51. On the revival of the white Legion kepi and more traditions invented by Rollet, see Douglas Porch, *The French Foreign Legion: A Complete History of the Legendary Fighting Force* (New York: Harper Collins, 1991), 410–440.

52. Wolfgang Muchitsch, ed., *Does War Belong in Museums? The Representation of Violence in Exhibitions* (Bielefeld: transcript Verlag, 2013).

53. David Prochaska, *Making Algeria French*, 72–74, 252; André Nouschi, "Notes sur la vie traditionelle des populations forestières algériennes," *Annales de Géographie* 86, no. 370 (1959): 525–535; and Diana K. Davis, *Resurrecting the Granary of Rome: Environmental History and French Colonial Expansion in North Africa* (Athens: Ohio University Press, 2007), 31. The early twentieth century saw Algerian losses of more than half of Kabylia's cork forests according to Andrea E. Duffy, "Civilizing through Cork: Conservationism and *la Mission Civilisatrice* in French Colonial Algeria," *Environmental History* 23, no. 2 (2018): 270–292.

54. Mark Letteney and Matthew D. C. Larsen, "A Roman Military Prison at Lambaesis," *Studies in Late Antiquity* 5, no. 1 (2021): 65–102.

55. Bonnie Effros, *Incidental Archaeologists: French Officers and the Rediscovery of Roman North Africa* (Ithaca, NY: Cornell University Press, 2018); Monique Dondin-Payre, "Réussites et déboires d'une œuvre archéologique unique: Le colonel Carbuccia au nord de l'Aurès (1848–1850)," *Antiquités africaines* 32 (1996): 145–174; and Michael Greenhalgh, *The Military and Colonial Destruction of the Roman Landscape of North Africa, 1830–1900* (Leiden: Brill, 2014).

56. A drawing of the tomb in Lambaesis is in Léon Renier, "Notice sur le tombeau de T. Flavius Maximus, préfet de la Légion III Auguste," *Revue archéologique* 7, no. 1 (1850):186–187. According to Bonnie Effros, citing the work of Nacéra Benseddik, Carbuccia's tomb was destroyed in 1983, see Effros, *Incidental Archaeologists*, 294n82.

57. Nacéra Benseddik, "Histoire colonial: Les tribulations des collections archéologiques de l'Algérie," *Libyan Studies* 50 (2019): 174. See also Elisabeth Fontan and Catherine Metzger, "History of the North African Collections of the Musée du Louvre," in *From Hannibal to Saint Augustine: Ancient Art of North Africa from the Musée du Louvre*, ed. Monique Seefried Brouillet (Atlanta: Michael C. Carlos Museum, Emory University, 1994), 13–15; Bonnie Effros, "Colliding Empires: French Display of Roman Antiquities Expropriated from Postconquest Algeria, 1830–1870," in *Objects of War: The Material Culture of Conflict and Displacement*, ed. Leora Auslander and Tara Zahra, 50–77 (Ithaca NY: Cornell University Press, 2018).

58. Unlike the 2018 Sarr-Savoy report detailing artifact spoliation for sub-Saharan colonies, the Stora Report of 2021 is inadequate to this task, see Susan Slyomovics, "Commissioning Memorial Reconciliation: The Stora Report and Algeria's Ottoman Canon in France," *Modern and Contemporary France* 31, no.1 (2023): 17–32.

59. Henri Lefebvre, *La production de l'espace* (Paris: Anthropos, 1974), 254.

60. Henri Grégoire, *Second rapport sur le vandalisme par Grégoire, séance du 8 brumaire, l'an III: Suivi du décret de la Convention nationale, et imprimé par son ordre* (Paris: De l'Imprimerie nationale, 1794).

61. William Dalrymple, *The Anarchy: The East India Company, Corporate Violence, and the Pillage of an Empire* (London: Bloomsbury, 2019).

62. Dorothy Mackay Quynn, "The Art Confiscations of the Napoleonic Wars," *American Historical Review* 50, no. 3 (1945): 437–460; Lynn Meskell, "Negative Heritage and Past Mastering in Archaeology," *Anthropological Quarterly* 75 (2002): 557–574; and Margaret M. Miles, *Art as Plunder: The Ancient Origins of Debate about Cultural Property* (New York: Cambridge University Press, 2008).

63. Kirrily Freeman, *Bronzes to Bullets: Vichy and the Destruction of French Public Statuary, 1941–1944* (Stanford, CA: Stanford University Press, 2008). A fascinating historical conjuncture occurred when spoliated French colonial statues from Algeria were used to replace statues melted down under Vichy; for example, the statue of General Frédéric Henri Le Normand de Lourmel erected in Al Amria, Algeria (formerly Lourmel) was placed in the general's hometown of Pontivry, Brittany.

64. See William Logan and Keir Reeves, eds., *Places of Pain and Shame: Dealing with "Difficult Heritage"* (London: Routledge, 2009); and Sharon Macdonald, *Difficult Heritage: Negotiating the Nazi Past in Nuremberg and Beyond* (London: Routledge, 2009), 2–8.

65. Since the mid-1970s, the legal status of the Catholic Church conformed over time with laws governing associations according to the Algerian state. Catholic institutions such as clinics and schools were successively nationalized beginning with Algeria's universal national healthcare system, and by 1976, all educational establishments were integrated into the Algerian national education system, see Oissila Saaidia, "Les catholiques d'Algérie: Minorités d'hier et d'aujourd'hui," *Les Cahiers d'EMAM* 32 (2020), http://journals.openedition.org/emam/2434.

66. On the recursive structure of the settler colonial "soliloquy," see Patrick Wolfe, *Settler Colonialism and the Transformation of Anthropology* (New York: Continuum, 1998), 4. On the "repatriated" Virgin Mary statue of Oran, Algeria, to Nîmes, Frances, see Susan Slyomovics, "The Virgin Mary of Algeria: French Mediterraneans *En Miroir*," *History and Anthropology* 31 (2020): 22–42.

67. On settlers claims to their property in Algeria and Algerian counterclaims of *biens vacants* (abandoned property), see Robert P. Parks, "From the War of National Liberation to Gentrification: Conflicting Claims over Property in Algeria," *MERIP / Middle East Report* (2018), https://merip.org/2018/08/from-the-war-of-national-liberation-to-gentrification/; and Susan Slyomovics, "Repairing Colonial Symmetry: Algerian Archive Restitution as Reparation for Crimes of Colonialism?" In *Time for Reparations: A Global Perspective*, ed. Jacqueline Bhabha, Margareta Matache, and Caroline Elkins, 201–218 (Philadelphia: University of Pennsylvania Press, 2021).

68. See Article 19 in "Algeria: France-Algeria Independence Agreements (Evian Agreements)," *International Legal Materials* 1, no. 2 (1962): 225.

69. Arnold Esch, "On the Reuse of Antiquity: The Perspectives of the Archaeologist and of the Historian," in *Reuse Value: Spolia and Appropriation in Art and Architecture from Constantine to Sherrie Levine*, ed. Richard Brilliant and Dale

Kinney (Farnham, Surrey: Ashgate, 2011), 19. See also, Arnold Esch, "Spolien: Zur Wiederverwendung antiker Baustücke und Skulpturen im mittelalterlichen Italien,"*Archiv für Kulturgeschichte* 51 (1969): 1–64.

70. Dale Kinney, "Introduction," in *Reuse Value*, 4.

71. Alexis de Tocqueville, "Second Letter on Algeria (22 August 1837)," in *Writings on Empire and Slavery*, ed. and trans. Jennifer Pitts (Baltimore, MD: Johns Hopkins University Press, 2001), 15.

72. Wolfe, *Settler Colonialism and the Transformation of Anthropology*.

73. Patricia M. E. Lorcin and Todd Shepard, "Introduction," in *French Mediterraneans: Transnational and Imperial Histories*, ed. Patricia M. E. Lorcin and Todd Shepard, 1–18 (Lincoln, Nebraska: University of Nebraska Press, 2016). See also the notion of the "colonial Mediterranean" in Hélène Blais and Florence Deprest, "The Mediterranean, a Territory between France and Colonial Algeria: Imperial Constructions," *European Review of History / Revue européenne d'histoire* 19, no. 1 (2012): 33–57.

74. Mohamed Mir, "Le mystère toujours entoure à Sidi-Bel-Abbès: La disparition de la statue fameuse 'La Chure d'Icare,'" *La Voix de l'Oranie* 5093, August 17, 2016, 6. On the public garden and its sculptures, see Ouldennebia, *Histoire de Sidi-Bel-Abbès*, 252–259.

75. Brahim Hasnaoui, interview with author, Sidi-Bel-Abbès, May 2017. Djillali Tahraoui and Boutkhil Beghdadi, "Batisseur: Brahim Hasnaoui, homme d'engagement," *Madinati* 1 (2016): 11–15. Alsatians came to Algeria before and after France's defeat in the 1871 Franco-Prussian War; indeed, 45 percent of Legion recruits were Alsatians escaping Prussian conscription, see Fabienne Fischer, *Alsaciens et Lorrains en Algérie, histoire d'une migration, 1830–1914* (Nice: Éditions Jacques Gandini, 1999).

76. Abdelkader Ghalem-Sardi, "Historique du site du rectorat de l'Université Djillali Liabes de Sidi Bel Abbès," *al-Jamiʿa wa-al-mujtamʿ*, November 2009, 29–32. Ghalem-Sardi's museum is recognized by AFMA (Association Française des Musées d'Agriculture) and AIMA (Association Internationale des Musées de l'Agriculture), although concerns were expressed during my visit about the museum's future in light of his eventual retirement. On local historians and curators, see Christina Kreps, "Non-Western Models of Museums and Curation in Cross-Cultural Perspective," in *A Companion to Museum Studies*, ed. Sharon Macdonald (Oxford: Blackwell, 2003), 457–472.

77. Amicale des anciens élèves des écoles d'agriculture d'Algérie, *L'œuvre agricole française en Algérie (1830–1962)* (Versailles: Atlanthrope, 1990).

78. "Visite de l'École d'Agriculture," *Amicale des anciens élèves des écoles d'agriculture d'Algérie: Bulletin* 59 (October 2009): 8–11.

79. See Douglas Hollan, "Who Is Haunted by Whom: Steps to an Ecology of Haunting," *Ethnos* 47, no. 4 (2019): 451–464.

80. R. Douglas Hurt, "Agricultural Museums: A New Frontier for the Social

Sciences," *The History Teacher* 11, no. 3 (1978): 367–375. On the roots of the colonial agronomy school and the Jardin Botanique de Paris (Nogent-sur-Seine, France) in relation to environmentalist movements, see Isabelle Lévêque, Michel Griffon, and Dominique Pinon, *Le jardin d'agronomie tropicale: De l'agriculture colonial au développement durable* (Arles: Actes Sud, 2005).

81. On the paradigmatic museum and sculpture to memorialize the Algerian Revolution in Algiers, see Emmanuel Alcaraz, "La mise en scène de la mémoire nationale: De la guerre d'indépendance algérienne au maqam al-chahid d'Alger," *Autour des morts de guerre: Maghreb—Moyen-Orient*, ed. Raphaëlle Branche, Nadine Picaudou and Pierre Vermeren, 21–45 (Paris: Éditions de la Sorbonne, 2013).

Chapter 4: Creating Provenance

1. On Algerian painters excavating the colonial visual archive, see Émilie Goudal, *Des damné(é)s de l'histoire: Les arts visuels face à la guerre d'Algérie* (Dijon, France: Les presses du réel, 2019).

2. For expansive important biographies and bibliographies of the artist, see Benjamin Barbier, "Benyahia, Ahmed," *Dictionnaire des artistes algériens, Hypotheses* (blog), https://patmagh.hypotheses.org/201; Malika Dorbani-Bouabdallah, *Ahmed Benyahia: Rétrospective* (Algiers: Ministry of Culture, 2015), 17–33. On Issiakhem and introductions to Algeria art, see François Pouillon, "150 Years of Algerian Painting: Relevance for Understanding on the Post-Colonial Situation," *French Politics, Culture & Society* 20, no. 2 (2002), 141–158; and Mary Vogl, "Algerian Painters as Pioneers of Modern Art," in *A Companion to Modern African Art*, ed. Gitta Salami and Monica Blackmun Visonà, 197–217 (Oxford: Wiley Blackwell, 2013).

3. On Benyahia's stamp, see Dorbani-Bouabdallah, *Ahmed Benyahia*, 21; and Salim Hamza, "Empreintes: Ahmed Benyahia," *Philnews: Algerian Philatelic News* 38 (August-September 2002): 10–11. On the history of Algerian philately, see Boudjemaa Haichour, *The Encyclopedia of the Postage Stamp of Algeria* (Algiers: Ministry of Post and Information Technology and Communication, 2008). On the Cold War context of the first fair, see Jean-François Kahn, "La première foire international d'Alger sera un nouvel épisode de la rivalité sino-soviétique," *Le Monde*, September 28, 1964, www.lemonde.fr/archives/article/1964/09/28/la-premiere-foire-internationale-d-alger-sera-un-nouvel-episode-de-la-rivalite-sino-sovietique_2127550_1819218.html. On postage stamps as lieux de mémoire, see David Scott, "Post and the Postage Stamp," in *Postcolonial Realms of Memory: Sites and Symbols in Modern France*, ed. Etienne Achille, Charles Fosdick, and Lydie Moudileno, 351–359 (Liverpool: Liverpool University Press, 2020); and Emmanuel Alcaraz,"Les timbres algériens de 1962 à nos jours, lieux de mémoire de la guerre d'Indépendance algérienne," *Cahiers de la Méditerranée* 91 (2016): http://journals.openedition.org/cdlm/8217.

4. Foreigners were deported; see the autobiography about her years in Algiers by Elaine Mokhtefi, *Algiers, Third World Capital: Freedom Fighters, Revolutionaries, Black Panthers* (London: Verso, 2020). See also Jeffrey James Byrne, *Mecca of Revolution: Algeria, Decolonization, and the Third World Order* (Oxford: Oxford University Press, 2016).

5. Historical accounts and analyses are by Alistair Horne, *A Savage War of Peace: Algeria 1954–1962* (London: Macmillan, 1977), 119–123; Daho Djerbal, "Mounadiline et mousebbiline: Les forces auxiliaires de l'ALN du Nord-Constantinois," in *Des hommes et des femmes en guerre d'Algérie*, ed. Jean-Charles Jauffret, 282–296 (Paris: Autrement, 2003); Claire Mauss-Copeaux, *Algérie, 20 août 1955: Insurrection, répression, massacres* (Paris: Payot, 2013); Daho Djerbal, *Lakhdar Bentobbal, mémoires de l'intérieur* (Algiers: Chihab: 2021), 2 vols; and Natalya Vince, *The Algerian War, the Algerian Revolution* (London: Palgrave Macmillan, 2020).

6. Ahmed Benyahia, phone interview with author April 9, 2021. See James McDougall, "Culture as War by Other Means: Community, Conflict and Cultural Revolution, 1967–81," in *Algeria Revisited: History, Culture and Identity*, ed. Rabah Aissaoui and Claire Eldridge, 235–252 (London: Bloomsbury Academic, 2018).

7. Natalya Vince and Walid Benkhaled, "The Long History of a Short-Lived Statue," interview with Ahmed Benyahia. YouTube. Uploaded November 11, 2019 by Vince and Benkhaled. I thank Natalya Vince, Walid Benkhaled, and their team of creators for this video, permission to reproduce materials, and readings of an early draft. Quotes in English by Ahmed Benyahia drawn from their subtitled video are numbered according to their online time codes. Subtitled in English, French, and Arabic: https://www.youtube.com/watch?v=wllPtQNYwo4&feature=youtu.be&fbclid=IwAR3ArOU_oyfojpNfMhWEHFOui73bw-1VEcrNUoDQ5kqvYNsKGfqoHOTAfLY. On Vince, Benkhaled, and their interview series, see Susan Slyomovics, "On the Wings of the Gallic Cockerel: Ahmed Benyahia and the Provenance of an Algerian Public Sculpture," in *Reframing Postcolonial Studies: Concepts—Methodologies—Scholarly Activisms*, ed. David D. Kim, 69–92 (London: Palgrave MacMillan, 2021). I thank Anissa Bouayed for putting me in touch with Ahmed Benyahia.

8. "À Constantine: Inauguration du monument aux combattants," *L'Afrique du Nord Illustrée* 77, October 21, 1922, 8.

9. On the rooster's symbolism, archaeologist Naomi Sykes sees the global spread of the chicken (of which the rooster stands as the adult male) into new societies was more because of cockfighting prowess and less for meat: "These introduced animals, so different from the native fauna and coming from remote realms, were seemingly imbued with cosmological power. Everywhere the chicken was introduced—Asia, Africa, America and Europe—it was quickly incorporated into magic and ritual practices," Naomi Sykes, "A Social Perspective on the Introduction of Exotic Animals: The Case of the Chicken," *World Archaeology* 44, no. 1

(2012): 165. See also Michel Pastoureau, "Le coq gaulois," in *Les lieux de mémoires*, ed. Pierre Nora, vol. 3: 507–539 (Paris: Gallimard, 1986).

10. Vince and Benkhaled, "The Long History of a Short-Lived Statue," 10:51–13:13.The bronze rooster, forged in the colonial Duplan foundry (founded by Claude Duplan in 1866), shaped Benyahia's Zighoud Youcef statue. To build Duplan's factory, a vast antique necropolis was destroyed and objects were sent to the museum of Constantine; see Jean Lassus, "L'archéologie algérienne en 1955," *Libyca: Bulletin du Service des Antiquités, Archéologie, Epigraphie* 4, no. 1 (1956): 169–189.

11. A succinct historical account of this period is by James McDougall, *A History of Algeria* (Cambridge: Cambridge University Press, 2017), 179–233.

12. Charles Sanders Peirce, *The Collected Papers*, ed. Charles Hartshorne and Paul Weiss (Cambridge, MA: Harvard University Press, 1931–1935), vol. 3: 361. Indexicality is characteristic of 1970s artwork, according to art historian Rosalind Krauss who cites Marcel Duchamp's last painted canvas *Tu m'* (1918) as an early example featuring a mechanical arm, blue sleeve, and a finger pointing rightward, see Rosalind Krauss, "Notes on the Index: Seventies Art in America," *October* 3 (1977): 68–81.

13. Vince and Benkhaled, "The Long History of a Short-Lived Statue," 13:20–14:22.

14. Vince and Benkhaled, 13:20–14:22.

15. A record of contravening and obstructing policies behind the back of serving presidents concerns the "DAFS," Algerian deserters from the French army (*Déserteurs de l'armée française* in French); see the section on DAF involvement in the coup d'états of 1963 and 1965 in Abdelhamid Brahimi, *Aux origines de la tragédie algérienne (1958–2000): Témoignage sur hizb França* (Geneva: Hoggar, 2000), 93-124.

16. Abdelghani is believed to have been one of the "Déserteurs de l'armée française" (DAFs) according to Amrane Ahdjoudj, *Algérie, etat, pouvoir et société (1962–1965)* (Paris: Arcantère, 1991), 122: "Sa force principale: L'armée des frontières, encadrée par d'anciens officiers et sous-officiers de l'armée française (Ben Chérif, S. Hoffman, Abdelghani, Chadli, Zerguini, Chabou, etc.)."

17. Algerian sociologist Ahmed Rouadjia contends that President Boumédiène bestowed this nickname on Abdelghani, who was acting in Constantine "à sa guise" (as he pleased), see his *Les frères et la mosquée: Enquête sur le mouvement islamiste en Algérie* (Paris: Karthala, 1990), 66. Stopping commemorative activities related to heroes of the army of the interior, such as Zighoud Youcef, during the era of Boumédiène, especially by the aforementioned DAFs is supported by Emmanuel Alcaraz, *Les lieux de mémoire de la guerre d'indépendance algérienne* (Paris: Karthala, 2017), 280. Abdelghani went on to a stellar political career as prime minister under President Chadli Bendjedid.

18. Benyahia's account of the statue's disappearance first appeared in the news-

paper article by C. B. [pseud. Abdelmadjid Merdaci], "Qui a peur de Zighout Youcef?" *Revolution africaine* 1331, September 8, 1986, 46.

19. Vince and Benkhaled, "The Long History of a Short-Lived Statue," 17:36–21:53.

20. Vince and Benkhaled, 19:32–21:14.

21. Salman Arslan [pseud. Mounji Farid], "Statue de Zighoud Youcef, histoire d'une oeuvre d'art et de mémoire," *El Watan* (August 19, 2021): 14–15.

22. Coq de la Grande Bosse website: http://www.guer-coetquidan-broceliande.fr/bisto/coet/coq_bosse.html.

23. See chapter 1 in Alain Amato, *Monuments en exil* (Versailles: Éditions de Atlanthrope, 1979).

24. Abdeljelil Temimi, *Le Beylik de Constantine et Ḥādj ʾAḥmed Bey (1830–1837)* (Tunis: Revue d'histoire maghrébine, 1978).

25. See Ordonnance of 9 June 1844: "Ordonnance du Roi qui règle le mode d'administration de la ville de Constantine, et régularise les prohibitions dont sont frappées les transactions immobilières dans cette ville." Article 1 maps out the urban racial divides: "La ville de Constantine sera divisée en deux quartiers, un quartier indigène et un quartier européen," see Ordonnance of 9 June 1844: "Ordonnance du Roi qui règle le mode d'administration de la ville de Constantine, et régularise les prohibitions dont sont frappées les transactions immobilières dans cette ville." In *Corps du droit francais, ou recueil complet des lois, décrets, ordonnances . . . publies depuis 1789 jusq'a nos jours*, ed. C.-M. Galliset (Paris: Imprimerie et librarie générale de jurisprudence de Cosse et N. Delamotte, 1847), vol 8: 188–189. This royal order effectively launched the creation of the European city, allowing settlers to move in, and ended the military jurisdiction over Constantine which had hitherto prohibited European settlement.

26. A recreation of Constantine before the 1837 conquest was attempted in Ernest Mercier, *Constantine avant la conquête française* (Constantine: A Braham, 1878). On colonial repurposing in Constantine, see Bernard Pagand, *La Médina de Constantine (Algérie): De la ville traditionnelle au centre de l'agglomération contemporaine* (Poitiers, Éditions du Centre Inter-universitaire d'Études Méditerranéennes, 1989), 124; Yasmina Boudjada, "L'église catholique de Constantine de 1839 à 1859: Cas de l'appropriation de la mosquée Souk el Ghzel par les Français," in *Villes rattachées, villes reconfigurées: xvi*[e]*-xx*[e] *siècles*, ed. Denise Turrel, 285–303 (Tours: Presses Universitaires François-Rabelais, 2003); and Abdelkrim Badjadja, *La Bataille de Constantine 1836–1837* (Algiers: Chihab, 2016).

27. Zeynep Çelik, *Urban Forms and Colonial Confrontations: Algiers under French Rule* (Berkeley: University of California Press, 1997), 26–38; and Zeynep Çelik, "Colonial/Postcolonial Intersections: *Lieux de mémoire* in Algiers," *Third Text* 49 (1999): 63–72.

28. Daniel Milo, "Street Names," in *Realms of Memory: Rethinking the French Past*, under the direction of Pierre Nora, vol 2: 363–389 (New York: Columbia University Press, 1996).

29. On laws to commemorate those who died for France, see chapter 2. The ANOM GGA 6G/2 files document Constantine name changes approved by the colonial municipality.

30. In France, battles over street names related to Algeria continue to beleaguer French municipal authorities faced with public outcries about removing or restoring a name commemorating contested people or events in Franco-Algerian history. French streets named "March 19," the date of the Évian Accords that signaled the process toward independence, are contested. For former settlers and their allied populations such street names and dates are signs of mourning rather than celebration.

31. See http://les-quatre-elements.over-blog.com/2017/05/le-boulevard-joly-de-bresillon-constantine.html.

32. Currently, retaining French names in Algerian urban centers is parsed as a form of the politics of "grievance" against the Algerian government according to anthropologist Stephanie V. Love, "The Poetics of Grievance: Taxi Drivers, Vernacular Placenames, and the Paradoxes of Post-Coloniality in Oran, Algeria," *City & Society* 33, no. 3 (2021), https://doi.org/10.1111/ciso.12412.

33. Badia Belabed Sahraoui, "Politique municipale et pratique urbaine: Constantine au XIXe siècle," *Insaniyat* 35/36 (2007): 109–129; and Hélène Blais, Claire Fredj, and Emmanuelle Saada, "Introduction, Un long moment colonial: Pour une histoire de l'Algérie au XIXe siècle," *Revue d'histoire du XIXe siècle* 41 (2010): 7–24.

34. Attila Kotányi and Raoul Vaneigem, "Basic Program of the Bureau of Unitary Urbanism," in *Situationist International Anthology,* 2006, https://theanarchistlibrary.org/library/raoul-vaneigem-attila-kotanyi-basic-program-of-the-bureau-of-unitary-urbanism. I follow Soyoung Soo's translation of *trou positif,* not as "positive void" but "positive hole," see Soyoung Soo, "Cinema against the Permanent Curfew of Geometry: Guy Debord's *Sur le passage de quelques personnes à travers une assez courte unité de temps* (1959)," *Grey Room* 52 (2013): 38–61

35. Situationist International, "Definitions," *Internationale situationniste: Bulletin central édité* 1 (June 1958): 13: "Détournement d'éléments esthétiques prefabriqués. Intégration de productions actuelles ou passées des arts dans une construction supérieure du milieu. Dans ce sens il ne peut y avoir de peinture ou de musique situationniste, mais un usage situationniste de ces moyens. Dans un sens plus primitif, le détournement à l'intérieur des sphères culturelles anciennes est une méthode de propagande, qui témoigne de l'usure et de la perte d'importance de ces sphères."

36. On the formulaic, mechanical characteristics of kitsch, see Clement Greenberg, "Avant-Garde and Kitsch" *Partisan Review* (1939): 34–49.

37. Cherif Ben Boulaïd, WhatsApp interview with author after Cherif interviewed his uncle, Abdelhak Ben Boulaïd, July 8, 2021, who provided the family perspective from Batna. For a similar argument about instrumentalizing the forgotten regional heroes of the Algerian revolution, see Benjamin Stora, "Algérie:

Les retours de la mémoire de la guerre d'indépendence," *Modern & Contemporary France* 10, no. 4 (2002): 461–468. On the Algerian regime's "monopolization of martyrdom," see Emmanuel Alcaraz, "Les monuments aux martyrs de la Guerre d'Indépendance Algérienne: Monumentalité, enjeux de mémoire et commémorations," *Guerres Mondiales et Conflits Contemporains* 237 (2010/11): 125–146; and Ouanassa Siari Tengour and Fouad Soufi, "Les Algériens écrivent, enfin, leur guerre," *Insaniyat* 25/26 (2004): 267–272.

38. The movement of statues in the Tlemcen square cuts across eras: Ben Bella was deposed by Boumédiène in a coup d'état in 1965. Around the same time, in the Tlemcen square where Ben Bella's statue stands is a replacement statue for the town's spoliated French colonial interwar memorial after it was removed to the French town of Fréjus by a former European settler (see chapter 1).

39. New statues (and new biographies) of resistance fighters proliferate in twenty-first-century Algeria. New local commemorative monuments are attributed to the waning influence of former independence war combatants by the 1990s, according to Thomas DeGeorges, "The Shifting Sands of Revolutionary Legitimacy: The Role of Former Mūjāhidīn in the Shaping of Algeria's Collective Memory," *Journal of North African Studies* 14, no. 2 (2009): 273–288.

40. Nadira Laggoune-Aklouche, "Résistance, appropriation et réappropriation dans l'art algérien," *Modern and Contemporary France* 19, no. 2 (2011): 179–193.

41. On traffic circles, see Éric Alonzo, *Du rond-point au giratoire* (Marseille, Lyon: Édition Parenthèses, Édition du Certu, 2005); Laurent Jeanpierre, *In Girum: Les leçons politiques des rond-points* (Paris: La Découverte, 2019); Eyal Weizman, *The Roundabout Revolutions* (Berlin: Sternberg Press, 2015); and Marc Augé, "Roundabouts: The Revenge of the Local," in *City A–Z*, ed. Nigel Thrift and Steve Pile, 206–207 (London: Routledge, 2000). For Constantine, see Mohamed Foura and Yasmina Foura, "Les places publiques dans la ville de Constantine," *Villes en parallèle* 36/37 (2003): 331–336; and Marc Côte, *L'Algérie ou l'espace retourné* (Paris: Flammarion, 1988).

42. According to architectural historian Amine Kasmi, Oran's Zabana statue is the work of Algerian sculptor Mohamed Karoub (personal communication).

43. François Pouillon, "Les images de l'Émir Abdelkader: De l'Algérie coloniale à l'Algérie algérienne," in *Le corps du leader: Construction et représentation dans les pays du Sud*, ed. Omar Carlier and Raphaëlle Nollez-Goldbach, 163–170 (Paris: L'Harmattan, 2008).

44. César Baldaccini, Benyahia's mentor in Paris, strongly recommended Benyahia as a young artist "displaying such firmness and intransigence, a self-discipline so powerful when it comes to his artistic work," see Letter of César Baldaccini to Fernand Pouillon, April 27, 1972, Ahmed Benyahia Archives. See also Abdelhamid Lemili "Ahmed Benyahia ou l'art de l'Anticonformisme," *La Tribune*, May 11, 2012, https://www.djazairess.com/fr/latribune/67486.

45. On Niemayer in Algeria, see Jason Oddy, *The Revolution Will Be Stopped Halfway* (New York: Columbia Books on Architecture and the City, 2019). On Pouillon, see Daphné Bengoa and Leo Fabrizio, *Fernand Pouillon et l'Algérie: Bâtir à l'hauteur des hommes* (Paris: Éditions Macula, 2019); and Myriam Maachi Maïza, "L'architecture de Fernand Pouillon en Algérie," *Insaniyat* 42 (2008), http://journals.openedition.org/insaniyat/6707.

46. Critical scholarship on Algerian *camps de regroupement* is not exhausted by key works such as the wartime ethnography published in French in 1964 by Pierre Bourdieu and Abdelmalak Sayad, *Uprooting: The Crisis of Traditional Agriculture in Algeria* (Cambridge, UK: Polity Press, 2020); remarkable postindependence films, graphic novels, and scholarly literatures proliferate, such as Samia Henni, *Architecture of Counterrevolution: The French Army in Northern Algeria* (Zürich: gta Verlag, 2017); and Fabien Sacristie, *Les camps de regroupement en Algérie: Une histoire des déplacements forcés (1954–1962)* (Paris: Presses de Sciences Po, 2022). For recent Algerian filmed testimonial works, see Dorothée-Myriam Kellou (chapter 2).

47. Ahmed Benyahia, interview with author, July 29, 2020, Constantine.

48. Willy Jansen, *Women without Men: Gender and Marginality in an Algerian Town* (Leiden: Brill, 1987), 263–264. For contemporary social science studies from the 1970s and 1980s, see François Burgat and Michel Nancy, *Les villages socialistes de la révolution agraire algérienne (1972–1982)* (Paris: Éditions du Centre National de la Recherche Scientifique, 1984); and Djafar Lesbet, *Les 1000 villages socialistes en Algérie* (Algiers: Office des publications universitaires; Paris: Syros, 1983).

49. Ordonnance 71-73 du 8 novembre 1971 portant à la revolution agraire (Order 71-73 on the Agrarian Revolution) *JORA*, November 30, 1971, 1282. Article 1 begins: "La terre appartient à ceux qui la travaillent." The slogan appears earlier, drawn from Ben Bella's autogestion programs according to Thomas L. Blair, *"The Land to Those Who Work It": Algeria's Experiment in Workers' Management* (Garden City, NY: Doubleday, 1969).

50. Ahmed and Abderrezak Benyahia interviewed together, June 1, 2022, Constantine. Benyahia's sculpture is on the cover of *Dix années de réalisations (19 juin 1965–19 juin 1975)* (Algiers: Ministère d'Information et de la Culture, 1976).

51. On the memory of Salah Bey by the people of Constantine, see Ouanassa Siari Tengour, "Salah Bey et la cité d'oubli," *Insaniyat* 3 (1998): 71–89.

52. As the literature and films on May 8, 1945 are vast, my selective references are Jean-Pierre Peyroulou, *Guelma, une subversion française dans l'Algérie coloniale* (Paris: La Découverte, 2009); and Boucif Mekhaled, *Chronique d'un massacre: 8 mai 1945, Sétif, Guelma, Kherrata* (Paris: Éditions Syros, 1995).

53. On French "aphasia," see Anne Laura Stoler, "Colonial Aphasia: Race and Disabled Histories in France," *Public Culture* 23, no. 1 (2011): 121–156.

54. Contextualizing Benyahia's monument within a long history of Algerian commemorations and ceremonies to May 9, 1945, see Jean-Pierre Peyroulou, "Les

métamorphoses du martyrologe algérien du 8 mai 1945: 1945–2009," in *Autour des morts de guerre: Maghreb-Moyen-Orient*, ed. Raphaëlle Branche, Nadine Picadou, and Pierre Vermeren, 97–118 (Paris: Éditions de la Sorbonne, 2013).

55. On long-standing Algeria-Palestine links, see Arthur Asseraf's chapter, "Palestine the Martyr: Distance and 'Proxy Nationalism,' 1911–48," in his *Electric News in Colonial Algeria* (Oxford: Oxford University Press, 2019), 156–182.

56. Reasons why Timgad is a UNESCO World Heritage Site since 1982 overlap with French Algeria's understandings of Trajan's Arch as a model for Constantine's interwar monument; see https://whc.unesco.org/en/list/194. See also chapter 4; Bonnie Effros, *Incidental Archaeologists: French Officers and the Rediscovery of Roman North Africa* (Ithaca, NY: Cornell University Press, 2018); and Nabila Oulebsir, *Les usages du patrimoine: Monuments, musées et politiques coloniale en Algérie (1830–1930)* (Paris: Éditions de la Maison des sciences de l'homme, 2004).

57. On Epstein and his Algerian statues—- missing, removed, or destroyed—see chapter 1. See also Amato, *Monuments en exil.*

58. On Ebstein's teachers, see June Hargrove, *The Statues of Paris: An Open-Air Pantheon* (Antwerp: Mercatorfonds, 1989), 169.

59. Auguste Cherbonneau, *Album du Musée de Constantine* (Constantine: Alessi et Arnolet Libraires, 1862), 7; and August Audollent, "Victoire Ailée du musée de Constantine," *Revue Archéologique* 16 (1890): 66–75.

60. Benjamin Stora, "Hacène Boudjenana," *Dictionnaire biographique de militants nationalistes algériens*, 145, https://issuu.com/azizmebarki/docs/dictionnaire_biographique_des_militants_national/397.

61. On the colonial conscripted army, see Dominique Lormier, *C'est nous les Africains: L'épopée de l'armée française d'Afrique (1940–1945)* (Paris: Calmann-Lévy, 2006).

62. Again, Benyahia was instrumental in refurbishing the monument in 2014, as part of European commemorations of the 1914 centenary of the outbreak of World War I. In 2015, representatives from France and Germany, two former enemies, as Benyahia remarked to me during my 2022 Constantine visit, participated in laying wreaths, a first for Algeria. Both the monument and site are deteriorating, see Oumnia Bouameur and Nadia Chabi, "The War Memorial of Constantine Facing Risks and Vulnerability," *Journal of Science and Technology* 4, no. 2 (2019): 7–14.

63. Valée tried to establish a protectorate rather than military rule beginning with Constantine, according to Charles-Robert Ageron, "Administration directe ou Protectorat: Un conflit de méthodes sur l'organisation de la province de Constantine (1837–1838)," *Revue français d'Outre-mer* 50 (1963): 5–40.

64. Djerbal, *Lakhdar Bentobbal, mémoires de l'intérieur*, vol. 2: 83n77.

65. The French military removal date from Algeria, according to files at Château Vincennes archives, is confirmed as January 1963, see SHD 1R368–2: "Souvenir Militaires," dossier 17 on "Maréchal Valée [2eme Div.] Affaire réglée le janvier 1963."

66. Ahmed Benyahia, interview with author, June 18, 2022, Constantine.

67. On changes in laws of associations, see Andrea Liverani, *Civil Society in Algeria: The Political Functions of Associational Life* (Abingdon, UK: Routledge, 2008).

68. Loi du 1er juillet 1901 relative au contrat d'association (Law of July 1, 1901 on the contract of association) *JORF*, July 2, 1901, 4025–4027, or France's 1901 law of associations abolished restrictions on all associations except religions ones. In Algeria, in contrast, numerous Algerian Islamic associations were formed, see Omar Carlier, *Entre nation et Jihad: Histoire sociale des radicalismes algériens* (Paris: PFSP, 1995), 43–65.

69. Restrictions on membership and oversight began to emerge in Ordonnance 71-79 du 3 décembre 1971 relative à l'association (Order 71-79 of December 3, 1971 on associations), *JORA*, December 12, 1971, 1410, which was revised in *JORA*, January 18, 1972, 8.

70. Nora Gueliane and Kaouther Bouchemal, "Algeria and Its Heritage: Inventory of the Various Heritage Policies, from the Pre-colonial to Colonial and Post-colonial Times," in *Transcultural Diplomacy and International Law in Heritage Conservation*, ed. Olimpia Niglio and Eric Yong Joong Lee, 257–272 (Singapore: Springer, 2021). On graphic design in the Arab world, see Bahia Shehab and Haytham Nawar, *A History of Arab Graphic Design* (Cairo, Egypt: American University in Cairo Press, 2020).

71. Bernard Pagand and Assïa Malki Allouani, "Un quartier colonial à Constantine (Algérie): Le Coudiat Aty," in *Villes maghrébines en situations colonials*, ed. Charlotte Jelidi, 59–76 (Paris, Karthala, 2014); Tewfik Guerroudj, "La question du patrimoine urbain et architectural en Algérie," *Insaniyat* 12 (2000): 31–43; and Djamel Dekoumi, "Pour une nouvelle politique de conservation de l'environnement historique bâti algérien: cas de Constantine," (PhD thesis, Constantine University, 2007).

72. Arrêté du 2 mars 1992 portant ouverture d'instance en vue du classement des monuments et sites historiques (Order of March 2, 1992 on opening the inscription in the list of historical monuments and sites) *JORA*, April 11, 1990, https://www.joradp.dz/FTP/Jo-Francais/1990/F1990015.pdf.

73. Although laws in 1990 governing the commune and wilaya granted important powers to both the president of the commune and the wali (see Loi 90-08 de 7 avril 1990 relative à la commune and Loi 90-08 de 7 avril 1990 relative à la wilaya), Benyahia argued that the requirement to publicize changes in safeguarding housing was never met.

74. See archives and oral histories gathered from his grandparent's generation in Abdelkrim Badjadja, *La bataille de Constantine, 1837–1837* (Algiers: Chihab, 2016), 92–93.

75. Abdelhamid Lemili, "Ahmed Benyahia ou l'art de l'Anticonformisme," *La Tribune*, May 11, 2012, https://www.djazairess.com/fr/latribune/67486.

76. "Le nouveau casino municipal de Constantine," *L'Afrique du Nord Illustrée* 431, August 3, 1929, 13. For photos of the inauguration and building, see "Casino municipal de Constantine," *L'Echo d'Alger* 8750, July 20, 1934, 4.

77. Marc André and Susan Slyomovics, "L'inévitable prison: Éléments introductifs à une étude du système carcéral en Algérie de la conquête coloniale à la gestion de son héritage aujourd'hui," *L'Année du Maghreb*, 20 (2019): 9–31.

78. On the colonial prison, see "Maison d'arrêt et centre pénitentiaire de Constantine (1853–1962)," ANOM 93 2Y 554–839.

79. Ahmed Benyahia, *Projet de transformation de la Prison du Coudiat et de la Gendarmerie en Musée de la Mémoire et de la Resistance* (Constantine: unpublished report, June 23, 2010), 10 pages.

80. Jean-Robert Henry, "L'histoire aux prises avec les mémoires: L'exemple du musée avorté de Montpellier sur l'histoire de la France et de l'Algérie," *L'Année du Maghreb* 19 (2018): 133–164.

81. Barkahoum Ferhati, "Le musée national Nasr Ed-din Etienne Dinet de Bou Saada: Un expérience avortée," *al-Naqd* 17 (2003): 73–96; and François Pouillon, *Étienne Dinet, peintre en Islam: L'Algérie et l'héritage colonial* (Boumerdès, Algeria: Edition Frantz Fanon, 2021), 253–278.

82. Marc André, *Une prison pour mémoire: Montluc, de 1944 à nos jours* (Lyon: ENS Éditions, 2022).

83. See Alcaraz, *Les lieux de mémoire*, 83–121.

84. Décret exécutif 18-102 du 11 Rajab 1439 correspondant au 29 mars 2018 portant création d'un musée public national "Prison Serkadji" 17 Rajab 1439 (Executive Decre 18-1-2 corresponding to March 29, 2018 on creating a national public museum "Prison Serkadji) *JORA*, April 4, 2018, 6–7. See Article 3: "Le musée public national 'Prison Serkadji' reflète la lutte et les sacrifices du peuple algérien pour recouvrer sa liberté et témoigne des pratiques pénitentiaires inhumaines, cruelles et dégradantes ainsi que des différentes formes de torture physiques et psychologiques du colonialisme. Le musée comprend des lieux de détention, des cellules et d'autres espaces ainsi que des collections muséales historiques, des objets, des documents ethnographiques, des photographies et des enregistrements audiovisuels relatifs aux pratiques pénitentiaires coloniales. Il est chargé de leur conservation, valorisation et exposition au public."

85. Édouard Glissant and Hans Ulrich Obrist, *The Archipelago Conversations* (New York: Isolarii, 2021); André Malraux, *Les voix du silence, Écrits sur l'art (I)*, ed. Jean-Yves Tadié, 2 vols. (Paris: Gallimard, 2004), vol. 1:203 passim; and Katarzyna Pieprzak, *Imagined Museums: Art and Modernity in Morocco* (Minneapolis: University of Minnesota Press, 2010). See the critique of Malraux's project in Hannah Feldman, *From a Nation Torn: Decolonizing Art and Representation in France 1945–1962* (Durham, NC: Duke University Press, 2014), 19–40.

86. Ahmed Benyahia, interview with the author, Constantine, June 10, 2022. See also according to the "ontology of imperial looting . . . objects are the eternal proofs of the crime," in Ariella Aïsha Azoulay, *Potential History: Unlearning Imperialism* (London: Verso, 2019), 142.

87. Albert Camus, *The First Man*, trans. David Hapgood (Toronto: Alfred Knopf, 1996), 180.

88. Éric de Chassey, "Une discussion entre Moncef Ben Moussa, Meriem Berrada, Malika Dorbani-Bouabdellah, Taher Ghalia et Abdellah Karroum," *Perspective: Actualité en histoire de l'art* 2 "Le Maghreb" (2017): http://journals.openedition.org/perspective/7476: "La réclamation par les Algériens de ces œuvres est une preuve de leur volonté de patrimonialiser le legs français." See also Andrew Bellisari, "The Art of Decolonization: The Battle for Algeria's French Art, 1962–70," *Journal of Contemporary History* 52, no. 3 (2017): 625–645.

89. Felwine Sarr and Bénédicte Savoy, *The Restitution of African Cultural Heritage: Toward a New Relational Ethics*, 2018, https://www.about-africa.de/images/sonstiges/2018/sarr_savoy_en.pdf. See their introductory chapter, footnote 4, unpaged.

90. Susan Slyomovics, "Commissioning Memorial Reconciliation: The Stora Report and Algeria's Ottoman Canon in France," *Modern and Contemporary France* 31, no.1 (2023): 17–32.

91. On the archive of French Algeria that remains largely in French hands, see Susan Slyomovics, "Repairing Colonial Symmetry: Algerian Archive Restitution as Reparation for Crimes of Colonialism?" In *Time for Reparations: A Global Perspective*, ed. Jacqueline Bhabha, Margareta Matache, and Caroline Elkins (Philadelphia: University of Pennsylvania Press, 2021), 201–218. See also Benjamin Stora, "Rapport: Les questions mémorielles portant sur la colonisation et la guerre d'Algérie," January 2021, https://www.elysee.fr/admin/upload/default/0001/09/0586b6b0ef1c2fc2540589c6d56a1ae63a65d97c.pdf.

92. John A. Templer, *The Staircase: History and Theories* (Cambridge, MA: MIT Press, 1992).

93. Ahmed Benyahia, interview with author, June 18, 2022, Constantine.

94. The pun is *hawāʾ* to mean "air" or *hawa* for "love."

95. Lorenzo Veracini. "Introducing," *Settler Colonial Studies* 1, no. 1 (2011): 1–12.

96. Lorenzo Veracini, "Telling the End of the Settler Colonial History," in *Studies in Settler Colonialism: Politics, Identity, and Culture*, ed. Fiona Bateman and Lionel Pilkington, 204–218 (New York: Palgrave Macmillan, 2011).

97. Ahmed Benyahia, phone interview with author, September 11, 2021. The work of Stoler and Cooper influences the ways in which metropole and colony are mutually forged, see Ann L. Stoler and Frederick Cooper, "Between Metropole and Colony: Rethinking a Research Agenda," in *Tensions of Empire: Colonial Cultures in a Bourgeois World*, ed. Ann L. Stoler and Frederick Cooper , 1–56. (Berkeley: University of California Press, 1997)

98. A large literature on the decoloniality of art and decolonial aesthesis has emerged including the quote from Walter Mignolo and Rolando Vasquez, "Decolonial AestheSis: Colonial Wounds/Decolonial Healings," *Social Text* (2013), special issue, https://socialtextjournal.org/periscope_article/decolonial-aesthesis-colonial-woundsdecolonial-healings/.

Conclusion: Settler Remains

1. Sigmund Freud, "Five Lectures on Psycho-Analysis (1910)," *Collected Works,* vol. 11 (London: Hogarth Press, 1957), 16–17. See also Victor Burgin, "Monument and Melancholia," in *Memory Culture and the Contemporary City,* ed. Uta Staiger, Henriette Steiner, and Andrew Webber, 17–31 (London: Palgrave Macmillan, 2009).

2. André Akoun, *Né à Oran: Autobiographie en troisième personne* (Paris: Bouchène, 2004), 26–27.

3. On Bertagna's political career, see David Prochaska, "The Political Culture of Settler Colonialism in Algeria: Politics in Bone (1870–1920)," *Revue de l'Occident musulman et de la Méditerranée* 48/49 (1988): 293–311. For photos of the inauguration of the Bertagna statue and its large pediment in 1907, see *Illustration Algérienne, Tunisienne er Marocaine,* April 13, 1907: cover, 2, 4–7. On the CDHA, see Claire Eldridge, "Feature Archive: Centre de documentation historique sur l'Algérie (CDHA)," http://frenchhistorysociety.co.uk/blog/?p=1856.

4. See Mohammed Khadda, *Éléments pour un art nouveau* (Algiers: Société Nationale d'Édition et de Diffusion, 1972); Anissa Bouayed, *Art et l'Algérie insurgée: Les traces de l'épreuve 1954–1962* (Algiers: ENAG, 2005); Anissa Bouayed, "Peinture moderne et patrimoine, Une position subsidiaire: la période charnière des années 60," *Insaniyat* 12, (2002): 65–75; Mary Vogl, "Algerian Painters as Pioneers of Modernism," in *A Companion to Modern African Art,* ed. Gitti Salami and Monica Blackmun Visonà, 197–217 (Hoboken, NJ: Wiley Blackwell, 2013); and Natasha Marie Llorens, ed., *Waiting for Omar Gatlato: A Survey of Contemporary Art from Algeria and Its Diaspora* (New York and Berlin: Wallach Art Gallery and Sternberg Press, 2019). On the history and biographies of French artists and art institutions in Algeria, see Élisabeth Cazenave, *Les artistes de l'Algérie: Dictionnaire des peintres, sculpteurs, graveurs, 1830–1962* (Paris: Association Abd-el-Tif, 2001); and Malika Dorbani-Bouabdellah, "Les prémices de la peinture de la modernité et contemporaine en Algérie," *Horizons Maghrébins* 47 (2002): 161–168.

5. Frantz Fanon, *The Wretched of the Earth* (New York: Grove Press, 1963), 225.

6. Abdelkebir Khatibi, *Maghreb Pluriel* (Paris: Denoel, 1983).

7. François Pouillon, "150 Years of Algerian Painting: Relevance for Understanding on the Post-Colonial Situation," *French Politics, Culture & Society* 20, no. 2 (2002): 142; and François Pouillon, "Les miroirs en abyme: Cent cinquante ans de peinture algérienne," *NAQD* 17 (2003): 9–25.

8. Nadira Laggoune-Aklouche, "Résistance, appropriation et réappropriation dans l'art algérien," *Modern and Contemporary France* 19, no. 2 (2011): 179–193. This model contrasts with the extreme affirmation of the primacy of European ideas that underpin anti-colonial expression. Jacques Derrida, a francophone Algerian-born Jew, who left Algiers for good in 1961 wrote: "The anticolonial revolution can only liberate itself from factual Europe or the empirical West . . . and first win with its [Western] values, language, sciences, techniques, and weapons"; see Jacques

Derrida, "Cogito et histoire de la folie," *Revue de Métaphysique et de Morale* 68, no. 4 (1963): 466: "La révolution anti-colonialiste ne peut se libérer de l'Europe ou de l'Occident empiriques de fait . . . et en se laissant d'abord gagner par ses valeurs, son langage, ses sciences, ses techniques, ses armes."

9. Virginie Rey, *Mediating Museums: Exhibiting Material Culture in Tunisia (1881–2016)* (Leiden: Brill, 2019), 57.

10. Anthropologist-historian Fanny Colonna embodies French-Algerian "worlds of contact" in her life (a European settler who chose Algerian citizenship at independence) and her writings: Fanny Colonna, *Le meunier, les moines et le bandit: Des vies quotidiennes dans l'Aurès (Algérie) du XXe siècle* (Paris: Sindbad, 2010). See also Malika Rahal, "Fanny Colonna: Notes sur le Middle Ground," *Textures du temps*, November 30, 2014, https://texturesdutemps.hypotheses.org/1359.

11. Pierre Bourdieu and Abdelmalek Sayad, "Colonial Rule and Cultural Sabir," *Ethnography* 5, no. 4 (2004): 445–486.

12. David Prochaska, *Making Algeria French: Colonialism in Bône, 1870–1920* (New York: Cambridge University Press, 1990), 209.

13. Ferdinand De Jong, "Recycling Recognition: The Monument as *Objet Trouvé* of the Postcolony," *Journal of Material Culture* 13, no. 2 (2008): 195–214.

14. Andreas Huyssen, *Memory Art in the Contemporary World: Confronting Violence in the Global South* (London: Lund Humphries, 2022).

15. Paul Basu, "Recasting the National Narrative: Postcolonial Pastiche and the new Sierra Leone Peace and Cultural Monument," *African Arts* 46, no. 3 (2013): 13; and Paul Basu, "Palimpsest Memoryscapes: Materializing and Mediating War and Peace in Sierra Leone," in *Reclaiming Heritage: Alternative Imaginaries of Memory in West Africa*, ed. Ferdinand De Jong and Michael Rowlands, 231–259 (Walnut Creek, CA: Left Coast Press, 2007). See also Anissa Bouayed, "Histoire de la peinture en Algérie: Continuum et ruptures," *Confluences Méditerranée* 81, no. 2 (2012): 163–179.

16. E. Valentine Daniel, "Interview with Ann Stoler," *Public Culture* 24, no. 3 (2012): 493–514.

17. Bernard Stiegler, *For a New Critique of Political Economy* (Cambridge, MA: Polity, 2010), 29: "[I]t is impossible to oppose *living* memory to the *dead* memory of the *hypomnematon* . . . This impossibility opens the *pharmacological question*, according to which the hypomnesic is a *pharmakon*: at once poison and remedy."

18. To a certain extent, here I'm influenced here by Actor-Network Theory (ANT) in reference to architecture and sculpture. My focus is on the actions, conditions, negotiations, and artistic interventions that emerge around Algerian public art.

19. Lorenzo Veracini, *The World Turned Inside Out: Settler Colonialism as a Political Idea* (London: Verso, 2021), 54.

20. See Kouider Metaïr et al., *Oran la mémoire* (Paris: Mediterra, 2013). On Bel Horizon, see Diana Wylie, "The Importance of Being At-Home: A Defense of His-

toric Preservation in Algeria," *Change Over Time* 2, no. 2 (2012): 172–187; and Diana Wylie, ""Part of Who We Are': Using Old Buildings to Foster Citizenship in North Africa (Oran, Algeria, and Casablanca, Morocco)," *Buildings & Landscapes: Journal of the Vernacular Architecture Forum* 25, no. 1 (2018): 44–63. The concept of a shared French-Algerian heritage has long circulated in Algerian architectural circles, see for example, Boussad Aiche, Farida Cherbi, and Leila Oubouzar, "Patrimoine XIX è. et XX è. siècles en Algérie: Un héritage à l'avenir incertain," *Reconnaître et protéger l'architecture récente en Méditerranée*, ed. Alexandre Abry and Roméo Carabelli, 147–170 (Paris: Maisonneuve et Larose, Paris, 2006).

21. Habib Benkoula and Larbi Merhoum, "L'impossible ville algérienne: Entre état rentier et citoyens désemparés," December 17, 2020, https://topophile.net/savoir/limpossible-ville-algerienne-entre-etat-rentier-et-citoyens-desempares/: "L'élite d'Oran veut sauvegarder un décor européen, un morceau de la colonisation, tout en se dressant en bloc contre la colonisation et son caractère criminel. Aussi, la nostalgie de la toponymie européenne marque les esprits. Même soixante ans après l'indépendance, le territoire urbain de l'imaginaire social demeure européen et est pris pour référence. Beaucoup des plus âgés se mettent en valeur par rapport à des Européens qu'ils connaissaient à 'l'époque,' ne serait-ce que pour signifier leur supériorité sur ceux qui n'étaient pas encore là. C'est dire ô combien la définition du patrimoine dans le cas des territoires européens d'Algérie demeure compliquée. L'élite qui défend ce patrimoine universel n'arrive pas, à mon sens, à voir en quoi la population qui y loge ne se sent guère concernée par l'histoire qu'il incarne."

22. Indeed, it was thanks to French military control that Delacroix could travel to Oran and Algiers in 1832 where he journeyed for six months under army protection with the embassy of the Duke of Mornay. See also Malika Dorbani-Bouabdellah, *Eugène Delacroix: Femmes d'Alger dans leur appartement* (Paris: Musée du Louvre éditions and Somogy éditions d'art, 2008).

23. César [Baldaccini], "Recommencer, ce n'est pas refaire / Starting Over Is Not Repeating," *Opus International*, 120 (July/August 1990): 18.

24. Guy Debord and Gil J. Wolman, "A User's Guide to Détournement," *Les Lèvres Nues* 8, May 1956, https://www.cddc.vt.edu/sionline/presitu/usersguide.html.

25. Michael Rothberg, "Holocaust Memory after the Multidirectional Turn," *Berliner Zeitung*, February 21, 2021, https://www.berliner-zeitung.de/open-source/gegen-opferkonkurrenz-es-gibt-auch-in-deutschland-kein-isoliertes-gedenken-li.141816.

BIBLIOGRAPHY

Materials from archives are not cited in the bibliography, only in the footnotes.

"À Constantine: Inauguration du monument aux combattants." *L'Afrique du Nord Illustrée* 77 (October 21, 1922): 8.

À nos grands hommes: La sculpture publique française jusqu'à la seconde guerre mondiale à travers la carte postale. Paris: Musée d'Orsay et l'Institut National d'Histoire de l'Art, 2004, CD-ROM.

AbiMershed, Osama W. *Apostles of Modernity: Saint-Simonians and the Civilizing Mission in Algeria*. Stanford, CA: Stanford University Press, 2010.

Adoue, Léon. *La ville de Sidi-Bel-Abbès: Histoire, légende, anecdotes*. Sidi-Bel-Abbès: René Roidot, Imprimeur-Editeur, 1927.

Agamben, Giorgio. *The Kingdom and the Glory: For a Theological Genealogy of Economy and Government*. Stanford, CA: Stanford University Press, 2011.

Ageron, Charles-Robert. "Administration directe ou Protectorat: Un conflit de méthodes sur l'organisation de la province de Constantine (1837–1838)." *Revue français d'Outre-mer* 50 (1963): 5–40.

Ageron, Charles-Robert. *Les Algériens musulmans et la France (1871–1919)*, 2 vols. Paris: Presses universitaires de France, 1968.

Ageron, Charles-Robert. "Décolonisation," *Encyclopaedia Universalis*, https://www.universalis.fr/encyclopedie/decolonisation/.

Ageron, Charles. "Enquête sur les origines du nationalisme algérien: L'émir Khaled, petit-fils d'Abd El-Kader, fut-il le premier nationaliste algérien?" *Revue de l'Occident musulman et de la Méditerranée* 2 (1966): 9–49.

Agulhon, Maurice. *Marianne au combat*. Paris: Flammarion, 1979.

Agulhon, Maurice. *Les metamorphoses de Marianne: L'imagerie et la symboliques républicaines de 1914 à nos jours*. Paris: Flammarion, 2001.

Agulhon, Maurice. "La 'statuomanie' et l'histoire," *Ethnologie française* 8, no. 2/3, (1978): 145–172.

Ahdjoudj, Amrane. *Algérie, etat, pouvoir et société (1962–1965)*. Paris: Arcantère, 1991.

Aiche, Boussad, Farida Cherbi, and Leila Oubouzar. "Patrimoine XIX è. et XX è. siècles en Algérie: un héritage à l'avenir incertain." In *Reconnaître et protéger l'architecture récente en Méditerranée*, edited by Alexandre Abry and Roméo Romeo Carabelli, 147–170. Paris: Maisonneuve et Larose, Paris, 2006.

Ainad-Tabet, Redouane. *Le 8 mai 1945 en Algérie*. Algiers: OPU, 1987.

Ainad-Tabet, Redouane. "Sidi-Bel-Abbès: des mythes fondateurs de la colonisation à la libération." *Insaniyat* 3 (1998):7–24.

Aîssaoui, Mohammad. "L'hommage émouvant de Régis Debray à Kamel Daoud." *Le Figaro,* May 5, 2015, https://www.lefigaro.fr/livres/2015/05/05/03005-20150505 ARTFIG00249-l-hommage-emouvant-de-regis-debray-a-kamel-daoud.php.

Akoun, André. *Né à Oran: Autobiographie en troisième personne*. Paris: Bouchène, 2004.

Alazard, Jean. "Le sculpteur Albert Pommier." *L'Art et les artistes* 31, new series no. 160 (1935): 89–94.

Albers, Kate Palmer, and Jordan Bear. "Photography's Time Zones." In *Before-and-After Photography: Histories and Contexts*, edited by Jordan Bear and Kate Palmer Albers, 1–11. London: Bloomsbury, 2017.

Alcaraz, Emmanuel. *Les lieux de mémoire de la guerre d'indépendance algérienne*. Paris: Karthala, 2017.

Alcaraz, Emmanuel. "La mise en scène de la mémoire nationale: De la guerre d'indépendance algérienne au maqam al-chahid d'Alger." In *Autour des morts de guerre: Maghreb—Moyen-Orient*, edited by Raphaëlle Branche, Nadine Picaudou and Pierre Vermeren, 21–45. Paris: Éditions de la Sorbonne, 2013.

Alcaraz, Emmanuel. "Les monuments aux martyrs de la guerre d'indépendance algérienne: Monumentalité, enjeux de mémoire et commémorations." *Guerres mondiales et conflits contemporains* 237 (2010/11): 125–146.

Alcaraz, Emmanuel. "Les timbres algériens de 1962 à nos jours, lieux de mémoire de la guerre d'Indépendance algérienne," *Cahiers de la Méditerranée* 91 (2016): http://journals.openedition.org/cdlm/8217.

"Algeria: France-Algeria independence agreements (Évian agreements)." *International Legal Materials* 1, no. 2 (1962): 214–230.

Alloa, Emmanuel. "Seeing-as, Seeing-in, Seeing-with: Looking through Images." In *Handbook of Image Studies*, edited by K. Purgar, 483–499. London: Palgrave Macmillan, 2021.

Alloula, Malek. *The Colonial Harem*. Minneapolis: University of Minnesota Press, 1986.

Alonzo, Éric. *Du rond-point au giratoire*. Marseille, Lyon: Édition Parenthèses, Édition du Certu, 2005.

Amato, Alain. *Monuments en exil*. Versailles: Éditions de Atlanthrope, 1979.

Amicale des anciens élèves des écoles d'agriculture d'Algérie. *L'œuvre agricole française en Algérie (1830–1962)*. Versailles: Atlanthrope, 1990.

Anderson, Benedict. *Imagined Communities: Reflections on the Origins and Spread of Nationalism*. London: Verso, 1983.

Andolenko, Serge. *Une visite aux Salles D'Honneur et au Musee du Souvenir de la Légion Etrangère*. Sidi-Bel-Abbès: Presse Regimentaire, 1938.

André, Marc. *Une prison pour mémoire: Montluc, de 1944 à nos jours*. Lyon: ENS Éditions, 2022.

André, Marc. "Les rapatriés d'Algérie et la presse: Le cas lyonnais." *Outre-mers* 97, no. 368/369 (2010):421–438.

André, Marc, and Susan Slyomovics. "L'inévitable prison: Éléments introductifs à une étude du système carcéral en Algérie de la conquête coloniale à la gestion de son héritage aujourd'hui." *L'Année du Maghreb* 20 (2019): 9–31.

Appadurai, Arjun, ed. *The Social Life of Things: Commodities in Cultural Perspective*. Cambridge: Cambridge University Press, 1986.

Appert-Sarrabezolles, Geneviève, Marie Odile Lefèvre, et al. *Carlo Sarrabezolles, sculpteur et statuaire 1888–1971*. Paris: Somogy Éditions d'Art, 2003.

Arrêté 21 octobre 2011 modifiant l'arrêté du 23 juin 2011 relatif au regroupement de sépultures civiles françaises en Algérie [Order of October 21, 2011 modifying the order of June 23, 2011 on regrouping civilian French tombs in Algeria] *JORF*, October 27, 2011, https://www.legifrance.gouv.fr/jorf/id/JORFTEXT000024717650.

Arrêté du 2 mars 1992 portant ouverture d'instance en vue du classement des monuments et sites historiques [Order of March 2, 1992 on opening the inscription in the list of historical monuments and sites] *JORA*, April 11, 1990, https://www.joradp.dz/FTP/Jo-Francais/1990/F1990015.pdf.

Arslan, Salman [pseud. Mounji Farid]. "Statue de Zighoud Youcef, histoire d'une oeuvre d'art et de mémoire." *El Watan*, August 19, 2021, 14–15.

Ashworth, Gregory John, and John E. Tunbridge. *Dissonant Heritage: The Management of the Past as a Resource in Conflict*. New York: Wiley, 1996.

Asseraf, Arthur. *Electric News in Colonial Algeria*. Oxford: Oxford University Press, 2019.

Audollent, August. "Victoire Ailée du musée de Constantine." *Revue Archéologique* 16 (1890): 66–75.

Augé, Marc. "Roundabouts: The Revenge of the Local." In *City A–Z*, edited by Nigel Thrift and Steve Pile, 206–207. London: Routledge, 2000.

Azoulay, Ariella. *The Civil Contract of Photography*. New York: Zone Books, 2008.

Azoulay, Ariella Aïsha. *Potential History: Unlearning Imperialism*. London: Verso, 2019.

Azoulay, Paul. *La nostalgérie française (Collections "Les cartes postales de l'histoire")*. Paris: Eric Baschet Editions, 1980.

Bacha, Myriam. *Architectures au Maghreb (XIXe–XXe siècles): Réinvention du patrimoine*. Tours, France: Presses universitaire François Rabelais, 2011.

Badjadja, Abdelkrim. *La bataille de Constantine, 1837–1837*. Algiers: Chihab, 2016.

Baghdad, Mohamed Hirreche. "Les inscriptions funéraires au cimetière d'Aïn El-Beida (Oran): État des lieux." *Insaniyat* 62 (2013), http://journals.openedition.org/insaniyat/14376.

Balafrej, Lamia. "Islamic Iconoclasm, Visual Communication and the Persistence of the Image." *Interiors* 6, no. 3 (2015): 351–366.

Balibar, Etienne. "Algérie, France: Une ou deux nations?" *Lignes* 30 (1997): 7–22.

[Baldaccini], César, "Recommencer, ce n'est pas refaire / Starting Over Is Not Repeating." *Opus International*. 120 (July–August 1990): 10–21.

Barbier, Benjamin. "Benyahia, Ahmed." *Dictionnaire des artistes algériens, Hypotheses* (blog), https://patmagh.hypotheses.org/201.

Barcellini, Caroline. *Le musée de l'Armée et la fabrique de la nation: Histoire militaire, histoire nationale et enjeux muséographiques*. Paris: L'Harmattan, 2010.

Barclay, Fiona. "The Sidi-Ferruch Monument Revisited," August 30, 2022, https://www.pieds-noirs.stir.ac.uk/sidi-ferruch-revisited/.

Basch, Sophe."La postérité littéraire et artistique de la Victoire de Samothrace: petite anthologie." *Revue d'histoire littéraire de la France* 3 (2019): 615–627.

Bastide, Léon. *Bel Abbés et son arrondissement: Histoire administrative*. Oran: Imprimerie Perrier, 1880.

Basu, Paul. "Palimpsest Memoryscapes: Materializing and Mediating War and Peace in Sierra Leone." In *Reclaiming Heritage: Alternative Imaginaries of Memory in West Africa*, edited by Ferdinand De Jong and Michael Rowlands, 231–259. Walnut Creek, CA: Left Coast Press, 2007.

Basu, Paul. "Recasting the National Narrative: Postcolonial Pastiche and the new Sierra Leone Peace and Cultural Monument." *African Arts* 46, no. 3 (2013): 10–25.

Beaugé, Florence. "Paris reconnaît que le massacre de Sétif en 1945 était 'inexcusable.'" *Le Monde*, March 9, 2005, https://www.lemonde.fr/international/article/2005/03/09/paris-reconnait-que-le-massacre-de-setif-en-1945-etait-inexcusable_400904_3210.html.

Becker, Annette. *Les monuments aux morts: Patrimoine et mémoire de la Grande Guerre*. Paris: Éditions Errance, 1988.

Bekkouche, Ammara. "Enjeux coloniaux et projection urbaine en Algérie: le cas de Sidi-Bel-Abbès." *Insaniyat* 13 (2001): 45–59.

Bekkouche, Ammara. "Un quartier nommé Ville Nouvelle: Du village nègre colonial à la Medina J'dida des Oranais." *Les annales de la recherche urbaine* 98 (2005): 114–121.

Bellisari, Andrew. "The Art of Decolonization: The Battle for Algeria's French Art, 1962–70." *Journal of Contemporary History* 52, no. 3 (2017): 625–645.

Belmessous, Saliha. *Assimilation and Empire: Uniformity in French and British Colonies, 1541–1954*. Oxford: Oxford University Press, 2013.

Beloufa, Neil. "L'ennemi de mon ennemi," 2018. https://www.paul-landowski.com/en/2018/04/02/algiers-war-memorial-palais-de-tokyo/.

Benaidja, Idir. "Le rapport ordinaire à l'héritage bâti de l'époque de la colonisation française en Algérie: L'exemple de l'hôtel de ville de Kherrata (Bejaia)." *L'Année du Maghreb* 19 (2018): 81–98.

Bendix, Regina F., Aditya Eggert, and Arnika Peselmann. *Heritage Regimes and the State*. Göttingen: Universitätsverlag Göttingen, 2012.

Bengoa, Daphné, and Leo Fabrizio. *Fernand Pouillon et l'Algérie: Bâtir à l'hauteur des hommes*. Paris: Éditions Macula, 2019.

Benjamin, Roger. *Orientalist Aesthetics: Art, Colonialism, and French North Africa, 1880–1930*. Berkeley: University of California Press, 2002.

Benjamin, Walter. "The Work of Art in the Age of Its Technological Reproducibility." In *The Work of Art in the Age of Its Technological Reproducibility, and Other Writings on Media*, 19–55. Cambridge, MA: Harvard University Press, 2008.

Benkada, Saddek. "La création de Médina Jdida, Oran (1845): Un exemple de la politique coloniale de regroupement urbain." *Insaniyat* 5 (1998): 103–111.

Benkoula, Habib, and Larbi Merhoum. "L'impossible ville algérienne: Entre état rentier et citoyens désemparés," December 17, 2020. https://topophile.net/savoir/limpossible-ville-algerienne-entre-etat-rentier-et-citoyens-desempares/.

Benramdane, Farid. "'Qui es-tu? J'ai été dit': De la destruction de la filiation dans l'état civil d'Algérie ou éléments d'un onomacide sémantique." *Insaniyat* 10 (2000): 79–87.

Benseddik, Nacéra. "Histoire colonial: Les tribulations des collections archéologiques de l'Algérie." *Libyan Studies* 50 (2019): 165–177.

Benyahia, Ahmed. *Projet de Transformation de la Prison du Coudiat et de la Gendarmerie en Musée de la Mémoire et de la Resistance*. Constantine: unpublished report, June 23, 2010, 10 pages.

Benyoucef, Messaoud. "L'été meurtrier: Rio Salado, Août 1962." *Socialgerie*, April 27, 2013. https://socialgerie.net/spip.php?article1168.

Berbrugger, Adrien. *La Bibliothèque-musée d'Alger: Livret explicative des collections diverses de ces deux établissements*. Algiers: Imprimerie Bastide, Libraire Editeur, 1860.

Bérenguer, Alfred. *Un curé en Amérique latine (1959–1960)*. Algiers: SNED, 1966.

Bérenguer, Alfred. *En toute liberté: Entretiens avec Geneviève Dermenjian*. Paris: Centurion, 1994.

Berque, Jacques. *Le Maghreb entre deux guerres*. Paris: Seuil, 1962.

Blair, Thomas L. *"The Land to Those Who Work It": Algeria's Experiment in Workers' Management*. Garden City, NY: Doubleday, 1969.

Blais, Hélène, and Florence Deprest, "The Mediterranean, a Territory between France and Colonial Algeria: Imperial Constructions." *European Review of History / Revue européenne d'histoire* 19, no. 1 (2012): 33–57.

Blais, Hélène, Claire Fredj, and Emmanuelle Saada. "Introduction: Un long moment colonial: pour une histoire de l'Algérie au XIXe siècle." *Revue d'histoire du XIXe siècle* 41 (2010): 7–24.

Boualam Bachaga. *Les Harkis au service de la France*. Paris: Édition, 1963.

Boualam, Bachaga. *Mon pays, la France*. Paris: Édition, 1962.

Bouameur, Oumnia, and Nadia Chabi. "The War Memorial of Constantine Facing Risks and Vulnerability." *Journal of Science and Technology* 4, no. 2 (2019): 7–14.

Bouayed, Anissa. *Art et l'Algérie insurgée: Les traces de l'épreuve 1954–1962*. Algiers: ENAG, 2005.

Bouayed, Anissa. "Histoire de la peinture en Algérie: continuum et ruptures." *Confluences Méditerranée* 81 (2012): 163–179.

Bouayed, Anissa. "Peinture moderne et patrimoine, une position subsidiaire: La période charnière des années 60." *Insaniyat* 12 (2002): 65–75.

Boudjada, Yasmina. "L'église catholique de Constantine de 1839 à 1859: Cas de l'appropriation de la mosquée Souk el Ghzel par les Français." In *Villes rattachées, villes reconfigurées: xvi*[e]*–xx*[e] *siècles*, edited by Denise Turrel, 285–303. Tours: Presses Universitaires François-Rabelais, 2003.

Bouniceau-Guesmon, Prosper. *M. F. de Saint-Vidal et sa fontaine: Étude critique*. Paris: A. Lemerre, 1889.

Bourdieu, Pierre. *The Algerians*. Boston: Beacon Press, 1961.

Bourdieu, Pierre, and Marie-Claire. "The Peasant and Photography." *Ethnography* 5, no. 4 (2004): 601–616.

Bourdieu, Pierre, and Abdelmalek Sayad. "Colonial Rule and Cultural Sabir." *Ethnography* 5, no. 4 (2004): 445–486.

Bourdieu, Pierre, and Abdelmalak Sayad. *Uprooting: The Crisis of Traditional Agriculture in Algeria*. Cambridge, UK: Polity Press, 2020.

Bourdin, Gérard. "Les ambiguïtés d'un rapprochement: parrainages et jumelages, 1956–1962." In *La France en guerre 1954–1962: Expériences métropolitaines de la guerre d'indépendance algérienne*, edited by Raphaëlle Branche and Sylvie Thenault, 82–100. Paris, Autrement, 2008.

Bourouiba, Rachid. *L'art religieux en Algérie*. Algiers: SNED, 1973.

Boyer, Pierre. "Historique des Béni Amer d'Oranie, des origines au Senatus Consulte." *Revue de l'Occident musulman et de la Méditerranée* 24 (1977): 39–85.

Boym, Svetlana. *The Future of Nostalgia*. New York: Basic Books, 2002.

Brahimi, Abdelhamid. *Aux origines de la tragédie algérienne (1958–2000): Témoignage sur hizb França*. Geneva: Hoggar, 2000.

Branche, Raphaëlle. "The Martyr's Torch: Memory and Power in Algeria." *Journal of North African Studies* 16 (2011): 431–43.

Branche, Raphaëlle. "La sexualité des appelés en Algérie." In *Des hommes et des femmes en guerre d'Algérie*, edited by Jean-Charles Jauffret, 402–415. Paris: Autrement, 2003.

Breuer, Tilmann. "Ensemble: Konzeption und Problematik eines Begriffes des

Bayrischen Denkmalschutzgesetzes." *Deutsche Kunst und Denkmalpflege* 34 (1976): 21–38.
Brazzoduro, Andrea. "Towards a Postmodern National Narrative? The Algerian War Memorial and Contemporary French Landscapes of Memory." *Memory Studies* 15, no. 4 (2022): 858–882.
Bullukian, Napoléon. *De l'Ararat à Napoléon*. Lyon: Éditions La Pensée Universelle, 1975.
Burgat, François, and Michel Nancy. *Les villages socialistes de la révolution agraire algérienne (1972–1982)*. Paris: Éditions du Centre National de la Recherche Scientifique, 1984.
Burgin, Victor. "Monument and Melancholia." In *Memory Culture and the Contemporary City*, edited by Uta Staiger, Henriette Steiner, and Andrew Webber, 17–31. London: Palgrave Macmillan, 2009.
Bussière, A. "Le Maréchal Bugeaud et la colonization de l'Algérie: Souvenirs et récits de la vie colonial en Afrique." *Revue des Deux Mondes (1829–1971)* 4, no. 3 (1853): 449–506.
Byrne, Jeffrey James. *Mecca of Revolution: Algeria, Decolonization, and the Third World Order*. Oxford: Oxford University Press, 2016.
Calmein, Maurice. *Les associations pieds-noirs, 1962–1994*. Carcassonne: SOS Outre Mer, 1994.
Calmein, Maurice, and Thierry Rolando. *Les français d'Algérie de 1962 à 2014*. Friedberg: Atlantis, 2014.
Campt, Tina. *Listening to Images*. Durham, NC: Duke University Press, 2017.
C. B. [pseud. Abdelmadjid Merdaci]. "Qui a peur de Zighout Youcef?" *Revolution africaine* 1331 (September 8, 1986): 46.
Camus, Albert. *L'étranger*. Paris: Gallimard, 1942.
Camus, Albert. *The First Man*. Translated by David Hapgood. Toronto: Alfred Knopf, 1996.
Cap, D. "Le Tessala (Actacilis?) et ses ruines." *Revue Africaine* 8, no. 2 (1857): 81–85.
Carlier, Omar. "'Homme fétiche' ou 'Homme-symbole'? Un notable-militant: Houari Souiah, Premier préfet d'Oran (1915–1990)." *Cahiers de la Méditerranée* 46/47, no. 1 (1993): 203–247.
Carlier, Omar. *Entre nation et Jihad: Histoire sociale des radicalismes algeriens*. Paris: PFSP, 1995.
"Casino municipal de Constantine." *L'Echo d'Alger* 8750 (July 20, 1934): 4.
Cazenave, Élisabeth. *Les artistes de l'Algérie: Dictionnaire des peintres, sculpteurs, graveurs, 1830–1962*. Paris: Association Abd-el-Tif, 2001.
Cazenave, Élisabeth. *La villa Abd-el-Tif: Un demi-siècle de vie artistique en Algérie, 1907–1962*. Saint Raphael, France: Association Abd-el-Tif, 1998.
Cazenave, Élisabeth, and Jean Christian Serna. *Le patrimoine artistique français de*

l'Algérie: Les oeuvres du Musée nationale des Beaux-arts d'Alger de la constitution à la restitution. Chire-en-Montreuil, France: Éditions Abd-el-Tif, 2017.

Çelik, Zeynep. "Colonial/Postcolonial Intersections: *Lieux de mémoire* in Algiers." *Third Text* 49 (1999): 63–72.

Çelik, Zeynep. "Colonial Statues and Their Afterlives." *Journal of North African Studies* 25, no. 5 (2020): 711–726.

Çelik, Zeynep. "A Lingering Obsession: The Houses of Algiers in French Colonial Discourse." In *The Walls of Algiers*, edited by Zeynep Celik, Julia Clancy-Smith, and Frances Terpak, 134–160. Seattle: University of Washington Press, 2009.

Çelik, Zeynep. *Urban Forms and Colonial Confrontations: Algiers under French Rule*. Berkeley: University of California Press, 1997.

"Cérémonie patriotique: Inauguration du monument aux morts." *Le Tell: Journal politique et des intérêts coloniaux* 63, no. 6163 (July 8, 1925): 1–2.

Chassey, Eric de. "Une discussion entre Moncef Ben Moussa, Meriem Berrada, Malika Dorbani-Bouabdellah, Taher Ghalia et Abdellah Karroum." *Perspective: Actualité en histoire de l'art* 2 "Le Maghreb" (2017). http://journals.openedition.org/perspective/7476.

Cherbonneau, Auguste. *Album du Musée de Constantine*. Constantine: Alessi et Arnolet Libraires, 1862.

Chevallier, R. "La centuriation et les problèmes de la colonization Romaine." *Études rurales* 3 (1961): 54–80.

Chigudu, Simukai. "'Colonialism Had Never Really Ended': My Life in the Shadow of Cecil Rhodes." *The Guardian*, January 14, 2021. https://www.theguardian.com/news/2021/jan/14/rhodes-must-fall-oxford-colonialism-zimbabwe-simukai-chigudu.

Chouadra S. et al. "Le patrimoine colonial entre la problématique du renouvellement urbain et la préservation de la mémoire des lieux, cas de la ville de Sétif, Algérie." *Sciences & Technologie D* 42 (2015): 9–19.

Choay, Françoise. *L'allégorie du patrimoine*. Paris: Seuil, 1992.

Choay, Françoise. *The Invention of the Historic Monument*. Cambridge: Cambridge University Press, 2001.

Choi, Sung-Eun. "The Muslim Veteran in Postcolonial France: The Politics of the Integration of Harkis after 1962." *French Politics, Culture, and Society* 29, no. 1 (2011): 24–45.

Choi, Sung-Eun. *Decolonization and the French of Algeria: Bringing the Settler Colony Home*. New York: Palgrave Macmillan, 2016.

Colonna, Fanny. *Le meunier, les moines et le bandit: Des vies quotidiennes dans l'Aurès (Algérie) du XXe siècle*. Paris: Sindbad, 2010.

Conklin, Alice L. *A Mission to Civilize: The Republican Idea of Empire in France and West Africa, 1895–1930*. Stanford, CA: Stanford University Press, 1997.

Cooper, Frederick, and Ann Stoler. *Tensions of Empire: Colonial Cultures in a Bour-*

geois World, edited by Frederick Cooper and Ann Laura Stoler. Berkeley: University of California Press, 1997.

Conseil National de la Révolution Algérienne [CNRA, National Council of the Algerian Revolution]. "Tripoli Program," 1962. http://www.el-mouradia.dz/francais/symbole/textes/tripoli.htm.

"Coq de la Grande Bosse" website. http://www.guer-coetquidan-broceliande.fr/bisto/coet/coq_bosse.html.

Corps du droit francais, ou recueil complet des lois, décrets, ordonnances . . . publies depuis 1789 jusq'a nos jours, edited by C.-M. Galliset. Paris: Imprimerie et librarie générale de jurisprudence de Cosse et N. Delamotte, 1847.

Côte, Marc. *L'Algérie ou l'espace retourné*. Paris: Flammarion, 1988.

"Courage mes amis, défendez-vous jusqu'à la mort!" In *Le Sergent Blandan et le combat d'El-Mechdoufa (près de Beni-Mered)*. Algiers: Adolphe Jourdan, 1887.

Cupers, Kenny. *The Social Project: Housing Postwar France*. Minneapolis: University of Minnesota Press, 2014.

Dalisson, Rémi. *En mémoire du 11 novembre: Vie et mort d'une fête nationale des origines à nos jours*. Paris: Armand Colin, 2013.

Dalrymple, William. *The Anarchy: The East India Company, Corporate Violence, and the Pillage of an Empire*. London: Bloomsbury, 2019.

Daniel, E. Valentine. "Interview with Ann Stoler." *Public Culture* 24, no. 3 (2012): 493–514.

Daoud, Kamal. *Meurseult, contre-enquête*. Arles: Actes Sud, 2014.

Darot, Joseph. "Les sacrifices de l'Oranie durant la Grande Guerre 1914–1918." *Le livre d'or de l'Oranie* 74. Algiers: Éditions de *l'Afrique du Nord Illustrée*, 1925.

Davis, Diana K. *Resurrecting the Granary of Rome: Environmental History and French Colonial Expansion in North Africa*. Athens: Ohio University Press, 2007.

De Jong, Ferdinand. "Recycling Recognition: The Monument as *Objet Trouvé* of the Postcolony." *Journal of Material Culture* 13, no. 2 (2008): 195–214.

Décret 63-105 du 4 Avril 1963 relatif aux hommages publics [Decree 65-105 of April 4, 1963 on public commemorations] *JORA*, April 12, 1963, p. 339.

Décret 3668 du 3 février 1912 relatif au recrutement des indigènes algériens [Decree 3668 of February 3, 1912 for the Recruitment of Algerian Natives] *JORF*, (February 7, 1912, 1208.

Décret 68-728 du 7 août 1968 portant publication de l'échange de lettres entre la France et l'Algerie des 29 avril et 30 juin 1968 concernant le regroupement des sepultures civiles françaises situées dans certains cimetières d'Algérie [Decree 68-728 on the publication of letters exchanged between France and Algeria concerning regrouping civilian French tombs situated in certain Algerian cemeteries] *JORF*, August 7, 1968, 7799.

Décret 2017-433 du 28 mars 2017 relatif au label "Architecture contemporaine remarquable" pris en application de l'article L. 650-1 du code du patrimoine [Decree 2017-433 of March 28, 2017 on the label "remarkable contemporary architecture" issued pursuant to article L. 650-1 of the heritage code], *JORF*, March 31, 2017. https://www.legifrance.gouv.fr/loda/id/JORFTEXT000034308019/?isSuggest=true.

Décret exécutif 18-102 du 11 Rajab 1439 correspondant au 29 mars 2018 portant création d'un musée public national "Prison Serkadji" 17 Rajab 1439 [Executive Decree 18-1-2 corresponding to March 29, 2018 on creating a national public museum "Prison Serkadji"] *JORA*, April 4, 2018, 6–7.

Debord, Guy, and Gil J. Wolman. "A User's Guide to Détournement." *Les Lèvres Nues* 8 (May 1956). https://www.cddc.vt.edu/sionline/presitu/usersguide.html.

Deifenbacher, Michel. *Rapport Parachever l'effort de solidarité nationale envers les rapatriés: Promouvoir l'oeuvre collective de la France outre-mer.* Paris: Documentation française, December 18, 2003.

DeGeorges, Thomas. "The Shifting Sands of Revolutionary Legitimacy: The Role of Former mūjāhidīn in the Shaping of Algeria's Collective Memory." *Journal of North African Studies* 14, no. 2 (2009): 273–288.

Dekoumi, Djamel. "Pour une nouvelle politique de conservation de l'environnement historique bâti algérien: Cas de Constantine." PhD thesis, Constantine University, 2007.

Deluz, Jean-Jacques. *Le tout et le fragment.* Algiers: Barzakh, 2010.

Demarchi, Luc. "Le Monument aux Morts d'Oran." Lyon: Cercle algérianiste de Lyon, posted August 9, 2007. http://www.cerclealgerianiste-lyon.org/mamo.html.

Denis, Jean-Christophe. *Le Souvenir Français à travers les siècles, 1887–2017.* Paris: Éditions Bernard Giovanangeli, 2017.

"Déplacement du monuments aux morts Promenade de Letang." *Travaux nord-africains* (February 22, 1939): 2.

Derderian, Richard L. "Algeria as a *lieu de memoire*: Ethnic Minority Memory and National Identity in Contemporary France." *Radical History Review* (2002): 28–43.

DeRoo, Rebecca J. "Colonial Collecting: French Women and Algerian *Cartes Postales.*" In *Postcards: Ephemeral Histories of Modernity,* edited by David Prochaska and Jordana Mendelson, 85–92. University Park: Pennsylvania State University Press, 2010.

Derrida, Jacques. *La carte postale.* Paris: Flammarion, 1980.

Derrida, Jacques. "Cogito et histoire de la folie." *Revue de Métaphysique et de Morale* 68, no. 4 (1963): 460–494.

Derrida, Jacques, and Safaa Fathy. "Contre-jour." Translated by Max Cavitch. *PMLA* 131, no. 2 (2016): 540–550.

Desplanques, G. "Les migrations extérieures, les rapatriés d'Algérie." *Les collections des de l'Institut national de la statistique et des études économiques* 39 (June 1975): 63–72.

Didi-Huberman, Georges. *Images malgré tout.* Paris: Minuit, 2003.

Dix années de realizations (19 juin 1965–19 juin 1975). Algiers: Ministère d'Information et de la Culture, 1976.

Djerbal, Daho. *Lakhdar Bentobbal, mémoires de l'intérieur.* Algiers: Chihab: 2021, 2 vols.

Djerbal, Daho. "Mounadiline et mousebbiline: Les forces auxiliaires de l'ALN du Nord-Constantinois." In *Des hommes et des femmes en guerre d'Algérie,* edited by Jean-Charles Jauffret, 282–296. Paris: Autrement, 2003.

Djerbal, Daho. "Processus de colonisation et évolution de la propriété foncière dans les plaines intérieures de l'Oranie (subdivisions de Mascara et Sidi-bel-Abbès, 1850–1920)." PhD thesis, Université Paris-VII, 1979.

Dondin-Payre, Monique. "*L'exercitus Africae* inspiratrice de l'armée française d'Afrique: *Ense et aratro.*" *Antiquités africaines* 27 (1991): 141–149.

Dondin-Payre, Monique. "Réussites et déboires d'une œuvre archéologique unique: Le colonel Carbuccia au nord de l'Aurès (1848–1850)." *Antiquités africaines* 32 (1996): 145–174.

Donop, Raoul-Marie. *Lettres sur l'Algérie (1907–1908).* Paris: Plon, 1908.

Dorbani-Bouabdallah, Malika. *Ahmed Benyahia: Rétrospective.* Algiers: Ministry of Culture, 2015.

Dorbani-Bouabdellah, Malika. *Eugène Delacroix: Femmes d'Alger dans leur appartement.* Paris: Musée du Louvre éditions and Somogy éditions d'art, 2008.

Dorbani-Bouabdellah, Malika. "Les prémices de la peinture de la modernité et contemporaine en Algérie." *Horizons Maghrébins* 47 (2002): 161–168.

Dreyfous, Maurice. *Dalou: Sa vie et son oeuvre.* Paris: Librairie Renouard, 1903.

DuBois, W. E. B. "Returning Soldier." *The Crisis,* 1919. https://glc.yale.edu/returning-soldiers.

Duffy, Andrea E. "Civilizing through Cork: Conservationism and *la Mission Civilisatrice* in French Colonial Algeria." *Environmental History* 23, no. 2 (2018): 270–292.

Duhamel, Jérôme, and Réné Pétillon. *Grand inventaire du génie français en 365 objets.* Paris: Albin Michel, 1992.

Edwards, Elizabeth. "Material Beings: The Objecthood of Ethnographic Photographs." *Visual Studies* 17, no. 1 (2002): 69–75.

Edwards, Elizabeth. "Objects of Affect: Photography beyond the Image." *Annual Review of Anthropology* 41, no. 1 (2012): 221–234.

Edwards, Peter. "'*Mort pour la France*': Conflict and Commemoration in France after the First World War." *Journal of Contemporary History* 1 (2000): 1–11.

Effros, Bonnie. "Colliding Empires: French Display of Roman Antiquities Expropriated from Postconquest Algeria, 1830–1870." In *Objects of War: The Material Culture of Conflict and Displacement*, edited by Leora Auslander and Tara Zahra, 50–77. Ithaca, NY: Cornell University Press, 2018.

Effros, Bonnie. *Incidental Archaeologists: French Officers and the Rediscovery of Roman North Africa*. Ithaca, NY: Cornell University Press, 2018.

Eldridge, Claire. "Feature Archive: Centre de documentation historique sur l'Algérie (CDHA). http://frenchhistorysociety.co.uk/blog/?p=1856.

Eldridge, Claire. "'The Forgotten of This Tribute': Settler Soldiers, Colonial Categories and the Centenary of the First World War." *History and Memory* 31, no. 2 (2019): 3–44.

Eldridge, Claire. *From Empire to Exile: History and Memory Within the Pied-Noir and Harki Communities*. Manchester: Manchester University Press, 2016.

Emsalem, René. "Les villages indigènes d'Oran." *Revue de géographie jointe au Bulletin de la Société de géographie de Lyon et de la région lyonnaise* 25, no. 4 (1950): 289–299.

Esch, Arnold. "On the Reuse of Antiquity: The Perspectives of the Archaeologist and of the Historian." In *Reuse Value: Spolia and Appropriation in Art and Architecture from Constantine to Sherrie Levine*, edited by Richard Brilliant and Dale Kinney, 13–32. Farnham, Surrey: Ashgate, 2011.

Esch, Arnold. "Spolien: Zur Wiederverwendung antiker Baustücke und Skulpturen im mittelalterlichen Italien." *Archiv für Kulturgeschichte* 51 (1969): 1–64.

Estoublon, Robert and Adolphe Lefébure. *Code de l'Algérie annoté: Recueil chronologique des lois, ordonnances, décrets, arrêtés, circulaires, etc., formant la législation algérienne actuellement en vigueur, avec les travaux préparatoires et l'indication de la jurisprudence*. Algiers: A. Jourdan, 1896.

Fanon, Frantz. *A Dying Colonialism*. New York: Grove Press, 1965.

Fanon, Frantz. *The Wretched of the Earth*. New York: Grove, 1963.

Feigenbaum, Gail, and Inge Resit. "Introduction." In *Provenance: An Alternate History of Art*, edited by Gail Fegenbaum and Inge Reist, 1–5. Los Angeles: The Getty Research Institute, 2012.

Feldman, Hannah. *From a Nation Torn: Decolonizing Art and Representation in France 1945–1962*. Durham, NC: Duke University Press, 2014.

Ferhati, Barkahoum. "Le musée national Nasr Ed-din Etienne Dinet de Bou Saada: Un expérience avortée." *al-Naqd* 17 (2003): 73–96.

Finnegan, Cara A. *Making Photography Matter: A Viewer's History from the Civil War to the Great Depression*. Urbana: University of Illinois Press, 2015.

Fischer, Fabienne. *Alsaciens et Lorrains en Algérie, histoire d'une migration, 1830–1914*. Nice: Éditions Jacques Gandini, 1999.

Flood, Finbarr Barry. "Lost Histories of a Licit Figural Art." *International Journal of Middle East Studies*, 45, no. 3 (2013): 566–569.

Flood, Finbarr Barry. "Refiguring Iconoclasm in the Early Indian Mosque." In *Ne-*

gating the Image: Case Studies in Iconoclasm, edited by Anne L. McClanan and Jeffrey Johnson, 15–40. Aldershot: Ashgate, 2005.

Fogarty, Richard S. *Race and War in France: Colonial Subjects in the French Army, 1914–1918*. Baltimore, MD: Johns Hopkins University Press, 2008.

Foliard, Daniel. *The Violence of Colonial Photography*. Manchester: Manchester University Press, 2022.

Fonfrède, Henri. "De la décolonisation d'Alger." In *Oeuvres de Henri Fonfrède: Recueillies et mises en ordre par Charles-Alcée Campan, son collaborateur*, vol. 8, 233–249. Bordeaux: Chaumas-Gayet, 1846.

Fontan, Elisabeth, and Catherine Metzger. "History of the North African Collections of the Musée du Louvre." In *From Hannibal to Saint Augustine: Ancient Art of North Africa from the Musée du Louvre*, edited by Monique Seefried Brouillet, 13–15. Atlanta: Michael C. Carlos Museum, Emory University, 1994.

Forcada, Eric. "Le monument de Sidi Ferruch d'Émile Gaudissard: Oeuvre de mémoires, mémoires d'une oeuvre (1830–2012)." *Mirmanda: Revista de cultura* 7 (2012): 78–88.

Förster, Larissa. "Plea for a More Systematic, Comparative, International and Long-Term Approach to Restitution, Provenance Research and the Historiography of Collections." *Museumskunde* 81 (2016): 49–54.

Forty, Adrian. *The Art of Forgetting*. New York: Berg, 1999.

Foura, Mohamed, and Yasmina Foura. "Les places publiques dans la ville de Constantine." *Villes en parallèle* 36/37 (2003): 316–339.

Freeman, Kirrily. *Bronzes to Bullets: Vichy and the Destruction of French Public Statuary, 1941–1944*. Stanford, CA: Stanford University Press, 2008.

Freha, Mohamed. *Oran: Une ville témoine*. Oran: Enadar, 2017.

Frémeaux, Jacques. *La France et l'Algérie en guerre, 1830–1870, 1954–1962*. Paris: Economica et Institut de Stratégie Comparée, 2002.

Freud, Sigmund. "Five Lectures on Psycho-Analysis (1910)." In *Collected Works*, vol. 11, 9–56. London: Hogarth Press, 1957.

Frey, Jean-Pierre. "Figures et plans d'Oran 1931–1936, ou les années de tous les Danger." *Insaniyat* 23–24 (2004): 111–134.

Fried, Michael. "Art and Objecthood." *Artforum* 5, no. 10 (1967): 12–23.

Fried, Michael. *Absorption and Theatricality: Painting and Beholder in the Age of Diderot*. Berkeley: University of California Press, 1980.

Fuller, Mia. "Difficult How? Italy's *Inertia Memoriae* of Fascism." In *Difficult Heritage? The Afterlife of Colonial and Fascist Architecture, Monuments, and Works of Art in Contemporary Italy*, edited by Carmen Belmonte, 15–23. Milan: Silvano, 2023.

Gallois, William. *A History of Violence in the Early Algerian Colony*. New York: Palgrave Macmillan, 2013.

Gamboni, Dario. *The Destruction of Art: Iconoclasm and Vandalism since the French Revolution*. New Haven, CT: Yale University Press, 1997.

Garcia, Claire. "Migrations, transferts et réécritures: Le destin des monuments publics d'Algérie après l'Indépendance." *Les Cahiers de l'École du Louvre* 12 (2018). https://journals.openedition.org/cel/920.

Gauzence de Lastours [Étienne-Philippe-Jules]. "L'Algérie et le service en campagne algérienne." *Revue du génie militaire* 42, no. 2 (1911): 377–428.

Geertz, Clifford. "Art as a Cultural System." *Modern Language Notes* 91, no. 6 (1976): 1473–1499.

Geertz, Hildred. *The Life of a Balinese Temple: Artistry, Imagination, and History in a Peasant Village*. Honolulu: University of Hawaii Press, 2004.

Ghalem-Sardi, Abdelkader. "Historique du site du rectorat de l'Université Djillali Liabes de Sidi Bel Abbès." *al-Jamiʿa wa-al-mujtamʿ* (November 2009): 29–32.

Gibbon, Edward. *Memoirs of My Life*. Hartnolls, UK: Ryburn Publications, [1796] 1994.

Gillet, Fanny. " 'Il suffira d'ouvrir la coquille pour le récupérer': Histoires développées du Monument aux Morts d'Alger de Paul Landowski." In *L'Algérie au présent: Entre résistances et changements*, edited by Karima Dirèche, 549–573. Paris: Karthala, 2019.

Glissant, Édouard, and Hans Ulrich Obrist. *The Archipelago Conversations*. New York: Isolarii, 2021.

Goody, Jack. *The Myth of the Bagre*. Oxford: Clarendon Press, 1972.

Goudal, Émilie. *Des damné(é)s de l'histoire: Les arts visuels face à la guerre d'Algérie*. Dijon, France: Les presses du réel, 2019.

Graulle, E. *Insurrection de Bou-Amama (avril 1881)*. Paris: H. Charles-Lavauzelle, 1905.

Greenberg, Clement. "Avant-Garde and Kitsch." *Partisan Review* (1939): 34–49.

Greenblatt, Stephen. *Marvelous Possessions: The Wonder of the New World*. New York: Clarendon Press, 1991.

Greenhalgh, Michael. *The Military and Colonial Destruction of the Roman Landscape of North Africa, 1830–1900*. Leiden: Brill, 2014.

Greenhalgh, Michael. "The New Centurions: French Reliance on the Roman Past during the Conquest of Algeria." *War & Society* 16, no. 1 (1998): 1–28.

Grégoire, Henri. *Second rapport sur le vandalisme par Grégoire, séance du 8 brumaire, l'an III: Suivi du décret de la Convention nationale, et imprimé par son ordre*. Paris: De l'Imprimerie nationale, 1794.

Groupe interreligieux Abraham de la Duchère, "Déclaration," May 28, 2012. http://www.christianismesocial.org/Declaration-du-Groupe.html.

Gruber, Christiane. "Idols and Figural Images in Islam: A Brief Dive into a Perennial Debate." In *The Image Debate: Figural Representation in Islam and across the World*, edited by Christiane Gruber, 9–29. London: Gingko Press, 2019.

Gruber, Christiane. "The Missiri of Fréjus as Healing Memorial: Mosque Metaphors and the French Colonial Army (1928–64)." *International Journal of Islamic Architecture* 1, no. 1 (2012): 25–60.

Gruber, Christiane. *The Praiseworthy One: The Prophet Muhammad in Islamic Texts and Images*. Bloomington: Indiana University Press, 2019.

Gsell, Stephane. *Atlas archéologique de l'Algérie*. Algiers: Adolphe Jourdan, 1911.

Gueliane, Nora, and Kaouther Bouchemal. "Algeria and Its Heritage: Inventory of the Various Heritage Policies, from the Pre-colonial to Colonial and Post-colonial Times." In *Transcultural Diplomacy and International Law in Heritage Conservation*, edited by O. Niglio and E. Y. J. Lee, 257–272. Springer: Singapore, 2021.

Guerroudj, Tewfik. "La question du patrimoine urbain et architectural en Algérie." *Insaniyat* 12 (2000): 31–43.

Guignard, Didier. *L'abus de pouvoir dans l'Algérie colonial*. Nanterre: Presses universitaires de Paris-Ouest, 2010.

Guisnel, Jean. *Les généraux: Enquête sur le pouvoir militaire en France*. Paris: Édition de La Découverte, 1990.

Haichour, Boudjemaa. *The Encyclopedia of the Postage Stamp of Algeria*. Algiers: Ministry of Post and Information Technology and Communication, 2008.

Hamza, Salim. "Empreintes: Ahmed Benyahia." *Philnews: Algerian Philatelic News* 38 (August-September 2002): 10–11.

Hargrove, June. *The Statues of Paris: An Open-Air Pantheon*. Paris: Vendôme Press, 1990.

Hassett, Dónal. *Mobilizing Memory: The Great War and the Language of Politics in Colonial Algeria, 1918–39*. Oxford: Oxford University Press, 2019.

Hassett, Dónal. "A Tale of Two Monuments: The War Memorials of Oran and Algiers and Commemorative Culture in Colonial and Post-Colonial Algeria." In *Commemorating Race and Empire in the Great War Centenary*, edited by Shanti Sumartojo and Ben Wellings, 151–168. Liverpool: Liverpool University Press, 2018.

Henni, Samia. *Architecture of Counterrevolution: The French Army in Northern Algeria*. Zürich: gta Verlag, 2017.

Henni, Samia. "Black Color and 'Negro Village:' Why Skin Color Still Matters in Architecture?" *Trans Magazin: Farbe* 30 (2017): 158–161.

Henry, Jean-Robert. "L'histoire aux prises avec les mémoires: L'exemple du musée avorté de Montpellier sur l'histoire de la France et de l'Algérie." *L'Année du Maghreb* 19 (2018): 133–164.

Héraut, H. "Charles-Henri-Pourquet, statuaire de la Légion étrangère." *Légion étrangère* 38, no. 6 (1938): 22–23.

Herrmann Jr., John J., Donato Attanasio, Robert H. Tykot, and Annewies van den Hoek. "Aspects of the Trade in Colored Marbles in Algeria." *L'Africa romana* XIX, Sassari 2010, Roma (2012): 1331–1342.

Hollan, Douglas. "Who Is Haunted by Whom: Steps to an Ecology of Haunting." *Ethnos* 47, no. 4 (2019): 451–464.

Horne, Alistair. *A Savage War of Peace: Algeria 1954–1962*. London: Macmillan, 1977.

Horowitz, Maryanne Cline. "Rival Interpretations of Continent Personifications." In *Bodies and Maps: Early Modern Personifications of the Continents*, edited by Maryanne Cline Horowitz and Louise Arrizoli, 1–24. Leiden: Brill, 2020.

Hubbell, Amy L. "Remembering the 5 July 1962 Massacre in Oran, Algeria." In *Places of Traumatic Memory: A Global Context*, edited by Amy Hubbell, Natsuko Akagawa, Sol Rojas-Lizana, and Annie Pohlman, 219–240. Cham, Switzerland: Springer International Publishing, 2020.

Hubbell, Amy L. "(Re)turning to Ruins: *Pied-Noir* Visual Returns to Algeria." *Modern & Contemporary France* 19, no. 2 (2011): 147–161.

Hurt, R. Douglas. "Agricultural Museums: A New Frontier for the Social Sciences." *The History Teacher* 11, no. 3 (1978): 367–375.

Huyssen, Andreas. *Memory Art in the Contemporary World: Confronting Violence in the Global South*. London: Lund Humphries, 2022.

"Inauguration du monument aux morts à Sidi Bel Abbès." *Le Progrès de Sidi-Bel-Abbès*, 2550, December 11, 1928, 1.

"Inauguration du monument aux morts à Sidi-Bel-Abbès." *L'Echo d'Oran*, December 10, 1928, 2–3.

"L'inauguration du monument départemental de la Victoire." *L'Echo d'Oran*, May 23, 1927, 2.

Ingold, Tim. "Temporality of Landscape." *World Archaeology* 25, no. 2 (1992): 152–74.

Institut National de l'Audiovisuel (INA) Video Archive. *L'inauguration du monument aux morts d'Oran transporté à La Duchère*. Rhône Alpes actualités, ORTF, July 16, 1968. http://www.ina.fr/video/LXF04042372.

Ivey, Beatrice. "The Landowski-Issiakhem Pavois." *Narratives and Representations of the French of Algeria*, Stirling University (blog), November 28, 2018. https://www.pieds-noirs.stir.ac.uk/the-landowski-issiakhem-pavois/.

Ivey, Beatrice. "The Monument of Sidi-Brahim." *Narratives of French Algeria* (blog), December 10, 2018.
https://www.pieds-noirs.stir.ac.uk/the-sidi-brahim-monument/.

Ivey, Beatrice. "Virtual Returns: Colonial Postcards Online and Digital 'Nostalgérie' among the Former European Settlers of Algeria." *Humanities and Social Science Communications* 9, no. 112 (2022): DOI: 10.1057/s41599-022-01134-3.

Janon, Michel. *Lambèse: Capitale militaire de l'Afrique romaine*. Ollioules: Nerthe, 2005.

Jansen, Jan C. "Une autre 'Union Sacrée'? Commémorer la Grande Guerre dans l'Algérie colonisée (1918–1939)." *Revue d'histoire moderne et contemporaine* 2, no. 2 (2014): 32–60.

Jansen, Jan C. "Celebrating the Nation in a Colonial Context: Bastille Day and the Contested Public Space in Algeria, 1880–1939." *Journal of Modern History* 85, no. 1 (2013): 36–68.

Jansen, Jan C. "Creating National Heroes: Colonial Rule, Anticolonial Politics and

Conflicting Memories of Emir 'Abd Al-Qadir in Algeria, 1900–1960s." *History and Memory* 28, no. 2 (2016): 3–46.

Jansen, Jan C. "1880–1914; une statuomanie à l'algérienne." In *Histoire de l'Algérie à la période colonial (1830—1962)*, edited by Abderrahmane Bouchène, 261–265. Paris: Découverte, 2012.

Jansen, Jan C. *Erobern und Erinnern. Symbolpolitik, öffentlicher Raum und französischer Kolonialismus in Algerien, 1830–1950*. Munich: Oldenbourg, 2013.

Jansen, Jan C. "Fête et ordre colonial: Centenaires et résistance anticolonialiste en Algérie pendant les années 1930." *Vingtième Siècle* 1, no. 121 (2014): 61–76.

Jansen, Jan C., and Manuel Borutta. *Vertriebene and Pieds-Noirs in Postwar Germany and France: Comparative Perspectives*. Basingstoke: Palgrave-Macmillan, 2016.

Jansen, Jan C., and Jürgen Osterhammel. *Decolonization: A Short History*. Princeton, NJ: Princeton University Press, 2017.

Jansen, Willy. *Women without Men: Gender and Marginality in an Algerian Town*. Leiden: Brill, 1987.

Jeanpierre, Laurent. *In Girum: Les leçons politiques des rond-points*. Paris: La Découverte, 2019.

Jennings, Eric. T. *Free French Africa in World War II: The African Resistance*. Cambridge: Cambridge University Press, 2015.

Jordi, Jean-Jacques. *De l'exode à l'exil: Rapatriés et Pieds Noirs en France*. Paris: L'Harmattan, 1993.

Jouhaud, Edmond. *O mon pays perdu: Mémoires de Bou-Sfer à Tulle*. Paris: Fayard, 1969.

Jouin, Henri Auguste. "About the Genius of Statuary." *Sculpture Journal* 27, no. 1 (2018): 117.

Julien, Charles-André. *Histoire de l'Algérie contemporaine*. Paris: PUF, 1979.

Kahn, Jean-François. "La première foire international d'Alger sera un nouvel épisode de la rivalité sino-soviétique." *Le Monde,* September 28, 1964. www.lemonde.fr/archives/article/1964/09/28/la-premiere-foire-internationale-d-alger-sera-un-nouvel-episode-de-la-rivalite-sino-sovietique_2127550_1819218.html.

Kahn, Louis. "Monumentality." In *New Architecture and City Planning: A Symposium,* edited by Paul Zucker, 577–588. New York: Philosophical Library, 1944.

Kameli, Katia. *Trou de mémoire,* 2018. https://www.katiakameli.com/photos/trou-de-memoire/.

Kammen, Michael G. *Digging Up the Dead*. Chicago: University of Chicago Press, 2010.

Kasmi, Amine. "Masjid Hassan el-Pacha, Oran, Algeria." *Archnet*. https://archnet.org/sites/6350/media_contents/136299.

Kasmi, Amine. "The Plan as a Colonization Project: The Medina of Tlemcen under French Rule, 1842–1920." *Planning Perspectives* 34, no.1 (2019): 25–42.

Kateb, Kamel. *Européens, "indigènes," et juifs en Algérie (1830–1962)*. Paris: Éditions de l'Institut National d'Études Démographiques, 2001.

Kellou, Dorothée Myriam. "Algérie coloniale: Le silence de nos pères." *Orient XXI* (2019). https://orientxxi.info/lu-vu-entendu/algerie-coloniale-le-silence-de-nos-peres,3367.

Kellou, Dorothée Myriam. *À Mansourah, tu nous a séparés*, film, 2019, 1 hour 11 min.

Kettaf, Fadila. *La fabrique des espaces publics en Algérie*. Paris: L'Harmattan, 2019.

Khadda, Mohammed. *Éléments pour un art nouveau*. Algiers: Société Nationale d'Édition et de Diffusion, 1972.

Khadra, Yasmina. *Ce que le jour doit à la nuit*. Paris: Julliard, 2008.

Khadra, Yasmina. *What the Day Owes the Night*. Translated by Frank Wynne. London: Vintage, 2011.

Khatibi, Abdelkebir. *Maghreb Pluriel*. Paris: Denoel, 1983.

Kinney, Dale. "Introduction." In *Reuse Value: Spolia and Appropriation in Art and Architecture from Constantine to Sherrie Levine*, edited by Richard Brilliant and Dale Kinney, 1–12. Farnham, Surrey: Ashgate, 2011.

Kopytoff, Igor. "The Cultural Biography of Things: Commoditization as Process." In *The Social Life of Things*, edited by Arjun Appadurai, 64–92. Cambridge: Cambridge University Press, 1986.

Kosseleck, Reinhart. *L'expérience de l'histoire*. Paris, Gallimard/Le Seuil, 1997.

Kotányi, Attila, and Raoul Vaneigem. "Basic Program of the Bureau of Unitary Urbanism." In *Situationist International Anthology*, 2006. https://theanarchistlibrary.org/library/raoul-vaneigem-attila-kotanyi-basic-program-of-the-bureau-of-unitary-urbanism.

Krauss, Rosalind. "Notes on the Index: Seventies Art in America." *October* 3 (1977): 68–81.

Krauss, Rosalind. "Sculpture in the Expanded Field." *October* 8 (1979): 30–44.

Kreps, Christine. "Non-Western Models of Museums and Curation in Cross-Cultural Perspective." In *A Companion to Museum Studies*, edited by Sharon Macdonald, 457–472. Oxford: Blackwell, 2003.

"La Duchère 1948–2014." Special issue of the *Bulletin de la société académique d'architecture de Lyon* 17–18 (2009).

Lacroix, Annick. "La poste au douar: Usagers non citoyens et État colonial dans les campagnes algériennes de la fin du xixe siècle à la Seconde Guerre Mondiale." *Annales: Histoire, Sciences Sociales* 71, no. 3 (2016): 709–740.

Laggoune-Aklouche, Nadira. "Résistance, appropriation et réappropriation dans l'art algérien." *Modern and Contemporary France* 19, no. 2 (2011): 179–193.

Lamare, Nicolas. *Les fontaines monumentales en Afrique romaine*. Rome: École française de Rome, 2019.

Landowski, Paul. *Journal*, November 5, 1926. http://journal.paul-landowski.com/node/363.

Laqueur, Thomas W. *The Work of the Dead: A Cultural History of Mortal Remains*. Princeton, NJ: Princeton University Press, 2015.

Lassus, Jean. "L'archéologie algérienne en 1955." *Libyca: Bulletin du Service des Antiquités, Archéologie, Epigraphie* 4, no. 1 (1956): 169–189.

Le Cour Grandmaison, Olivier. "Bugeaud: bourreau des 'indigènes' algériens et ennemi de la République." *Blog de Olivier Le Cour Grandmaison*. Mediapart, September 4, 2017. https://blogs.mediapart.fr/olivier-le-cour-grandmaison/blog/040917/bugeaud-bourreau-des-indigenes-algeriens-et-ennemi-de-la-republique.

Le Cour Grandmaison, Olivier. *De l'indigénat, anatomie d'un "monster" juridique: Le droit colonial en Algérie et dans l'Empire français*. Paris: La Découverte, 2010.

Le Men, Ségolène. "La statuaire publique en images: Une pédagogie civique par le manuel scolaire et par la carte postale." In *La statuaire publique XIXe siècle*, edited by Ségolène Le Men and Aline Magnien, 32–55. Paris: Centre des monuments nationaux / Monument Éditions du Patrimoine, 2004.

"Le Monument aux morts de Constantine." *L'Afrique du Nord Illustrée* 443 (October 26, 1929): 5.

"Le monument aux morts de la légion étrangère a Sidi-Bel-Abbès: Le sculpteur Henri Pourquet presidera à la mise en place du monument." *L'Echo d'Alger* 7831 (March 19, 1931): 1.

"Le Monument aux Morts d'Oran rapatrié à Lyon dans le quartier de la Duchère." Le Cercle Algérianiste de Lyon website. https://www.cerclealgerianiste-lyon.org/le-monument-aux-morts-doran-rapatrie-a-la-duchere/.

"Le Monument aux Morts transféré à Lyon." *La Republique*, December 9, 1967, 14.

"Le nouveau casino municipal de Constantine." *L'Afrique du Nord Illustrée* 431, August 3, 1929, 13.

Le Sueur, James D. *Uncivil War: Intellectual and Identity Politics during the Decolonization of Algeria*. Lincoln: University of Nebraska, 2006.

Le Sueur, James D. *Between Terror and Democracy: Algeria since 1989*. London: Zed Books, 2010.

Lebovics, Herman. *Mona Lisa's Escort: André Malraux and the Reinvention of French Culture*. Ithaca, NY: Cornell University Press, 1999.

Lebovics, Herman. "Cultural Policy." In *The French Republic: History, Values, Debates*, edited by Edward Berenson, Vincent Duclert, and Christophe Prochasson, 344–354. Ithaca, NY: Cornell University Press, 2011.

Lefebvre, Henri. *La production de l'espace*. Paris: Anthropos, 1974.

Lemili, Abdelhamid. "Ahmed Benyahia ou l'art de l'Anticonformisme." *La Tribune*, May 11, 2012. https://www.djazairess.com/fr/latribune/67486.

Lepage, Jean-Denis G. G. *The French Foreign Legion: An Illustrated History*. London: McFarland, 2008.

Lesbet, Djafar. *Les 1000 villages socialistes en Algérie*. Algiers: Office des publications universitaires. Paris: Syros, 1983.

Leschi, Louis. *Etudes d'épigraphie, d'archéologie et d'histoire africaines*. Paris: Arts et Métiers graphiques, 1957.

Lespès, René. *Oran: Étude de géographie et d'histoire urbaines*. Paris: F. Alcan, 1938.

Letteney, Mark, and Matthew D. C. Larsen. "A Roman Military Prison at Lambaesis." *Studies in Late Antiquity* 5, no. 1 (2021): 65–102.

Lévêque, Isabelle, Michel Griffon, and Dominique Pinon. *Le jardin d'agronomie tropicale: De l'agriculture colonial au développement durable*. Arles: Actes Sud, 2005.

Liverani, Andrea. *Civil Society in Algeria: The Political Functions of Associational Life*. Abingdon, UK: Routledge, 2008.

Llorens, Natasha Marie. "The Other Battle of Algiers: Overcoming an Architecture of Oppression." *World Policy Journal* 35, no. 2 (2018): 63–69.

Llorens, Natasha Marie, ed. *Waiting for Omar Gatlato: A Survey of Contemporary Art from Algeria and its Diaspora*. New York and Berlin: Wallach Art Gallery and Sternberg Press, 2019.

Logan, William, and Keir Reeves, eds. *Places of Pain and Shame: Dealing with "Difficult Heritage"*. London: Routledge, 2009.

Loi 98-04 du 20 Safar 1419 correspondant au 15 juin 1998 relative à la protection du patrimoine culturel [Law 98-04 of 20 Safar 1419 corresponding to June 15, 1998 on cultural heritage] *JORA*, June 17, 1998, 3–15.

Loi 99-07 du 19 Dhou El Hidja 1419 correspondant au 5 avril 1999 relative au moudjahid et au chahid [Law 99-07 of 19 Dhou El Hidja 1419 corresponding to April 5, 1999 on moudjahid and chahid], *JORA*, April 12, 1999, 3–9. See especially article 54, p. 8.

Loi du 1er juillet 1901 relative au contrat d'association [Law of July 1, 1901 on the contract of association] *JORF*, July 2, 1901, 4025–4027.

Loi du 25 octobre 1919 *relative à la commémoration et à la Glorification pour la France au cours de la Grande Guerre* [Law of October 26, 1919 for the commemoration and glorification of France during the Great War] *JORF*, October 26, 1919, 11910.

Loi 61-1439 du 26 décembre 1961 relative à l'accueil et à la réinstallation des Français d'outre-mer [Law 61-1439 of December 26, 1961 on the reception and resettlement of overseas French] *JORF*, December 28, 1961, 11996.

Loi 62-880 du 31 juillet 1962 relative à la restauration de grands monuments historiques [Law 62-880 of July 11, 1962 on restoring great historical monuments] *JORF*, August 2, 1962, 7651.

Longeaux, Guy de. "Naissance d'un grand ensemble: Genèse d'une société nouvelle." *Études* (1964): 375–392.

Lorcin, Patricia M. E. "France and Rome in Africa: Recovering Algeria's Latin Past." *French Historical Studies* 35, no. 2 (2002): 295–329.

Lorcin, Patricia M. E. "The Nostalgias for Empire." *History and Theory* 57, no. 2 (2018): 269–285.

Lormier, Dominique. *C'est nous les Africains: L'épopée de l'armée française d'Afrique (1940–1945)*. Paris: Calmann-Lévy, 2006.

Love, Stephanie V. "The Poetics of Grievance: Taxi Drivers, Vernacular Place-names, and the Paradoxes of Post-Coloniality in Oran, Algeria." *City & Society* 33, no. 3 (2021). https://doi.org/10.1111/ciso.12412.

"M. Violette à Oran." *L'Afrique du Nord Illustrée* 318, June 4, 1927, 3–4.

Macdonald, Sharon. *Difficult Heritage: Negotiating the Nazi Past in Nuremberg and Beyond*. London: Routledge, 2009.

Madani, Said. "Le tramway de Sétif: Projet urbain ou simple projet de transport." *Cahiers Géographiques de l'Ouest* 12–13 (2017): 169–178.

Maïza, Myriam Maachi. "L'architecture de Fernand Pouillon en Algérie." *Insaniyat* 42 (2008): http://journals.openedition.org/insaniyat/6707.

Malraux, André. *Les voix du silence, Écrits sur l'art (I)*. Edited by Jean-Yves Tadié, 2 vols. Paris: Gallimard, 2004.

Malverti, Xavier. "Les officiers du Génie et le dessin de villes en Algérie (1830–1870)." *Revue du monde musulman et de la Méditerranée* 73/74 (1994): 229–244.

Malverti, Xavier, and Aleth Picard. "Algeria: Military Genius and Civic Design (1830–70)." *Planning Perspective* 6, no. 2 (1991): 207–234.

Mammeri, Abdelkrim. "Sidi Bel Abbes: Début de la démolition des anciennes maisons closes." *El Watan*, December 20, 2010. https://www.elwatan.com/regions/ouest/bel-abes/sidi-bel-abbes-debut-de-la-demolition-des-anciennes-maisons-closes-20-12-2010.

Mann, Gregory. "Locating Colonial Histories: Between France and West Africa." *American Historical Review* (2005): 409–434.

Mann, Michelle. "The Young Algerians and the Question of the Muslim Draft, 1900–1914." In *Algeria Revisited: History, Culture and Identity*, edited by Rabah Aissaoui and Claire Eldridge, 39–54. London: Bloomsbury, 2017.

Mansouri, Kh. "Hammam-bou-Hannifa." *Encyclopédie berbère* 22 (2000): 3345–3349.

Martinet, Chantal. "Le Concours." In *La sculpture française au xixe siècle*, 216–217. Paris: Éditions de la Réunion des musées nationaux, 1986.

Martinet, Chantal. "La Souscription." In *La sculpture française au xixe siècle*, 231–238. Paris: Éditions de la Réunion des musées nationaux, 1986.

Martinez, Luis. *La guerre civile en Algerie*. Paris: Karthala, 1998.

Mauss-Copeaux, Claire. *Algérie, 20 août 1955: Insurrection, repression, massacres*. Paris: Payot, 2013.

McAllister, Ed. "Algeria's Belle Epoque (1) Postcards and Nostalgia: Images of Algiers in the 1970s." *Texture du temps* (2012). https://texturesdutemps.hypotheses.org/414.

McDougall, James. "Culture as War by Other Means: Community, Conflict and Cultural Revolution, 1967–81." In *Algeria Revisited: History, Culture and Identity*, edited by Rabah Aissaoui and Claire Eldridge, 235–252. London: Bloomsbury Academic, 2018.

McDougall, James. *History and the Culture of Nationalism in Algeria*. Cambridge: Cambridge University Press, 2006.

McDougall, James. *A History of Algeria*. Cambridge: Cambridge University Press, 2017.

McDougall, James. "The Impossible Republic: The Reconquest of Algeria and the Decolonization of France, 1945–1962." *Journal of Modern History* (2011): 790–811.

McQueen, Alison. "Politics and Public Sculpture in Nineteenth-Century Colonial French Algeria." *Sculpture Journal* 28, no. 1 (2019): 7–34.

Méheut, Constant. "France Returned 24 Skulls to Algeria: They Weren't What They Seemed." *New York Times,* October 18, 2022. https://www.nytimes.com/2022/10/17/world/europe/france-algeria-restitution-skulls.html.

Mekhaled, Boucif. *Chroniques d'un massacre: 8 Mai 1945, Sétif, Guelma, Kherrata*. Paris: Syros/Au Nom de la Mémoire, 1995.

Memmi, Albert. *The Colonizer and the Colonized*. Translated by Howard Greenfeld. New York: Orion Press. 1965.

Menia, Amina. "Enclosed @Mosaic Rooms." https://aminamenia.com/works/enclosed-at-mosaic-rooms/.

Menia, Amina. "Monuments in Exile." https://aminamenia.com/works/monuments-in-exile/.

Merbouh, Hadjer. "Toponymes urbains à Sidi Bel Abbès-ville (Algérie): Usages, représentations et identités sociolinguistiques." *Nouvelle revue d'onomastique* 53 (2011): 127–141.

Mercier, Ernest. *Constantine avant la conquête française*. Constantine: A Braham, 1878.

Merle, Isabelle. "De la 'légalisation' de la violence en contexte colonial: Le régime de l'indigénat en question." *Politix* 17, no. 66 (2004): 137–162.

Meskell, Lynn. "Negative Heritage and Past Mastering in Archaeology." *Anthropological Quarterly* 75 (2002): 557–574.

Messimy, Adolphe. "Le service militaire des indigènes algériens." *Bulletin de la réunion d'études algériennes* 10, nos. 2/3 (1908): 79–93.

Metaïr, Kouider, et al. *Oran la mémoire*. Paris: Mediterra, 2013.

Metair, Nabila. "Twentieth Century Architecture in Oran: Its Contemporary Heritage-Value." *Journal of North African Studies* 26, no. 3 (2021): 404–425.

Meynier, Gilbert. *L'Algérie révélée: La guerre de 1914–1918 et le premier quart du XXe siècle*. Geneva: Droz, 1981.

Michel, M. "Alaphilippe." *Notre rive: Revue nord-africaine illustrée,* January 1, 1927, 20.

Michels, Eckard. "From One Crisis to Another: The Morale of the French Foreign Legion During the Algerian War." In *The Algerian War and the French Army: Experiences, Images, Testimonies,* edited by Martin S. Alexander, Martin Evans, J. F. V. Keiger, 88–100. New York: Palgrave Macmillan, 2002.

Michon, Jean. "Sidi-bel-Abbès: Capitale légionnaire." *Guerres mondiales et conflits contemporains* 237, no. 1 (2010): 25–38.

Mignolo, Walter, and Rolando Vasquez. "Decolonial AestheSis: Colonial Wounds/

Decolonial Healings." *Social Text* (2013), special issue. https://socialtextjournal.org/periscope_article/decolonial-aesthesis-colonial-woundsdecolonial-healings/.

Miles, Margaret M. *Art as Plunder: The Ancient Origins of Debate about Cultural Property*. New York: Cambridge University Press, 2008.

Milo, Daniel. "Street Names." In *Realms of Memory: Rethinking the French Past*, under the direction of Pierre Nora, vol 2: 363–389. New York: Columbia University Press, 1996.

Mir, Mohamed. "Le mystère toujours entoure à Sidi-Bel-Abbès: La disparition de la statue fameuse 'La Chure d'Icare.'" *La Voix de l'Oranie* 5093, August 17, 2016, 6.

Mirzoeff, Nicholas. *The Right to Look: A Counterhistory of Visuality*. Durham, NC: Duke University Press, 2011.

Mitchell, W. J. T. "The Violence of Public Art: Do the Right Thing." *Critical Inquiry* 16, no. 4 (1990): 880–899.

Mohand-Amer, Amar. "Les monuments aux martyrs en Algérie." In *Dictionnaire de la guerre d'Algérie*, edited by Tramor Quemeneur, Ouanassa Siari-Tengour, and Sylvie Thénault, 831–832. Paris, Éditions Bouquins, 2023.

Mokhtefi, Elaine. *Algiers, Third World Capital: Freedom Fighters, Revolutionaries, Black Panthers*. London: Verso, 2020.

Monument Lab. *National Monument Audit*, 2021. https://monumentlab.com/projects/national-monument-audit.

"Monuments as Monsters: Michael Rakowitz and Erin L. Thompson in Conversation." *Art Journal Open*, June 16, 2022. http://artjournal.collegeart.org/?p=16895.

Moumen, Abderrahman. *Les Harkis*. Paris: Éditions Le Cavalier Bleu, 2008.

Moussaoui, Abderrahmane. *De la violence en Algérie: Les lois du chaos*. Arles: Actes Sud/MMSH, 2006.

Mouton, Claude. *Lamoricière: De l'Algérie française aux zouaves pontificaux: Vendéen, africain, romain, un grand soldat de la chrétienté*. Montsurs, France: Résiac, 1990.

Muchitsch, Wolfgang, ed. *Does War Belong in Museums? The Representation of Violence in Exhibitions*. Bielefeld: transcript Verlag, 2013.

Musée Franchet d'Espérey Alger (Casbah). *Livre-guide pour la visite du musée*. Algiers: Baconnier-Hélio, ca. 1941.

Natif, Mika. "The Painter's Breath and Concepts of Idol Anxiety." In *Idol Anxiety*, edited by Josh Ellenbogen and Aaron Tugenhaft, 41–55. Stanford, CA: Stanford University Press, 2011.

Naylor, Philip. *France and Algeria: A History of Decolonization and Transformation*. Gainesville: University Press of Florida, 2000.

"Nécrologie: Le Général Prudon." *Revue du génie militaire*, January 1, 1892, 267.

Nilsen, Micheline. *Architecture in Nineteenth-Century Photographs: Essays on Reading a Collection*. Farnham: Ashgate, 2011.

Nouschi, André. "Notes sur la vie traditionelle des populations forestières algériennes." *Annales de Géographie* 86, no. 370 (1959): 525–535.

Oddy, Jason. *The Revolution Will Be Stopped Halfway*. New York: Columbia Books on Architecture and the City, 2019.

"Une oeuvre patriotique départementale: Le monument commémoratif de la victoire (Hommage aux morts de la Grande Guerre), Un Appel aux Populations de l'Oranie." *L'Echo d'Oran*, January 8, 1922, 2.

Offenstadt, Nicolas. "(Hi)stories and Memories of the Great War in France (1914–2018)." In *Writing the Great War: The Historiography of World War I from 1918 to the Present*, edited by Christoph Cornelissen and Arndt Weinrich, 11–49. New York: Berghahn Books, 2021.

Olusoga, David. *The World's War: Forgotten Soldiers of Empire*. London, Head of Zeus, 2014.

Onderdonk, F. S. *The Ferro-concrete Style: Reinforced Concrete in Modern Architecture*. New York: Architectural Book Publishing, 1928.

Ordonnance 71-79 du 3 décembre 1971 relative à l'association [Order 71-79 of December 3, 1971 on associations], *JORA*, December 12, 1971, 1410; revised in *JORA*, January 18, 1972, 8.

Ordonnance 71-73 du 8 novembre 1971 portant Révolution agraire [Order 71-73 on the Agrarian Revolution] *JORA*, November 30, 1971, 1281.

Ouagueni, Yassine. "The Birth of the Notion of *Patrimoine* (through the Generations) in Algeria." *Journal of North African Studies* 25, no. 5 (2020): 753–770.

Ouldennebia, Karim. "La commune mixte de la Mekerra (1874–1962)." *Bel-Abbes Info*, November 24, 2014. http://bel-abbes.info/les-lundis-de-lhistoire-la-commune-mixte-de-la-mekerra-1874-1962/.

Ouldennebia, Karim. *Histoire de Sidi-Bel-Abbès: Le face à face Koubba-Redoute*. Oran: Edition Dar AlQods, 2022.

Oulebsir, Nabila. *Les usages de patrimoine: Monuments, musées et politique coloniale en Algérie (1830–1930)*. Paris: Édition de la Maison des sciences de l'homme, 2004.

Pagand, Bernard. *La Médina de Constantine (Algérie): De la ville traditionnelle au centre de l'agglomération contemporaine*. Poitiers: Éditions du Centre Interuniversitaire d'Études Méditerranéennes, 1989.

Pagand, Bernard, and Assïa Malki Allouani. "Un quartier colonial à Constantine (Algérie): Le Coudiat Aty." In *Villes maghrébines en situations colonials*, edited by Charlotte Jelidi, 59–76. Paris, Karthala, 2014.

Parks, Robert P. "Claiming Bits and Pieces of the State: Squatting and Appropriation of Public Domain in Algeria." *Middle East Law and Governance* 11 (2019): 103–135.

Parks, Robert P. "From the War of National Liberation to Gentrification: Conflicting Claims over Property in Algeria." *MERIP / Middle East Report*, 2018. https://merip.org/2018/08/from-the-war-of-national-liberation-to-gentrification/.

Pastoureau, Michel. "Le coq gaulois." In *Les lieux de mémoires*, edited by Pierre Nora, vol. 3: 507–539. Paris: Gallimard, 1986.

Paul, Georges-Emile. *Hammam-Bou-Hadjar 1874–1962: Petite chronique de mon village algérien et de son environnement*. Montpellier: Transcomp Éditions, 1988. http://hammambouhadjar.free.fr/le_village.htm.

Paulin, Michel. "François-Régis Cottin: L'oeuvre." *Bulletin de la société academique d'architecture de Lyon* 21 (2013): 26–37.

Peckham, Robert Shannan. "Introduction to the Politics of Heritage and Public Culture." In *Rethinking Heritage, Politics, and Culture in Europe*, edited by Robert Shannan Peckham, 1–13. London: I. B. Tauris 2003.

Peirce, Charles Sanders. *The Collected Papers*, edited by Charles Hartshorne and Paul Weiss. Cambridge, MA: Harvard University Press, 1931–1935.

Perrier, Aurelie Evengeline. "Intimate Matters: Negotiating Sex, Gender and the Home in Colonial Algeria." PhD diss. Georgetown University, 2014.

Peters, Vincent. "Legion of Violent Lovers." *Whisper*, May 1950, 10–11. https://monlegionnaire.files.wordpress.com/2012/02/legion-of-violent-lovers.jpg.

Peyroulou, Jean-Pierre. *Guelma, une subversion française dans l'Algérie coloniale*. Paris: La Découverte, 2009.

Peyroulou, Jean-Pierre. "Les métamorphoses du martyrologe algérien du 8 mai 1945: 1945–2009." In *Autour des morts de guerre: Maghreb-Moyen-Orient*, edited by Raphaëlle Branche, Nadine Picadou, and Pierre Vermeren, 97–118. Paris: Éditions de la Sorbonne, 2013.

Pieprzak, Katarzyna. *Imagined Museums: Art and Modernity in Morocco*. Minneapolis: University of Minnesota Press, 2010.

Pinol, Jean Luc. "Le monument aux morts d'Oran transporté à La Duchère." Fresques INA. https://fresques.ina.fr/rhone-alpes/fiche-media/Rhonal00121/le-monument-aux-morts-d-oran-transporte-a-la-duchere.html.

Porch, Douglas. *The French Foreign Legion: A Complete History of the Legendary Fighting Force*. New York: Harper Collins, 1991.

Pouillon, François. *Abdelkader, l'émir de la resistance*. Ghent, Belgium: Snoeck, 2019.

Pouillon, François. *Étienne Dinet, peintre en Islam: L'Algérie et l'héritage colonial*. Boumerdès, Algeria: Edition Frantz Fanon, 2021.

Pouillon, François. "Les images de l'Émir Abdelkader: De l'Algérie coloniale à l'Algérie algérienne." In *Le corps du leader: Construction et représentation dans les pays du Sud*, edited by Omar Carlier and Raphaëlle Nollez-Goldbach, 163–170. Paris: L'Harmattan, 2008.

Pouillon, François. "Les miroirs en abyme: Cent cinquante ans de peinture algérienne." *NAQD* 17 (2003): 9–25.

Pouillon, François. "150 Years of Algerian Painting: Relevance for Understanding on the Post-Colonial Situation." *French Politics, Culture & Society* 20, no. 2 (2002): 141–158.

Pouillon, François, and Michel Mégnin. "Le miroir aux alouettes: Destin sociologique des images du nu indigène." *L'Année du Maghreb* 6 (2010): 19–45.

Prochaska, David. "The Archive of *Algérie imaginaire*." *History and Anthropology* 4, no. 2 (1990): 373–420.

Prochaska, David. *Making Algeria French: Colonialism in Bône, 1870–1920*. New York: Cambridge University Press, 1990.

Prochaska, David. "The Political Culture of Settler Colonialism in Algeria: Politics in Bone (1870–1920)." *Revue de l'Occident musulman et de la Méditerranée* 48/49 (1988): 293–311.

Prost, Antoine. "The Algerian War in French Collective Memory." In *War and Remembrance in the Twentieth Century*, edited by Jay Winter and Emmanuel Sivan, 161–176. Cambridge: Cambridge University Press, 1999.

Prost, Antoine. *Les anciens combattants*. Paris: Gallimard, 1977.

Prost, Antoine. "Monuments to the Dead." In Pierre Nora, *Realms of Memory: Rethinking the French Past*, vol 3: 307–330. New York: Columbia University Press, 1996.

Puissegur, Jean. "Mémorial Sidi Ferruch." *Commando Guillaume* (blog). http://www.commandoguillaume.com/html/fra/page-42.html.

Pyne, Lydia. *Postcards: The Rise and Fall of the World's First Social Network*. London: Reaktion Books, 2021.

Quynn, Dorothy Mackay. "The Art Confiscations of the Napoleonic Wars." *American Historical Review* 50, no. 3 (1945): 437–460.

Rabbat, Nasser. "Identity, Modernity, and the Destruction of Heritage." *International Journal of Middle East Studies* 49 (2017): 739–741.

Rahal, Malika. *Algérie 1962: Une histoire populaire*. Paris: La Découverte, 2022.

Rahal, Malika. "Fanny Colonna: Notes sur le Middle Ground." *Textures du temps*, November 30, 2014. https://texturesdutemps.hypotheses.org/1359.

Rahal, Malika. "A Local Approach to the UDMA: Local-level Politics during the Decade of Political Parties, 1946–56." *Journal of North African Studies* 18, no. 5 (2013):703–724.

Rahal, Malika. "Oran 1962: Des trois dimensions du souvenir." *Textures du temps*, July 16, 2018. https://texturesdutemps.hypotheses.org/2731.

Recham, Belkacem. *Les musulmans algériens dans l'armée française, 1919–1945*. Paris: L'Harmattan, 1996.

Renan, Ary. "Les Arts arabes dans le Maghreb, Tlemcen." *Gazette des Beaux-Arts* (1892): 383–401.

Renier, Léon. "Notice sur le tombeau de T. Flavius Maximus, préfet de la Légion III Auguste." *Revue archéologique* 7, no. 1 (1850): 186–187.

Rey, Jacques. *Lyon, cité radieuse: Une aventure du Mouvement moderne international*. Lyon: Libel, 2010.

Rey, Robert. "Le Monument de Hammam-Bou-Hadjar." *Art et Décoration* 42 (July-December 1922): 157–160.

Rey, Virginie. *Mediating Museums: Exhibiting Material Culture in Tunisia (1881–2016)*. Leiden: Brill, 2019.

Rey-Goldzeiguer, Annie. *Le royaume arabe: La politique algérienne de Napoléon III, 1861–1870*. Algiers: SNED, 1977.

Riboud, Marc. "Interview by Sylvie Hugues." http://marcriboud.com/en/texte/algiers-july-1962-marc-riboud/.

Riegl, Alois. "The Modern Cult of Monuments: Its Character and Its Origin." *Oppositions* 25 (1982 [1903]): 20–51.

Roberts, Hugh. *The Battlefield Algeria 1988–2002: Studies in Broken Polity*. London: Verso, 2003.

Rodhain, Jean. "Les cloches d'Algérie." *Messages du Secours Catholique* 163 (1966). https://fondationjeanrodhain.org/jean-rodhain-textes-de-jean-rodhain/1966/les-cloches-dalgerie.

Rof, Gilles. "À Marseille, l'école Bugeaud bientôt rebaptisée du nom d'un tirailleur algérien." *Le Monde*, May 10, 2021. https://www.lemonde.fr/politique/article/2021/05/11/a-marseille-l-ecole-bugeaud-debaptisee-pour-porter-le-nom-d-un-tirailleur-algerien_6079825_823448.html.

Rojon, Sarah. "La renovation de l'habiter dans le grand ensemble de la Duchère: Pour en finir avec la figure des nouveaux habitants." *Recherches sociologiques et anthropologiques* 1 (2014): 47–67.

Rothberg, Michael. "Holocaust Memory after the Multidirectional Turn." *Berliner Zeitung*, February 21, 2021. https://www.berliner-zeitung.de/open-source/gegen-opferkonkurrenz-es-gibt-auch-in-deutschland-kein-isoliertes-gedenken-li.141816.

Rouadjia, Ahmed. *Les frères et la mosquée: Enquête sur le mouvement islamiste en Algérie*. Paris: Karthala, 1990.

Rousso, Henry. *Face au passé: Essais sur la mémoire contemporaine*. Paris: Éditions Belin, 2016.

Ruin, Hans. *Being with the Dead: Burial, Ancestral Politics, and the Roots of Historical Consciousness*. Stanford, CA: Stanford University Press, 2019.

Ruscio, Alain. "Pour une statue à la gloire de l'émir Abd El-Kader à Paris." *Orient XXI*, September 6, 2017. https://orientxxi.info/magazine/pour-une-statue-a-la-gloire-de-l-emir-abd-el-kader-a-paris,1985.

Saaidia, Oissila. "Les catholiques d'Algérie: Minorités d'hier et d'aujourd'hui." *Les Cahiers d'EMAM* 32 (2020). http://journals.openedition.org/emam/2434.

Sacristie, Fabien. *Les camps de regroupement en Algérie: Une histoire des déplacements forcés (1954–1962)*. Paris: Presses de Sciences Po, 2022.

Sahraoui, Badia Belabed. "Politique municipale et pratique urbaine: Constantine au XIXe siècle." *Insaniyat* 35/36 (2007): 109–129.

Sarr, Felwine, and Bénédicte Savoy. *The Restitution of African Cultural Heritage: Toward a New Relational Ethics*, 2018. https://www.about-africa.de/images/sonstiges/2018/sarr_savoy_en.pdf.

Sarrabezolles, Carlo. *De l'esquisse au colossal*. Montreuil, France: Éditions Gourcuff-Gradenigo, 2008.

Sarrabezolles, Carlo. *La sculpture sans maquette par taille directe du béton en prise*. Paris: Société d'Encouragement pour l'Industrie Nationale, 1933.

Scheid, Kirsten. "Start with Art: New Ways of Understanding the Political in the Middle East." In *Handbook for Political Science in the Middle East*, edited by Larbi Sadki, 432–444. New York: Routledge, 2022.

Schor, Naomi. "*Cartes Postales*: Representing Paris 1900." *Critical Inquiry* 18, no. 2 (1992): 188–244.

Schwartz, Annie. *La Duchère, 40 ans*. Lyon: Audacce, 2003.

Scioldo-Zürcher, Yann. "The Cost of Decolonization: Compensating the Pieds-Noirs." In *France Since the 1970s: History, Politics and Memory in an Age of Uncertainty*, edited by Emile Chabal, 93–114. London: Bloomsbury, 2015.

Scioldo-Zürcher, Yann. *Devenir métropolitain, parcours et politique d'intégration de rapatriés d'Algérie en métropole, de 1954 au début du XXI° siècle*. Paris: Éditions de l'École des hautes études en sciences sociales, 2010.

Scott, David. "Post and the Postage Stamp." In *Postcolonial Realms of Memory: Sites and Symbols in Modern France*, edited by Etienne Achille, Charles Fosdick, and Lydie Moudileno, 351–359. Liverpool: Liverpool University Press, 2020.

Sealy, Mark. *Decolonising the Camera: Photography in Racial Time*. London: Lawrence and Whishart, 2019.

Sebbar, Leïla. *Mes Algéries en France*. Saint-Pourçain-sur-Sioule, France: Éditions Bleu Autour, 2005.

Segalla, Spencer. *Empire and Catastrophe: Decolonization and Environmental Disaster in North Africa and Mediterranean France since 1954*. Lincoln: University of Nebraska Press, 2020.

Serres, Michel. *Statues: The Second Book of Foundations*. Translated by Randolph Burks. London: Bloomsbury, 2015.

Shanan, Abdo. "The Right to Memory." *Flare*, September 4, 2020. https://medium.com/flare-photoforum/the-right-to-a-memory-d7bb72a5a731.

Shehab, Bahia, and Haytham Nawar. *A History of Arab Graphic Design*. Cairo, Egypt: American University in Cairo Press, 2020.

Shepard, Todd. *The Invention of Decolonization: The Algerian War and the Remaking of France*. Ithaca, NY: Cornell University Press, 2006.

Shepard, Todd. " 'Of Sovereignty': Disputed Archives, 'Wholly Modern' Archives, and the Post-Decolonization French and Algerian Republics, 1962–2012." *American Historical Review* 120, no. 3 (2015): 869–883.

Sherman, Daniel J. "Bodies and Names: The Emergence of Commemoration in Interwar France." *American Historical Review* 103 (1998): 443–466.

Sherman, Daniel J. *The Construction of Memory in Interwar France*. Chicago: University of Chicago Press, 1999.

"Sidi Bel Abbes." *Képi blanc*, no. 382bis (September 1979).

Situationist International. "Definitions." *Internationale situationniste: Bulletin central édité* 1 (June 1958): 13.

Skander, Nabila. "Pour M. Tebboune, l'histoire n'est qu'un enjeu politique (Hosni Kitouni, historien)." *Algérie Cultures*, May 9, 2020. https://algeriecultures.com/actualite-culturelle/pour-m-tebboune-lhistoire-nest-quun-enjeu-politique-hosni-kitouni-historien/.

Slama, Samir. *Arbres et paysages remarquables*. Oran: Bel Horizon Editions, 2019.

Slyomovics, Susan. "Commissioning Memorial Reconciliation: The Stora Report and Algeria's Ottoman Canon in France." *Modern and Contemporary France* 31, no. 1 (2023): 17–32.

Slyomovics, Susan. "The Ethnologist-Spy Was Hanged, At That Time We Were a Little Savage': Anthropology in Algeria with Habib Tengour." *Boundary 20: An online journal* 3 (2018). https://www.boundary2.org/2018/12/susan-slyomovics-the-ethnologist-spy-was-hanged-at-that-time-we-were-a-little-savage-anthropology-in-algeria-with-habib-tengour/.

Slyomovics, Susan. " 'False Friends?': On Algeria, the Algerian Jewish Question, and Settler Colonial Studies." In *Race, Place, Trace: Essays in Honour of Patrick Wolfe*, edited by Lorenzo Veracini and Susan Slyomovics, 58–89. London: Verso, 2022.

Slyomovics, Susan. "Female Winged Victory Statues of North Africa: Roman Provenance, French Colonial Appropriations, and Algerian Preservation." In *Breaking the Bronze Ceiling: Women, Memory, and Public Space*, edited by Valentina Rozas-Krause and Andrew M. Shanken, 230–252. New York: Fordham University Press, 2024.

Slyomovics, Susan. "French Restitution, German Compensation: Algerian Jews and Vichy's Financial Legacy." *Journal of North African Studies* 17, no. 5 (2012): 881–901.

Slyomovics, Susan. "On the Wings of the Gallic Cockerel: Ahmed Benyahia and the Provenance of an Algerian Public Sculpture." In *Reframing Postcolonial Studies: Concepts—Methodologies—Scholarly Activisms*, edited by David D. Kim, 69–92. London: Palgrave MacMillan, 2021.

Slyomovics, Susan. "Repairing Colonial Symmetry: Algerian Archive Restitution as Reparation for Crimes of Colonialism?" In *Time for Reparations: A Global Perspective*, edited by Jacqueline Bhabha, Margareta Matache, and Caroline Elkins, 201–218. Philadelphia: University of Pennsylvania Press, 2021.

Slyomovics, Susan. "The Virgin Mary of Algeria: French Mediterraneans *En Miroir*." *History and Anthropology* 31 (2020): 22–42.

Slyomovics, Susan. "Visual Ethnography, Stereotypes, and Photographing Algeria." In *Orientalism Revisited: Art, Land, and Voyage*, edited by Ian Richard Netton, 128–150. London: Routledge, 2012.

Smith, Andrea L. *Colonial Memory and Postcolonial Europe: Maltese Settlers in Algeria and France*. Bloomington: Indiana University Press, 2006.

Smith, Andrea L. "Introduction: Europe's Invisible Migrants." In *Europe's Invisible*

Migrants, edited by Andrea L Smith. Amsterdam: University of Amsterdam Press, 2003.

Smith, Andrea L. "Settler Sites of Memory and the Work of Mourning." *French Politics, Culture & Society* 31, no. 3 (2013): 65–92.

Smith, Shawn Michelle. *At the Edge of Sight: Photography and the Unseen.* Durham, NC: Duke University Press, 2013.

Soo, Soyoung. "Cinema against the Permanent Curfew of Geometry: Guy Debord's *Sur le passage de quelques personnes à travers une assez courte unité de temps* (1959)." *Grey Room* 52 (2013): 38–61.

Souaidia, H. *La sale guerre.* Paris: La Découverte, 2012.

Stewart, Susan. *The Ruins Lesson.* Chicago: University of Chicago Press, 2020.

Stiegler, Bernard. *For a New Critique of Political Economy.* Cambridge, MA: Polity, 2010.

Stoler, Anne Laura. "Colonial Aphasia: Race and Disabled Histories in France." *Public Culture* 23, no. 1 (2011): 121–156.

Stoler, Ann L. *Duress: Imperial Durabilities in Our Times.* Durham, NC: Duke University Press, 2016.

Stoler, Ann Laura. " 'The Rot Remains': From Ruins to Ruination." In *Imperial Debris: On Ruins and Ruination,* edited by Ann Laura Stoler, 1–37. Durham, NC: Duke University Press, 2013.

Stoler, Ann L., and Frederick Cooper. "Between Metropole and Colony: Rethinking a Research Agenda." In *Tensions of Empire: Colonial Cultures in a Bourgeois World,* edited by Ann L. Stoler and Frederick Cooper, 1–56. Berkeley: University of California Press, 1997.

Stora, Benjamin. "Algérie: Les retours de la mémoire de la guerre d'independence." *Modern & Contemporary France* 10, no. 4 (2002): 461–468.

Stora, Benjamin. *La guerre des mémoires: La France face à son passé colonial (entretiens avec Thierry Leclere).* La Tour d'Aigues: Éditions de l'Aube, 2007.

Stora, Benjamin. "Hacène Boudjenana." *Dictionnaire biographique de militants nationalistes algériens,* 145. https://issuu.com/azizmebarki/docs/dictionnaire_biographique_des_militants_national/397.

Stora, Benjamin. "Pied noirs." In *Les mots de la colonisation,* edited by Sophie Dulucq et al. Toulouse: Presses universitaires du Mirail, 2008.

Stora, Benjamin. *Rapport: Les questions mémorielles portant sur la colonisation et la guerre d'Algérie,* 2021. https://www.elysee.fr/admin/upload/default/0001/09/0586b6b0ef1c2fc2540589c6d56a1ae63a65d97c.pdf.

Surkis, Judith. *Sex, Law, and Sovereignty in French Algeria, 1830–1930.* Ithaca, NY: Cornell University Press, 2019.

Sykes, Naomi. "A Social Perspective on the Introduction of Exotic Animals: The Case of the Chicken." *World Archaeology* 44, no. 1 (2012): 158–169.

Tahraoui, Djillali, and Boutkhil Beghdadi, "Batisseur: Brahim Hasnaoui, homme d'engagement." *Madinati* 1 (2016): 11–15.

Taraud, Christelle. *La prostitution coloniale: Algérie, Maroc, Tunisie (1830–1962)*. Paris, Éditions Payot, 2003.

Taussig, Michael. *Defacement: Public Secrecy and the Labor of the Negative*. Stanford, CA: Stanford University Press, 1999.

Temimi, Abdeljelil. *Le Beylik de Constantine et Ḥādj ʾAḥmed Bey (1830–1837)*. Tunis: Revue d'histoire maghrébine, 1978.

Templer, John A. *The Staircase: History and Theories*. Cambridge, MA: MIT Press, 1992.

Tengour, Ouanassa Siari. "Salah Bey et la cité d'oubli." *Insaniyat* 3 (1998): 71–89.

Tengour, Ouanassa Siari, and Fouad Soufi. "Les Algériens écrivent, enfin, leur guerre." *Insaniyat* 25/26 (2004): 267–272.

Tillier, Bertrand. *La disgrâce de statues: Essai sur les conflits de mémoire, de la Révolution française à Black Lives Matter*. Paris: Payot, 2022.

Tin, Louis-Georges. "Mémoire de l'esclavage: 'Débaptisons les collèges et les lycées Colbert!'" *Le Monde*, September 17, 2017. https://www.lemonde.fr/idees/article/2017/09/17/debaptisons-les-colleges-et-les-lycees-colbert_5186813_3232.html.

Tocqueville, Alexis de. "Second Letter on Algeria (22 August 1837)." In *Writings on Empire and Slavery*, edited and translated by Jennifer Pitts, 14–36. Baltimore, MD: Johns Hopkins University Press, 2001.

Tony [pseud.]. "La vraie figure du meeting de Dimanche." *Oran-Spectacles* 230, October 14, 1933, 7.

Tournier, J-O. "Nouveau Marbre Onyx d'Algerie à Sidi Hamza près Tlemcen." *Le monde du travail de l'Afrique française, L'économiste algérien-tunisien technique et scientifique. Bulletin officiel des adjudications*, January 10, 1897, 2.

Trigg, Dylan. *The Memory of Place: A Phenomenology of the Uncanny*. Columbus: Ohio University Press, 2012.

"Un Monument aux Morts de l'Oranie." *Art et Décoration* 45 (1924): 5–6.

Upton, Dell. *What Can and Can't Be Said: Race, Uplift, and Monument Building in the Contemporary South*. New Haven, CT: Yale University Press, 2015.

Vaillant, Alberic. "Récit des anciens: De Bel Abbès à Aubagne et à la Corse. " *Le Trait d'union: Journal de l'Amicale des anciens de la Légion Etrangère de Paris* 84 (2012): 7–10.

Veracini, Lorenzo. "Settler Collective, Founding Violence and Disavowal: The Settler Colonial Situation." *Journal of Intercultural Studies* 29, no. 4 (2008): 363–379.

Veracini, Lorenzo. "Introducing." *Settler Colonial Studies* 1, no. 1 (2011): 1–12.

Veracini, Lorenzo. "Telling the End of the Settler Colonial History." In *Studies in Settler Colonialism: Politics, Identity, and Culture*, edited by Fiona Bateman and Lionel Pilkington, 204–218. New York: Palgrave Macmillan, 2011.

Veracini, Lorenzo. *The World Turned Inside Out*. London: Verso, 2021.

Vayrou, Georges. "Sur la route de Dijon: parcours croisés de deux militants anticolonialistes." *Cahiers d'histoire: Revue d'histoire critique*,123 (2014): 157–162.

Veyne, Paul. "Conduites sans croyances et oeuvres d'art sans spectateurs." *Diogène* 143 (1988): 3–22.

Viala, Claire. "Oeuvre d'un artiste marbrier Oranais: Sainte-Germaine veille sur le cimetière de Mers-El-Kebir." *L'Echo d'Oran,* November 2, 1950. http://www.merselkebir.org/annonces_1950.htm.

Vince, Natalya. *The Algerian War, the Algerian Revolution.* London: Palgrave Macmillan, 2020.

Vince, Natalya, and Walid Benkhaled. "The Long History of a Short-Lived Statue." YouTube. Uploaded November 11, 2019 by Vince and Benkhaled. https://www.youtube.com/watch?v=wllPtQNYwo4&feature=youtu.be&fbclid=IwAR3ArOU_oyfojpNfMhWEHFOui73bw-1VEcrNUoDQ5kqvYNsKGfqoHOTAfLY.

"Visite de l'École d'Agriculture." *Amicale des anciens élèves des écoles d'agriculture d'Algérie: Bulletin* 59 (October 2009): 8–11.

Vogl, Mary. "Algerian Painters as Pioneers of Modernism." In *A Companion to Modern African Art,* edited by Gitti Salami and Monica Blackmun Visonà, 197–217. Hoboken, NJ: Wiley Blackwell, 2013.

Von Sivers, Peter. "Secular Anxieties and Religious Righteousness: The Origins of the Insurrection of 1881 in the Nomadic and Sedentary Communities of the Algerian Southwest." *Peuples Méditerranéens* 18 (1982): 145–162.

Warmington, B. H. *The North African Provinces from Diocletian to the Vandal Conquest.* Cambridge: Cambridge University Press, 1954.

Warner, Marina. *Monuments and Maidens: The Allegory of the Female Form.* London: Weidenfeld and Nicolson, 1985.

Weizman, Eyal. *The Roundabout Revolutions.* Berlin: Sternberg Press, 2015.

Widrich, Mechtild. *Performative Monuments: The Rematerialisation of Public Art.* Manchester: Manchester University Press, 2014.

Wolfe, Patrick. "Settler Colonialism and the Elimination of the Native." *Journal of Genocide Research* 8, no. 4 (2006): 387–409.

Wolfe, Patrick. "Recuperating Binarism: A Heretical Introduction." *Settler Colonial Studies* 3, no. 3/4 (2013): 257–279.

Wrigley, Richard. "Breaking the Code: Interpreting French Revolutionary Iconoclasm." In *Reflections of Revolution: Images of Romanticism,* edited by Alison Yarrington and Kelvin Everest, 182–195. London: Routledge, 1993.

Wylie, Diana. "The Importance of Being At-Home: A Defense of Historic Preservation in Algeria." *Change Over Time* 2 no. 2 (2012): 172–187.

Wylie, Diana. " 'Part of Who We Are': Using Old Buildings to Foster Citizenship in North Africa (Oran, Algeria, and Casablanca, Morocco)." *Buildings & Landscapes: Journal of the Vernacular Architecture Forum* 25 no. 1 (2018): 44–63.

Young, James L. *The Texture of Memory: Holocaust Memorials and Meaning.* New Haven, CT: Yale University Press, 1992.

INDEX

Note: page references for figures are presented in italics

WORLDING THE MIDDLE EAST

Emily Gottreich and Daniel Zoughbie, editors

Arang Keshavarzian, *Making Space for the Gulf: Histories of Regionalism and the Middle East*
2024

Paraska Tolan-Szkilnik, *Maghreb Noir: The Militant-Artists of North Africa and the Struggle for a Pan-African, Postcolonial Future*
2023

Jacob Norris, *The Lives and Deaths of Jubrail Dabdoub: Or, How the Bethlehemites Discovered Amerka*
2023

Nadim Bawalsa, *Transnational Palestine: Migration and the Right of Return before 1948*
2022

Carel Bertram, *A House in the Homeland: Armenian Pilgrimages to Places of Ancestral Memory*
2022

Susan Gilson Miller, *Years of Glory: Nelly Benatar and the Pursuit of Justice in Wartime North Africa*
2021

Amélie Le Renard, *Western Privilege: Work, Intimacy, and Postcolonial Hierarchies in Dubai*
2021